# SECRETS

*from the Jerry Baker*

# Test Gardens

**www.jerrybaker.com**

**Other Jerry Baker Good Gardening Series™ books:**

*Jerry Baker's All-American Lawn Book*
*Jerry Baker's Backyard Bird Feeding Bonanza*
*Jerry Baker's Bug Off!*
*Jerry Baker's Terrific Garden Tonics!*
*Jerry Baker's Year-Round Bloomers*
*Jerry Baker's Giant Book of Garden Solutions*
*Jerry Baker's Flower Garden Problem Solver*
*Jerry Baker's Perfect Perennials!*
*Jerry Baker's Backyard Problem Solver*
*Jerry Baker's Green Grass Magic*
*Jerry Baker's Terrific Tomatoes, Sensational Spuds, and Mouth-Watering Melons*
*Jerry Baker's Great Green Book of Garden Secrets*
*Jerry Baker's Old-Time Gardening Wisdom*

**Jerry Baker's Good Health Series™ books:**

*Nature's Best Miracle Medicines*
*Jerry Baker's Supermarket Super Remedies*
*Jerry Baker's The New Healing Foods*
*Jerry Baker's Cut Your Health Care Bills in Half!*
*Jerry Baker's Amazing Antidotes*
*Jerry Baker's Anti-Pain Plan*
*Jerry Baker's Homemade Health*
*Jerry Baker's Oddball Ointments, Powerful Potions & Fabulous Folk Remedies*
*Jerry Baker's Giant Book of Kitchen Counter Cures*

**Jerry Baker's Good Home Series™ books:**

*Jerry Baker's Home, Health, and Garden Problem Solver*
*Grandma Putt's Old-Time Vinegar, Garlic, Baking Soda, and 101 More Problem Solvers*
*Jerry Baker's Supermarket Super Products!*
*Jerry Baker's It Pays to Be Cheap!*
*Jerry Baker's Eureka! 1,001 Old-Time Secrets and New-Fangled Solutions*

# SECRETS
## *from the Jerry Baker*
# Test Gardens

*Over 1,436 Tips, Tricks, and Tonics from America's Master Gardener®*
*for Lush Lawns, Amazing Annuals, Eye-Popping Perennials,*
*Beautiful Bulbs, Vibrant Veggies, and Much, Much More!*

**by Jerry Baker,**
**America's Master Gardener®**

Published by American Master Products, Inc.

**IMPORTANT**—Study all directions carefully before taking any action based on the information and advice presented in this book. When using any commerical product, always read and follow label directions. When reference is made to any trade or brand name, no endorsement by Jerry Baker is implied, nor is any discrimination intended.

**Published by American Master Products, Inc. / Jerry Baker**

**Executive Editor:** Kim Adam Gasior
**Managing Editor:** Cheryl Winters-Tetreau
**Copy Editor:** Barbara McIntosh Webb
**Interior Design and Layout:** Sandy Freeman
**Cover Design:** Kitty Pierce Mace
**Indexer:** Lina Burton

**Publisher's Cataloging-in-Publication**
***(Provided by Quality Books, Inc.)***

Baker, Jerry.
Secrets from the Jerry Baker test gardens :
over 1,436 tips, tricks, and tonics from america's master gardener®
for lush lawns, amazing annuals, eye-popping perennials,
beautiful bulbs, vibrant veggies, and much, much more!
/ by Jerry Baker.
p. cm.
Includes index.
ISBN 978–0–922433–55–1

1. Gardening. I. Title.

SB453.B3177 2005 635
QBI04–200487

Printed in the United States of America
2 4 6 8 10 9 7 5 3 hardcover

# CONTENTS

PART TWO

# Fantastic Flowers...59

PART THREE

# Just Veggin'...183

Chapter 10 **Love Those Leaves...211**

Chapter 11 **The Roots Are What Matter...232**

Chapter 12 **Classic Veggie Crops...254**

Chapter 13 **Heavenly Herbs...300**



Chapter 14 **The Best of the Rest...328**

**PART FOUR**

# Mix It Up Tonics...346

# Introduction

Back when I was growing up, I had the best gardening teacher around: my Grandma Putt. Working by her side, I learned the real secrets of how to make plants thrive—not through book learning, but through solid, hands-on experience. And when I got older and had a yard of my own, you can bet I put Grandma's teachings to good use. As I made friends with other folks and started asking about the secrets to their success, they all said the same thing: The best source of dependable, no-nonsense gardening know-how is another gardener—someone who's actually *done* whatever it is you want to know about. And that's what gave me the idea for the Jerry Baker test gardens: real-life plantings where real gardeners could try out tips to see what works (and yes, what *doesn't* work, too)!

Well, time sure flies, and when I look back on over 60+ years of gardening grow-how, my biggest thrill isn't from the whopper tomatoes I've raised, or the picture-perfect lawns, or the blue-ribbon zinnias at the county fair. Nope—it's from the adventures I've shared with the folks I've worked beside in our test gardens. We've had lots of successes over the years, rediscovering forgotten old-time tips, fine-tuning our everyday gardening skills, and experimenting with the latest and greatest new varieties on the market each year. We've had our share of failures, too—including weather-related disasters, plagues of bad bugs, and marauding critters that mowed down entire plantings overnight. But we've always come up with solutions to stop those problems from ever happening again. So finally, we decided it was time to put this treasure trove of garden-tested wisdom down on paper, so we could share it with folks like you!

We all want the same things: lush lawns, fabulous flowers, and veggie gardens packed with great things to eat. But it isn't enough to simply *want* them; we have to get out there and make 'em happen. Whether you're a gardening greenhorn or a seasoned pro, *Secrets from the Jerry Baker Test Gardens* is the best guide you'll find to getting the job done right—right from the get-go!

# Part One

# Luxurious Lawns

I've been looking after lawns for well over 60 years now, and you can bet your bottom dollar that I've learned a thing or two in all that time about getting grass to grow its very best. Whether you're tending a tiny patch of turf or a yard large enough for a regulation football game, the basics are the same: Feed with forethought, water wisely, and mow at the right height. Nine times out of ten, well-tended turf will be able to take whatever life throws at it—whether it's hungry bugs, deadly diseases, vicious varmints, or wild and woolly weather. To help keep your yard in blue-ribbon condition, I've pulled together my favorite time-tested tips for growing gorgeous green grass. And if trouble *does* strike, well, we've got you covered there too, with handy hints, terrific tonics, and our very best test-garden secrets to get your grass back on track and growin' like gangbusters—*guaranteed!*

# Chapter 1

# Super Lawn Secrets

Having a gorgeous, emerald green lawn doesn't take a lot of hocus-pocus—just good, old-fashioned know-how! It all comes down to the three basics: feeding, mowing, and watering your lawn just the right amount and at just the right time. Whether you're new to the grass-care game or an old hand who's hoping to pick up some helpful hints, you'll find this chapter packed with time-tested tips that are sure to make your yard the envy of the neighborhood!

# It's Chow Time!

## FEEDING FRENZY

Whenever we talk to our test-garden visitors about the benefits of a regular lawn-feeding program, there's always one person in the crowd who thinks we're crazy—at least at first. After all, it just makes sense that the more you feed the grass, the more it grows, and the more work you make for yourself, right? Well, one look at our gorgeous green grass tells the real story: A properly fed lawn is a healthy lawn, and a healthy lawn actually needs *less* mowing than scrawny, sickly, weed-infested turf!

## WASH UP FIRST

I'll bet you didn't know that *what* you feed a lawn with isn't nearly as important as what you do *before* and *after* you fertilize. Here at our test gardens, we've found that treating our turf with a soapy water solution (1 cup of dishwashing liquid in a 20 gallon hose-end sprayer) before *and* after we feed the grass works wonders with any kind of fertilizer. This simple mixture washes off dust and pollution, helps the fertilizer stick to the lawn better, slows down soil compaction, and helps prevent the fertilizer from burning your grass, too. Plus, it helps discourage some lawn insects. Now *that's* what I call a perfect solution!

### COLOR CUES

Not sure if your lawn is hungry? Trust me—it'll let you know! As the soil warms up in the spring, plant roots stretch farther out in the soil, seeking food. If they can't find enough, their growth is stunted and the plants start to show signs of starvation. So if your green lawn becomes spotty or lighter in color, pay attention—it's begging for food!

### Grass Greener-Upper Elixir

When I see a lawn that needs immediate help, I always suggest a good dose of this elixir as a super-quick fix. Trust me, this liquid lunch never fails to get a hungry lawn back on track!

**1 can of beer**
**1 can of regular cola (not diet)**
**1 cup of apple juice**
**1 cup of lemon-scented dishwashing liquid**
**1 cup of ammonia**
**1 cup of all-purpose plant food**

Mix these ingredients in a large bucket, then pour 1 quart into a 20 gallon hose-end sprayer. Apply to your yard to the point of run-off every three weeks during the growing season for fantastic growing results!

JERRY'S Q&A

Q My lawn's not looking quite as good as I'd like, so I'm thinking I should get my soil tested. Can I get good results from the soil-test kits I've seen at my local garden center?

A You bet! Do-it-yourself soil-test kits aren't as accurate as professional lab tests, of course, but the research staff here agrees that they're fine if you don't suspect a major problem with your soil. They'll give you a pretty good idea of the pH and sometimes, the N-P-K (nitrogen, phosphorus, potassium) levels.

# YEAR-ROUND LAWN FEEDING

If you're serious about having the best-looking lawn on the block, follow our garden-tested, year-round feeding program:

**Step 1.** Start with our Lawn Wake-Up Mix (on the opposite page) in spring: It's an all-organic dry blend followed up with a liquid elixir to kick things into high gear.

**Step 2.** Within two weeks of applying our Lawn Wake-Up Mix, feed the lawn with a mix of 3 pounds of Epsom salts per bag of 20-5-10 dry lawn food (enough for 2,500 square feet). Apply half of this mixture at *half* the recommended rate on the package label, moving north to south in rows across your yard. Note: If you're using a synthetic, slow-release fertilizer, spread the salts and the lawn food separately.

**Step 3.** Within two days of applying the dry lawn food/Epsom salts mix, follow up with our Fertilizer Energizer Elixir (see page 6).

**Step 4.** One week later, apply another dose of the dry lawn food/Epsom salts mix (again at half the recommended rate), this time spreading it in rows going from east to west.

**Step 5.** To keep your grass growing like gangbusters, apply our All-Season Green-Up Tonic (see page 69) every three weeks, right up through the first hard frost in fall.

**Step 6.** Get your lawn ready for winter with a final feeding: Use 1½ pounds of Epsom salts per bag of slow-release, 5-10-5 dry lawn food (enough for 2,500 square feet). Apply half of the lawn food mixed with ½ cup of gentle dry laundry soap at half the recommended rate on the package label, moving north to south in rows across your yard. Then apply the Epsom salts in the same direction.

**Step 7.** Finish up with a good dose of our Fertilizer Energizer Elixir (see page 6) within two days of your final lawn feeding. You won't believe the results!

## TIMING IS EVERYTHING

Nothing's worse than going to all the effort of fertilizing your lawn, then having it look worse than it did before. But it can happen in a flash if you're not careful about *when* you make the application. At our test gardens—and in our own yards, too—we make it a habit to apply lawn fertilizer (either liquid or dry) first thing in the morning. That gives the fertilizer a chance to work its way down to the soil and off of the grass before the hot afternoon sun burns those gorgeous green lawns!

## HOORAY FOR SPRAY

One time, we asked our test-garden staff: If you could keep only one lawn-care tool (besides the mower), what would it be? The vote was unanimous: A 20 gallon hose-end sprayer! No, that doesn't mean we like to lug 20 gallons of tonic all over the place! You see, this sprayer's plastic container holds just 1 quart of liquid mix. It attaches to the end of an ordinary garden hose with a mechanism that allows water to flow through the container. While the water's flowing, it picks up just the right amount of ingredients from the jar to make 20 whole gallons of spray—and it's light enough to hold in one hand. Now that's what we call livin' easy!

### Lawn Wake-Up Mix

Want to give your lawn a root-rousing wake-up call? We make it a habit to apply this tonic as soon as possible in spring, and trust us—the results are *amazing!*

**50 lb. of pelletized gypsum**
**50 lb. of pelletized lime**
**5 lb. of bonemeal**
**2 lb. of Epsom salts**

Mix these ingredients in a wheelbarrow, and apply with your handheld broadcast spreader. Next, follow up with this energizing mix:

**1 cup of baby shampoo**
**1 cup of ammonia**
**1 cup of regular cola (not diet)**
**4 tbsp. of instant tea granules**

Mix these ingredients in a 20 gallon hose-end sprayer, and apply to the point of run-off. Within two weeks of this treatment, follow up with a good feeding of your favorite dry lawn fertilizer to get your grass off to a great start.

## Fertilizer Energizer Elixir

Within two days of putting down our lawns' main meal in spring and fall, we like to give that dry food a kick in the grass with this beery tonic.

**1 can of beer**
**1 cup of dishwashing liquid**
**Ammonia**

Mix these ingredients in a 20 gallon hose-end sprayer, and fill the balance of the jar with ammonia. Overspray your lawn to the point of run-off. The best time to apply this mix is early in the morning, anytime before noon. It'll get your lawn up and growin' like gangbusters.

## WHO NEEDS THE STRESS?

When hot weather settles in for the summer, we know it's time to hold off on fertilizing the lawn areas around our test gardens. One year, one of our over-enthusiastic fellow gardeners went ahead and kept feeding during a dry spell; before we knew it, the fertilized areas looked just awful. That was a good lesson for all of us: Stressed-out grasses are much more prone to fertilizer burn during the "dog days"!

## SPREADING THE WEALTH

If you have a tiny lawn, you can get away with scattering dry fertilizers by hand (while wearing gloves, of course). But here at our test gardens, and for my own lawn at home, handheld or walk-behind broadcast spreaders are the tool of choice for even, consistent coverage. Whichever method you use, always wait for a calm day to feed your lawn, or the wind will scatter the fertilizer hither and yon. The result? A patchy-looking lawn, with areas of overfed turf next to weak, pale grass that didn't get anything to eat—definitely *not* the effect you're looking for!

## DON'T OVERDO IT

If a little lawn fertilizer is good, a lot is even better, right? Don't you believe it! Too much fertilizer can be even worse than too little, causing brown or burnt-looking patches in your turf. This is especially true when you're working with concentrated dry or liquid fertilizers. Fortunately, it's easy to avoid overdoing things; simply follow label instructions carefully, and make sure your spreader is on the right setting. Still worried about applying too much? Then stick with organically based dry fertilizers or our liquid lawn tonics; they're a lot less likely to harm your yard even if you overdo them a bit!

## CLEAN-UP IN AISLE ONE!

Yikes! You were filling your broadcast spreader with dry fertilizer, and a bunch spilled on your lawn by accident. You need to get it cleaned up right away, or you'll be looking at an ugly bare spot for the rest of the season. Here's what our test-garden experts suggest:

**Step 1.** Pick up as much of the loose fertilizer as you can, then drench the soil with soapy water (1/2 cup dishwashing liquid per gallon of water).

**Step 2.** Let the soapy water soak in for a few minutes, then grab the hose and give the area a good dousing. Follow up with plenty of water daily for several days.

**Step 3.** Finish up by applying gypsum at the rate recommended on the package. Your grass should perk up in a month or two and be as good as new.

*If you keep goldfish, you need to periodically change the water in their tank. Instead of pouring the old water down the drain, pour it on your plants. It makes an excellent fertilizer, since it is full of ammonia, fish waste, algae, uneaten bits of food, and beneficial bacteria. We tested it on our lawn, and the treated patch turned a deep, dark green in only a few days!*

Maureen S., Philadelphia, PA

## HOMEMADE LAWN FOOD

Back in the good old days, folks couldn't just drop in at their local garden center to pick up a bag of fertilizer for their lawn. Instead, they had to make do with materials they could find around home or get from their local mill. Here's one simple blend that we find works just as well today as it did back then! Just mix 2 parts alfalfa meal with 1 part bonemeal and 1 part wood ashes. Apply this mix at a rate of 25 pounds per 1,000 square feet of lawn area last thing in the fall, and watch for the greenest grass you'll ever see next spring!

**W**hy do I suggest applying fertilizers by walking north to south, then east to west? It's a trick I learned from Grandma Putt back when I was a boy. Using this crisscross pattern guarantees that every inch of turf gets fed, and you're not left with any obvious light green spots where the grass has gone hungry.

### Octoberfeast Lawn Food

Cool fall weather may be slowing things down in the rest of your yard, but your lawn is getting ready for a new growth spell. So give it a taste of this fortified lawn food, and be prepared for a great-looking lawn that'll sail right through the worst weather winter can throw at it!

**1 bag of low-nitrogen, dry lawn food (enough for 2,500 sq. ft.)**
**3 lb. of Epsom salts**
**1 cup of gentle dry laundry soap (not detergent)**

Mix these ingredients together, and apply at half of the rate recommended on the lawn-food bag. Within two days, overspray this dry feeding with our Fertilizer Energizer Elixir (see page 6) to wash it down into the soil, where the hungry grass roots can gobble it up.

## HIGH AND DRY

If you're like us, you've probably left a bag or two of partially used lawn food in your garage or garden shed at the end of the growing season. Chances are you, too, have come back in spring to find that fertilizer in one hard-as-a-rock chunk that's no good for anything! Over the years, we've learned to place our opened bags on boards or pallets to keep them off of the concrete floor, because dampness can seep through the bag and ruin the fertilizer. Or better yet, we place them in plastic trash cans with tight-fitting lids for the winter. Either way, the fertilizer stays in great shape for next year's spring feeding!

## WINTERIZE WHEN YOU FERTILIZE

You'll often hear folks talking about fertilizing their lawns in fall, and it can be a great idea—*if* you've got the right stuff! In our test gardens, we've found that fall applications of regular (high-nitrogen) lawn fertilizer can spur tender new grass growth that isn't tough enough to stand up to winter cold. That means the fertilizer actually does more harm than good! We've had much better results using an organic or "winterizer" fertilizer that has more phosphorus than nitrogen (such as 4-12-4, 5-10-5, or 6-10-4). For best results, use that type of fertilizer as part of our Octoberfeast Lawn Food, at left.

## LIME-AID

One of the most common questions we get about lawn care is about "feeding" grass with lime. Contrary to popular belief, lime is not a lawn food! It's a soil amendment that changes the acidity of the soil. So use it only if a soil test indicates that your soil is acidic (sour).

## HONE, SWEET HONE

What's the No. 1 mistake most folks make when mowing? Forgetting to keep their mower blades sharp! A blunted blade makes jagged cuts, leaving torn grass blade tips that are an open invitation to pesky pests and funky fungi.

To ensure clean cuts that'll heal quickly and prevent problems, the folks at our test gardens recommend sharpening rotary-mower blades every four to six weeks during the mowing season. If we don't have the time to tackle the job ourselves, we never hesitate to have a pro do it. In fact, we like to keep two blades for each of our mowers, so that we can keep mowing with one while we leave the other at the shop for sharpening!

## MAKE A CLEAN SWEEP

When it comes to mowing your lawn, haste can make waste—or even worse! Fast-spinning mower blades will kick out rocks, sticks, and other debris at high speeds, which can damage your mower, you, and anyone or anything nearby. For safety's sake, we always take a stroll through our lawn areas to scout for potential hazards *before* we start mowing—and so should you!

- Pick up any sticks, stones, bark chips, and other loose materials.
- Watch out for anthills—especially those fire ant mounds! Ants get mighty agitated when you run over their homes, and they'll retaliate by swarming and biting your feet, ankles, and legs.
- Don't forget to give your mower a good once-over, too. Check for loose screws, caps, and nuts and bolts, and tighten them up.

### Clipping Clean-Up Tonic

Do you like to leave the clippings on your lawn after you mow? Then spray it with this clean-up tonic at least twice a year. It'll help the clippings break down more quickly and let your lawn breathe better, too!

**1 can of beer**
**1 can of regular cola (not diet)**
**1 cup of ammonia**
**1 cup of dishwashing liquid**

Mix these ingredients in a bucket and pour them into a 20 gallon hose-end sprayer. Apply to the point of run-off. This'll really help speed up the decomposition process for any clippings left littering your lawn, and help minimize thatch buildup as well.

## BEAT THE HEAT

Do your lawn—and yourself—a favor: Don't even *think* of mowing between noon and 3 P.M., if you can help it! Grass clipped when the sun is at its fiercest is exposed to the blazing heat and drying power of direct sunlight and may get burned. Whenever possible, we schedule our mowing for either late in the afternoon or early in the evening, and we suggest you do the same. Trust us—it'll be easier on both you *and* your lawn!

## GREEN GOLD FOR YOUR GARDEN

Whoa, pardner—don't you dare toss those grass clippings in the trash! They make a fantastic free mulch that's good as gold for your trees, shrubs, flowers, and vegetables! Just make sure you never use contaminated clippings in your gardens. If you've applied a chemical weed control to your lawn, our test-garden experts suggest waiting at least a month after each application before using any grass clippings as mulch or tossing them into your compost pile.

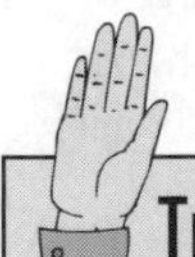

### TRIED-AND-TRUE

**W**hen the weather was hot and dry, Grandma Putt always had me raise the mower blade a notch before I headed out to mow her lawn. Why? She knew that taller grass withstands drought better, because the blades shade the soil. Less stress on the grass also means fewer pest problems in the long run!

## GET AN ANGLE ON MOWING

Lawn mowing gets to be such a routine that it's easy to follow the same pattern over and over—straight across in one direction, then back across in the other. But after a few weeks, this kind of mindless mowing can cause your turf to develop unsightly ridges. So at least once a month, make it a habit to mow in diagonal lines instead. We've found that this one simple trick can turn a lumpy-looking lawn into a smooth, even green that any homeowner would be proud of!

## MAKE THE MOST OF COMPOST

Have more grass clippings than you can use as mulch? Then toss 'em into your compost pile! Mix in discarded plants and other healthy yard fodder, and once they've broken down, you'll end up with crumbly, black compost that's a fantastic—and *free*—soil energizer.

Even with all of the compost we make here at the test gardens, we never seem to have enough, because we're always finding new ways to put it to work. We use it for patching bare spots, scatter it over established grass as a yearly top-dressing, and work it into the soil prior to seeding or sodding new lawn areas. Wherever it's applied, compost fortifies the soil, helps slow water evaporation, cools down soil temperatures, *and* suffocates weed seeds. Not bad for a bunch of unwanted yard and garden leftovers, huh?

### GO AGAINST THE GRAIN

Here's a super trick we picked up from one of the old-timers at our test gardens: When you're cleaning up clippings on a new-mown lawn, rake in the opposite direction of the way the grass blades are leaning. It makes them stand up straighter—and makes them easier to cut the next time you mow!

## TAKE A RAKE BREAK

Fed up with raking grass clippings after you mow? We've got some super news for you! We've found that by leaving the clippings on your lawn, you can actually cut the amount of fertilizer you need by up to 25 percent! Yes, 25 percent! That's because the nutrients in the clippings break down and become organic material for your grass plants to feed on. Besides saving time on raking, you'll be saving dough on fertilizer as well. So now when your neighbor asks why you aren't out there raking, you can say you're not lazy—you're thinking smart!

### Clipping Compost Booster

We're always in a hurry to make more compost, so every time we add a batch of grass clippings to our compost piles, we spray the heaps with this mixture.

**1 can of regular cola (not diet)**
**1/2 cup of ammonia**
**1/2 cup of liquid lawn food**
**1/2 cup of dishwashing liquid**

Mix these ingredients in a 20 gallon hose-end sprayer, and soak each new layer of grass clippings with this tonic. Every once in a while, toss the pile with a garden fork, just like it's a big salad, to mix in lots of air and speed up the composting process. The clippings will break down so quick, you'll have usable compost in weeks, instead of months!

## MOWING BY MEASURE

Here at our test gardens, we schedule mowing days by our lawns' needs, not by the calendar—and that's good advice for you, too. Remember our One-Third Rule: You should never cut off more than one-third of the grass blade at any one time. So, if you want to keep your grass at 2 inches, for instance, you need to cut before it gets more than 3 inches tall. When the grass is growin' like gangbusters (late spring and early fall), you may have to mow twice a week. But during the dog days, growth slows down, so you may need to cut your grass only twice a month.

JERRY'S Q&A

**Q** I have a few big trees in my yard, and mowing around their surface roots is a real hassle. Any suggestions?

**A** We had the same problem at some of our test gardens, and you know what we did? Got rid of the grass for good! We replaced the grass under our trees with groundcovers, or else simply put down a wide circle of bark mulch. It saved us a bunch of time, spared a lot of wear-and-tear on our mowers, and kept our trees a whole lot healthier, too!

## FIX THE MIX

Does your lawn always look a little ragged, even though you mow often and keep your mower blade nice and sharp? The problem isn't you or your mower—it's your mixed-up lawn. You see, some older varieties of tall fescue and Bahia grass grow faster than many other popular grasses. So if your lawn includes a mix of grasses (and most do), these oldsters may be going to seed while the other grasses in the mix are still much shorter. If your lawn looks thick and healthy overall, our test-garden experts suggest putting up with the less-than-perfect look. But if your yard just isn't up to your standards anyway, consider starting over with high-quality seed or sod—and steer clear of Bahia grass and tall fescue!

From Our Readers

*I hated cleaning the underside of my lawn mower deck because it always took so much time and effort to get all that grass off. Then I discovered this time- and labor-saving technique: The next time you clean your mower, dry off the underside and apply a heavy coat of silicone spray. No more cleaning—the grass doesn't cling!*

Ferne S., Bloomington, IN

## EASY DOES IT

Smooth and easy—that's the secret to getting a great cut when you're mowing around edges and obstacles in your yard. Sharp turns create uneven cuts and damage your grass, especially during dry spells. They'll also leave a pile of clippings at each turning point—and who needs *more* cleanup to do? Here are a few clever tricks my fellow gardeners have used to shave off significant mowing time *and* improve the looks of our test-garden lawns at the same time:

■ Reshape flower beds within your lawn to eliminate angled corners; smooth curves are much easier to mow around!

■ Place new garden beds in the corners of your yard, and shape the inner (lawn) sides of the beds with long, gentle curves. You'll never have to contend with tight corners again!

■ Encircle the base of trees and shrubs with a 3-foot-diameter, 3-inch-deep layer of shredded bark mulch. No more wasting time with dime-sized turns around each one—and your trees and shrubs will stay healthier, too.

## DON'T MISS OUT

When you're in a rush to finish mowing and get on to other things, it can be tempting to make as few passes as possible with the mower. Don't do it! Otherwise, you can easily end up with skipped strips that'll make your turf look just terrible. Over the years, we've found that overlapping each pass of the mower by at least 3 inches gives the very best results—it gets rid of wheel marks *and* gives your grass a neat, smooth cut that makes your place look great!

### Post-Mow Mixer

To keep your lawn looking its best, do what we do: Treat it to a cool drink once a month after you mow. This gentle but effective elixir will help your grass plants bounce right back from the shock of mowing.

**1 cup of baby shampoo**
**1 cup of ammonia**
**1 cup of weak tea water***

Mix these ingredients in a 20 gallon hose-end sprayer, filling the balance of the sprayer jar with warm water. Then apply it to your lawn to the point of run-off to soothe mowing stress and keep it growin' strong.

*To make weak tea water, soak a used tea bag in a solution of 1 gallon of warm water and 1 teaspoon of dishwashing liquid, until the mix is light brown. Store leftover liquid in a tightly capped jug or bottle for later use.

## HIT THE RIGHT HEIGHT

After you've put time and effort into growing a gorgeous green lawn, the last thing you want to do is ruin it by mowing carelessly. But that's all too easy to do—*if* you forget to check the height of your mower blade. A too-close-to-the-turf setting can quickly scalp your lawn, leaving you with bald spots all over your yard. Trust us—we learned this the hard way! So take our advice and check your mower blade before you start mowing each spring, and a few times during the summer, too. A properly set blade will cut off only the top third of the grass blades at any one time, leaving your lawn lovely and lush!

## WEATHER OR NOT

Those endless spring rains have finally stopped, and the grass is almost as high as an elephant's eye, so it's time to get out and mow that lawn, right? Not so fast, pardner! Trying to mow wet grass is a sure way to end up with a sticky, soggy mess. Wet clippings tend to clump together and sit on top of the lawn instead of sifting down in, where they can break down and help improve the soil. You run the risk of clogging your mower, too, by mowing damp grass. So take our advice and give the grass at least a few hours to dry after the rain or heavy dew.

## MEASURE ONCE, CUT TWICE

It happens to the best of us: We get a few days of bad weather, we go away for vacation, or we just get too busy, and before we know it, the lawn has gotten out of control. Whatever you do, resist the temptation to whack that wilderness back into submission in one fell swoop! Instead, adjust your mower to its highest setting, so you're taking off no more than half of what you need to. Then wait a few days, and mow again at the normal height. This trick will keep your lawn healthy and put a lot less stress on your mower, too!

Here at our test gardens, we like to experiment with old-time tricks and try out new techniques, but one rule is set in stone when it comes to caring for our lawns: *Never* add gasoline or oil to the mower while it's parked on the grass. Spilling this powerful stuff on the lawn is a recipe for disaster! That's why we always do this kind of mower maintenance on a flat, dry surface—a sidewalk, driveway, or other paved area is fine. Using a funnel and pouring slowly help, too. So go with the flow like we do, and you won't be crying over spilled gas!

## DON'T BE A DRIP!

There's nothing like a little drink every day to keep your lawn lush and lovely, right? Wrong! Believe it or not, the healthiest lawns are those that are watered infrequently, *not* every day. You see, frequent, light sprinkling encourages roots to stay close to the soil surface. So, if you go away for the weekend or forget to water for a few days, your lawn will start suffering right away. That's what we call killing with kindness! You and your lawn will both be better off if you remember this simple rule: Water *deeply,* not *often!*

## DOUBLEHEADER

Lawn care calls for lots of water-related equipment, including hoses, sprinklers, and hose-end sprayers. But chances are, you have only *one* outdoor faucet. There's no need to spend hundreds of dollars to get additional faucets installed—we've found a great solution! Go to your favorite hardware store or home-improvement center and pick up a two-headed faucet adapter. Attach your hose to one of the heads and leave the other one open for when you need the water faucet to fill up a bucket. Trust us—this will be the best few bucks you've ever spent!

## UNDER THE SURFACE

Don't want to bother keeping track of rainfall or weather reports? Here at the test gardens, we let our *lawns* tell us when they need watering. Our rule is to water slowly and deeply to moisten the top 6 to 8 inches below the surface; then we wait until the top 2 inches are dry before watering again. This thorough watering encourages roots to go down deep, and deep roots help all plants survive better in times of drought.

JERRY'S Q&A

**Q** I just got a new water softener, and I've heard that the salt in softened water is harmful to grass. Is this true? And if so, how can I protect my lawn?

**A** Yes, it's true. Too much salt can make a lawn go belly up. Fortunately, the answer to your problem is simple: Just make sure your outdoor faucets aren't connected to the softener system. Besides saving your grass, you'll save a bundle on water-softener salt!

## CAN IT!

On average, lawns need about 1 inch of water a week to get a good soaking, but they aren't fussy about where it comes from—rain, irrigation, or a combination of the two. An inexpensive rain gauge is a handy tool for measuring rainfall. If you need to make up for any lack on Mother Nature's part, figure that it'll take between 30 minutes and an hour to thoroughly water your lawn. Or, for a more accurate approach, do what we do: Set a couple of empty cat-food or tuna-fish cans in the path of your sprinkler, and let the water run until the depth of the water in the cans matches the quantity you wanted to apply. (If you had a half-inch of rain, for instance, leave the sprinkler on until there is a half-inch of water in the cans, to get a full inch for the week.)

## BE AN EARLY BIRD

When it comes to watering a lawn, the folks at our test gardens all agree: Timing really *is* everything!

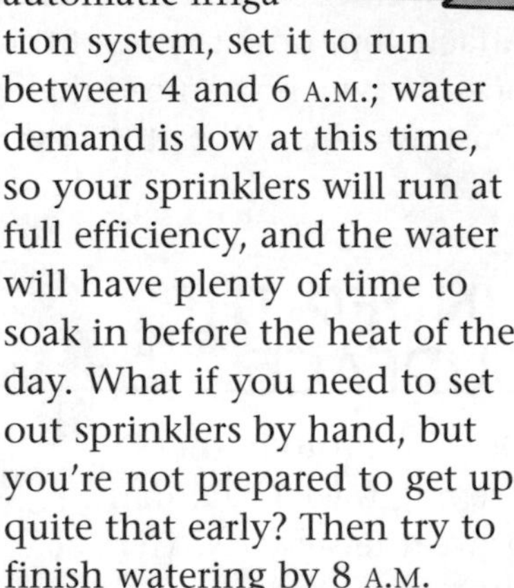

If you're using an automatic irrigation system, set it to run between 4 and 6 A.M.; water demand is low at this time, so your sprinklers will run at full efficiency, and the water will have plenty of time to soak in before the heat of the day. What if you need to set out sprinklers by hand, but you're not prepared to get up quite that early? Then try to finish watering by 8 A.M.

Don't water in the evening. Putting your lawn to bed when it's wet is an open invitation to diseases!

### Summer Soother Tonic

If you're like us and enjoy watering your yard by hand from time to time, then why not kill two birds with one stone? By that we mean to water *and* soothe your grass at the same time with a nice relaxing shower.

**2 cups of weak tea water***
**1 cup of baby shampoo**
**1 cup of hydrogen peroxide**

Mix these ingredients in a 20 gallon hose-end sprayer, and give everything in sight a good soaking. It makes for a really delightful summer shower, and your grass will thank you for it!

*To make weak tea water, soak a used tea bag in a solution of 1 gallon of warm water and 1 teaspoon of dishwashing liquid, until the mix is light brown. Store leftover liquid in a tightly capped jug or bottle for later use.

## SLOW AND STEADY

If you ever see puddles forming while watering your lawn, STOP! The same goes if you spot water running off onto your sidewalk or driveway. It may mean you're applying too much water too fast, or it may be the sign of a more serious problem. We like to let the area sit overnight, then try watering more slowly next time. If puddling or run-off keeps happening, that's a good sign that the soil has gotten compacted, so water can't soak in fast enough. That's your clue to strap on your aerating lawn sandals and take a walk around your yard, or else bring home a core aerator from the rental center to loosen things up. Aeration is a surefire way to perk up a squashed-down lawn!

*I used to water each section of my lawn for one 30-minute sitting. Now, I've found better results by watering each section twice for a total of 15 minutes each time. By the time I get around to the second watering, the moisture from the first watering has had time to soak in, so the second watering gets down deep instead of running off.*

Raymond L., Apoka, FL

## THE WAY IT IS

Often, reducing lawn watering woes is simply a matter of changing your standards. For those of us in the middle and northern parts of the country, some midsummer browning is a natural reaction of our cool-season grasses to summer heat. No matter how much we water, they simply won't look as lush in July and August as they do in spring and fall. With water restrictions becoming more common every year, it makes sense to cut down on watering your lawn during the hottest weeks of summer. Just imagine all the time and water you'll save! Come cooler weather, your grass will green up in no time and look just as good as lawns watered all summer long.

### TRIED-AND-TRUE

**W**ant to get your watering done faster? Don't blow your budget buying a bigger lawn sprinkler! Simply try this quick trick I learned from Grandma Putt: Set the sprinkler you already have on top of a box or overturned bucket. The higher it sits, the more area it'll cover—and the less you'll have to water!

Here at our test gardens, high-quality garden hoses are among our most important lawn-care tools. Even if you don't have as much ground to cover as we do, it's still worthwhile to invest in a good hose right from the get-go. We've tried a bunch, and we've found that for lawn-care chores, the best bet is a hose with at least a ⅝-inch diameter and a psi (pounds per square inch) minimum rating of 500. Brass couplings are a must, too; breakable plastic parts are no bargain at any price!

## WATER, WATER EVERYWHERE

Believe it or not, *overwatering* causes way more lawn problems than underwatering ever could! When the soil is totally saturated with water, your grass roots can't get any air, and their deepest roots suffocate. That teaches 'em to stay close to the surface, which then makes them more dependent on watering during dry spells. The research staff here at our test gardens tells me that a stressed-out lawn is also far more prone than usual to the triple threat of bad bugs, funky fungi, and wicked weeds. And if all that weren't enough, overwatering washes nutrients out of reach of grass roots, so you'll have to fertilize more often, too!

### THE RAIN DRAIN

Want to make the most of Mother Nature's bounty? Direct your gutter downspouts *away* from your foundation or driveway and *toward* lawn areas where the water can soak in. We've found that this simple step helps cut down on watering *and* reduces water run-off from the yard at the same time!

## PUT IT ON AUTO

Unless you have a postage-stamp-sized yard, using a handheld hose just isn't a practical option for effective lawn watering. For areas up to 1,000 square feet, a portable sprinkler does a fine job with a lot less hassle than hand-watering. But for larger lawns, we've found that an automatic system is a much more sensible option. Sure, it'll be pricey up front, but think of all the time you can spend fishing, playing ball with the kids, or simply relaxing instead of watering all summer long!

## GIVE IT A CHECKUP

When you water with hoses and sprinklers, it's easy to see when your grass has had enough. But if you use an automatic irrigation system like we do for our test-garden lawns, you'll need to keep an eye out for leaks and other problems on a regular basis. Here are some routine checks we do to keep our system in top-notch condition:

■ Always test the irrigation system after mowing to make sure you didn't damage any parts with your mower.

■ Test sprinkler heads or drip emitters weekly throughout the growing season, and make any needed adjustments or repairs right away.

■ If your system doesn't have a rain sensor, get one installed *pronto!* This handy-dandy switch shuts your system off automatically when it's raining, saving a whole lot of water and keeping your lawn from getting flooded at the same time.

### Wonderful Watering Tonic

Not sure whether it's time to water your lawn? Strap on your aerating lawn sandals or golf shoes, and take a stroll around your yard. If the grass doesn't spring back from your footsteps, it's definitely thirsty. Give it a good, long drink with this wonder tonic to help it recover and get back to health.

**1 can of beer**
**1 cup of baby shampoo**
**$^1/_2$ cup of ammonia**
**$^1/_2$ cup of weak tea water***

Mix these ingredients in a 20 gallon hose-end sprayer, and apply to the point of run-off. You'll be amazed to see how quickly this simple solution can bring even the most tired-looking lawn back to life!

*To make weak tea water, soak a used tea bag in a solution of 1 gallon of warm water and 1 teaspoon of dishwashing liquid, until the mix is light brown. Store leftover liquid in a tightly capped jug or bottle for later use.

MORE TIPS

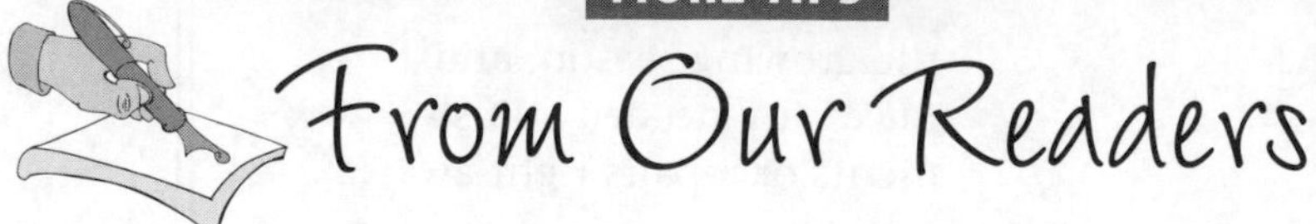

# From Our Readers

## CLOBBER CLAY

When we moved into our home in 1995, we found that we had a yard full of hard, clay soil that we couldn't grow anything in. We dug a hole, filled it with food scraps, vegetable scraps, peels, etc. (but not meat or fats). When the hole was full, we dug another hole about 4 feet away, and did this again and again until our yard was teeming with worms. This took us a bit over three years, but now our whole yard is lush with healthy grass and other plants!

***Mineko C., Lemon Grove, CA***

## DROUGHT DORMANCY

When a drought hits my area, we stop watering our lawn for a couple of weeks and let the grass go dormant. After that, we only need to give the lawn about ½ inch of water every two weeks (enough to keep the roots alive, but not enough to encourage them to grow). When the rain starts falling again, the grass springs right back to life!

***Thelma C., Tulsa, OK***

## MOWER MAGIC

Make cleaning your mower deck a real breeze by using a product found in your kitchen cabinet. Just spray PAM®, or any other nonstick cooking spray, on the underside of the deck. After mowing, simply spray away any stuck grass with a hose. This makes your mower cut better and keeps the deck from rusting.

***Clay C., Charleston, WV***

## KEEP YOUR CLIPPINGS

In many parts of the country, a newly seeded lawn is covered with cow manure to provide nitrogen and keep the birds from eating the seeds. This has been a problem for us in Alaska, because manure costs too much. Recently, I discovered that a light covering of grass clippings will do the same job, and it's free.

***Mark A., Kenai, AK***

# From Our Readers

## FANTASTIC FERTILIZER

Here is my recipe for a fabulous green lawn. Fertilize on one day with granular fertilizer and water in. The next day, mix up one bag of granular Revive®, 2 cups of Tide® powdered laundry detergent, and 3 cups of sugar. Mix well in two clean 5-gallon buckets, and apply to your lawn with a hand-held spreader set on a number 4 setting. Apply in a crisscross fashion to completely cover the lawn. Water well, and watch your neighbors' eyes pop out. You'll have the finest lawn on the block!

***Judy R., Englewood, CO***

## CLOVER TO THE RESCUE

I've found that clover is much more drought-resistant than grass. If you live in a drought-prone area like I do, try letting a little clover grow in your lawn to keep your yard green all summer long.

***Lucy S., Richmond, VA***

## EASY EDGING

I got tired of clipping lawn edges, so I buried railroad ties so their tops are at ground level around my beds. Now my mower goes right over them with no trouble—and I don't have any edges to clip!

***Stacy B., Boston, MA***

## CALLING ALL COMPOST

I spread ½ inch of compost over my lawn every spring and fall. Try it—compost works wonders on your grass, just like it does in your gardens!

***Adam W., Denver, CO***

## SIMPLE SHARPENING TEST

If you aren't sure whether your mower blade needs to be sharpened, just look at your grass. If the grass tips are shredded instead of cleanly sliced, it's time to sharpen your blade.

***Alex T., North Platte, NE***

# Chapter 2

# No Lawn to New Lawn

Whether you're landscaping around your new home or giving your tired old yard a new lease on life, starting a new lawn from scratch doesn't have to be a big hassle. With a little time-tested know-how and some handy hints from us, you'll have your new grass up and growing in no time! We haven't forgotten about those of you with already-established lawns, either: When cars, critters, or other nogoodniks tear up your beautiful turf, try these quick tricks to patch things up in a hurry!

## LAWN PREP, STEP-BY-STEP

We've put in a lot of lawns in our time, and you can bet that we've learned a fair bit in the process! If there's one thing that never fails to amaze us, it's the difference that good soil preparation can make in the life of a lawn—not just in the getting-started phase, but for years to come. We simply can't stress enough how important it is to do the job right from the get-go! Here's a simple four-step system we swear by for getting any new turf off to a tip-top start at our test gardens:

**Step 1.** Collect some soil samples from the area where you plan to plant, and send them off to a testing lab to check the pH and fertility levels.

**Step 2.** While you're waiting for the results, loosen the soil with a rotary tiller, then rake the whole area to break up any big clods of dirt.

### Lawn Jump-Start Tonic

Once you've got the soil in great shape for your new lawn, treat it to a taste of this power-packed potion. By the time you're ready to plant, your soil will be rarin' to get that grass growin'!

**1 cup of fish emulsion**
**1/2 cup of ammonia**
**1/4 cup of baby shampoo**
**1/4 cup of clear corn syrup**

Mix these ingredients in a 20 gallon hose-end sprayer, and saturate the soil. Wait several days before you sow seed or lay sod. After planting, spray the area lightly with water three or four times a day. Pretty soon, you'll be rollin' in the green—grass, that is!

**Step 3.** When you get the report back from the lab, apply the appropriate starter fertilizer, organic matter, and pH adjusters as recommended by the test results.

**Step 4.** Three weeks after the first tilling, till and rake again to aerate the soil and remove any weeds. Finish up the job by overspraying the soil with our Lawn Jump-Start Tonic, above, and you'll be all set to sow!

## TIP-TOP TOPSOIL

If you're starting a new lawn around a just-built home, you can be pretty sure that the good topsoil was scraped off the site before the construction process started. If you're lucky, the builder put it all back—but don't count on it! Unless you know that the topsoil was replaced, we suggest ordering enough to spread a good 2- to 3-inch-thick layer over your entire yard-to-be. Here's an extra tip: Make sure you get a good look at the soil you're buying *before* it's dumped in your yard. Steer clear of any soil that's chock-full of rocks, weeds, and other litter; this junky stuff isn't going to do your new lawn any good!

*A great way to test your soil for lime is to mix 1 tbsp. of dry soil and 1 tbsp. of white vinegar in a teacup. As the vinegar and soil mix, shake the cup and hold it to your ear. If you have excess lime in your soil, you will hear a strong fizzing sound as the acidic vinegar mixes with the alkaline lime. To correct this situation, add either leaf mold, sawdust, or peat moss to your soil.*

Gerald M., Mascoutah, IL

## BUILD YOUR LAWN FROM THE GROUND UP

A healthy lawn will stay in place for many years to come, so it just makes sense to improve the soil under it as much as you can before planting. Here at the test gardens, we make it a habit to work a 1- to 2-inch layer of compost into the soil before starting any new lawn area, and we're always pleased as punch with the results. If you want to try this for yourself, you first need to know that compost is sold by the cubic yard. To figure out how much to buy, we use this handy-dandy rule of thumb: It takes 3 cubic yards of compost to get a 1-inch layer of compost for each 1,000 square feet of soil.

## PICK IT UP, PLEASE

New homeowners have another special challenge to getting their lawn going: namely, getting rid of construction debris. Even the most careful construction crews are likely to miss small items that could eventually kill the grass or damage lawn-care equipment, and no one wants that! So before sowing seed or laying sod, search carefully for nails, bits of wood, chunks of cement, pieces of wallboard, and any other stuff that simply doesn't belong in a lawn. The hour or so you spend now will save you a lot of grief in the future!

## CHOICES, CHOICES

When it comes to starting a new lawn, we all have the same decision to make: seed or sod? Here's how we choose whenever we need to get grass growing at the test gardens:

**Sow seed?** This is the option we prefer when we need to cover a good-sized area, but don't want to spend a lot of money. It's easy for us for find the perfect varieties for our site and climate, too, which bodes well for the long-term health and happiness of our turf.

**Lay sod?** When we need an "instant lawn" in a small or highly visible area (like a front entrance, for instance), we spring for sod. Sure, we pay a lot more for the convenience, and we don't have many options of grass types to choose from. But the result is a lawn that looks great right away and doesn't need much special care to get settled in—which is a big plus!

## BUY THE BEST

Here's some investment advice you can bank on: *Always* buy the best-quality seed you can get your hands on for your new lawn. Read the label carefully for details like the age of the seed (it should be packed for the current year), the expected germination rate (the higher the better), and how much weed seed might be mixed in with the grass seed (less is best).

You folks know that I love to save money, but this is one time I *never* cut corners—and you shouldn't either. When you figure that a thick, healthy lawn can easily last for decades, trying to save a few bucks on bargain seed just doesn't "make cents"!

**Test Garden SECRET**

Our best advice for starting a new lawn from seed? *Diversify!* Instead of sowing just one kind of grass seed, we always use a mix of two or three different varieties. We've found that each one is a little different in its resistance to pests, diseases, drought, and other troublesome turf problems. So, if something comes along that weakens or wipes out one variety, we don't have to worry about losing the whole lawn in the process!

## Grass Seed Starter Tonic

The secret to getting your grass seed off to a great start is first giving it a good soaking with this tonic. It'll guarantee almost 100 percent germination every time!

**1 gal. of weak tea water***
**1/4 cup of baby shampoo**
**1 tbsp. of Epsom salts**

Mix these ingredients in a large container, drop in your grass seed, and put the whole shebang into your refrigerator. After 48 hours, take the seed outside and spread it out on a smooth, flat surface, such as a clean-swept area of your driveway. Once the seed is dry, it's ready to sow.

*To make weak tea water, soak a used tea bag in a solution of 1 gallon of warm water and 1 teaspoon of dishwashing liquid until the mix is light brown.

## BREAK IT UP

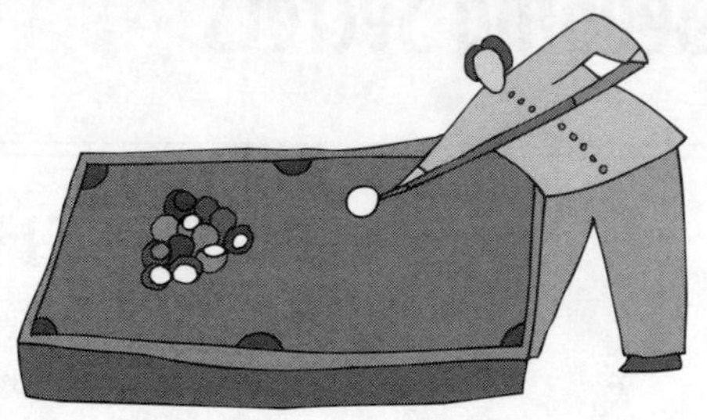

If you've got an extra-large lawn to get going (more than an acre or so), the idea of seeding the whole thing at once can be totally overwhelming. To make the job easier, do what we do: Break it up into sections. Do the front yard one weekend, the side yards the next weekend, and the backyard a week or two later. After a month or so, you'll hardly be able to tell that they were planted at different times—and you'll still have enough energy to admire all your hard work!

## THE SEASON'S THE REASON

What's the secret to giving grass seed a super-quick start? Get it in the ground just before it naturally kicks into its fastest growth spurt. For warm-season grasses—Bermuda grass, carpet grass, and Bahia grass—our test-garden experts say the season to sow is late spring, when the temperatures are consistently about 75° to 80°F during the day. In cool-season-grass country—growing Kentucky bluegrass, perennial ryegrass, creeping fescue, and the like—we sow seeds during the late summer or early fall.

## HAVE A SPRING FLING

If you cool-season folks miss the fall seed-sowing window, don't worry. It's time for Plan B: Sow the seed in early spring. It's not as mistake-proof as sowing in late summer or early fall, but the seeds still have a good chance of getting established and growing strong enough before the dog days of summer.

## HERE'S A HOT TIP

We're mighty fond of the companionship and fun that dogs can provide, but we *sure* don't like the damage they can do to a newly seeded lawn! Here at our test gardens, we've tried all kind of tricks to keep 'em from digging in the dirt, and we've found that, like people, dogs are sensitive to the capsaicin found in hot peppers. So, all you have to do is sprinkle our Don't Dig Here Tonic (see page 28)—or even just straight chili powder—on newly seeded soil where you don't want dogs to dig. After a try or two, Fido will associate bare ground with a burning nose and won't try to dig where you've just planted—whether the pepper is there or not!

### TRIED-AND-TRUE

**T**ime to reseed your lawn, and you've got no spreader? Try this trick that Grandma Putt used all the time: Punch holes in the bottom of a coffee can, then pour your grass seed inside. Put on the plastic lid, and walk all over your yard, shaking the can as you go!

## MULCH MADNESS

You know about all the great things mulch does for veggies and flowers—so why not try it on your lawn-to-be? A thin layer of mulch will provide consistent moisture and cool temperatures during the growing period, speeding up sprouting and promoting quick cover. Here are some of our favorites:

**Old sawdust, peat moss, screened compost, or shredded bark.** A little goes a long way, so all you need is a $1/4$-inch layer. That comes out to 1 cubic foot of mulch for every 50 square feet of lawn area.

**Hay or straw.** I've always sworn by straw for my own yard, but several readers have told me that they get great results with hay, too. Whichever you choose, shake it out thoroughly and spread it evenly. One bale of either is enough to cover 1,000 square feet.

After mulching with any of these materials, hose the whole area down with water to help settle it and keep it from blowing away before your grass seeds sprout. They'll appreciate their cozy cover and be up before you know it!

## A LITTLE ON THE TOP

As the growing season winds down, we like to buck up our test-garden lawns with a fresh supply of seed. So about six weeks before the first frost is expected, we reseed our cool-season turf with Kentucky bluegrass, perennial ryegrass, or tall fescue. Early fall planting gives these grasses time to germinate and grow strong enough to survive the freezing temperatures of winter—and it gives us super-thick lawns the following spring!

### Don't Dig Here Tonic

Dogs may be man's best friend, but they certainly aren't a lawn's best pal. Fortunately, this simple solution can help keep cruisin' canines at bay.

**3–4 hot peppers**
**2–3 garlic cloves**
**2–3 drops of dishwashing liquid**
**2 gal. of water**

Puree the peppers and garlic in a blender, then mix them with the dishwashing liquid and water. Dribble the elixir around the edges of your lawn, driveway, and sidewalks. Repeat frequently, especially after each rain, to keep those marauding paws off your newly planted turf.

## TLC FOR NEW TURF

You've gotten your grass seed sown and mulched—good for you! Now, there's one thing left to do to ensure that your grass gets off to a great start: Keep it well watered. We don't mean just one heavy watering each weekend, or whenever you remember; we're talking about a light, but even, sprinkling three or four times *every day* (unless it rains) until the grass is up and growing. Sounds like a lot of bother, maybe, but trust us—your watering schedule can make or break a lawn. We like to think of a new lawn kind of like a newborn baby: It needs lots of pampering (but at least you don't have to change any diapers)!

## HASTE MAKES WASTE

After all your hard work getting your new lawn going, you'll want to mow that new patch of grass *very* carefully. The experts at our test gardens suggest waiting for at least three weeks, and preferably six weeks, after planting to allow the roots to get a good grip. If you've planted a cool-season grass, like Kentucky bluegrass, it should be at least 2½ inches tall before its first mowing. For warm-season grasses, like Bermuda grass, hold off until the blades are 3 inches tall. And for *all* grasses, be sure to set your mower blade higher than normal the first few times you mow: The *last* thing you want to do is give your baby grass a buzz cut!

## GET GROUNDED

Here at our test gardens, we get all kinds of questions from visitors about starting new lawns. And when we find folks who've had trouble using sod, we always bet where they went wrong: thinking that they could skimp on soil preparation! Remember, sod is living grass that's ready to grow right away, so it needs smooth, crumbly soil that it can send its roots into, right from the get-go.

## BE A SMART SOD SHOPPER

Want to get the best grass for your buck? Of course you do! So I asked the folks at our test gardens to share their favorite sod-shopping tips, and here's what they told me:

**Do the touch test.** Healthy sod will feel cool to the touch. If it feels warm or hot, *don't buy it.*

**Look under the hood.** Properly handled sod is thick and springy, with roots that are abundant, but not overcrowded. Tightly matted roots are a sign that the sod's been sitting around far too long—you don't want it for your new lawn.

**Check the depth.** Look for roots that are least ½ inch long. The total thickness of the sod (grass blades, roots, and soil) should be between 1 and 3 inches.

**Go for the green.** When it comes to color, not just any hue will do! Stick with sod that is a rich green color; say no to any with a yellowish or brownish cast.

**Compare apples to apples.** Once you've found the top-quality sod you're looking for, get each supplier to give you an estimate. When you're comparing them, make sure the prices cover *all* costs, including delivery. Hidden charges can turn that bargain sod into an expensive lesson.

**Q** Since sod is ready to grow when it arrives, that means I can plant it anytime, right?

**A** Yep, you *can* lay sod anytime during the growing season. But for quickest rooting, keep in mind that cool-season grasses take hold best when planted in mid- to late spring, while warm-season sod settles in quickest in early spring and early fall. No matter where you live, do your work on a cool, cloudy day; that means less stress on your sod and on you, too!

## Sod Revitalizer Tonic

Sod is living, breathing grass that's just rarin' to get growin', so you'll want to get it on the ground ASAP! But in the meantime, treat it to this terrific tonic to keep it cool until you're ready to plant.

**1 gal. of weak tea water***
**1/4 cup of dishwashing liquid**
**1/4 cup of ammonia**

Mix these ingredients together, then spray on your newly delivered sod pieces to keep them as fresh as a daisy. When you're done planting, sprinkle the leftovers on the newly placed sod.

*To make weak tea water, soak a used tea bag in a solution of 1 gallon of warm water and 1 teaspoon of dishwashing liquid until the mix is light brown.

## THE LEVEL BEST

When they prepare a site for laying sod, most folks rake the soil even with their driveway and sidewalks. But at our test gardens, we've found it works better to keep the soil level 3/4 to 1 inch below these hard surfaces. This gives us a nice, smooth transition between the pavement and the grass—just what we're after. Plus, it practically eliminates the need for tedious trimming later on to keep those edges looking sharp!

## ROLLIN', ROLLIN', ROLLIN'

Here's a great garden-tested trick that can make sod settle in lickety-split: Run a lawn roller over the prepared soil *before* you lay the sod. That'll allow full contact between the sod and the soil, without any air pockets that can kill roots and leave you with ugly, dead patches in your beautiful new turf.

## SODDING SECRETS

Want to install a sod lawn just like the pros at our test gardens do? Here are some handy hints they've given me over the years:

■ Make sure the ends of the sod strips butt together tightly. *Don't* leave gaps or try to stretch the pieces to cover more ground with less sod!

■ Lay the strips in a staggered pattern, to make sure that the ends of adjacent pieces don't form straight lines. (In other words, set them out like bricks in a wall.)

■ On slopes, run the strips lengthwise across the area; that way, they'll be less likely to slide out of place.

## NO TIME TO LOSE

When it comes to installing sod, remember: Wait makes waste! Figure on getting it fitted into your yard no more than 48 hours after it arrives. If you absolutely have to wait a couple of days, store the sod in a shady place, and mist it lightly with water or our Sod Revitalizer Tonic (opposite page) a couple of times a day to keep it moist. *Never cover it with sheets of plastic!* This will suffocate the roots, adding stress that sod simply doesn't need.

**Test Garden SECRET**

It's a snap to cut sod into whatever shape you need to fit along edges and around corners. Unfortunately, those small pieces are far more prone to drying out than the rest of your sod, leaving tattered-looking edges all around your lawn if you're not careful. Well, I challenged the folks in our test gardens to solve this puzzle, and they came up with a great solution: Lay sod strips all the way around the outline of your lawn *first*, then fill in the middle. That way, you won't end up with lots of little pieces along the edge!

## KEEP SOME SAND ON HAND

If you find gaps in your finished sod lawn, don't despair—do what we do, and simply sweep some sand into the cracks. That'll eliminate any ruts and keep the edges of the sod from drying out, so those ugly gaps will grow together in no time!

## POST-PLANTING POINTERS

Newly laid sod takes a lot less care than seeded areas, but it still needs some TLC to get off to a great start. For the first two or three weeks, we suggest watering it every morning to keep the top 6 to 8 inches of soil evenly moist. That'll encourage those tender new roots to grow down deep ASAP. And to give it an extra boost, give it a good drink of our All-Season Green-Up Tonic (see page 69) every three weeks to promote faster, thicker growth.

**TRIED-AND-TRUE**

After we laid sod in her yard, Grandma would have me run over the whole area again with her lawn roller to make sure there was good contact between the sod roots and the soil beneath. But she'd make sure we emptied out most of the water first, so that the heavy weight wouldn't damage the sod. We found that leaving the roller just one-third full of water was just right for the grass—and it made that roller a lot easier for me to move, too!

## FILLING THE GAPS

Have a couple of ugly bare spots in your lawn? Instead of tearing up the turf, just get some new grass growing, and your lawn will be back in business before you know it! Here are two good ways to go:

**Start from seed.** This is the obvious way to go for most lawn repairs. It's readily available and inexpensive, too. On the downside, it can be slow to fill in, especially when the weather doesn't cooperate.

**Consider plugs and sprigs.** These are pieces of already-growing grasses, with both tops and roots, so they fill in lickety-split compared to seed. They're usually available only for warm-season grasses, like zoysia; don't expect to find them for cool-season grasses, like perennial rye.

## GOING TO PIECES

Hey, you cool-climate folks! If you want faster fill than you get from seed, try this quick trick we use often at our test gardens: Pick up a piece of sod at your local garden center, then make your *own* plugs by pulling or cutting it into pieces that are 2 to 4 inches square. Voilà—perfect plugs for pennies!

## THINK SPRING

Plugs are pretty flexible as far as planting time; but whatever you do, don't plant them within two months of the average first frost date in your area. Those poor little plugs may not be able to settle in quickly enough before the rough winter weather arrives. Then come next spring, you'll have the whole patch job to do all over again. Believe us, when it comes to grass plugs, spring to early summer is a *much* better bet!

MIX IT UP!

### Plug Power Mix

Whether you use store-bought plugs or make your own, treat them to some TLC while they're getting their roots down. Water them once or twice a day for the first month, then apply this nourishing mix five weeks after planting.

**3 lb. of Epsom salts**
**1 bag of dry lawn food (enough for 2,500 sq. ft.)**

Apply this mix at half the rate recommended on the lawn-food bag with your broadcast spreader, being sure to evenly cover the whole lawn area. Before you know it, the repaired area will look as good and healthy as the rest of your lawn!

## GET PLUGGED IN

When it comes time to perk up a sorry-looking lawn with plugs of new grass, our test-garden staff have a simple routine that we swear by. First, we prep the soil just as we would for seeding or sodding (see our Lawn Jump-Start Tonic on page 23). Then we set out the plugs in a checkerboard pattern, spacing them 4 to 6 inches apart, and water them in thoroughly. And the key step: On the day we plant the plugs, we skip forward on our garden calendar and put a big red X on the date that's five weeks later. We've found that that's the optimal time to apply our Plug Power Mix (on the opposite page).

## SPOT REMOVER

Want to use seed to repair a bald spot (in your lawn, that is)? With our garden-tested technique, it's as easy as 1-2-3!

**Step 1.** Start by cleaning up the dead grass and debris, then loosen the soil a bit with a rake or hoe.

**Step 2.** Mix the seeds with a little potting soil and sand, then spread the mix over the bare area.

**Step 3.** Lightly cover the seed mix with soil, tamp it down with the back of your rake, and spray with a mixture of 1 cup of beer, 1 cup of baby shampoo, and 4 tablespoons of instant tea granules, using a 20 gallon hose-end sprayer.

Here's a bonus hint: Add enough soil to create a slight mound. That way, when the soil settles over time, it will be level with the rest of your lawn, instead of leaving a telltale dip!

## BE A MATCHMAKER

When we plant grass seed in bare spots, we always try to select a variety that matches the green hue and leaf width of the other grasses in our lawns. We have the same standards for our test-garden turf as we do for our own lawns, and the last thing we want is the new stuff sticking out like a sore thumb!

*You can let your lawn fill in its own bare spots—and it won't cost you one cent! See, if you let your grass grow long, it will go to seed. Those seeds will grow up into new grass plants. Last year, my backyard was looking a little thin, so I laid off the mower, and let my grass go to seed. The next spring, I had a lush, grassy backyard!*

Max C., Dayton, OH

# From Our Readers

## MADE IN THE SHADE

I used to curse up and down because grass just wouldn't grow in the shade under one of my big, beautiful trees. Then I finally came to my senses and decided to lay bricks down in that area, making a nice little patio. It's nothing fancy, and it's just enough to cover the shadiest center area. But, now I don't have to struggle to grow grass, and I have a lovely, shady sitting area where I can sip my morning coffee.

***Katie S., Madison, WI***

## LEAF BAG LIFTER

I always rake fallen leaves off my lawn. I bag any leaves that I cannot put into my compost pile, but have always had trouble removing the bag from the trash can when full. But I have found an easy way to do it. Rather than attempting to lift the bag out of the can (an almost impossible task), just bunch up the top of the bag, and grab it with one hand. Tilt the trash can over, lay it on the ground, and easily pull the full bag of leaves out. It's even easier if you position the trash can so it's facing downhill. Try it!

***Ken C., Charlotte, NC***

## GRASS WITH A GRIP

I had a big bare spot in my front yard where the water would constantly wash away my grass seed. So, after a good night's rain, I put the seed on the bare spots and "stomped" it into the mud. From that point on, when I watered the grass or it rained, the seed was in the ground, not on the surface. It didn't wash away! Now I have beautiful grass, even in the run-off areas.

***K. W., Spring Hill, TN***

## IT'S TEA TIME!

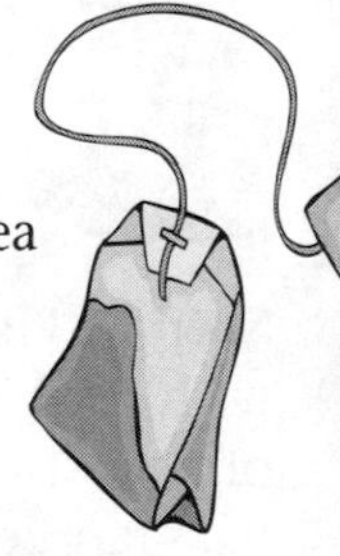

To repair a small bare spot in your lawn, set a moist, used tea bag right on the spot. Then sow grass seed onto the tea bag. The bag will provide moisture, as well as fertilizer, as it decomposes.

***Mark M., St. Ignace, MI***

## SEED SHAKERS

Save those plastic Parmesan cheese shakers! They're great for spreading small amounts of grass seed to patch bare spots.

***Brian J., Minneapolis, MN***

# From Our Readers

## READY-MADE REPAIRS

If a lawn edge next to a sidewalk gets damaged, fixing it is easy! Just cut out a rectangular patch of the grass that includes the damaged part, and turn it around so the worn spot is on the inside of the lawn, away from the sidewalk. Water well, and the spot will quickly fill in.

***Phil B., Memphis, TN***

## WIRE'S THE SEED?

To keep dogs, cats, birds, and other animals off of your newly planted lawn patches after planting, just cover the area with chicken wire. It'll give your seedlings protection, and will also help you remember where to water!

***Charles B., Springfield, IL***

## RUGGED TURF

To make areas of your lawn resistant to damage from heavy use, add finely chopped tires to the top-dressing when seeding. (Shredded-tire mulch is available at home improvement stores and landscaping centers.)

***Rob G., Mesa, AZ***

## "HAY" THERE!

Take a tip from an old nurseryman—cover newly seeded lawns with hay, not straw. Put the hay on, then run over it with a rotary mower so it doesn't look so shabby. The hay won't blow around like straw. Plus, best of all, hay contains nourishment, while straw is sterile. As soon as water goes through the hay, it's like going through a tea bag—it gives the seeds an instant start. Many times, farmers have hay that has been wet, or is old, and can be bought cheaply.

***L. M., Angola, IN***

## GRASS SEED COVER

Use an old window screen (painted green) as a protector for newly planted grass seed. Sprinkle grass seed over the bare spots in your lawn, and tamp it down. Then place the window screen on top and water right through it. Now you've got a nice, green, almost unnoticeable cover to protect the seed from varmints. Remove the screen once the grass has sprouted.

***Eileen H., Philadelphia, PA***

# Chapter 3

# LAWN RX

Luckily, lawn grasses are pretty forgiving. They'll let you walk all over them, and they can stand up to just about anything good ol' Mother Nature can dish out. But sometimes, even the toughest turf needs a little help from you to look its best. In this chapter, we've rounded up a bunch of our best grass-care tips, along with some great pointers that we've discovered at our test gardens. So if your lawn is lookin' a little under the weather, you've come to the right place. Working together, we'll set it right in no time!

## "A" IS FOR APHIDS

You might expect to see aphids on your veggies or flowers, but did you know that they can suck the life out of your lawn, too? Also known as greenbugs and plant lice, these tiny, pear-shaped bugs feed on plant sap, causing grass blades to turn yellow, then orange, and finally, dead brown. We've found that natural predators usually keep these little buggers at bay, but if they do get out of hand, we simply douse them with our Aphid-Away Spray (at right).

## BUG-FIGHTING BLOOMS

Why spend time or money on lawn pest controls when Mother Nature can do the work for you? Here at our test gardens, we depend on allies, like lacewings and lady beetles, in the fight against aphids and other nasties. Besides saving us loads of time and money on nasty chemical sprays, we never have to worry about the safety of our visitors! To attract more of these good guys to our turf areas, we fill our flower beds with lots of the daisy-like bloomers that beneficial bugs prefer: Black-eyed Susans (*Rudbeckia*), purple coneflowers (*Echinacea purpurea*), and cosmos are just a few of their favorites.

### BUG OFF, BUGS!

It's often possible to stop lawn problems in their tracks simply by changing the way you take care of your turf! We've experimented with a variety of techniques over the years, and we've found that we can send many pests packin' just by adjusting the amount of water or fertilizer we give to our lawns. (Some bugs, for instance, love to munch on underwatered lawns, while the tender shoots of overfertilized grass invite lots of insect pests.) Setting our mower blades slightly higher and keeping our lawns clear of thatch have also proven to be top-notch bug-off tactics!

### Aphid-Away Spray

Aphids can strike anywhere at any time, but they're particularly active in northern lawns, especially in shady places during the heat of summer. If they start bugging your yard, give this spray a try.

**2 cups of water**
**2 medium cloves of garlic, chopped finely**
**1 small onion, chopped finely**
**1 tbsp. of baby shampoo**

Put all of these ingredients into an old blender, and blend on high. Let it sit overnight, and then strain through a coffee filter. Pour the liquid into a hand-held sprayer bottle, and apply liberally at the first sign of aphid trouble to send these little suckers scurryin'!

# THE EARLY BIRDS

When we see flocks of birds feeding on our test-garden lawns, we know that's our cue to check for caterpillars in our turf. Cutworms are plump, brownish black, striped caterpillars that particularly love the tender shoots of new lawns, while sod webworms are grayish or tan, black-spotted caterpillars that thrive in heavily thatched or dry areas of established lawns. Both culprits can cause similar-looking damage: small, irregular dead patches of grass that slowly get larger and larger. If you find these bad boys in your own yard, do what we do—fight back with beneficial nematodes, Btk (*Bacillus thuringiensis kurstaki*), or, for really serious infestations, my Squeaky Clean Tonic (on the opposite page).

## Test Garden SECRET

Lots of folks come to our test gardens looking for help, so we have lots of practice identifying common lawn problems from just a few basic clues. When we hear about symptoms like chewed-up grass blades, brown spots, and even whole patches of loose sod, we can pretty much guarantee that chinch bugs are at work. But to make sure, we always suggest this simple test: Take a metal coffee can and remove the top and bottom. Then stick the open can shell 3 to 4 inches deep into your lawn. Fill the can with water, and watch for signs of tiny insects floating to the surface. Baby chinch bugs are all red, while adults are black with a white spot on their backs.

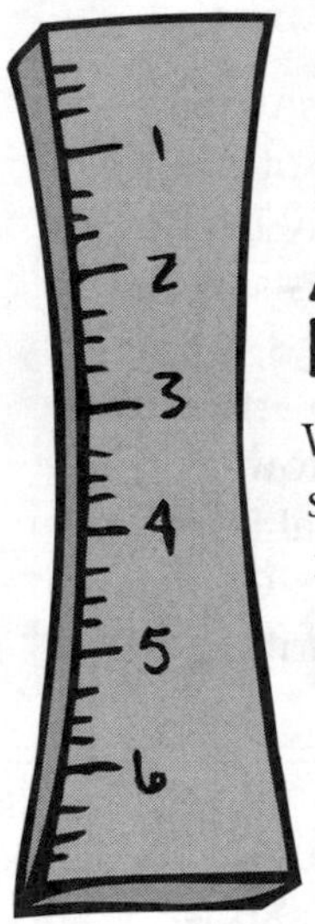


# DON'T GIVE CHINCH AN INCH

When you start seeing spots, it's definitely time to worry—about your lawn, that is! Scattered patches of yellowish or brownish dead spots are often a sign of chinch bugs. These nasty nogoodniks suck the nourishing juice from grass blades, causing them to wither and die. To stop the damage *now,* and prevent it in the future, too, follow our simple three-step program:

**Step 1.** Mix 1 cup of dishwashing liquid with 3 cups of warm water in a 20 gallon hose-end sprayer, then saturate your lawn to send these sap-suckers scurryin'.

**Step 2.** Rake out the damaged grass, then reseed the bald spots with endophytic grass varieties such as 'Tribute' tall fescue and 'Palmer II' perennial ryegrass, which chinch bugs won't eat.

**Step 3.** Chinch bugs thrive in poorly maintained lawns, so pay careful attention to watering and fertilizing. Watch out for thatch buildup, too—our Thatch-Blaster Tonic (see page 53) can really help here.

## LOVE DEM NEMATODES

Want to battle bugs the natural way? Try beneficial nematodes! These microscopic worms are best known as plant pests themselves, but the truth is that many nematodes are actually good guys. Beneficial nematodes hang out in the soil and feed on some of the most common and destructive lawn pests, including cutworms, Japanese beetles, and sod webworms.

Here at our test gardens, we've been using beneficial nematodes on our lawn areas for several years with super results. If you want to put 'em to work for you, too, buy 'em from garden-product suppliers and apply to your lawn with a 20 gallon hose-end sprayer. These worms really work wonders!

### Squeaky Clean Tonic

When you catch pest problems early, a mild tonic will usually clean things up lickety-split. If not, then it's time to pull out the big guns with this more potent version of our All-Season Clean-Up Tonic (see page 111).

**1 cup of antiseptic mouthwash**
**1 cup of tobacco tea***
**1 cup of chamomile tea**
**1 cup of urine**
**1/2 cup of Murphy's Oil Soap®**
**1/2 cup of lemon-scented dishwashing liquid**

Mix these ingredients in a bucket, then pour into a 20 gallon hose-end sprayer, and apply to the point of run-off. No matter what bad guys are buggin' your yard, this potent brew will stop 'em dead in their tracks!

*To make tobacco tea, place half a handful of chewing tobacco in an old nylon stocking and soak it in a gallon of hot water until the mixture is dark brown. Pour the liquid into a glass container with a tight lid for storage.

## THE RUB ON GRUBS

If moles and skunks like to call your yard home, you may have a serious grub problem and not even know it! A surer sign is dead clumps of grass that pull up like pieces of carpet, with no roots left underneath. The experts at our test gardens tell me that the best time to go gunning for lawn-chomping grubs is early spring or late summer. Let 'em have it with one of our favorite biological controls: milky spore disease. Or, release a horde of beneficial nematodes to get rid of greedy grubs in a flash! As an extra bonus, once you get rid of the grubs, chances are the moles and skunks will leave town, too!

## Rise 'n' Shine Clean-Up Tonic

Want to bag bad bugs before they get going? First thing in spring, spray down everything in your yard with this tonic.

- 1 cup of Murphy's Oil Soap®
- 1 cup of tobacco tea*
- 1 cup of antiseptic mouthwash
- 1/4 cup of hot sauce

Mix these ingredients in your 20 gallon hose-end sprayer, filling the balance of the jar with warm water. Apply to the point of run-off to nail any wayward bugs and thugs that were overwintering in your lawn.

*To make tobacco tea, place half a handful of chewing tobacco in an old nylon stocking and soak it in a gallon of hot water until the mixture is dark brown. Pour the liquid into a glass container with a tight lid for storage.

## FUNGUS AMONGUS

When it comes to foiling lawn pests, the best defense is often a good—*fungus?* The latest buzz word in the lawn-grass world is "endophytes," which are fungi that live inside grass blades. They don't bother the plants, but they *are* poisonous to chinch bugs, armyworms, sod webworms, and a whole slew of other pernicious lawn pests. We always choose endophytic grasses for new lawn areas, and we suggest you do, too. They send a clear message: *No bad bugs welcome here!*

*I use a couple of tricks that save a little money when I'm mixing Jerry's formulas. The beer that I use comes from the not-quite-empty beer kegs that are returned to the local liquor store. I supply the folks there with an empty milk jug and tell them what I need the beer for, and they are happy to donate the leftovers.*

*Another ingredient that you can get for free (sometimes) is loose tobacco. Get to know a tobacco company sales rep or maybe a convenience store manager, and when the expiration date on the tobacco passes, they might give you a can or pouch rather than trash it, if you explain what you will be using it for.*

Dennis M., Merrill, IA

## EEEW—SPIT!

Don't blame a neighborhood slob for that gob of frothy stuff on your lawn. The white spittle is actually the hiding place of immature leafhoppers—a pesky lawn pest. Both baby and adult hoppers cause small, white spots on individual blades of grass and eventually thin, stunted turf.

Luckily, here at the test gardens, we know just what to do: Mix 1 cup of Murphy's Oil Soap® and 1 cup of tobacco tea in a 20 gallon hose-end sprayer, then douse your lawn thoroughly at the first sign of damage. It never fails to send those hoppers hoppin' away! (To make tobacco tea, place half a handful of chewing tobacco in an old nylon stocking and soak it in a gallon of hot water until the mixture is dark brown.)

## STICK TO THE SCHEDULE

Believe it or not, it's possible to prevent most common lawn diseases no matter where you live, simply by paying attention to *when* you care for your yard. Here's a brief rundown of the lawn-care rules we always follow at our test gardens, with great results:

■ When we need to water lawn areas, we do it early in the morning—ideally between 5 and 8 A.M., but always before noon. We *never* water at night!

■ Every two weeks, we apply my All-Season Clean-Up Tonic (see page 111) in early evening to stop insects *and* diseases in their tracks.

■ Every three weeks, we apply my All-Season Green-Up Tonic (see page 69) before noon to keep our grass well fed and healthy.

### Summer-Patch Remedy

Hot, humid weather is hard on people and plants, but it's perfect for a host of foul fungi who just live to lunch on your lawn. One of the worst is a condition called summer patch. It looks just like it sounds: small, scattered, wilted patches of turf that turn tan. If you see any signs of it appearing in your lawn, give this tonic a try.

**1 cup of dishwashing liquid**
**1 cup of antiseptic mouthwash**
**1 cup of tobacco tea***
**1 cup of ammonia**
**3 tbsp. of saltpeter**

Mix these ingredients in a large bucket, and pour into your 20 gallon hose-end sprayer. Apply to the point of run-off every three weeks throughout the growing season to keep summer patch, dollar spot, and other fungal diseases from developing.

*To make tobacco tea, place half a handful of chewing tobacco in an old nylon stocking and soak it in a gallon of hot water until the mixture is dark brown.

## MAGICAL MILDEW REMOVER

Shady lawns are an easy target for powdery mildew, a fungus that produces a grayish white dust all over the grass. To fight this dastardly disease, the folks at our test gardens swear by the following formula: Mix 1 cup of baby shampoo, 1 cup of hydrogen peroxide, and 4 tablespoons of instant tea granules in a 20 gallon hose-end sprayer jar, then fill the balance of the jar with water. Spray the affected areas thoroughly every 7 to 10 days.

## FAIRY-FIGHTING FORMULA

If you notice mushrooms running rings around your yard, you've got a fungus called fairy rings. You don't have to put up with 'em, though: Just try our surefire, garden-tested, ring-remover program! First, get rid of the mushrooms as soon as you spot them, then puncture the turf with your golf shoes or aerating lawn sandals. Sprinkle a gentle dry laundry soap lightly over the area, then add 1 cup each of ammonia, antiseptic mouthwash, and baby shampoo to a 20 gallon hose-end sprayer, and douse the affected area. Want to prevent future problems? Make sure your lawn has adequate nitrogen to keep it lush and free of fairy rings!

### Test Garden SECRET

Looking for an all-natural way to stop nasty diseases before they start ruining your lawn? We've experimented with all kinds of potions and products at our test gardens, and guess what the surprise winner was: Good ol' garden compost! Compost is loaded with microorganisms that nurture plants while giving them the ammunition they need to defend themselves from the bad guys. We treat our turf to a light coating (about 1/3 inch deep) of screened compost each spring, and the results have been simply amazing. No doubt about it—compost is black gold when it comes to keeping lawns lush and healthy!

## JUST WALK AWAY

Golf shoes aren't just for golf courses anymore! We always try to wear ours whenever we're working in our test-garden lawns—and you should, too. (Don't have golf shoes? Pick up a pair of aerating lawn sandals from your favorite garden supplier.) Those metal spikes do a bang-up job keeping thatch under control, which in turn helps prevent disease problems. Please make sure, though, that you keep your special lawn shoes on your own turf and *off* of other folks' lawns! Funky fungi from their yard could hitchhike a ride on your shoes back to your home turf—and that definitely defeats the purpose!

### JERRY'S Q&A

**Q** My beautiful bluegrass lawn looked great going into last winter, but this spring, it's covered with gray patches! Can you tell me what the problem is, and how to fix it?

**A** Sounds like your lawn has a classic case of snow mold. The fungus that causes this isn't active in warm weather, so there's no point in spraying for it. Here at our test gardens, we simply rake up the moldy patches as soon as we can in spring, then give our whole lawn a good feeding. By early summer, you'd never know there had been a problem!

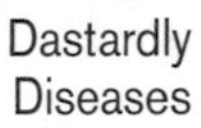

## DON'T LET THE BROWN GET YOU DOWN

When it comes to disease problems, brown patch ranks high on our Lawn Enemy Top-10 List. Be on the lookout for irregular, brownish patches of turf, with a grayish color on the grass at the outer edge of the brown patch. You may also notice filmy, white tufts covering the grass during the morning dew. This pesky fungus spreads on grass clippings, on mowing equipment, and even on your shoes, so don't take any chances—treat problem patches right away with our Brown Patch Brew (below). Then give your lawn equipment and your shoes a good scrubbing with warm, soapy water and let everything air-dry.

### Brown Patch Brew

Brown patch does the most damage during warm, wet weather, especially when the lawn's been fertilized with too much nitrogen, so go easy on the feeding where summers are hot and humid. If the disease still strikes, fight back with this super fix-it formula.

**1 tbsp. of baking soda**
**1 tbsp. of instant tea granules**
**1 tbsp. of horticultural or dormant oil**
**1 gal. of warm water**

Mix these ingredients together in a large bucket, then apply with a hand-held sprayer by lightly spraying the turf. *Do not* drench or apply to the point of run-off. Repeat in two to three weeks, if necessary. If brown patch persists even with treatment, follow up with a fungicide to knock this disease down before it spreads to your entire lawn.

## GOT MILDEW?

If you find yourself battling powdery mildew year after year, it's time to consider a more permanent fix for your problem. One option is to prune or remove shrubs and trees to let more light in. Or, do what we did in one of our shadiest spots, and grow a moss lawn instead. It's a great disease-free replacement for unhealthy grass, and it's green all year long, too!

Moss grows best if you sour the soil a bit to bring the pH to a level of 5.5 or so. Do this by adding sulfur or aluminum sulfate at the rate recommended on the package, which will kill the grass and encourage moss to grow.

## Test Garden SECRET

Here at our test gardens, we have lots of folks helping out, which is great for the gardens, but possibly fatal to our plants if we're not careful. You see, if we use a sprayer for weed killer and then put a fertilizer or something else in it, the herbicide can contaminate our other sprays and kill our plants—and we *definitely* don't want that! To make sure this never happens, we always mark all parts of our weed sprayers—both head and jar—with a dab of red nail polish. That way, we all know it's been contaminated with herbicide and won't use it for anything else. We also keep a red or orange golf ball in the sprayer jar. Besides serving as an extra reminder, the ball helps keep the solution mixed up and flowing freely as we spray.

## WIN THE WEED WAR

Dealing with lawn weeds comes down to one basic fact: Mother Nature hates bare soil. So, if you have empty or thin spots in your yard and don't fill them with good lawn grass, you can be darn sure that weeds will appear. Paying close attention to proper feeding, watering, and mowing is by far your best weapon in the war on weeds, because they'll never even have a chance to get growin' in the first place!

## ROLLIN' IN THE CLOVER

For many folks, the perfect lawn is an expanse of grass, grass, and nothin' but grass. But here at our test gardens, we include a secret ingredient in our turf: white clover. Far from being a weed, this leafy wonder can do all kinds of great stuff for your yard. So take a tip from our test-garden pros, and treat white clover as a friend—not a foe!

Like its close relatives, peas and beans, clover can take nitrogen right from the air. That means that a lawn with clover needs less fertilizer than a lawn without it—a big plus if you often forget to feed your grass. Another plus: Clover tolerates low mowing well. In fact, mowing encourages it to spread *out,* rather than *up,* filling in any empty space it can find and keeping ugly weeds away.

While most cool-season lawns look brownish during summer droughts, those that include clover will still look nice and green. And the small white flowers attract beneficial insects to your yard—and beautiful, lawn-friendly butterflies, too! So what are you waiting for? Go plant some clover!

## SAY GOODBYE TO MOSS

Judging by the questions we get from visitors, a lot of you folks want to know the secret to getting rid of moss in your lawn. Well, our Get Lost, Moss! Tonic (at right) is a good first step, but don't stop there! You see, moss thrives in acidic soil, while grass prefers neutral to slightly alkaline soil. So if you kill the moss but don't change the soil pH, the grass won't grow and the moss will return. The secret is to get your soil tested to determine its pH, then add ground limestone according to the test recommendations. Reseed with the grass of your choice, and say goodbye to moss!

### Get Lost, Moss! Tonic

To get rid of moss once and for all, you have to make the soil a place where it doesn't like to grow. Our moss-busting tonic will get rid of unwanted moss in a hurry—*guaranteed!*

**1 cup of antiseptic mouthwash**
**1 cup of chamomile tea**
**1 cup of Murphy's Oil Soap®**

Mix these ingredients in a 20 gallon hose-end sprayer, and apply to the point of run-off every two weeks until the moss is history.

## MAKE THE MOST OF MOSS

Instead of fighting moss in shady parts of your yard, why not just enjoy it? In my own yard, I reluctantly gave up trying to grow decent grass in one shady corner; instead, I added some interesting rocks, and used a few pieces of driftwood to separate the mossy garden from the rest of my lawn. Guess what—this former problem area is now one of my favorite places to hang out on hot summer days! If you try this yourself, just remember not to use limestone rocks, because they are alkaline; moss prefers acidic conditions.

### Tried-and-True

Lawn-care pros pay close attention to weather reports to time their applications of crabgrass control just right (before temperatures reach 60°F). I use a less scientific, but equally dependable, method that old-timers swear by: I wait until the forsythias and dogwoods start blooming. When these flowers appear, it's a sure sign that soil temperatures are almost warm enough for crabgrass seeds to sprout!

## WEEDING THE EASY WAY

The surest way to get rid of lawn weeds is the old-fashioned way: by hand-to-hand combat. To make the job a snap, remember that the early gardener gets the weeds! It's easier to pull weeds in the morning, when the ground is still moist, than it is later in the day, after things dry out.

## Wild Weed Wipeout Tonic

When you've got lawn weeds that won't take no for an answer, fill a hand-held sprayer with this tonic and take it with you every time you go out to mow your lawn. Zap those pesky weeds right on the spot, and before you know it, your weeds will be history!

**1 tbsp. of white vinegar**
**1 tbsp. of baby shampoo**
**1 tbsp. of gin**
**1 qt. of warm water**

Mix these ingredients in a bucket, and then pour into a hand-held sprayer. Drench each weed to the point of run-off, taking care not to get any spray on the surrounding plants. For particularly stubborn weeds, use apple cider vinegar instead of white vinegar.

## DON'T BE LATE

If the weather warms up before you can get your preemergent crabgrass control down in spring, don't bother applying it this year; it won't do a darn bit of good once the seeds start to sprout. Instead, our test-garden experts recommend setting your mower blade a little higher than usual, and being extra-careful with your feeding and watering this summer. Thick, healthy turf grass is your best defense against that crabby foe!

## KEEP OFF THE GRASS!

Get ten gardeners together, and they'll have ten different ways to accomplish the same task. But there's one hard-and-fast rule we *all* follow at our test gardens: When we pour granular herbicides or weed-and-feed products into a spreader, we make sure that the spreader is on a hard surface—never on our lawn. If we're ever in a hurry and are tempted to take a chance, we just remember these two little words: *Spills kill!* You can bet we'd rather take a few extra minutes to move the spreader than to spend months looking at damaged turf!

## WEED 'EM AND REAP

Believe it or not, you can weed your lawn and help prepare dinner at the same time! Young dandelions make mighty tasty salad fixings, so pluck 'em out by the roots and turn the tops into a delicious, fresh garden salad. Or simmer them in chicken or vegetable broth until tender. My herbalist friends tell me that the ingredients in dandelion leaves actually help you digest food. I like 'em just because they taste so good!

If you try this yourself, always be sure to use dandelions only from *unsprayed* lawns—no chemicals, please!

## STAY CALM, PLEASE

Whenever you apply any kind of weed control, *always* do it on a calm, windless day. Even the tiniest breeze can scatter those chemicals, possibly damaging nearby shrubs and flowers (not to mention kids and pets) before you realize what is happening. For extra protection when spot-spraying, keep the sprayer's nozzle close to the weed, and use a piece of cardboard or plastic to shield healthy grass, flowers, and shrubs from the spray. When it comes to chemicals, I always say it's better to be safe than sorry!

**Test Garden SECRET**

You've heard the saying that if something sounds too good to be true, it probably is, right? Well, here's one case where the reality is just as good as the hype! I'm talking about using corn gluten as an all-natural, chemical-free way to stop weeds before they start. We've been applying corn gluten to the lawn areas at our test gardens for a few years now, and the results speak for themselves. Applied in midspring, this "a-maize-ing" stuff stops crabgrass, dandelions, and other weed seeds from sprouting, so summer weed woes are a thing of the past. Best of all, this powdery material is a byproduct of corn processing, so you can't get any safer. It's fine for kids and pets to play on your lawn right away!

You can find corn gluten at your local feed store, or order it from suppliers that specialize in natural pest controls.

## CUT IT OUT

Even great-looking grass is a weed if it's growing where you don't want it to. But here at our test gardens, we've found a way to put even unwanted grass to work! When we find a clump of turf grass that's crept into our garden beds, we cut it out with an old, dull but sturdy carving knife that we keep on hand for this very purpose. The knife makes it a snap to slice the grass roots about a half-inch below the soil line. Then we use those handy pieces of sod as an instant (and *free*) fix for bare spots in our lawn!

### Weed-Killer Prep Tonic

Sometimes, you need to call in the heavy artillery to tackle a major weed invasion—and that's where chemical herbicides come in. To really zing a lot of weeds in a large area, overspray your turf with this tonic first.

**1 cup of dishwashing liquid**
**1 cup of ammonia**
**4 tbsp. of instant tea granules**

Mix these ingredients in a 20 gallon hose-end sprayer, filling the balance of the sprayer jar with warm water. Apply to the point of run-off, then spread or spray on the herbicide. This one-two punch will make those wily weeds wither away before you know it! And one more tip: *Don't* water the grass for at least six hours following the herbicide application.

## THE BEST DE-FENCE

Of all the problems that can affect a lawn, everyone on our test-gardens team agrees that animal pests are the most troublesome. Why? Well, with good general care—regular feeding, proper mowing, and careful watering—most lawns can fight off pests and diseases before you ever know there's a problem. But where grass-gouging critters are concerned, preventing their damage is often more trouble than repairing it!

The one exception is for those of you trying to garden in gopher country: Your best option by far is to defend your territory with a secure fence *before* these varmints move in. Most of the structure goes underground, because that's where gophers travel. To erect your barrier, bury a length of chicken wire or hardware cloth 18 inches below the surface, leaving 6 to 12 inches rising above ground level.

### From Our Readers

*If your readers live on a lake and are bothered by ducks and geese coming up on their lawns, here's how to get rid of the waterfowl. Put in some small stakes at the water's edge, then wrap string on them about 6 inches off the ground across the front. The ducks and geese will not cross this line!*

Robert W., Detroit, MI

## WORMS AWAY

Now, don't get us wrong—we're big fans of earthworms! These wiggling wonders do a bang-up job keeping our soil in good shape; plus, they feed our grass with their droppings (called "castings"). But sometimes, we can have too much of a good thing—an overabundant worm population that spoils the look of our fine lawn.

To reduce their numbers a bit, we put 2 pounds of mustard powder into a coarse canvas bag (you can use cheesecloth or old pantyhose), and soak it in a bucket of water. Then, we drain off the mustard water and sprinkle it over our lawn. This brings the worms to the surface, where we can easily gather 'em up for our compost piles—or use 'em for some mighty good fishin'!

## MOLE CONTROLS

If you're looking for some surefire ways to convince pesky moles to move on, give any or all of these three quick tricks a try. We've had good luck with 'em, and so should you!

- Place whole castor bean seeds, or cotton balls soaked in castor oil, in and along their tunnels.
- Stick pieces of rose canes or other thorny stems into the holes.
- Mix mothball crystals with human hair, and scatter this mix in and along the mole tunnels.

### GUM 'EM UP

Are you seeing lumpy spots, raised ridges of soil, and other evidence of gophers or moles excavating in your yard? The folks in our test gardens swear by this great trick to get rid of 'em, and I use it myself: Simply insert sticks of unwrapped Juicy Fruit® gum, slit lengthwise, into the gopher or mole runs. These pesky critters will eat the gum, but cannot digest it, and will die within a few weeks.

## DOGGIE DAMAGE REPAIR

Ready to fix those ugly brown or yellow spots in your lawn caused by dog urine or droppings? It's easier than you think! Simply rake out the dead or dying grass in the affected area, spray the turf with 1 cup of baby shampoo per 20 gallons of water, and then apply gypsum at the recommended rate. A week later, mix 1 can of beer, 1 can of regular cola (not diet), and 1 cup of ammonia in a 20 gallon hose-end sprayer, and spray your turf every other week. It'll be lush and green again before you know it! To prevent future problems, take a stroll over your lawn every day or so, and dispose of the droppings you find before they can damage your grass.

### Moles-No-Mo' Tonic

Not sure whether you have moles or gophers? Take a good look at the culprit. Moles are much smaller than gophers, with a pointed snout and large, clawed front paws that are well suited for intense digging. You rarely see them, but you'll know they are there when you see the mounds of dirt they push out as they dig their tunnels. To send 'em on their way, try this tonic.

**2 tbsp. of hot sauce**
**1 tbsp. of dishwashing liquid**
**1 tsp. of chili powder**
**1 qt. of water**

Mix these ingredients in a bucket, then pour a little of the tonic every 5 feet or so in the mole runways to make the critters run away!

## DOG GONE-IT!

A few years ago, some of our test-garden helpers started bringing their dogs to work with them. We all enjoyed playing with the pups, but we sure weren't pleased to see the damage their urine was doing to our beautiful blue-grass lawn! Our long-term solution was to reseed the turf with a tougher grass, but in the meantime, we needed a quick fix. One of our old-timers suggested feeding the dogs a bit of brewer's yeast. Just a teaspoon a day was all it took to do the trick—no more dead spots in our lawn. And our dog owners reported an extra benefit: fewer flea problems, too!

*Cut off the bottom half of a half-gallon plastic milk jug, and use the remaining part with the handle as a "poop scooper" to remove animal droppings left in your yard. It's easy to rinse off and save for the next time you need it.*

Helen R., Beaverton, OR

You may love your dog, but I can guarantee that your lawn doesn't! Dogs' nitrogen-packed urine can be strong enough to burn roots, leaving telltale spots of dead grass surrounded by rings of bright green turf. In our test gardens, we found that Bermuda grass and Kentucky bluegrass are particularly prone to damage; so if you have a dog in your family, think twice about using these grasses in your yard. Look for tougher types like fescue and perennial ryegrass, which in our tests were far less likely to show Fido's favorite potty spots!

## SPRAY 'EM AWAY

Want to know the quickest way to protect a lawn from dog-urine damage? Keep a hose handy! I've found that watering down my dog's favorite spots immediately after the deed is done helps dilute the urine, so most times, I never have to worry about fixing bare spots later on.

## GET CATTY

Most of the cats that visit our test gardens are purr-fectly well behaved, but every once in a while, one decides to leave little "gifts" on our lawn. To discourage this, we sprinkle ground black pepper, cayenne pepper, or mothball flakes in and around the places we particularly want to protect. Cats are very scent-oriented, so these strong-smelling materials send 'em scurrying right out of our yard!

## GIVE IT A BREAK

Sometimes, it just seems like ol' Ma Nature is out to get our lawns. One of her cruelest tricks has to be those darn summer dry spells that suck the life right out of the grass, leaving the turf limp and tired-looking. You'll know that your turf is summer-stressed when it doesn't spring back after you walk on it, like healthy, well-watered grass does. That's your cue to give your yard a good, slow drink of our Drought Recovery Tonic (at right). And in the meantime, do what we do, and be sure to keep people and pets off the lawn until it recovers.

## MULCH MAGIC

When the weather forecasts predict a dry summer ahead, we don't head for our sprinklers—we head for our compost pile! We run finished compost through a ¼-inch mesh screen to get a good supply of fine, crumby stuff, then spread it over our lawns in late spring. We've found that a layer about ½ inch deep, raked in and then watered thoroughly, gets our grass through those damaging summer droughts.

## STICK IT TO YOUR LAWN

Not sure whether your soil is packed down? Try this quick trick that we swear by at the test gardens: Just poke a large screwdriver or a sturdy stake into the ground. If it goes in easily, the soil is still in good shape. But if it only goes in with difficulty, that's a clear signal that the soil is compressed and needs some breathing room in a hurry.

MIX IT UP!

### Drought Recovery Tonic

If the dog days of summer are doing a real number on your lawn, don't despair—this refreshing tonic will soon set things right!

**1 can of regular cola (not diet)**
**1 cup of baby shampoo**
**1 cup of ammonia**

Mix these ingredients in a 20 gallon hose-end sprayer, and saturate the turf to the point of run-off every two weeks until the grass returns to normal. And remember that every time you water, moisture needs to reach 6 to 8 inches below the surface. This deep watering will encourage strong, deep roots that can stand up to periodic droughts.

The turf at our test gardens gets a whole lot of foot traffic, but we never seem to have compaction problems. What's our secret? We mix 1 cup of dishwashing liquid and 1 cup of beer in a 20 gallon hose-end sprayer, fill the balance of the sprayer jar with warm water, and spray all our turf once a month to the point of run-off. This one simple step really does the trick!

## AFTER THE FLOOD

Sometimes, our lawns don't get enough water; other times, they get way too much! If excess rain has turned your stunning green lawn into a soggy mess, don't get upset—there's hope for it yet. First of all, keep off the grass until all of the water has soaked in; you don't want to make muddy footprints or compact the soil. Once things have firmed up a bit, our test-garden experts suggest applying gypsum to your yard, at the rate of 50 pounds for every 2,500 square feet of turf. This will help loosen the soil and encourage better drainage in future—kind of like an army of little rototillers going to work right under your feet!

*I was trying to find a way to store and dispense tonics that are made in large quantities (like the tobacco tea). Then I remembered those liquid laundry detergent bottles (the gallon-sized ones). Now when we empty one, I label it and use it to store the tobacco tea or one of the other mixes. Then I can easily measure the amount I need, and save the rest for later use.*

Kerry S., Kent, WA

## LET IT BREATHE

Some folks just like to look at their lawn; others practically *live* on it. But with romping kids and pets, not to mention routine chores like mowing, even the best-prepared soil can get packed down over time. Fortunately, the answer is simple: *aeration!* That's a 50-cent word for poking holes into the soil to allow food, water, oxygen, and my terrific tonics to get down to the grass roots. Golf spikes are the simplest form of aerators—that's why I'm always reminding you to wear them when you mow. Aerating lawn sandals are also helpful, or you can rent a power aerator to do the job in a flash.

## TRY THIS!

Aerating your lawn really helps liven it up, but why stop there? Do what we do, and give your grass a super boost by top-dressing it with some sifted peat moss, dried manure, or compost after you aerate it. Using a broadcast spreader, we apply a layer about 1/4 inch thick to the whole area, then water thoroughly to help wash it down into the soil. Try it for yourself, and you'll see the amazing results in just a few days—*guaranteed!*

## DON'T LEAVE THE LEAVES

Crisp, cool days and drifting fall leaves may signal the end of the mowing season at our test gardens, but we know better than to put our tools away—there's still work to be done! We make it a point to get those leaves cleaned up pronto, before they pile up and smother our lovely lawns. There are as many ways to pick up leaves as there are folks who have to do it, but our favorite way is to rake them into a few long rows, then run over them with a mower a few times to chop 'em up. Or, if we're in a hurry, we use a bagging mower and eliminate the raking. We toss those chopped-up leaves into our compost piles, and come spring, we have an ample supply of top-notch compost.

## THATCH MATTERS

Folks who take lawn care seriously know that thatch is one of the biggest threats to the health of their grass. So, what is thatch, anyway? It's a tightly packed layer of undecomposed organic matter—leaves and grass roots, stems, stolons, and rhizomes—that lodges itself in your lawn. This nasty stuff crowds your grass plants, blocks water and nutrients from reaching grass roots, and makes mowing a hassle, too. How do you know if you have a thatch problem? The pros at our test gardens recommend cutting out a small plug of turf with a sharp knife and measuring the depth of the thatch. If it's more than 3/4 inch thick, it's time to take action, quick!

### Thatch-Blaster Tonic

Instead of waiting for thatch to build up in our lawns, we stop it from starting in the first place by spraying regularly with this power-packed tonic. Give it a try, and we know you'll be as pleased with the results as we are!

**1 cup of beer**
**1 cup of regular cola (not diet)**
**1/2 cup of dishwashing liquid**
**1/4 cup of ammonia**

Mix these ingredients in a 20 gallon hose-end sprayer, filling the balance of the sprayer jar with warm water. Saturate the entire turf area. Repeat once a month during summer, when grass is actively growing, and that nasty thatch will soon be a thing of the past!

## JERRY'S Q&A

**Q** My neighbor sprayed his lawn with a sudsy solution made from an antibacterial dish detergent. Now his lawn has yellowish streaks all over it. How can I stop this from happening to my yard?

**A** Thanks for asking, because this is important information. In recipes that call for soap, never substitute detergent—especially antibacterial detergent. In recipes that call for dishwashing liquid, be sure it is not the antibacterial kind. You see, soap (such as Ivory® flakes) is made from fats and oils, while detergent is often made from synthetic materials that can damage plant leaves. Antibacterial detergents have an added ingredient that makes them even more likely to burn plants. If you ever do use detergent by mistake, overspray your lawn with our All-Season Green-Up Tonic (see page 69), and the grass should recover quickly.

## DON'T BUY IT!

The folks at our test gardens all agree: The best way to tackle a serious thatch problem in a hurry is with a motorized dethatcher. But don't blow your whole lawn-care budget buying one, because we've found that dethatching isn't something you'll need to do very often. When it comes to power, renting is definitely the way to go!

## IT'S EASY BEING GREEN

While cool-season grasses stay nice and green through winter weather, the warm-season types that make up southern lawns turn brown soon after the first frost. If you've got a southern lawn and you don't like the brown look, try this garden-tested trick: Overseed your warm-season turfgrass in October with annual ryegrass. This cold-hardy grass will establish itself quickly, stay green all winter, then die away just as your warm-season lawn is greening up in spring. No more brown!

## SPILL-REPAIR SOLUTION

What's our No. 1 rule for mower maintenance here at the test gardens? *Never* add gasoline to the mower when it's parked on the lawn! But if you take the risk yourself and end up spilling gas on your grass, our experts suggest drenching the soil with soapy water (1/2 cup of dishwashing liquid per gallon of water). Let it soak in for a few minutes, then give the area a good dousing of water. If brown spots develop despite this treatment, cut out the dead grass and soil to a depth of at least 5 inches. Fill with new soil and reseed the area. If you have to do this once, we bet you'll think twice the next time you go to gas up your mower!

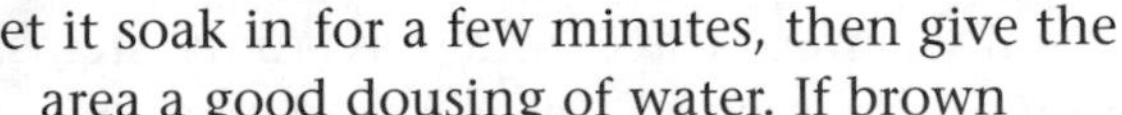

# GET BACK AT TRACKS

In mere seconds, a careless driver can undo the many hours of work you've put into making your lawn the best on the block. Believe me, we've had a few of these unfortunate incidents in lawn areas that adjoin the driveway and parking lot at our test gardens, and we know *exactly* how frustrating it can be! But you don't have to live with a lumpy lawn; just give these come-back tricks a try:

■ If the ruts are shallow (about 3/4 inch or less), they're the easiest to fix. Simply sprinkle some new topsoil on the damaged area. The grass will grow right up through the topsoil in no time at all, and those ruts will be just a memory.

■ If you're faced with deep ruts in your turf, or if a car sat there for a while and compacted the soil, you have a bit more work ahead. The first step is to loosen up the soil with a spade, then fill in with good topsoil to make the area level again. Rake it smooth, water the soil lightly to settle it, and then sow grass seed or cover the area with a fresh piece of sod. Water lightly for a week to 10 days until the new grass gets established. Then post a "No Parking" sign!

## Tire-Track Eraser Elixir

Trying to get rid of tire tracks in your lawn, but feeling like you're spinning your wheels? Walk over the damaged area with golf shoes or aerating lawn sandals to allow the soil to expand a bit, then sprinkle gypsum over the damaged area at the recommended rate. Follow up by overspraying the area with our special elixir.

**1 cup of ammonia**
**1 cup of beer**
**1/2 cup of baby shampoo**
**1/4 cup of weak tea water***

Mix these ingredients in a 20 gallon hose-end sprayer, filling the balance of the sprayer jar with warm water. Apply to the point of run-off. Repeat this treatment every three weeks, and before you know it, your lawn will be on the road to recovery.

*To make weak tea water, soak a used tea bag in a solution of 1 gallon of warm water and 1 teaspoon of dishwashing liquid until the mix is light brown. Store leftover liquid in a tightly capped jug or bottle for later use.

## Winter Turf Protection Tonic

After you sprinkle grassy areas with gypsum, give 'em a good drink of this tonic to help set 'em up right for the tough winter ahead.

**1 cup of dishwashing liquid**
**1/2 cup of ammonia**
**1/2 cup of beer**

Mix these ingredients in a 20 gallon hose-end sprayer, and then apply it over the turf to the point of run-off. Want to provide even more protection? One week after you apply this tonic, follow up by applying an anti-transpirant like our WeatherProof™ to help your grass shrug off sunscald, windburn, and salt and pollution damage all winter long.

## YOU CAN WALK ALL OVER 'EM!

Heavy foot traffic is tough on turf, but there's a way to help reduce the chance of bare spots popping up: Plant grasses that can really take a beating. Over the years, we've tried all different kinds in the lawns at our test gardens, and we've found that Kentucky bluegrass, perennial ryegrass, and tall fescue are the top choices for cool-season regions. In warm-season areas, Bahia grass, Bermuda grass, and zoysia grass are your best bets.

## STOP SALT DAMAGE

Deicing salts can be a great help for keeping winter sidewalks safe, but they sure don't do lawns any favors! No matter how careful we are, we always seem to spill some salt onto the lawns bordering our driveway and walkways here at the test gardens, causing yellowed, brownish, or even totally dead grass. We asked our turf experts to come up with a solution, and they found a winner: To stop salt damage before it even starts, we go out in late fall and liberally sprinkle gypsum in a 5-foot-wide band all over the grass that's next to any paved areas. Then we overspray the treated areas with our Winter Turf Protection Tonic (at left). Voilà—no more salt damage!

## SAFER WINTER WALKWAYS

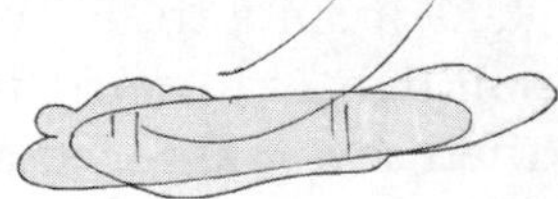

This winter, why not try some natural alternatives to melting the ice—like clean cat litter (not the clumping kind) or sand? We've found that both provide good traction on slippery surfaces, and they're cheap, effective, and lawn-friendly, too. There's also a whole slew of new ice melters that are salt-free. Some even contain fertilizers that add nutrients to your lawn as they take away the ice!

# From Our Readers

## GRASS SHIELD

I've found a great trick to protect my grass from the spray of Roundup®, or any other weed killers that wipe out everything they touch. Just take a large piece of cardboard, and cut different-sized holes all over it (leaving a good foot between each hole). Then you can select which size hole fits best over the weeds, and the cardboard can be used as a shield to protect the grass around it. For extra caution, mark a big "X" on the side that catches all the spray, so you always know which side is up.

***Kelly S., St. Louis, MO***

## GOPHERS-BE-GONE

To get rid of gophers, I pour a cup of ammonia into a 2-gallon watering can. Then I open up a gopher hole, pour in the contents, and put soil back over the opening. You may need to repeat this treatment, but that's how I got rid of one stubborn gopher that was determined to stay!

***Mary N., Tulsa, OK***

## FAIRY RING CURE

Here's a surefire remedy for fairy rings in your lawn: Mix ½ cup of baking soda in a quart of water, then sprinkle or spritz it over the rings. Presto! The fairy rings are gone.

***T. B., North Battleford, CA***

## ANT ANNIHILATOR

If you're bothered by fire ants in your lawn, get a long piece of plastic pipe (about 2 inches in diameter and 2 feet long). Seal one end with a wooden plug or duct tape, and secure it on the handle of your push mower or the steering column of your riding mower—sealed end down. Buy a dozen surveyors' flags from a hardware store (wires about 30 inches long with a small flag attached to the top). Put these flags in the pipe on your mower. When you're mowing the lawn and the blade chops off the top of an ant mound, take out one of your flags and stick it into the center of the nest. After finishing the mowing, walk around the yard, treat each nest with fire ant killer, and pick up the flags. In a short time, you'll have an ant-free lawn, and you'll be able to keep it that way all season long.

***Norman K., Greenville, MS***

MORE TIPS

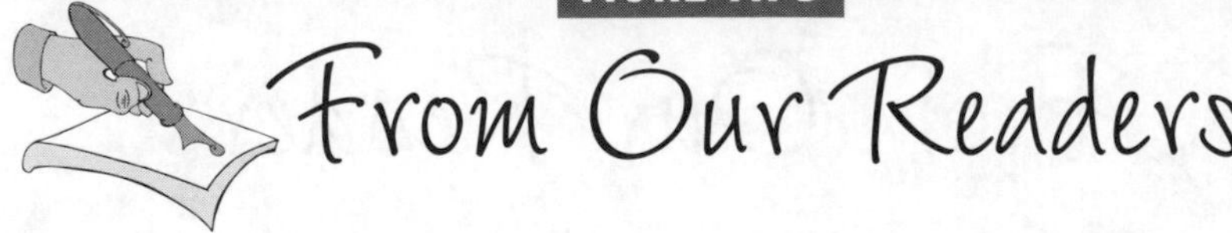

# From Our Readers

## CATS AWAY!

I add a capful of concentrated Lysol® to Jerry's famous All-Season Clean-Up Tonic (see page 111) to keep my neighbors' cats from using my lawn as their litter box. It works great!

***Jerry H., Dunmore, PA***

## LET THEM EAT GRUBS

To cut down on my grub problem, I set out a birdbath. Now, all sorts of birds stop by for a drink. While they're there, they often stay to feast on grubs in the lawn!

***Sadie M., Allendale, MI***

## FEEL THE VIBRATIONS

Moles don't like vibrations. So, set 5-foot-long metal stakes in the ground by their tunnels, and then hang an empty plastic bottle from the top of each stake so the wind can blow it around. The moles'll move out in a big hurry!

***Andy R., Albion, IN***

## ERADICATE DANDELIONS

When there is no rain in the forecast for at least a couple days, I head outside and dig out the center of the dandelions (all the buds, flowers, and stems), deposit them in a small plastic bag, and fill the cavity in the dandelion with table salt. This has not damaged surrounding vegetation, and it kills the dandelion—taproot and all. This method costs less, is quicker, and is environmentally safer than store-bought remedies.

***Nancy W., Dalton, MA***

## LIMEY LAWN

Here is my solution to the problem of dead brown spots in my lawn caused by dog urine. I place about 2 cups of ordinary garden lime in a clean, empty 1-gallon milk jug, and fill it with water. Then, I accompany my dog on her excursions in the yard, and simply pour about a cup of the lime-water on the area where she urinates. It really helps.

***Charles V., Shavertown, PA***

# Part Two

# Fantastic Flowers

Lucky for us gardeners, most blooming plants are pretty forgiving. You can stick 'em in just about any part of your yard, and you'll probably get a few flowers for your trouble. But if I told you that you could get *bigger* blooms, and *lots* more of them, for *longer* than you ever imagined, wouldn't you want to know my secrets? Of course you would—and I'm rarin' to share them with you!

If there's one thing I've learned in my many years of gardening, it's that flowers always appreciate a little extra TLC, and they'll repay you for it by blooming their fool heads off. From surefire soil preparation pointers to garden-tested tonics for feedin', weedin', and pest-pulverizin', I've gathered over 60 years' worth of terrific tips from my own yard and from working side-by-side with the folks in our test gardens. So whether you want to grow amazing annuals, perfect perennials, bodacious bulbs, or ravishing roses, the answers you need are right here at your fingertips!

# Chapter 4

# Fill Your Yard with Flowers

Who says you have to be born with a green thumb to fill your yard with beautiful blooms? There's no better way to learn about the basics of growing a fabulous flower garden than by getting out there and trying it yourself—except maybe having an experienced gardener right by your side to help you! Well, that's what this chapter is all about: handy hints and time-tested tips that my helpers and I have learned the hard way, so you won't make the same mistakes we've made. And that means you can skip right to the fun part: growing the best-looking beauties on the block!

## GETTING ROPED IN

When you start digging a new flower bed, it's awfully easy to get carried away—and awfully *hard* to get those curves and edges just right! So try this trick that we depend on: Use a clothesline rope (or a long electrical extension cord) to lay out the edges of your garden *before* you dig. That way, you can get the size and shape just right from the start, with no wasted effort working up a bigger bed than you can handle.

### From Our Readers

*When I'm laying out a new garden, if I know how I want it shaped, I mark the outline with wild birdseed. If I'm undecided, I use slices of stale bread, which makes it easier to rearrange. After I'm satisfied with the shape, I cut along the outline with a spade, then return to the house to watch the birds and squirrels feast on my leavings. What a great way to relax after all that hard work!*

Patricia W., Bethlehem, PA

## LIVIN' ON THE EDGE

I'll bet you didn't know that you can save yourself hours of tedious trimming every year, simply by changing the shape of your flower beds! Here at our test gardens, we have a little ritual: Whenever a new person wants to put in a new bed with scalloped or zigzag edges, we let 'em do it, but they have to agree to be the one to maintain the lawn around it. After spending a few hours on their knees hand-trimming the fussy edges that a mower can't reach, you can bet our helper has learned the same lesson we have: Gentle, easy-to-mow curves are *way* less trouble to keep tidy—and straight edges are the easiest option of them all!

MIX IT UP!

### Bed-Builder Mix

If you have a site that you'd like to fill with flowers someday, it's never too soon to start the soil-building process. Scrape off the weeds and grass with a sharp spade, then add this nutritious mix.

**40 lb. of bagged topsoil**
**10 lb. of compost**
**5 lb. of bonemeal**
**1 lb. of Epsom salts**

Mix these ingredients in a wheelbarrow, spread a 2- to 3-inch layer over the entire site, and then top the bed with mulch. Add the plants whenever you're ready!

Q I have lots of plans for my new perennial garden, but not a lot of money to buy the plants. Any suggestions on how to get the perennials I need without breaking my budget?

A Do what I do: Wait for end-of-the-season sales to buy potted perennials at a deep discount, then divide them before you plant. By next year, you'll have two, three, four, or even more great-looking perennials for less than the normal price of one clump!

## GETTING A GRASP ON YOUR SOIL

Nothing can make a good flower garden go bad quicker than working the earth when it's either too wet or too dry. So in our gardens, we *never* dig in until we've done this quick and easy test to make sure the soil's in tip-top shape: Simply trowel up a handful of soil from the site, and give it a good squeeze. If it crumbles apart when you open your hand, it's too dry. If it clumps into a solid shape, it's too wet. But if it holds together without packing, it's just right—and you can get on with your digging. Trust us—this simple 30-second test will save you years of trying to fix spoiled soil later on!

## TOODLE-OO, TURF!

You *have* grass, and you *want* flowers—so now what? You've got to get rid of the turf to make room for those beautiful bloomers. Digging up the sod is a lot of work, but we've found that it's worth the trouble: The grass you remove, and the roots and soil that come with it, are fantastic compost ingredients! Just do what we do, and lay the pieces of sod upside down (roots up) on your compost pile, then keep adding your kitchen scraps and other common compostables. As they decompose, those pesky pieces of grass produce pure garden gold—nutrient-rich compost to feed your flowers next year!

## IT'S ABOUT TIME

For most folks, spring is a super time to start a new garden, no matter what you want to grow. But for those of you who live in hot-summer areas, setting out baby perennial plants right before the steamy season can be a recipe for disaster. Instead, our experts recommend digging your new flower garden in late winter or early spring, then letting the site sit until fall. That way, you can get the perennials settled in when the weather's likely to be mild and moist, rather than hot and dry.

## DON'T GET SOAKED

If there's one thing flowers hate more than not having enough water, it's having too much! So, when we put in new beds here at our test gardens, we don't play guessing games with our future flower garden; we use a super-simple sogginess test instead. We dig a hole about 10 inches deep and 4 to 6 inches wide, fill it with water, and let it drain overnight. The next day, we fill the hole with water again, then wait 10 hours and recheck it.

If the hole is dry, we can be confident that drainage isn't a problem. If the hole still has water sitting in it, we consider a couple of options: limiting ourselves to growing flowers that can tolerate "wet feet," improving the drainage of the area, or looking for a new site. Nine times out of ten, our choice is to improve the drainage by spreading several inches of topsoil over the site. Why? Because we've found that raised soil provides perfect growing conditions for a wide range of flowers, while the steady moisture underneath keeps the plants lush and healthy without any extra watering from us!

## PUT YOUR FLOWERS TO WORK

If you're like us, your flower beds-to-be aren't blessed with great soil to start with. But we've found a trick that's made flower gardening a lot more fun and a lot less work: We let annuals do the soil improvement for us! The first spring, we dig a 1-inch layer of compost into the soil as best we can, then we fill the bed with annual flowers. After frost, we cut off the tops of the plants (leaving their roots in place), then work some more compost into the soil. We do the same thing the next year, and by the end of that growing season, the combination of digging, compost, and decaying annual roots leaves us with loose, rich soil that's just perfect for all kinds of beautiful bloomers!

### Bed-Energizing Mix

When the gardening bug bites in spring, there's nothing to do but grab a shovel and get your garden started. Whip up a batch of this bedding mix, spread it over your planting area, and then get busy digging!

**50 lb. of peat moss**
**25 lb. of gypsum**
**10 lb. of organic garden food (such as 5-10-5)**
**4 bushels of compost**

Mix these ingredients in a large wheelbarrow, then work the mixture into the soil before you plant. This combination provides a steady supply of nutrients that are well suited for just about any annual or perennial you'll put in.

## FORGET THE FLOWERS

We flower gardeners want color, and we want it fast—so it just makes sense to buy plants that are already in bloom, right? WRONG! Flower-filled annuals and perennials are busy putting their energy into their blossoms instead of growing new roots, which is what they need to do to settle into your garden. When we buy plants for our test gardens, we always go for those that have lots of healthy leaves and stems, but few or no blooms. That way, we know they'll adjust quickly to their new home, and we'll have months of easy-care color to look forward to!

Those of you who grow flowers in sandy soil know how quickly compost can disappear when you work it into the soil. Well, you'll love this trick we swear by in our test gardens—we've found that unused, "all-natural" cat box filler, made from alfalfa, corn husks, or other plant-based materials, is a super addition for bulking up sandy soil. It adds both organic matter and nutrients to the soil—and that means less watering and feeding as far as your flowers are concerned!

## THE ROOTS OF THE MATTER

When it's planting time at the test gardens, we always like to have a little review session before we send our helpers out with trowel in hand. You can spot the new folks, because they're shocked to see us use a knife or screwdriver to make shallow cuts along the sides of the rootball after we remove each plant from its pot. To prove we're not just being mean to our poor plants, we'll leave one with the roots uncut, and then plant it next to the others for comparison. When folks see the difference that loosening the roots makes in the health and vigor of our flowers, you can be sure they think our tough-love treatment isn't as cruel as it looks!

## SOAK IT TO 'EM

Want to speed the sprouting time of your flower seeds? Do what we do, and give 'em a good soak. Place the seeds in a piece of old nylon stocking and tie it up with a twist-tie. Then soak the stocking in a mix of 1 teaspoon of dishwashing liquid, 1 teaspoon of ammonia, and 1 teaspoon of instant tea granules in 1 quart of warm water for 24 hours. Let the seeds dry out, remove them from the stocking, and plant 'em. They'll be up before you know it!

## Test Garden SECRET

When folks see our flower-filled test gardens, they often expect to find some fancy-schmancy greenhouse there, too. But the truth is, we start most of our seedlings right in our homes and offices, using inexpensive 4-foot shop lights (the kind with two fluorescent tubes) from our local home-improvement center. Using the chains and the S-hooks they come with, we hang 'em over a table or bench so they're no more than 2 inches above the pots to start with. As the seedlings grow, we adjust the chains so the lights are 4 to 6 inches above their tops. Within a few weeks, we've got all the seedlings we can use—*without* the expense and hassle of a greenhouse!

# A TOOTHSOME TRICK

My old eyes aren't what they used to be, so when it comes to sowing my flower seeds in pots, I take all the help I can get! The folks at our test gardens shared this great tip with me for sowing tiny seeds: Pour 'em into a small dish, then wet the very tip of a wooden toothpick and stick it into the seeds. Touch the tip of the toothpick to the seed-starting mix in the pot to transfer the seeds, and presto—perfectly sowed seeds every time!

# SPREAD THE WEALTH

One of the hardest parts of getting a new garden started is figuring out what to plant where. Generally, we like to suggest that folks put the shortest plants near the front or edge of the bed, and the tallest ones near the back or middle. But we've noticed that the earliest-flowering perennials also tend to be the shortest in stature, so if you put 'em all at the front of your garden, it'll look ho-hum boring for 11 months of the year. To get around that, we like to scatter the early risers throughout our beds and borders. That spreads out the spring show, plus gives us room for some colorful late-bloomers at the border's edge later on!

## Super Seed-Starting Mix

Regular potting soil is way too rich for small seedlings, and it can foster a bunch of funky fungi that'll quickly wipe out your baby bloomers. To get your flower seeds up and growing safely, we suggest blendin' up a batch of this mix.

**2 parts peat moss**
**1 part perlite or vermiculite**
**Warm water**

Mix the peat moss and perlite or vermiculite in a bag or bucket. The day before sowing seeds, moisten the mix by adding warm water—a few cups at a time—and working it in with your hands until the mix feels evenly moist to the touch. Fill your seed-starting pots with this mix and you're ready to sow!

## SHAKE THINGS UP

Around here, we know better than to throw away empty herb and spice jars—you know, the ones with those plastic shaker lids that have holes in them? The folks in our test gardens absolutely love these jars when it comes time to sow seeds in spring. First, they drop a seed through one of the holes to make sure it'll fit through, then fill the jars with the rest of the seeds and shake to sow. When I use this trick in my own garden, I like to add a pinch of unflavored, powdered gelatin to the seeds, too. The light-colored gelatin makes it a cinch for me to see where I've sown the seeds. Plus, it contains a bit of nitrogen that seedlings can use to grow strong!

## MOSS IS THE BOSS

Sowing flower seeds indoors gives them a real jump start: no bad bugs to chomp them, no cruel winds or hard rains to flatten them, and no nasty frosts to nip them. Unfortunately, they still have diseases to deal with—especially a fungal disease called damping-off, which rots seedlings right at the soil line. We used to have a problem with these fungi every year, until our test-garden experts finally found the solution: Simply sprinkle milled sphagnum moss (available at garden centers) over the entire surface of each pot, either before or right after you sow your seeds. Voilà—no more damping-off!

## DEFEATING DISEASE IS A BREEZE

Want to keep your indoor-sown seedlings short and sturdy? We've tried all kinds of tricks, and you know what works best? Setting up a small fan at the lowest setting to blow across their tops. The moving air does a bang-up job of keeping baby flowers low and bushy—*and* it puts a stop to disease problems, too!

### Seedling Saver

The tender stems and soft leaves of flower seedlings are easy targets for dastardly diseases, so it's smart to be prepared ahead of time. Put out the "Not Welcome" mat with a batch of our special solution.

**4 tsp. of chamomile tea**
**1 tsp. of dishwashing liquid**
**1 qt. of boiling water**

Mix these ingredients in a bowl, and let steep for at least an hour. Strain out the solids and pour the liquid into a hand-held sprayer. Mist your seedlings as soon as their little green heads poke out of the soil to foil attacks by foul fungi.

# Easy-Care Flower Secrets

## START SMALL

Our best piece of advice for beginning flower gardeners? Start small! When you're dreaming of a yard full of flowers, we know it's easy to get carried away digging up new beds in spring. But at one time or another, all of us here at the test gardens have learned the hard way: A small bed that's easy to look after will make you much happier than a gigantic one that's overrun by weeds come July. It's always possible to make the garden bigger later, but it's tough to admit defeat and turn failed flower beds back to lawn!

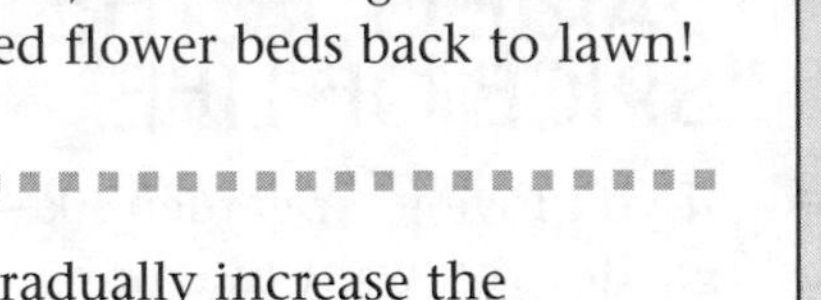

## READY, SET, GO!

Whether we buy annual transplants at a greenhouse or grow 'em ourselves, we make it a point to give 'em a little special care before their move to the great outdoors. A few days before we put them out, we cut back on their water a bit to start toughening them up. Then on the big day, we give 'em a good drink and set 'em outside in a shady, protected spot outdoors for an hour or so before bringing 'em back in. Over the next week or so, we gradually increase the amount of sun they receive and the number of hours they stay outside. Once our youngsters can stay outdoors all day without drooping, we know they're ready for the garden!

### Transplant Recovery Tonic

A sip of this soothing drink will set *all* your seedlings up right at transplanting time!

**1 tbsp. of fish emulsion**
**1 tbsp. of ammonia**
**1 tbsp. of Murphy's Oil Soap®**
**1 tsp. of instant tea granules**
**1 qt. of warm water**

Mix these ingredients in a bucket and pour into a hand-held sprayer. Mist your little plants several times a day until they're off and growing again.

It may not be a good idea to look a gift horse in the mouth, but it's *definitely* smart to look carefully at gift plants from friends. Before we add any new plant to our test gardens, we check it closely to make sure it looks healthy, with no signs of pest or disease problems. We also ask questions or do some research to find out whether the plant produces lots of unwanted seedlings, or if its roots spread far and wide. Unless we're 100 percent sure the plant is healthy and well behaved, we plant it in a small "quarantine" bed, where we can keep a close eye on it for a year or two. If it passes muster, it goes into our flower garden; if not, it goes in the trash!

## FUN IN THE SUN

Did you know that plants can get sunburned, just like people? When tender leaves are suddenly exposed to strong sunshine, you'll see tan, bronzed, or scorched-looking patches on the leaves or flowers within a couple of hours. To prevent sun damage, we suggest exposing indoor-grown plants to sunshine gradually—a few hours more each day over a period of a week or two. If you see these symptoms on plants that are already in the garden, take our advice: Give 'em a long, cool drink *right away,* and move them to a shadier spot as soon as you can.

## VARIETY IS THE SPICE OF LIFE

If you love your garden like we do, you want to enjoy it as long as possible. Well, we've found that a typical flower bed offers little to look at through the winter, but a mixed border gives us something to enjoy every single day of the year! So whenever we can, we like to bulk up our test-garden plantings with shrubs and small trees featuring colorful bark, berries, and/or handsome branching habits to have beauty through the dreary winter months. Rounding out our flower gardens with a variety of different plants turned out to have a bonus benefit: It leaves less room for pesky weeds, which are always more than happy to take over if *we* don't fill the space first!

### A LITTLE OFF THE TOP, PLEASE!

Believe it or not, taking some of the top growth off your flower transplants can actually help them settle in faster. We've found that pinching or snipping off the tips of the stems, as well as any flower buds and open blossoms, encourages transplants to put more energy into growing new roots, so they'll settle in quicker. Plus, they'll come back a whole lot bushier, with many more blooms than before—and isn't that what flower gardening is all about?

## USE THESE CLUES

Wondering when to wet your bloomers? Listen to your plants—they'll tell you when they need water! Here are some signs to look for:

- Leaves that droop during the heat of the day but perk up again in the evening.
- Leaves that are duller or grayer than normal.
- Normally plump leaves that shrivel slightly or feel soft to the touch.

The experts at our test gardens want me to remind you that plants that have *too much* moisture can show the same symptoms as those that don't have enough.

So before you water, always take a look at the soil—pull the mulch aside, if you have to—and make sure the ground isn't actually waterlogged.

## BEAT 'EM UP!

Kitchen scraps are great compost ingredients, but if you have an open compost bin like we do at the test gardens, those tasty trimmings can attract skunks, mice, and other critters. So we've found another way to put these nutrient-rich leftovers to good use: Take any combination of plant-based kitchen scraps—like table scraps (no meat or fats), eggshells, and potato peelings—and put 'em in an old blender. Fill it to the top with water, blend it all up, then pour it around the base of your flowering plants. That gets the goodness right to plant roots *without* providing a buffet dinner for the neighborhood critters!

### All-Season Green-Up Tonic

If your plants are looking a bit peaked, give them a taste of this sweet snack. It's rich in nutrients and packed with energizers, too: just what plants need to stay happy and healthy all summer long. They'll green up in a jiffy!

**1 can of beer**
**1 cup of ammonia**
**1/2 cup of dishwashing liquid**
**1/2 cup of liquid lawn food**
**1/2 cup of molasses or clear corn syrup**

Mix these ingredients in a large bucket, pour into a 20 gallon hose-end sprayer, and spray everything in sight—not just your flowers, but also your trees, shrubs, lawn, and even vegetables. Apply this tonic every three weeks right up through the first hard frost, and your whole yard will come through the hot summer months with flying colors!

## WATER ON THE SPOT

Want to give a cherished plant buddy its own personal water supply? Here's what we do: Make a pinhole in the bottom of a 1-liter soda bottle, then sink the base of the bottle slightly into the soil next to the plant. Keep the bottle filled, and it'll leak a slow, but steady, supply of water—just what newly planted flowers need to get growing!

## AN EGG-CELLENT IDEA

Just like people, plants need calcium to grow sturdy and strong. To give your flowers a quick calcium fix, dry some eggshells in the microwave or oven and crush them underfoot on your garage floor, then add them to any planting mix. Or try this trick that one of the old-timers at our test gardens swears by: Soak the eggshells in water overnight and use the liquid to water *and* feed plants at the same time.

## DON'T DELAY—WEED TODAY

Whenever one of us is tempted to put off weeding our part of the test garden, the others never fail to remind us with a little poem: "One year's seeding makes seven years' weeding." We've all found that baby weeds are always easier to pull than full-grown adults, and we can be sure that they haven't had a chance to flower and set seed. So do what we do, and make it a habit to always pull weed seedlings as soon as you spot 'em. Trust us—you'll save yourself a whole lot of work in the long run!

### TRIED-AND-TRUE

**G**randma Putt always swore that nothin' fed her flowers better than a cup of compost tea. It's a breeze to brew your own at home, just the way Grandma did: Simply put several shovelfuls of compost into a large trash can, and fill the can to the top with water. Allow the mixture to sit for a day or two, stirring it several times each day. Give each plant about a cup of this tea every two weeks, and your plants will be filled with more flowers than you can believe!

*Save your plastic jugs after the milk is gone. Before you rinse them out, fill them to the top with tap water, and use it on your outdoor plants. This milky water will make them lush and green. Why? I don't know, but I know it works!*

Sharon B., Deland, FL

## RAINDROPS KEEP FALLIN' ON MY HEAD

And on our mulch, too! Mulch can do great things for your flowers—*if* you know the secret to applying it. The best time to mulch is after a heavy rain, before the weather gets too hot. One year, we learned the hard way never to apply mulch when the ground is dry. The mulch absorbed any rainwater that happened to come along and let it evaporate before it could soak into the soil, so we ended up having to water twice as much the rest of the summer. You can be darn sure we never did that again!

## MULCH MANAGEMENT

When it comes to mulching a flower garden, there's a right way and a wrong way. What we *don't* want you to do is pile it up around the base of your plants, so it looks like they're rising out of mini mulch mountains. That'll hold moisture against your plants' leaves and stems, which is an open invitation for fungi, as well as borers, mice, and various other critters. Through trial and error, we've found that keeping a 2- to 3-inch-wide mulch-free zone around the base of each plant prevents these problems but still gives us all the great soil-building benefits.

## THE PATH TO SUCCESS

Bark mulches might seem all the same at first glance, but if you're using them to cover a flower garden path, it pays to be picky. We strongly suggest sticking with *shredded* bark, because the pieces tend to knit together. We've found that makes for a much firmer path than bark *chips*, which tend to slide around underfoot and get pushed off the pathway.

### JERRY'S Q&A

**Q** I've often heard you say that newly planted flowers need careful watering until they "get established." What exactly does that mean?

**A** For annual transplants, that means watering once every five to seven days for the first month. Newly planted perennials need watering once a week for their first growing season in your garden. After that, your flowers should do fine all on their own.

## Mulch Moisturizer Tonic

Mulching your flower garden in spring will go a long way toward minimizing maintenance chores for the rest of the growing season. To really kick things into action, overspray your mulch with this fantastic formula.

**1 can of regular cola (not diet)**
**1/2 cup of ammonia**
**1/2 cup of antiseptic mouthwash**
**1/2 cup of baby shampoo**

Mix these ingredients in your 20 gallon hose-end sprayer, and give your mulch a long, cool drink. Add more mulch as needed through the season to keep it at the same depth. Treat it with this spray each time you re-mulch, then get ready to have the most bloom-filled flower beds on your block!

## DON'T WAIT TO STAKE

Of all the chores that need doin' around the flower garden, our least favorite by far is staking. We used to put it off as long as possible, then struggle to find ways to prop floppy stems; no matter what we did, the results always looked awful. Eventually, one of the new folks at our test gardens took pity on us and shared her secret: Do your staking in spring, when new shoots are no more than a few inches tall. Putting stakes in at this time of year takes just minutes, and the plants grow up through their supports in no time. By midsummer, the supports aren't even visible, but we know they're there, because now our proud perennials are standing straight and tall!

## PRUNING PROPS

We're always tickled when we can find a way to use things we already have, instead of spending hard-earned dough on store-bought gardening supplies. If you're as frugal as we are, you'll love this trick: Recycle tree and shrub prunings as supports for floppy flowers! Simply stick several stems into the ground—cut end down, twiggy end up—around each clump of plants in spring. Snap the branch tips over toward the center of the clump (don't break them off completely) for extra stem support, and get rid of any pointy ends sticking up. Your supply of stakes will be never-ending and, best of all, *free!*

*I came up with a wonderful idea for my bleeding heart plant. After the plant has died back for the winter and before it starts to grow in the spring, I put a tomato cage over it so that the plant will have something to hold it up. This trick works great for other bushy perennials, too!*

Karen W., Wentachee, WA

## THE TIES THAT BIND

Here's another super recycling tip from our clever test-garden crew: Save old pantyhose to make perfect plant ties! One ruined pair or two can supply all the ties you'll need for an entire year. Simply cut across each leg piece to get a bunch of 1- to 2-inch-wide loops. Slide the loops onto your wrist as you head out to the garden, and you've got a supply of soft but sturdy plant ties close at hand.

## THE BIG CHILL

Contrary to what you might think, the point of mulching your flower garden in winter *isn't* to keep the plants warm—it's to keep them *cold!* Soil that keeps freezing, thawing, and refreezing through the winter can break delicate roots, eventually pushing plants right out of the ground. But if you wait until the soil is frozen before you mulch, it will stay cold even during midwinter thaws, and your perennials will stay well grounded until it's safe for them to grow again in spring.

## 'SNO JOKE!

When the weather forecast calls for heavy snow, all the folks who work at our test gardens couldn't be happier. No, we're not crazy: We know (and now you will, too) that a nice, thick blanket of snow is one of the best winter mulches that flower beds could ask for. For even more insulation, feel free to pile extra snow on 'em as you clear your sidewalks and driveway. Just be sure you *don't* shovel snow on flower beds if it's likely to contain deicing salts, because the salt can harm plant roots.

**Test Garden SECRET**

You can bet that we've tried a multitude of mulches in our test gardens over the years, and you know what? We've found that it really doesn't matter what type of wood chips, bark chunks, or shavings you use to mulch your flower beds, as long as you put shredded cedar or eucalyptus mulch underneath them! For some reason, these aromatic woods seem to discourage insects from setting up shop when they're either worked into the soil or laid on top of it.

## GET WIRED

A few years ago, we tried to grow some hanging baskets at our test gardens, but a few pesky birds kept insisting on making their nests in them. Besides making it difficult for us to water, the birds left droppings all over the paved areas under the baskets—definitely not the effect we were going for. So the next year, we took pieces of chicken wire (roughly 1 foot square for an 8-inch basket) and covered the top of each basket right after planting, tucking the edges of the wire into the soil. The plants could easily pop up through the wire, but the birds couldn't get in to build their nests—a perfect solution!

### Year-Round Refresher Tonic

Do your flowers tend to go hog-wild for a while, then fade out by midsummer? We've found that feeding lightly, but often, with this refresher tonic gives much better results than one big supper of chemical fertilizer at planting time. Our plants grow more steadily, bloom better, and stay healthier than we ever dreamed possible—and now yours can, too!

**1 cup of beer**
**1 cup of baby shampoo**
**1 cup of liquid lawn food**
**1/2 cup of molasses**
**2 tbsp. of fish emulsion**
**Ammonia**

Mix the beer, shampoo, lawn food, molasses, and fish emulsion in a 20 gallon hose-end sprayer. Fill the balance of the sprayer jar with ammonia, then apply liberally to your flower beds to the point of run-off every three weeks from spring through fall. (In warm climates, you can use it year-round.)

## FOOD FROM YOUR FLOWER GARDEN

Have a tiny yard? You can still have a garden that's beautiful *and* bountiful—by planting pretty veggies and herbs among your flowers! Cherry tomato plants can hold their own in any beauty contest, and when you stake 'em up, they can easily take the place of a large perennial in a bed or border. For the middle of the garden, try eye-catching edibles such as kale, leeks, peppers, and Swiss chard. And down at the front, red and green leaf lettuces, along with curly parsley and spinach, make great edging plants.

## JUMP-START YOUR SPRING SHOW

On the first mild days after a long cold winter, my family always knows where to look for me—out in the yard, hunting for the earliest spring blooms. And I always know where to search first: those warm spots on the south side of my house, snugged up against the foundation wall. These southern spots thaw out early, so the perennials and bulbs I plant there always bloom a few weeks earlier than they do in other parts of my yard. If you want to get a jump start on spring in your own yard, give this southern-exposure trick a try—I guarantee you'll have the first flowers on the block!

## END YOUR WATERING WOES

Sandy-soil gardens are a dream to dig in, but a nightmare to keep watered. Well, we can free you from summer-long watering chores with a single word: *Mulch!* A 2- to 3-inch-deep layer of shredded bark, chopped leaves, or other mulch works wonders to keep even the sandiest soil moist and cool for great root growth. It adds organic matter, too, which helps your soil hold moisture. Just make sure you mulch *after* a rain or thorough watering, when the ground is totally moist. Otherwise, you'll have to water *more* to wet both the mulch and the soil!

## GIVE 'EM A LIFT

If your soil's too wet or rocky to dig down, then why not grow up—with raised beds! Build low frames with rocks or lumber (we make ours about 6 inches high), and fill 'em with a mix of topsoil and compost. The frames can be any length you want, but our test-garden experts suggest keeping the width no more than 6 feet if you can reach in from both sides, or 3 feet if you can reach in from only one side. That way, you'll never have to step into the beds, which can pack down and spoil that loose, crumbly soil!

### From Our Readers

*Instead of breaking your back trying to remove tree stumps, use them as planters. Gouge out the top of the stump 3 to 6 inches deep, then fill the hole with rich soil, mixing in well-rotted manure or compost. Transplant a few annuals into it, and water well for eye-catching color all summer long.*

Gerald M.,
Mascoutah, IL

## TRY A FEW LATER BLOOMERS, TOO

Do your flower beds tend to fizzle out by fall? When that happens here at our test gardens, we don't waste time studying books and nursery catalogs: We pile into our cars and go for a drive in the country! Wildflowers that adorn the roadsides in autumn are a super source of ideas for fall flower gardens. Asters top the list for autumn color, but goldenrods (*Solidago*) are great, too; 'Fireworks' has golden blooms that literally explode into flower in fall, just as its name suggests. And before you ask—our experts promise that goldenrods take a bum rap for causing fall hayfever; the real culprit is plain old ragweed, which blooms at the same time but blends into the background, so no one notices it!

### Perfect Partners Planting Mix

Whether you're using annuals as temporary fillers around new perennials or as beautiful bedmates every year, this planting mix will get the soil in great shape for *all* of your flowers.

**4 cups of bonemeal**
**2 cups of gypsum**
**2 cups of Epsom salts**
**1 cup of wood ashes**
**1 cup of lime**
**4 tbsp. of medicated baby powder**
**1 tbsp. of baking powder**
**Peat moss**

Mix these ingredients in a wheelbarrow with a bucketful of dried peat moss. Toss a handful into each planting hole, and scatter some over the soil around established clumps, too. Lightly scratch it into the soil, then water it in well before applying a 2- to 3-inch-thick layer of mulch over the whole area. Before you know it, your flower beds will be off to a rip-roarin' start!

## A VINE IDEA

Tired of looking at those boring, single-season shrubs in your yard? Forsythias, lilacs, flowering quince (*Chaenomeles*), and other spring-flowering shrubs are great for early color, but once they're done blooming, they're just taking up space. The folks at our test gardens found a great way to make our shrubs do double duty, by pairing them with annual vines. Some of our favorite shrub buddies include morning glories (*Ipomoea*), hyacinth bean (*Lablab purpureus*), and scarlet runner bean (*Phaseolus coccineus*). With just a little guidance, these climbers will quickly scramble up through shrub stems, then produce bunches of blooms from early summer clear through to frost.

## LIGHT UP THE NIGHT

With so much to get done during the day at our test gardens, we're lucky to find a few minutes to admire our home flower gardens before dark. If your schedule's as busy as ours, you'll love our secret strategy: Plan ahead for nighttime strolling! Plants with white and pale yellow flowers will show up with just the tiniest bit of light, as will silvery or white-variegated leaves. And try this trick we learned from one of my helpers: Outline your paths with white stones, or make them out of white gravel, so it's easy to see where you are going, even when light is lacking!

## PUT 'EM IN POTS

Are tree roots making digging too daunting? Potted plants are a perfect way to bring color to those tough sites in the shade. The shade-gardening experts at our test gardens recommend long-blooming annuals like begonias and impatiens for loads of showy flowers, or coleus for a spectacular show of brightly colored leaves. The larger the container, the better—half-whiskey barrels with holes drilled in the bottom are ideal—because big planters need watering way less often than small pots do.

## GET AN EDGE

None of us here at the test gardens would consider ourselves neatniks, but there's one thing we all agree on: There's nothing like crisply edged flower beds to make a yard look its blue-ribbon best. But that doesn't mean you have to spend hours cutting or trimming those edges by hand—do what we've done, and install edging strips! You can buy commercial plastic or rubber edging strips, or make your own from landscape timbers, stones, or bricks. Install the strips so that their top edge is just slightly above the soil surface. That way, you can mow around your beds with the wheels on one side riding along the strip, trimming as you go!

### From Our Readers

*Over the past several years, we have added newly gathered pine needles to all of our garden paths. They smell good, add color, and keep our feet dry and free of mud! Even after a rain, they are dry on top of the path. People who have seen our garden areas and walked on our special pine needle garden paths always remark, "What a great idea!"*

Elmer C.,
Portland, OR

## LEAF ROLL-UP

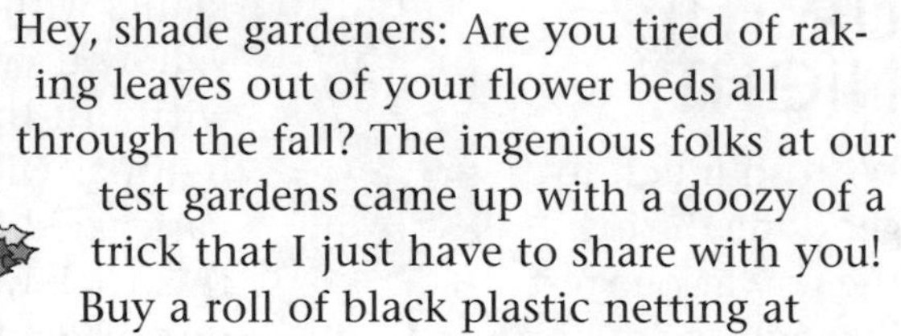

Hey, shade gardeners: Are you tired of raking leaves out of your flower beds all through the fall? The ingenious folks at our test gardens came up with a doozy of a trick that I just have to share with you! Buy a roll of black plastic netting at your local garden center (we used ½-inch mesh netting), and lay it over your flower beds as soon as the leaves start to fall. Once all the leaves are down, simply roll up the netting and carry the leaves right to your compost pile. How easy is that? This trick works great on lawn and groundcover areas, too!

## NO-MOW SLOPES

If you're tired of coping with tough-to-mow slopes, you'll love our quick stair-step trick! Head over to your local lumberyard and pick up a bunch of warped, discounted boards—pine 4 × 8s are ideal. Starting at the top of the slope, place the boards on edge running across the area, and drive wooden pegs to hold the boards in place. Make sure the boards fit firmly against the ground, then fill in behind them with soil to make level planting areas for flowering groundcovers. The boards will rot away after a few seasons, but by that time, your slope garden will be settled in and growin' strong—with no mowing required!

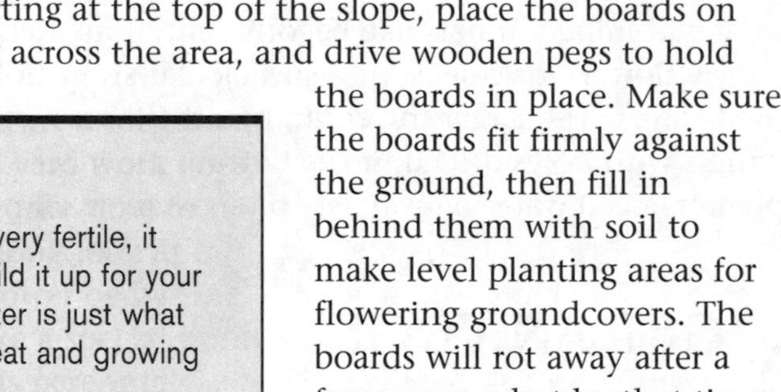

### Soil-Builder Tonic

Unless you're *sure* that your soil is naturally very fertile, it makes sense to take every opportunity to build it up for your flowers. This all-natural, home-blended fertilizer is just what you need to keep all your flowers looking great and growing their very best.

**6 parts greensand or wood ashes**
**3 parts cottonseed meal**
**3 parts bonemeal**
**Gypsum**
**Limestone**

Mix the greensand or wood ashes, cottonseed meal, and bonemeal together. Add 2 cups of gypsum and 1 cup of limestone per gallon-sized container of the resulting mixture. Apply 5 pounds of the mixture per 100 square feet of garden area a few weeks before planting, or work it into the soil around established perennials.

## BERM ME UP, SCOTTY!

A few years ago, we were trying to figure out a way to screen out both the noise and the view of street traffic from our test gardens without spending a fortune on a fence. We considered a clipped hedge, but none of us volunteered to do the tedious trimming; an evergreen screen would have been nice, but we didn't want to wait forever the trees to fill in. Finally, we found the perfect solution: a soil berm! (A berm, by the way, is a raised mound of ground spruced up with flowers and shrubs.)

To build a berm, we outlined the shape we wanted with a dusting of lime (you can use flour instead). We spread a base of several inches of gravel within the outline, and topped it with about 18 inches of heavy clay soil. We covered that with another foot of good topsoil, mixed with compost, and set out our chosen plants. A generous layer of mulch helped hold the soil in place and keep down weeds. We've been as pleased as punch with our pretty privacy screen (and with all the time and money we saved in the bargain)!

## MOVE OVER, MULCH

Here's one tip that can really be a time-saver in a large garden—or any size garden, for that matter. Lay your mulch down after you prepare the soil, but *before* you plant. Sounds crazy? Not really. For one thing, it takes less time to spread the mulch when you don't have to be careful around tender new transplants. And when the time comes to get those babies in the ground, you simply push the mulch aside, dig a hole for each plant, and pop the plant into the hole. Easy! Gently push the mulch around the new plants, and you're done.

**Q** Some people tell me that sand's great for loosening up my clay soil, while others insist the opposite's true. Who's right?

**A** Sand *can* help, but only if you add enough! Spread at least 3 inches of sand over the area, and work it into the top 6 inches of soil. Adding less than that won't turn your soil into cement—that's an old wives' tale—but it also won't make a difference in helping loosen up tough clay.

## WATCH OUT!

Are your flowering plants not looking as lush and green as usual? They might just need a snack; but before you reach for the fertilizer, it's smart to rule out possible pest problems first. Here are some clues we want you to watch for:

- If tiny white bugs fly up when you brush the plant with your hand, whiteflies are at work.
- Webbing on stems, webbing under leaves, and yellow-speckled leaves are sure signs of spider mites.
- Sticky leaves and stunted or distorted shoots are the calling cards of pesky aphids.

It's easy to send any and all of these pests packin'—just give 'em a shot of insecticidal soap or our Flower Defender Tonic (at left) to send 'em on their way!

### Flower Defender Tonic

Bad bugs feed on lots of different flowers, so it's smart to be ready for them. This power-packed mix will wipe out just about any bad bugs.

**1 cup of dishwashing liquid**
**1 cup of tobacco tea***
**1 cup of antiseptic mouthwash**
**1/4 cup of hot sauce**
**Warm water**

Mix these ingredients in a 20 gallon hose-end sprayer, filling the balance of the sprayer jar with warm water. Then bathe all of your bloomers with this bug-busting elixir to send those pesky pests running for the hills!

*To make tobacco tea, place half a handful of chewing tobacco in the toe of an old nylon stocking and soak it in a gallon of hot water until the mixture is dark brown. Pour the liquid into a glass container with a tight lid for storage.

## A QUICK FIX

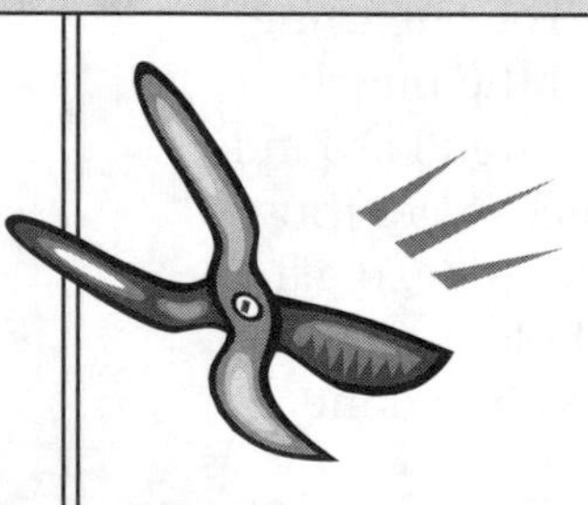

Want to know our all-time favorite way to get rid of any plant pest, *pronto?* Simply pinch or prune off the branches or leaves where they're hanging out! Drop the infested plant parts in a plastic grocery bag, tie it up, and throw it away.

## KEEP IT CLEAN

At our test gardens, we make it at habit to give our flower beds a good washing before applying *any* pest control spray (or any liquid fertilizer, for that matter). Why? Soapy water scrubs leaves clean of dust, dirt, and pollution, so it's easier for our plants to take up the good stuff that follows.

Best of all, it couldn't be easier to make: We just use 1 cup of dishwashing liquid applied with a 20 gallon hose-end sprayer. Try it for yourself, and you'll see your flowers turn into lean, green, growing machines!

## PICK A PECK OF BEETLES

Many beetles are actually good guys in the garden, eating bad bugs that spoil your flower fun. But there *are* a few that can cause problems—*big* problems—when they start feeding in your flower beds. When we spot beetles breakfasting on our bloomers, we pick them off by hand and drop them into soapy water. (We've found that early morning is the best time for beetle-hunting, by the way, because cooler temperatures make these pests sluggish and easier to catch.) Once you have a bunch of beetles, use them to whip up a batch of our Beetle Juice (see page 83).

## ROUGH 'EM UP

Have a woodworker or carpenter in your family? Ask 'em to save their used sandpaper disks for you, because they make super slug busters! Cut a slit up to the center of the disk, and put the disk on the ground around the stem of your plant, like a collar. We've been using this trick in our test gardens for a few years now, and our seedlings have been safe ever since, because slugs don't dare cross the scratchy surface!

**Q** I've heard a lot about all the great things that mulch can do for flowers, and it sounds too good to be true. So, what's the catch?

**A** Mulch *does* work like magic, holding in soil moisture, keeping roots cool, and stopping soil from splashing onto the plants. Unfortunately, the cool, damp conditions that are so good for root growth are also perfect for pesky soil-dwelling pests, like slugs, snails, and cutworms. I'd still suggest using mulch for all the benefits it provides, but if these creepy-crawlies start attacking your plants, rake away the mulch for a few weeks until things dry out a little, and you'll have the problem under control.

## DO THE JAVA JIVE

If slugs are destroying your daisies and making Swiss cheese out of your hostas, we've got some great news for you! Researchers have recently discovered that even diluted solutions of coffee can make slugs think twice about snacking on your bloomers. Nobody yet knows exactly why this works, but the important thing is that it *does!* So when you have a bit of coffee left over, don't dump it down the drain—toss it into your flower garden and say "So long!" to those slimy slitherers!

We've had great results using floating row cover in our vegetable gardens, so we decided to try it in our flower beds, too. And you know what? It worked great there, as well! Besides protecting our baby bloomers from chilly winds, strong sunshine, and pounding raindrops, the row cover also kept critters, like rascally rabbits, away. We left it on for just a week or two after planting; after that, the plants were settled in and ready to come out from under the covers, so to speak!

## SAY GOODBYE, SUCKERS!

Visitors to our test gardens often remark on how tidy our place looks, but you can bet they're absolutely speechless when they see us *vacuuming* our flowers! No, we don't do that to keep 'em free of dust and dirt; we do it to get rid of pesky plant pests. When we find a bunch of bugs bugging our bloomers, we run a handheld, rechargeable vacuum cleaner lightly over the infested plants, while using our free hand to gently brush the leaves and stems. (This encourages the pests to fly up and be caught in the suction.) When we're done, we simply dump the pests into a bucket of soapy water, away from our plants. Give this trick a try yourself—but make sure your neighbors aren't watching!

### THORNY PROTECTION

Grandma Putt never let anything go to waste in her home or in her garden. So when it came time to prune her roses, she didn't bother trying to bag, burn, or shred those thorny stems; instead, she cut 'em up and scattered 'em around her flower garden. They did a bang-up job of keeping rabbits and other hungry varmints away from her tender transplants!

## THE NATURAL SOLUTION

When the growing season's in full swing, it seems like we never have enough help in our test gardens. So last year, we decided to recruit some help—from our neighborhood toads. Our experts tell me that a single toad can eat between 10,000 and 20,000 insects and other creepy-crawlies a year! You can buy toad houses from garden-supply catalogs, but we made our own by using a hammer to chip a doorway out of the rim of an old clay pot. Nestled upside down in a cool, shady spot, these homemade abodes provide a perfect home for pest-munching toads!

### Beetle Juice

Are beetles chomping at your beautiful bloomers? A dose of this elixir can save the day. This recipe sure isn't for the squeamish, but we've found that nothing beats it for fighting bad beetles!

**1/2 cup of beetles (both larval and adult beetles, dead or alive)**
**2 cups of water**
**1 tsp. of dishwashing liquid**

Collect the beetles and whirl 'em up in an old blender (one that you'll never again use for food) with 2 cups of water. Strain the liquid through cheesecloth and mix in the dishwashing liquid. Pour about 1/4 cup of the juice into a 1-gallon hand-held sprayer, and fill the rest of the sprayer jar with water. Spray your plants from top to bottom, and make sure you coat both sides of the leaves. Wear gloves when handling this mixture, and be sure to clean the blender with hot, soapy water when you're done.

## OH, DEER!

Of all the troublesome critters that like to feed on flower beds, deer have to be one of the toughest to control. A tall fence is the most dependable option, but we didn't want to completely enclose all of our gardens, so we decided to depend on repellents instead, and we've been pleased as punch with the results. Within the gardens, we sprinkle bloodmeal or human hair trimmings on and around our plants. And for extra protection, we place stakes around the outermost parts of the gardens and hang bars of strongly scented deodorant soap at deer nose level. We've found that if we get 'em out early, *before* the deer develop a taste for our flowers, repellents do a fairly good job of keeping our bloomers from getting munched for lunch.

# KEEP CUTWORMS AT BAY

I still remember the first time I planted a flower garden at my first home—not because it was such a success, but because it was such a disaster! I planted all my carefully nurtured seedlings, and when I went out the next day to admire my handiwork, a good number of them had been nipped off right at ground level and left to wilt. Over the next few days, nearly all of the remaining seedlings fell prey to the same fate.

Eventually, I discovered the culprit: cutworms. These dastardly demons strike at night, chewing through stems at ground level. So now, before I set out new transplants, I cut a bunch of 1- to 2-inch-tall rings from the cardboard tubes inside paper towel or toilet tissue rolls. After planting, I slip one collar over each transplant, and push it into the soil a bit to keep the critters from slithering underneath it. Hooray—no more cutworm problems!

## All-Purpose Bug & Thug Spray

Very cold winter weather can strike a big blow against the bad bugs that plague your flower beds, but you can't depend on it to kill all of them. You *can* rely on our all-purpose spray to do the job!

**3 tbsp. of baking soda**
**2 tbsp. of Murphy's Oil Soap®**
**2 tbsp. of canola oil or other vegetable oil**
**2 tbsp. of vinegar**
**2 gal. of warm water**

Mix these ingredients in a bucket, pour into a hand-held sprayer, and mist-spray your plants until they are dripping wet. Apply in early spring, just when the bugs and thugs are waking up from their long winter's nap, and you'll say "So long!" to those bad boys.

# From Our Readers

## PLANT POOL

Before a rainstorm, I put a small plastic kiddie pool out on my patio. After the rainstorm fills it up, I put all of my potted plants in it for a refreshing dip. They love it!

*Lori L., Dothan, AL*

## POTTING PLANTS

When I'm potting plants in clay pots that have a drainage hole at the bottom, I cover the hole by placing a piece of my wife's discarded pantyhose inside the pot—enough to cover the hole and go up the sides of the pot as well. Then I add my potting soil and plants. The pantyhose will not let any soil leach out of the bottom, while excess water can still drain out.

*Ed V., Pella, IA*

## SUPER SEEDLINGS

An easy way to get seedlings up faster is to use hot water in a cooler chest. Put the seed trays in a 48-quart cooler, leaving about 5 inches of open space in the center. Then fill a large, zip-top plastic bag with hot water, and place it in the open space between the trays. Close the lid, and the heat from the water warms the cooler and seeds for 6 to 8 hours. Change the water three or four times a day, and the seeds will be up in no time at all!

*Gerald M., Mascoutah, IL*

## HOW LOW IS TOO LOW?

Sometimes, a brown lawn is the result of mowing too close, not from a lack of water. If you're watering like you should, but your lawn still looks brown, check the preferred mowing height for your kind of grass. You might find that you're cropping it too short, and you can green things up again just by mowing a little higher.

*Matthew D., Rock Springs, WY*

MORE TIPS

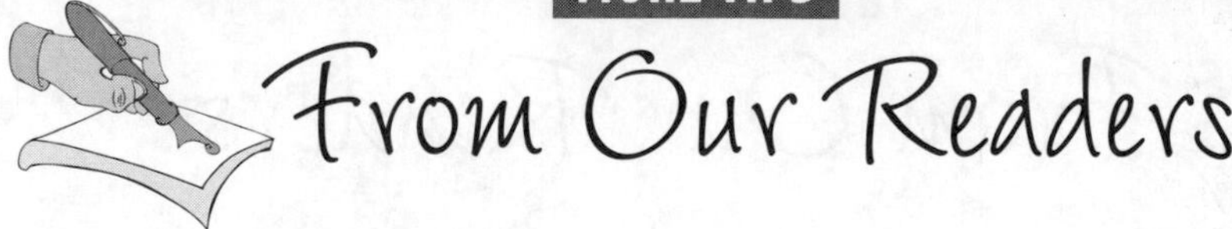

# From Our Readers

## WATER WONDER

I inherited a very special and different plant, which I think is an African primrose. It looks like a giant violet plant. It never did very well until I started using bottled water on it. Now it is absolutely beautiful. The ends of the leaves have stopped turning brown, and the blooms are huge. I have to use name-brand waters because I find that the store-brand water is not pure enough. This plant seems to be especially "allergic" to trace chlorine and fluoride in public water.

***Samantha S., Lakewood, CO***

## OXYGEN BOOST

For healthy, happy houseplants, I mix 1 ounce of 3-percent hydrogen peroxide in 1 quart of water. I mist the leaves with it and pour it on the soil. It gives plants that extra boost of oxygen to make them grow faster and have more blooms.

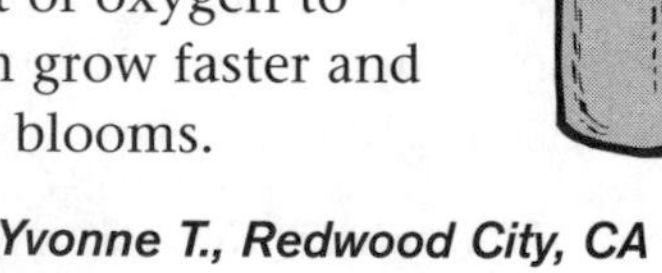

***Yvonne T., Redwood City, CA***

## SLUG BUSTER

If slugs are eating your garden up, get some grit for pet birds (it can be purchased at your local pet shop), and sprinkle it around your flowers. It not only keeps the slugs away, but it also helps plants grow because it contains lots of calcium and charcoal.

***Suzanne J., Twinsburg, OH***

## PLANT FILTER

A paper coffee filter makes a great liner in the bottom of flower pots with drainage holes. Put the filter inside the pot, with or without drainage gravel on top. You'll have no more soil draining into the plant saucer.

***Debbie L., Lansing, MI***

## THIRST QUENCHER

To help keep potted flowers quenched, I cut up unused disposable diapers and add them to the potting soil. They hold water longer, which is great if you have no one to water your flowers while on vacation!

***Julie S., Collinsville, IL***

# From Our Readers

## EASY OVER GRAVEL

I installed black plastic edging around my flower beds. In order to avoid having to trim around the edging, I dug a small moat, about 5 to 6 inches wide and 2 to 3 inches deep, butting up to the edging. I filled the moat with gravel to make it level with the lawn, and now I just run my lawnmower along that moat!

***Kathi K., Akron, OH***

## FISHY FERTILIZER

I use the water from my fish tank to water my plants, both indoors and out. I also use the bio-bag filters to cover drain holes in my pots.

***Kate M., Maryville, MO***

## SOIL STOPPER

Before planting seeds in a pot or repotting a plant, I place a used dryer sheet in the bottom of the pot (dryer lint is okay, too). Then when I water, the soil doesn't wash out of the pot and into the saucer.

***Doris B., Ghent, WV***

## QUICK SEED STARTS

To germinate seeds in as little as five days, steep five chamomile tea bags in 1 gallon of warm water for about 15 minutes. Then place a paper towel on a plate and pour the tea over the towel to soak it. Sprinkle the seeds on the wet paper towel, and fold the towel to cover the seeds. Add more tea, if necessary, to make sure the paper towel is wet on both sides, but leave the towel on the plate. Cover the plate with an inverted plate of the same size to retain the moisture, heat, and darkness. Put the covered plate somewhere it will not be disturbed. After 5 days, look at your seeds. Most seeds that require 14 to 21 days to germinate will already be growing! The great thing about using a paper towel is that you can plant the seeds, towel and all, without disturbing them.

***Sally V., Davison, MI***

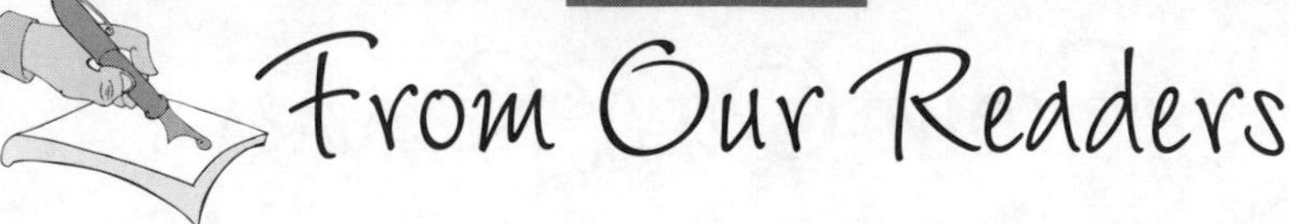

# From Our Readers

## CLEAR PROTECTION

When plants are just peeking through the dirt, and various bugs and birds have them on their menu, I use tall, clear, plastic drink cups, with the bottoms cut out, to cover them. Not only does it protect the plants, but it also provides hours of entertainment watching the birds try to peck through the clear cups!

***June H., Wentachee, WA***

## POTTED PLANT WATER

Our central air conditioner removes 5 to 10 gallons of water from the air each day from late spring to early fall, while cooling our home. The water is piped outside, where I catch it in gallon jugs and use it on our many potted flowers. Any water that is not used overflows from the jugs and goes into my garden.

***Parker C., Hastings, NE***

## DEER-FREE

To keep deer out of my flower beds, I sprinkle cinnamon and ground black pepper over the soil. Works like a charm!

***Brian D., Walla Walla, WA***

## FLICK OFF BLOSSOMS

Here's an easy way to head off blossom-end rot: Flick off the blossom from the bottom of the fruit with your finger. It costs nothing, and it works 100 percent of the time if done before the rot starts. I've shared this tip with my gardening friends, and they all agree that it works.

***Florian B., Princeton, IL***

## QUICK BUG CHECK

Whenever I'm out in my flower garden, I always carry a folded-up piece of white paper in my pocket. Then, whenever I see flowers that aren't doing so good, I hold the paper under the blooms, and tap the stems to see what bugs fall out. They're easy to spot that way!

***Kris D., Big Rapids, MI***

# Chapter 5

# Amazing Annuals

Of all the beautiful bloomers there are to choose from, annuals win the prize hands down for being the most versatile. They're great for new gardeners, bringing months of dependable color without demanding a lot of special fuss. But beginners aren't the only ones who appreciate annuals: Even pros like to pack their plantings full of these easy-care bloomers, with their bountiful flowers, lovely leaves, and fabulous fragrance. So whether you have a small flower bed, or great big borders like we have at our test gardens, you'll want to make the most of adaptable annuals.

Of course, we all know it's smart to give flowering plants the very best soil possible. But even after years of improving our beds at the test gardens, we still have some areas where the ground isn't yet as rich or loose as we'd like. If you have the same problem, do what we do, and save your best beds for hungrier plants like perennial flowers or vegetables. We've found that for most annuals, having full sun is a lot more important than having top-quality soil!

## THINK WARM THOUGHTS

After a long winter, we know just how tempting it is to get out in the garden and start sowing seeds everywhere. But take our word for it: Rushing the season for warmth-loving annuals like marigolds and morning glories (*Ipomoea*) isn't smart gardening; in fact, it's more like a recipe for disaster! Even though the air feels warm, the ground's still cold, and seeds are far more likely to rot than sprout in chilly soil. Here at the test gardens, we've had much better results by playing it safe with summer-loving annuals—we wait until the soil has warmed up to at least 50°F before sowing annual seeds outside. Far from being left behind, these late-sown seeds sprout and grow so quickly, they'll be in bloom weeks before those sown too soon!

## DIVIDE AND CONQUER

Here at the test gardens, we're big fans of nasturtiums (*Tropaeolum majus*), zinnias, and other annuals that are easy to grow by sowing the seeds right in the garden. No fussing with lights, no troublesome transplanting—just sow 'em and grow 'em! The only trick is spreading out those seeds to fill the area you need. I put the folks here to work on this little challenge, and they came up with a super solution that we all use now: Count up the number of patches you'd like to have of each flower, and divide the seeds in the packet into that many piles on pieces of scrap paper. Fold up each piece of paper to make a little carrying packet, then simply tap the seeds out over each patch. You'll get perfect results every time!

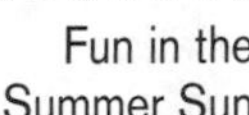

## NOTHIN' BUT NET

It can be fun to watch the antics of silly squirrels, but there's *nothin'* fun about the damage they can do to a newly planted flower bed! At one of our test gardens, we used to have problems every spring with these critters nipping off the best blooms, or even pulling whole plants out of the soil. Finally, out of desperation, one of our helpers tossed a piece of black netting over the bed that the squirrels bothered the most. After a day or two, we realized that the netting was keeping the critters away—and we promptly protected the rest of our beds the same way. We've found that leaving the netting on for just a week or two is enough to keep plants safe—and in the meantime, we hardly even notice that the net's there!

### Awesome Annual Feeder Formula

Lively annuals burn up a great deal of energy with their constant flowering, so they need to eat heartily to keep it up. For consistent color all through the growing season, stick with a liquid food that your plants can use right away, such as this terrific tonic.

**1 can of beer**
**2 tbsp. of fish emulsion**
**2 tbsp. of dishwashing liquid**
**2 tbsp. of ammonia**
**2 tbsp. of hydrogen peroxide**
**2 tbsp. of whiskey**
**1 tbsp. of clear corn syrup**
**1 tbsp. of unflavored gelatin**
**4 tsp. of instant tea granules**
**2 gal. of warm water**

Mix these ingredients together in a large bucket, and pour into a watering can. Feed all of the annuals in your yard with this mix every two weeks in the morning for glorious blooms all season long.

## FILL 'EM UP!

In the past, no matter how carefully we planned ahead, it seemed that come summer, we always ended up with a few gaps in our test-garden flower beds. Well, that's not a problem for us anymore, thanks to a great trick one of our clever helpers shared with us. Now, we pick up an extra cell-pack or two of our favorite annuals each spring, then plant them in individual pots. Then, when empty spaces appear in our beds and borders during the summer, we have a ready supply of perfect fillers to pop into those gaps!

# PERENNIAL ANNUALS

With so many flower beds to take care of, you can bet that the folks at our test gardens are always on the lookout for ways to save time and money. If it's the same for you, then try our favorite flower-gardening secret: self-sowing annuals. Plant 'em just once, and they'll come back year after year after year—kind of like perennials, but *without* the high price tag! There's nothin' second-best about these beauties, either; they have some of the prettiest flowers around. Ready to give 'em a try? Here's a list of our favorite garden-tested self-sowers:

**California poppy** (*Eschscholzia californica*)

**Corn poppy** (*Papaver rhoeas*)

**Cosmos** (*Cosmos bipinnatus*)

**Larkspur** (*Consolida ajacis*)

**Love-in-a-mist** (*Nigella damascena*)

**Shoofly plant** (*Nicandra physalodes*)

**Spider flower** (*Cleome hasslerana*)

**Sweet alyssum** (*Lobularia maritima*)

## TRIED-AND-TRUE

**W**hen it came time to sow seeds, one of Grandma Putt's favorite sayings used to be "Don't plant your corn until the oak leaf is as big as a squirrel's ear." What does that have to do with flower gardening? Well, sweet corn is a warm-weather annual, and it hates to sprout in chilly conditions. Grandma knew that once the weather was warm enough for oak leaves to reach a certain size, it was warm enough to sow corn seeds, as well as those of warm-weather annual flowers, like nasturtiums and zinnias.

## Test Garden

We get a lot of kids visiting our test gardens, so we always like to show them fun projects to get them excited about growing plants. One year, we sowed large seeds, like those of sunflowers (*Helianthus annuus*), on a moist paper towel instead of in soil, so the kids could see what newly sprouted seeds looked like. Rather than waste the baby plants, we then set them in individual pots. Imagine our surprise when those seedlings grew faster and bloomed weeks sooner than soil-sown seeds! We now sow all of our large seeds this way.

If you want to try this for yourself, here's how: Moisten a paper towel, and spread out the seeds on one side of it. Fold the other half of the towel over the seeds, then fold it in half again. Before sealing the whole package in a plastic bag, write the name of the plant on a label and tuck it in the paper towel. Set the bag in a warm place (70°F or so). Every two or three days, unfold the towel, and carefully transfer any seeds that have sprouted to pots filled with moist seed-starting mix. After that, grow 'em like you would any other seedlings.

# LET THERE BE LIGHT

Most annuals are a cinch to start from seed, but there are a few that can be tough to get going—unless you know the secret, of course! Over the years, we've experimented with growing just about every annual you can imagine, and we've found the usual practice of covering the seeds with soil can sometimes actually *discourage* sprouting. Four-o'clocks (*Mirabilis jalapa*), gloriosa daisies (*Rudbeckia hirta*), mignonette (*Reseda odorata*), portulaca (*Portulaca grandiflora*), stocks (*Matthiola*), and sweet alyssum (*Lobularia maritima*) all need light to germinate, so you definitely *don't* want to bury them when sowing. Just press them lightly into the soil surface, then mist with water often to keep them moist until they sprout.

## Bedding Plant Starter Brew

Whether you buy your annual bedding plants or grow 'em yourself, regular feeding is a must to keep 'em strong and healthy. We swear by this boozy brew to keep all of our bedding plants in top shape until transplanting time!

**2 tsp. of fish emulsion**
**2 tsp. of dishwashing liquid**
**1 tsp. of whiskey**
**1 qt. of water**

Mix these ingredients in a watering can, and feed this formula to your seedlings every other time you water them. Give them a good soak with it just before you set them out, too. Then stand back and enjoy the best-looking bloomers on the block.

# UNDERCOVER ANNUALS

What's the secret to successful transplanting? Making the transition as easy as possible on your baby plants! We always try to set out our annual transplants on cloudy days to avoid sun stress, but sometimes the weather just won't cooperate. So if Ol' Sol is shining down on us, we simply put our sun hats on our heads—and on our seedlings, too! We gather up bushel baskets, cardboard boxes, and whatever other lightweight covers we can find, and set 'em over the transplants as soon as we get 'em planted. (If we use boxes, we prop 'em up on one side with a rock to let some air in.) We give the little plants a day or two to settle in, then take off their covers and let 'em get busy growin'!

Are you planning to support your annual vines with string? Whatever you do, *don't* use the plastic kind! We tried this at one of our test gardens, thinking it would save us from having to put up new string every spring. Well, it did that, but it also left us stuck with unwinding all the dead vines when we put the garden to bed for the winter. Now, we *only* use biodegradable cotton string or uncoated jute. At the end of the season, we can simply cut down the whole mass of withered stems and string, and chuck it onto our compost pile. Talk about a time-saver!

## A CHEAT SHEET FOR WEEDERS

One of the trickiest parts of growing annuals from seed is figuring out which sprouts are the good guys and which are the weeds. Even those of us who have been gardening for years can have a tough time telling them apart! So, every time we sow seeds outdoors at our test gardens, we save a few of each kind and sow them in labeled pots indoors. When it's time to weed, we simply pick up the pot and take it out with us as a handy comparison. Now the weeds don't stand a chance—and we never pull out our baby flowers by accident!

## KEEP 'EM IN CHECK

To be fair, we should warn you that sometimes, self-sowing flowers can get a little *too* generous and produce more seedlings than you need. If we see that happening in our test gardens, we simply remove all of their flowers after the first main flush of blooms, then let only some of the follow-up flowers set seed. This works great with bushier plants, like bachelor's buttons (*Centaurea cyanus*) and cosmos (*Cosmos bipinnatus*). Spiky blooms, like larkspur (*Consolida ajacis*) and foxglove (*Digitalis purpurea*), call for a slightly different system—we cut their flower spikes back halfway after the flowers fade. That way, some seeds can form, but not *too* many!

*I live in Tennessee, where our summer heat makes it almost impossible to keep small flowerpots moist in the summer. I take a bag of cheap sponges and tear them into small pieces (1- or 2-inch squares) and put them in the bottom of my pots of annuals before I add the soil and plant. Now, I only have to water them once a day!*

C. K., Columbia, TN

## MARIGOLDS NOT VERY MERRY?

One of the annuals we get the most questions about is also one of the most popular: marigolds (*Tagetes*). These bright bloomers have a reputation for being no-fail flowers, so many folks are disappointed when their plants stop flowering in midsummer. You can be sure they're relieved when we tell them that the same thing happens in our gardens! See, marigolds like warm weather, but sometimes, things get a little too hot, even for them. So if your plants stop blooming during the dog days, do what we do: Just keep 'em watered, and be patient—they'll start flowering again when cooler weather arrives—we promise!

## TUNE IN TO PETUNIAS

When we think of classic annual flowers, petunias are among the first to come to mind. But did you know that petunias aren't true annuals? They're actually tender perennials. That means you can keep your favorite colors and flower forms from year to year if you bring 'em inside for the winter! Sometimes we dig up whole plants; other times, we take cuttings in late summer. We've found they do best indoors when we keep 'em in a bright, cool (55° to 65°F) place for the winter. When the weather warms up, we harden them off just like other indoor-grown annuals, and we're back in business! Here's a bonus hint: It's a snap to make dozens of new plants by taking cuttings from the overwintered plants in spring.

### JERRY'S Q&A

**Q** Our front yard is enclosed with a chain-link fence. It does a great job of keeping our dogs in, but it sure looks ugly! Any ideas on how to dress it up?

**A** You bet—annual vines! These quick-growing climbers will cover that fence in a flash, with lush foliage and fabulous flowers from early summer to frost. Morning glories (*Ipomoea*) and scarlet runner beans are two of our favorites, and we know you'll love 'em, too!

## SAVE THE LITTLE 'UNS!

Prefer to grow new petunias from seed? Then you *need* to know this trick that the experts at our test gardens discovered! Normally, when you pot up seedlings, you want to keep the most vigorous ones and toss the rest. But with petunias, the *smallest* seedlings are often the ones that'll produce the best blooms later on! This is especially true if you're trying to grow double-flowered petunias from seed. So next time you're potting up baby petunias, save some of the smallest, as well as the largest, and see if those little guys don't end up being the big winners in the long run!

MIX IT UP!

### Annual Protector Potion

Sap-sucking pests like aphids, leafhoppers, and spider mites can do a real number on your annuals. Besides causing yellowing or speckled leaves, distorted shoots, and overall poor growth, they can quickly spread dastardly diseases from one plant to another. To stop 'em in their tracks, try this simple but effective tonic.

**1 cup of vegetable oil**
**1 tbsp. of dishwashing liquid**
**1 cup of water**

Put 1 cup of water into a hand-held sprayer. Mix the vegetable oil and dishwashing liquid, and add 1 to 2 teaspoons of the mixture to the water in the sprayer. Shake well, then drench affected plants thoroughly—especially the undersides of the leaves, where sap-sucking pests particularly like to hide. This super solution will get rid of those bad boys, *pronto!*

## A FATAL FLAW

One of our favorite things about growing annuals is that they give so much beauty for so little bother. Sure, they might get a few pests, but for the most part, they're trouble-free. The one exception you need to watch out for is plants with stunted growth and deformed flowers: two classic signs of a nasty disease called aster yellows. Infected plants can't be cured, so pull 'em up, and toss 'em in the trash—*don't compost them!* To protect the rest of your plants, use our Annual Protector Potion (above) to control leafhoppers, aphids, and other pests that can spread this disease.

## IMPATIENS ARE A VIRTUE

Trust us—we know just how hard it can be to find top-notch flowering annuals for shady sites! You see, producing flowers takes a lot of energy, and where sun is scarce, most plants simply don't have what it takes to bloom abundantly. Fortunately, one of the exceptions to this rule is also one of the easiest-to-grow annuals around: impatiens! These trouble-free plants bear single or double blooms in bright and soft shades of pink, rose, salmon, lilac-pink, and white, from early summer all the way up to frost!

Best of all, impatiens are a snap to grow from cuttings; in fact, they'll even root sitting in a glass of water! So, instead of spending a bundle buying new plants each spring, do what we do: Keep your favorites from year to year by taking cuttings in late summer. Pot up the rooted cuttings, and keep 'em in a warm, bright spot for the winter. Come spring, take cuttings off of those impatiens, and you'll have dozens of new plants to fill your garden—all for free!

## HOW LOW CAN YOU GROW?

If you've had trouble with impatiens growing taller than you expected, you're not alone! They can get pretty rangy during the dogs days of summer—especially in the South. We've tried just about all the kinds out there, and we've found that looking for the word "compact" on the plant tag is a good clue that we'll get plants that stay dense and bushy. In our trials, impatiens in the 'Impulse' and 'Super Elfin' series turned out to be particularly dependable for putting their energy into flowers instead of tall stems!

### Test Garden SECRET

We know from experience that trying to dress up shady sites under trees can be a real headache! Surface roots make it almost impossible to dig there, and soil is so dry that the plants need watering several times a day. Well, we've found an easier way to bring bright blooms to dark corners—by placing big pots of annuals there instead! The only down side is that it can take a lot of potting soil to fill those king-size planters. So instead of filling 'em with new soil each year, we've found the perfect solution: Add 1 can of beer or one shot of bourbon, scotch, vodka, or gin—plus 1 ounce of dishwashing liquid—to 1 gallon of water. Use this mix to replace plain water whenever you make up your favorite plant food formulas. There's nothing like it to pep up that tired old soil and to keep your bloomers full of flowers!

### All-Star Annual Potting Mix

There's no need to spend money on prepackaged potting soil, 'cause you can mix your own right at home. Here's one of our favorite recipes for keeping potted annuals in tip-top shape.

**1 part topsoil**
**1 part peat moss**
**1 part vermiculite**
**1 part compost**

Mix these ingredients together in a wheelbarrow, and use it for potting up all kinds of annuals. Store any leftover mix in a closed bag, can, or box so you'll have it on hand for next year.

## FALL FROST COVER-UPS

Along with impatiens, we depend on annual begonias to fill our shady test gardens all through the growing season. We've found, though, that both of these shade stars are also among the first annuals to get nipped by cool temperatures in fall. So if the weather forecast calls for nighttime temperatures of 40°F or below, we cover our begonias and impatiens with old sheets or cardboard boxes before we head home at night. Once the temperature comes back up in the morning, we take the covers off. Since early fall frosts are often followed by a long, mild Indian summer, we've found that giving our annuals this extra TLC for a few nights often means that we get several more weeks of flowers in the fall.

## ANNUALS ON THE MOVE

Did you know that you can actually grow *any* annual in *full* shade? It's true—*if* you use this great trick: Just put 'em on wheels! Drill a few drainage holes in the bottom of an old kids' wagon or wheelbarrow, then fill it with potting soil and plant your favorite annuals inside. Set 'em in the sun for a few weeks to get 'em off to a good start, then wheel 'em to wherever you need to brighten a shady place. When they start producing fewer blooms, simply wheel 'em back into the sun until they're loaded with buds again.

## A WONDERFUL WINTER TREAT

If you love annual begonias as much as we do, you want to enjoy them as long as possible. So do what we do, and dig up a few of your plants in late summer or early fall, then cut 'em back about halfway, and pot 'em up. Set the potted begonias in a sunny east- or west-facing window, and they'll brighten your winter days with their beautiful blooms all winter long. Come spring, plant your potted buddies back out in the garden, and they'll be even bigger and better!

## MAKES SCENTS TO ME!

When folks come to see our test-garden flower beds, it's the color that draws 'em in—but it's the scent that makes them stay awhile. There's something about fragrance that makes any garden just a bit more special, so we like to work scented annuals into our beds and borders wherever we can. Don't make the same mistake we did the first year, though, when we planted as many scented flowers as we could all in one "fragrance garden." Instead of being pleasant, the effect was totally overwhelming—a hodgepodge of scents assaulted our senses! Now, we spread the fragrant flowers throughout our test gardens so that visitors can enjoy the different scents as they stroll along. Give it a try in your own garden and see if you don't agree!

## RAISE THE FRAGRANCE

When it comes to making scents, the only problem with annuals is that they're mostly on the short side. So unless you plan to spend a lot of time kneeling down to sniff your flowers, do what we do: Bring 'em up closer to nose level! Pots, planters, and hanging baskets are all great options for showcasing scented blooms. For something extra-special, try adding a few fragrant annuals to a window box outside your kitchen or bedroom window, so you can enjoy the delightful scents even when you're stuck indoors!

**Q** A couple of times now, I've bought plants that were supposed to be very fragrant, and I can't detect any scent at all! Is it me, or is the book wrong?

**A** Well, it's you—but it's not your fault! Some people can detect most or all of the chemical compounds that cause various scents, while others can smell only a few of them. The lesson here is that you shouldn't buy a plant just because someone else thinks it smells great—always sniff for yourself *before* you buy.

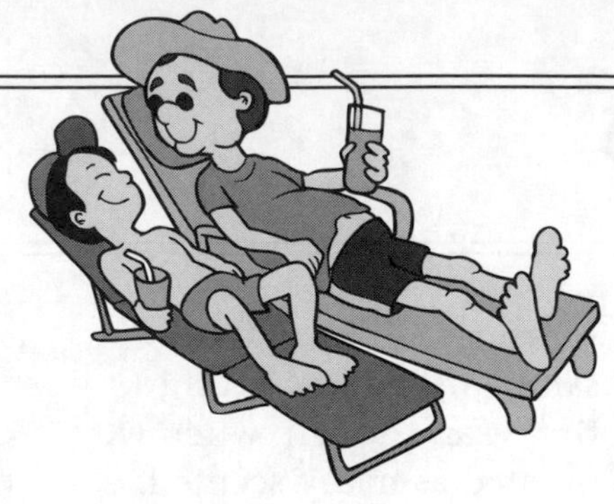

## CHILL OUT!

Come summertime, it's not unusual to find a number of our test-garden helpers lingering here long into the evening. No, it's not because we're workaholics! It's because we've noticed that many of our flowers are most fragrant just after sunset, when the air is still and humid, and the temperature begins to cool down. To make the most of this trait in your own garden, be sure to add a few fragrant flowers to the plantings around a porch, deck, patio, or wherever you like to spend summer evenings. Then sit back and enjoy the aroma.

## JUST RIGHT FOR NIGHT

For extra evening enjoyment, it's worth searching out annuals that are particularly prized for their nighttime scents. Here's a quick rundown on the top five favorites of our test-garden staff:

**Dame's rocket**
(*Hesperis matronalis*)

**Heliotrope**
(*Heliotropium arborescens*)

**Moonflower**
(*Ipomoea alba*)

**Night-scented stock**
(*Matthiola longipetala*)

**Woodland tobacco**
(*Nicotiana sylvestris*)

### Annual Perk-Me-Up Tonic

If summer's heat and humidity have gotten the best of your annual flowers, don't give them up for lost. You can enjoy several more weeks of blooms if you treat 'em right, right now! Cut them back by about half, water them thoroughly, and then dose them with a shot of this tonic. They'll be back in bloom before you know it!

**1/4 cup of beer**
**1 tbsp. of corn syrup**
**1 tbsp. of baby shampoo**
**1 tbsp. of 15-30-15 fertilizer**
**1 gal. of water**

Mix these ingredients in a watering can, then slowly dribble the solution onto the soil around all of your annuals. Within two weeks, they'll be real comeback kids—and you'll get to enjoy their lush leaves and beautiful blooms until mean, old Jack Frost makes a return appearance in mid-fall.

## A SITE FOR SCENTS

What's the secret to getting the best fragrance from your flowers? We can sum it up in three words: *location, location, location*! Okay—that's technically one word, but it's an important one. We've found that selecting the right site can make the difference between a garden that's full of fragrance and one that's slightly scented at best. Specifically, you need a site that's sheltered from wind, because wind blows away the scents you want to enjoy. So for best results, pick a spot protected from breezes—ideally near a window or outdoor sitting area. Hedges and shrub borders also help cut down on wind and keep fragrances lingering in the air. Trellises covered with vines are another good option for wind protection.

## LOVE THOSE LEAVES!

Here at the test gardens, we're crazy about geraniums (*Pelargonium*)—and not just about the ones that produce colorful flowers! (In fact, the best bloomers often have a strong scent that some people find unpleasant.) So, when we want to add fragrant foliage to our plantings, we turn to the "scented geraniums," a special group of geraniums that come in an amazing array of leaf scents and sizes. Most of them have names that describe their fragrance, like coconut geranium (*P. grossularioides*), lemon geranium (*P. crispum*), and rose geranium (*P. graveolens*), to name just a few! You'll usually find scented geraniums sold with herbs, rather than with regular geraniums. We've found that they're particularly nice in pots on a table or next to a bench, so we can easily reach 'em to rub the leaves and take a good whiff!

## FLORAL FREE-FOR-ALL

Considering how much time we spend in our test-garden flower beds, you might think that we're happy to be away from flowers when we're indoors. But you know, it seems that they're almost addictive: The more blooms we have, the more we want! That's why we always make it a point to grow extra annuals specifically for cut flowers to enjoy indoors. In one small area, we can grow enough blooms to keep us in beautiful bouquets all summer long.

If you, too, would like an abundance of garden-fresh cut flowers—all for free!—do what we do: Set aside a corner of your vegetable garden, or another sunny, well-drained spot that *isn't highly visible*. We used to snip blooms out of our regular flower beds, but we always felt bad about taking color away from our display. With a separate cutting garden, we've found that we can pick all the flowers we want—and still have a pretty-looking property, too!

### From Our Readers

*Here's a favorite trick of mine that I use when I send cut flowers to my friends: I take an ordinary potato, cut slits in it, and insert the stems into the slits, making sure that they are securely fastened in. Then I pack up the potatoed flowers for shipping. I've found that a potato will keep most flowers fresh for up to two weeks in moderate temperatures.*

Darla E.,
Tacoma, WA

## GET THE BLUES

To be honest, we've never seen a flower color that we *didn't* like for our bouquets. But we think there's something extra-special about true-blue blooms—maybe because it's just so hard to find them! One that's earned a permanent place in our cutting garden is the old-fashioned annual called bachelor's buttons (*Centaurea cyanus*). Their shaggy-petaled, daisylike flowers come in the purest shade of rich blue you can imagine, as well as pink and white. They're fantastic in fresh arrangements, and they dry beautifully, too! Best of all, they're incredibly easy to grow: Simply scatter the seeds directly in the garden in spring, and you'll have all the blooms you can use all summer long!

## TALL IS WHERE IT'S AT

When you're choosing annuals for your cutting garden, stay away from those described as "compact," "dwarf," or "low-growing." In our first cutting garden, we paid more attention to color than we did to plant size, and we learned our lesson—we had plenty of blooms, but we could only make tiny bouquets because the stems were so short! Now, we check the catalog description or plant tag to make sure we get the tallest plants we can find, so we have a lot more options when we make arrangements.

## DOUBLE THE FUN

Lots of annuals make great cut flowers, but we agree that our all-time favorite is cockscombs (*Celosia*). These sun lovers send up showy blooms that fill the garden with color and last for weeks in fresh arrangements. But even better, they're a snap to dry, so we can enjoy their bright colors in our homes all through the winter, too! The blooms of some cockscombs look like feathery plumes, while others supposedly resemble a rooster's comb. For something really different, we also like wheat celosia (*C. spicata*). It thrives in the same conditions, and its dense, cream-and-pink spikes look super in both fresh and dried bouquets. It's easy to dry any kind of celosia: Simply snip off the leaves, then hang the stems upside down in small bunches in a warm, dry place for two to three weeks.

### Cut-Flower-Saver Solution

To keep your home-grown cut flowers in florist-quality form right from the get-go, take a pail of tepid water into the garden when you go out to harvest, and place the cut stems in the water right away. Then, when you're done picking blooms and are ready to arrange them, mix up a batch of this drink to help them last as long as possible.

**1 cup of lemon-lime soda (not diet)**
**1/4 tsp. of household bleach**
**3 cups of warm water (110°F)**

Mix these ingredients in an old container, and pour the solution into a clean vase. It'll make those posies perk right up. Add more solution as needed every few days to keep the water level topped off. You'll be amazed at how much better your cut flowers look!

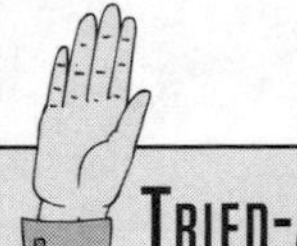

## Tried-and-True

Back when I was a boy, I loved to pick poppies, but I could never get them to last more than a day or two, while Grandma Putt's would easily last a week or more. Finally, she took pity on me and shared her secret: She'd cut the flowers just as the buds began to open, then dip the cut stem ends into an inch or two of boiling water for a few seconds, or else sear the ends with a match. Then she'd stand the flowers in cold water for several hours before adding them to her arrangements. Once I tried this trick, I never had droopy poppies again!

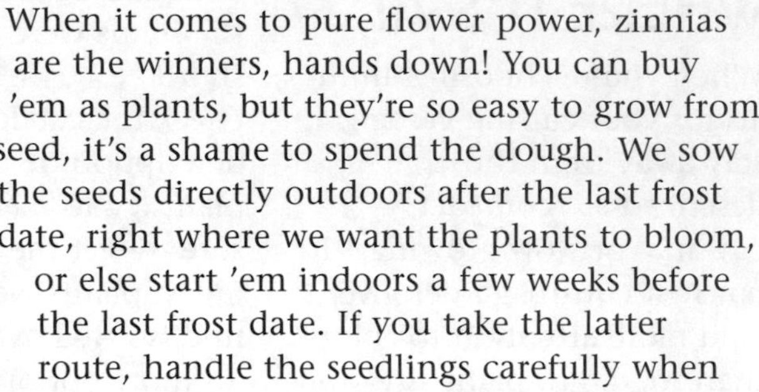

# WINNING ZINNIAS

When it comes to pure flower power, zinnias are the winners, hands down! You can buy 'em as plants, but they're so easy to grow from seed, it's a shame to spend the dough. We sow the seeds directly outdoors after the last frost date, right where we want the plants to bloom, or else start 'em indoors a few weeks before the last frost date. If you take the latter route, handle the seedlings carefully when you transplant them, because we've found that they don't appreciate having their roots disturbed too much. For lots of flowers, look for "cut and come again" zinnias, like our garden-tested favorite: the Oklahoma Series. The more we pick, the more they bloom!

# KEEP ON CUTTING

Please pick the daisies? You bet! Believe it or not, cutting a few blooms every few days for bouquets—or simply snipping off the dead ones—encourages your daisy-flowered plants to keep producing flower buds. More importantly, it also keeps them from dropping so many seeds, which we've found can be a problem with some daisies. Regular deadheading, plus pulling up any unwanted seedlings that appear, will keep your daisies from taking over your beds and borders—*and* give you bunches of beautiful bouquets in the process.

## Test Garden

We usually keep a couple of cans of lemon-lime soda on hand so we can whip up a batch of our Cut-Flower-Saver Solution (see page 103) on a moment's notice. But one hot day, a couple of thirsty test-garden helpers wiped out our entire soda stash! Luckily, one of the old-timers here remembered a trick from the days before handy canned sodas: a simple solution of 2 tablespoons of white vinegar mixed with 1 teaspoon of sugar in 1 quart of warm water. We added this tonic to the vase before we arranged our flowers, and the blooms stayed in great shape for over a week. Now we never have to worry about running out of soda again—at least as far as our cut flowers are concerned!

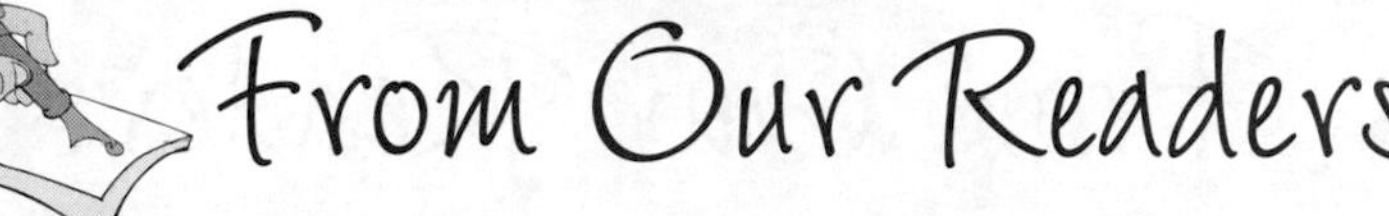

# From Our Readers

## PICK A POT OF FLOWERS

I like putting some of my annuals in flowerpots; that way, I can rearrange my flower beds for more color and design, and I can turn the pots if they need sun. Of course, if your plants are in the ground, you can't do this without digging them up! I also use large tree limbs to line my flower beds. It's natural looking, and it saves me money because I don't need to buy expensive edgings from the garden shop.

***Bootsie H., Richmond, VA***

## THE HEAT IS ON

To start annual seeds, I use my gas oven. I use only the pilot light, which heats the oven to 75° or 80°F. You might need to open the door a little, and be sure to use an oven thermometer to monitor the temperature. The seeds will usually sprout in three or four days.

***Bob H., Centrahoma, OK***

## "BERRY" SPECIAL PLANT

When I plant a special annual seedling that I don't want to lose among the existing plants, I place one of the little green baskets that berries come in over the seedling. Because of the mesh design, the plant gets all the light, air, and moisture it needs. And, the bright green basket is easy to find in the garden.

***Barbara N., Flint, MI***

## ANNUAL STARTER

I am 13 years old, and my grandparents love your radio and TV shows. I was reading one of your booklets, and you mentioned all kinds of seed-starting containers that I haven't thought of. But you didn't mention egg containers—they work great. I've started flowers in them and they are coming up beautifully. Thanks so much for your shows, tricks, and especially your tonics. P.S., I'm flooded with marigolds and morning glories in my egg cartons!

***Malynda M., Rogers, AR***

MORE TIPS

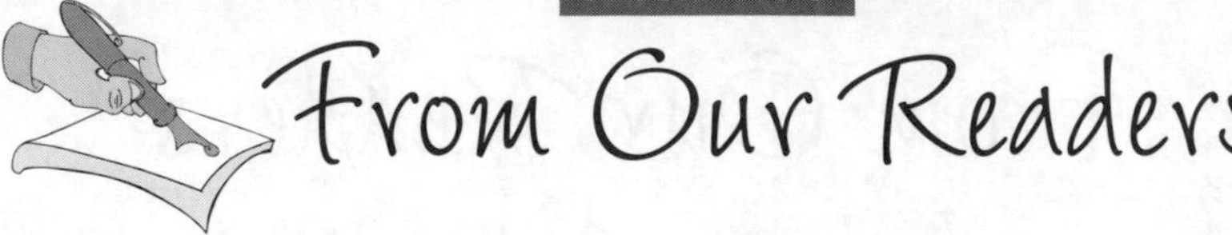

# From Our Readers

## WHITEFLY CONTROL

I've found that sweet alyssum keeps whiteflies away. Since I started planting it around my garden a few years ago, I've had no trouble with these little pests.

***Mildred K., Portola Valley, CA***

## STRING 'EM UP

I had an ugly back wall on my garage and decided to hide it with a trellis. I didn't want to build a huge trellis, so, instead, I made a string trellis. The strings are simply tied to nails. I planted morning glories, and shaped the strings to form a sunburst. The whole wall was loaded with flowers and vines from one little planted area. Then in the fall, I collected all of the seeds, and never had to buy morning glory seeds again. By the way, little fancy-labeled jars of these seeds make nice stocking stuffers for gardening friends.

***Sherry D., Green Bay, WI***

## PERFECT PANSIES

The next time you're arranging pansies, put them in a flower bowl that's half-filled with sand. Add water after the pansies are inserted. The flowers will remain standing tall.

***Pegeen B., Neodesha, KS***

## IMPATIENS A-PLENTY

When my impatiens get leggy, I cut the tops off and replant the cuttings in small pots. In a couple of weeks, I have new plants growing.

***Marian H., Orlando, FL***

## GARDEN STAKES

I have many annuals that flop right over, hiding their gorgeous blooms. To stake them upright, I discovered that nothing works better than yardsticks. I can get them free from many home shows and hardware shops, and they can be painted whatever color I like.

***Dorothy M., Roanoke, VA***

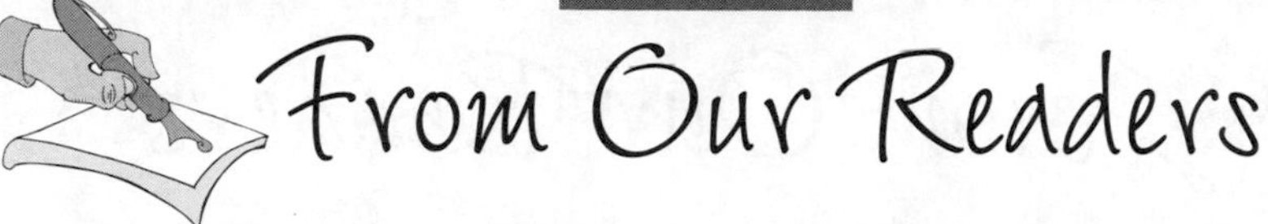


## MINI-GREENHOUSE

A 2-liter plastic soda bottle, cut off a few inches from the bottom, fits perfectly over a plant pot to make a mini-greenhouse and frost protector until planting time. And the screw-on cap can be used to regulate the heat.

***Paul K., Dover, NH***

## INCREASED IMPATIENS

Whenever I plant impatiens, I always cut the top third off immediately after planting. This encourages the plants to spread and not grow so tall and leggy. You end up with lots of large, bushy, beautiful flowers.

***Karen H., Henderson, NC***

## FOILED AGAIN!

To keep slugs off of your plants, use aluminum foil. For single-stemmed plants, put a 1-inch piece of foil around the bottom of the stem. For multi-stemmed plants, place a ring of crinkled foil around all of the stems. Slugs will not touch your plants.

***Patty E., North Bend, WA***

## SUNFLOWER TRELLIS

Don't get rid of sunflower stalks—you can use them as a trellis next year. After harvesting the sunflowers, strip off the leaves from the stalks, and let the stalks dry for a few weeks. Then chop them down, and keep them off the ground over winter. Next spring, use them to trellis your plants.

***Charles M., Posen, MI***

## GROWIN' GLORIES

When it's almost time to plant morning glory seeds, I soak them in water overnight. Then, I place the seeds on a damp paper towel, and seal them in a plastic bag for several days. When the roots appear, I plant them right into the warm garden soil.

***Marian S., Whitewater, WI***

MORE TIPS

# From Our Readers

## COZY COVER

I got the gardening itch early, and planted some pansies on my porch. The days were warm, but the nights froze. I put a paper bag over them as soon as the sun went down, and took it off as I left for work in the morning. They grew well, and even gave me new blooms!

***Rayne M., Springfield, OR***

## PAPER PRESCRIPTION

The easiest way to make cutworm collars is to cut the cardboard tube from a paper towel roll into 2-inch rounds; I use a utility knife. They are easy to use at planting time, and they do a good job of keeping cutworms away from my plants.

***Vicki Z., Rock City, IL***

## ANT AID

Every time I dug to plant my annuals, hundreds of ants would come pouring out of the dirt (and when they bite, boy does it sting!). I hate using chemicals, so I tried using bonemeal to get rid of them, and I saw amazing results. Now, anytime the ants are out of control, I just pour it right into the ant colony, and days later, no more ants!

***Cecilia H., Logan, WV***

## SUREFIRE SPROUTS

Here's how to get seedlings up in a week in an unheated room, with a little effort and some hot water. Put two one-gallon glass jugs full of hot water in a 2-foot × 3-foot cardboard box. Plant the seeds in small cups filled with potting soil, put the cups around the jugs of hot water, and cover the box with an old blanket. Then refill the jugs with hot water each morning and night.

***Evelyn T., Warren, MI***

# Chapter 6

# Eye-Popping Perennials

If annual bloomers are the stars of the flower garden, then perennials are the workhorses. Plant 'em once, and they'll come back to grace your yard with a bounty of blooms year after year. Many perennials are sturdy enough to survive with minimal care; but with just a little extra TLC from you, they can really grow like gangbusters and bloom better than you'd ever believe. With so many years of perennial gardening under our belts, you can bet we've learned all kinds of great tips and tricks for selecting and growing these versatile plants—and now we can share those tips with you!

Dividing overgrown clumps is one of *the* most important things you can do to keep your perennial flowers vigorous, healthy, and free-flowering. While it's possible to divide any perennial at any time during the growing season, we've found that early spring is by far the best time to divide plants that bloom in late summer or fall. It's a snap to separate the clumps before much top growth appears, and they'll have plenty of time to settle in before their flowering season. By late summer, you can hardly tell that they've been disturbed—except that they're filled with more blooms than before!

## THE KINDEST CUT

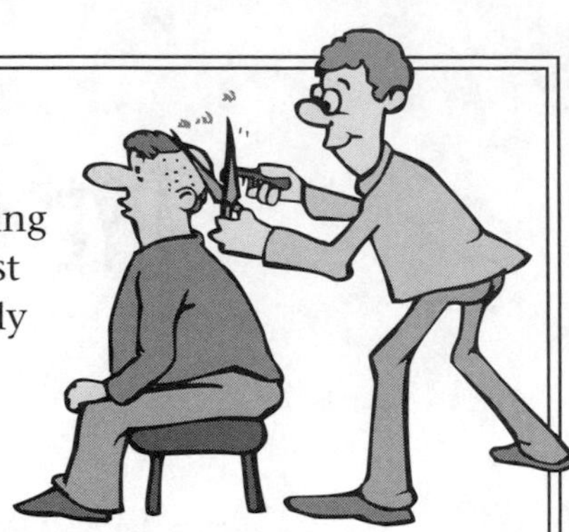

Every winter, we swear we're not going to add any new perennials to our test gardens—and every spring, we simply can't resist the urge to try just a few more! When we set out our chosen additions, though, we know not to expect much from them during the first year. Why? Because first-year perennials need to put their energy into making new roots, not seeds, so we snip off the flowers as soon as they fade. In fact, if we start with bare-root perennials, we cut off all the flower *buds* the first year, to direct energy to root growth. It seems harsh, but trust us—we've experimented with pinching some and leaving others alone, and we've found that the plants we removed the flowers from were *way* bigger, bushier, and more bloom-filled the following year!

## GET SPACEY

Over the years, we've heard all the "rules" for creating beautiful perennial gardens, and we've found that most of those rules are made to be broken. But there's *one* guideline that we always take seriously: the spacing recommendations given on the labels of the perennials we buy. Even though the plants are small when we put them in, we know that the care we give them will make 'em grow like gangbusters, so they'll fill that space lickety-split!

*Here's a neat trick for stimulating the roots of your transplants. Take some small willow twigs or chips, and soak them overnight in a 5-gallon bucket of water. Then skim out the twigs, and use the water on newly transplanted perennials, annuals, and vegetables. You can also use the chips as a fall mulch around transplanted trees and shrubs.*

Brad M., Flint, MI

# PARTING THOUGHTS

Dividing perennials has to be one of the most asked-about topics here at the test gardens, and one of the most popular questions is: "How do you know how many pieces you can make out of one clump?" As with many other questions, the answer to this one is, "It depends!"

■ If your goal is simply to reduce the size of a large clump, cutting it in half or thirds will give you two or three good-sized pieces that will recover quickly after replanting and look fantastic from the get-go.

■ If you want to get as many new plants as possible, you can divide all the way down to a single "eye," or bud," per piece. This can provide dozens of new plants from a single clump, but we've found that these tiny divisions do best when potted up and pampered for a few months before replanting. Generally, it'll take these small divisions a few years to get back their full flower power—but you'll have lots of them to look forward to!

■ In most cases, we like our divisions to have three to five eyes each, along with a good complement of roots, to boot. That gives us a fair number of new plants that are big enough to go right back into the garden and still bloom well that season.

## All-Season Clean-Up Tonic

This is the one tonic that you *absolutely* need to use religiously throughout the growing season. The mouthwash kills bad bacteria and discourages insects; the shampoo cleans your plants and helps the other ingredients stick better; and the tobacco tea contains nicotine, which does a double whammy on those pesky pests.

**1 cup of antiseptic mouthwash**
**1 cup of baby shampoo**
**1 cup of tobacco tea***

Mix these ingredients in a 20 gallon hose-end sprayer, and give everything in your yard a good shower every two weeks in the early evening throughout the growing season. You'll have the healthiest flowers in town—*guaranteed!*

*To make tobacco tea, place half a handful of chewing tobacco in an old nylon stocking and soak it in a gallon of hot water until the mixture is dark brown. Store leftover liquid in a tightly capped jug or bottle for later use.

Each summer, we gather up all our test-garden helpers and take them on a special field trip to thank them for all their hard work. We've been to county fairs, amusement parks, and nature centers; but you know which trip still gets talked about the most? The tour we took of some old graveyards! Believe it or not, graveyards—and old homesteads, too—are great places to see perennials that are growing and thriving without any special care whatsoever. We made a list of all the long-lived perennials we saw that day, and we still refer to it when we're planning a new perennial bed at one of our test gardens. We know that a garden based on these no-fail flowers will give us years of beauty without demanding much in the way of maintenance from us!

## FILLERS UP!

When we tell visitors at our test gardens about the need to space perennials properly, we know to expect a lot of skeptics—especially when we're standing in front of a first-year planting that's packed with flowers and foliage! What's our secret? Annuals! Each spring, we pick up a few extra transplants of our favorite annuals, then use them to fill in around newly planted perennials. Not only do the annuals provide lots of color, but they also do a bang-up job keeping down the weeds that would otherwise pop up in the empty spaces!

## HERE COMES THE GROOM

Our top trick for helping perennials look their best and bloom the longest is also the easiest: Simply remove the spent flowers every few days, so they don't set seed. You don't need any special equipment; in fact, our favorite tools for this grooming task are a good pair of garden clippers and a basic 5-gallon plastic bucket. (You can often find these buckets free for the asking, or for just a dollar or two, at fast-food restaurants, delis, and bakeries.)

Keep your clippers and bucket in a handy spot, and carry them with you each time you go out to your garden. As you admire your beautiful flowers, snip off the dead ones and toss them in the bucket. Finish your tour with a trip to the compost pile to dump the clippings, and your bucket will be ready and waiting for your next trip to the garden!

### TAKE A POWDER

Want to give your newly divided perennials extra protection from foul fungi? Then do what we do, and dust all the cuts you make with powdered sulfur (available at your local garden center). This amazing stuff is just the ticket to keep root-rotting nogoodniks from decimating your new divisions!

## PRECOCIOUS PERENNIALS

If you need a whole lot of perennials to fill a new garden, buying already-started plants can be a real budget-breaker! But you don't have to give up your dream garden, because we've found that many beautiful perennials are just as easy to start from seed as annuals are. Spend a buck or two per packet, and you can grow dozens of perennials for just pennies apiece.

Most perennials take at least two years to reach flowering size, but if you're in a hurry, here's the top-ten list of our favorite first-year bloomers. Give these fast-maturing perennials an early start by sowing their seeds indoors in late winter, then setting out as transplants after the last spring frost:

**Anise hyssop**
(*Agastache foeniculum*)

**Balloon flower**
(*Platycodon grandiflorus*)

**Black-eyed Susan**
(*Rudbeckia fulgida*)

**Carpathian harebell**
(*Campanula carpatica*)

**Fern-leaved yarrow**
(*Achillea millefolium*)

**Jupiter's beard**
(*Centranthus ruber*)

**'Lady' lavender**
(*Lavandula angustifolia* 'Lady')

**'Southern Charm' mullein**
(*Verbascum* 'Southern Charm')

**Tree lavatera**
(*Lavatera thuringiaca*)

**Tree mallow**
(*Malva sylvestris*)

## BE A CUTUP

When dividing perennials, it's critical to use clean, sharp tools. That way, you'll get nice, neat cuts instead of ripped or torn roots, which provide an open invitation for root rots and other dastardly diseases. One of our test-garden team's favorite tools is an old kitchen knife we picked up at a garage sale. It has a long, serrated blade that never seems to get dull, and it slices through even the toughest clumps like nobody's business!

**Q** I'd love to add some woodland wildflowers to my yard this spring. Is it okay to transplant them right from the woods?

**A** Digging even common plants from the wild can destroy natural stands and spoil the beauty for everyone. So if you'd like to add wildflowers to your yard, *please* grow them yourself from seed, buy them from reputable nurseries, or get them from friends who are already growing them in their garden. If you decide to purchase wildflower plants, make sure that they are "nursery-propagated," meaning that someone has grown them in cultivation and not simply dug them up and popped them into a pot for sale.

## From Our Readers

*To clean stubborn garden soil and grass stains from your hands and under your nails, use an old toothbrush and toothpaste. It works great, and it's gentle on skin and nails, too!*

Arline T., Watertown, CT

## FUN WITH FOLIAGE

When you're picking pretty flowers for your spring gardens, don't overlook the allure of leaves. We've found that perennials with showy foliage make super companions for delicate spring blooms—and their beauty goes on and on, long after the early flowers are gone! One of our favorites for spring foliage is variegated Solomon's seal (*Polygonatum thunbergii* 'Variegatum'). This charmer bears elegant, arching stems clad in green-and-white-striped leaves. It makes a perfect partner for the brushy white blooms of foamflowers (*Tiarella*), as well as colorful primroses and other shade-loving bloomers. There are lots of perennials with great foliage for spring color in sun, too! Try golden creeping Jenny (*Lysimachia nummularia* 'Aurea'), purple-leaved heucheras (*Heuchera*), and gardener's garters (*Phalaris arundinacea* var. *picta*), to name just a few.

## AFTER THE LAUGHTER

Don't count on spring bloomers to look good much after May—at least for a while. After flowering, many early-rising perennials tend to look tired and tattered, and they may even die back to the ground. That's why we make it a habit to trim back the foliage of all our spring bloomers as soon as it turns yellow. Often times, that one simple step is enough to encourage the plants to produce a flush of fresh new leaves that look great all through the summer!

It's a fact, though, that some early risers like to take a long rest after spring flowering. So if we don't see new leaves appear after we cut off the yellowed ones, we don't worry—we know that the plants will be back next year! In the meantime, we just pop in a few annual transplants to fill the empty space for the rest of the season.

## DELIGHTFUL DELPHINIUMS

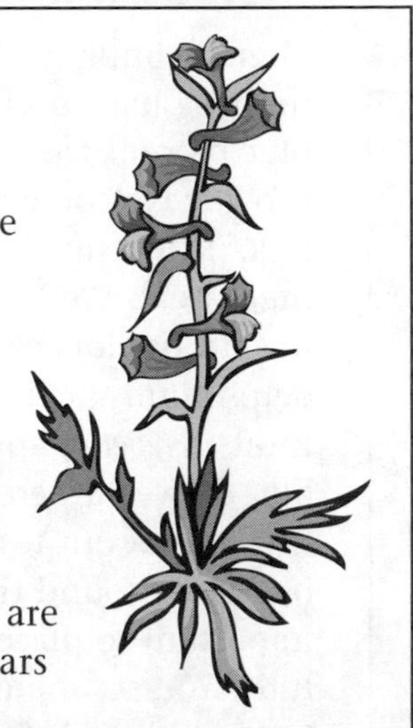

Of all the stunning summer flowers there are to choose from, we have to admit that the spire-like blue blooms of delphiniums are our favorites. Unfortunately, these border beauties can be tricky to grow unless you're lucky enough to live in an area with cool summers, like the Pacific Northwest. Still, we love 'em so much that it's worth a little extra effort to make them happy. Here are some of the tricks we've learned over the years to keep delphiniums doing their thing year after year, even where growing conditions are less than ideal:

- Where summers are hot, give your plants a site with morning sun and dappled afternoon shade.
- Mulch with compost in spring to keep the soil moist and cool.
- Feed with 5-10-5 fertilizer in spring when stems are 3 inches tall; repeat when blooms appear.
- Water deeply once a week through the summer.
- If all else fails, treat them like annuals or biennials—simply set out new plants every year or two!

### Blossom-Booster Tonics

When flowers fail to perform, it's typically because they're either dirty or tired (or both). Here's a great way to clean 'em up and green 'em up in a hurry. First, perk up your soil with this simple dry mixture.

**1/3 lb. of sugar**
**1/3 lb. of Epsom salts**
**1/3 lb. of gypsum**

Mix these ingredients in a bucket, and apply the mixture to your flower beds with a hand-held spreader. Now, it's time to get those leaves clean and shiny, so they can get back to their job of feeding your flowers.

**1 cup of apple juice**
**1 cup of Gatorade®**
**1/2 cup of ammonia**
**1/2 cup of Pedialyte®**

Mix these ingredients in your 20 gallon hose-end sprayer, and overspray your flower beds to the point of run-off. This'll wash the dirt right off those leaves—*and* help energize the dry mix at the same time. Before you know it, your flowers will be back to blooming like crazy!

## UP CLOSE AND PERSONAL

There's simply nothing like cool blue blooms to provide welcome relief from summer's heat. We love to use lots of delphiniums, catmints (*Nepeta*), and other blue-flowered perennials in the beds at our test gardens, but we've found that it's important to place them carefully. You see, blue flowers tend to blend into the background of green leaves, so unless you plant them up close, they hardly get noticed. So now, we keep our blue bloomers near the entrance to our test gardens, where they never fail to attract attention from staff and visitors alike. As a matter of fact, I use the same trick at home, too, placing the blues close to the house and keeping brighter colors in beds that are out farther in the yard. It's the best way to make the most of the blues!

## BACK TO BASICS

Sure, it's fun to try to try new perennials, but don't overlook the old favorites just because they're more common. One early summer bloomer we'd never be without, for instance, is dianthus. This old-fashioned classic comes in all shades of pink, plus white, maroon, ruby-red, and many combinations of two or more colors. We used to have trouble with our plants rotting out, until one of our helpers tried mulching them with gravel instead of compost. This one simple step did the trick, improving drainage around the base of the plants and keeping them in tip-top form. We've found that alkaline soil helps them stay happy, too, so we use limestone chips instead of regular gravel when we can, or else scatter some wood ashes around the base of the plants each spring.

Daylilies (*Hemerocallis*) are tough-as-nails perennials that grow quickly, so we like to divide our clumps about every three years to expand our collection. Still, we never seem to have as many as we want, so imagine our delight when we discovered a new way to make more of them! We've found that 'Fairy Tale Pink', 'Prairie Blue Eyes', 'Siloam Red Toy', and some of our other hybrid daylilies sometimes produce miniature plants, called *proliferations,* on their normally leafless flower stems. We cut off these little plants right where they join the stem, then stick the base of each one in some moist potting soil and treat them like cuttings. By fall, they've produced roots, and we have brand-new plants that are identical to the daylilies they came from!

# SO LONG, SPOTS!

If powdery mildew makes unsightly white spots on your garden phlox (*Phlox paniculata*) or bee balm (*Monarda didyma*), don't be too quick to pull out the chemical sprays! We've found a great way to prevent most mildew problems: Simply snip off one-third to one-half of the stems in the clump, right at ground level, in late spring. This reduces crowding and improves air circulation around the leaves, so those funky fungi can't get a grip!

# WONDERFUL WORK-SAVERS

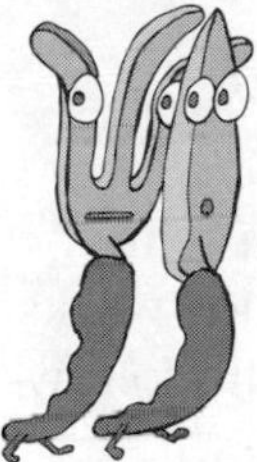

We're lucky to have lots of dedicated helpers here at the test gardens, but when summer's in full swing, there are still more jobs to do than there are hands to do them! You can imagine, then, that we're always on the lookout for ways to have bushels of blooms with a minimum of maintenance. If you're in the same boat in your own yard, do what we're doing: Replace some of those high-care flower beds with gorgeous, flowering groundcovers! These sturdy bloomers look super even in tough growing conditions, and once you get 'em going, they need almost no care. Here are eight great sun-loving groundcovers we've used with great success:

**Bellflowers** (*Campanula portenschlagiana* and *C. poscharskyana*)

**Candytuft** (*Iberis sempervirens*)

**Daylilies** (*Hemerocallis*)

**Hardy geraniums** (*Geranium*)

**Lamb's ears** (*Stachys byzantina*)

**Moss phlox** (*Phlox subulata*)

**Plumbago** (*Ceratostigma plumbaginoides*)

**Sedums** (*Sedum*)

## TRIED-AND-TRUE

I'm actually embarrassed that it took me so long to suggest we use more groundcovers in our test gardens, because I now remember how Grandma Putt always made the most of these versatile perennials in her own yard. She'd never waste much time, mulch, or fertilizer on 'em; just a single yearly trim was all they needed to stay in top form all season long. Grandma used hedge shears or hand pruners to cut the whole patch back by about a third of its height; but today, we use a string trimmer to do the job extra-quick. The trick is in the timing: Clip summer- or fall-flowering groundcovers in the spring, and trim spring-bloomers right after they finish flowering.

## WHACK 'EM BACK

When we're out demonstrating some of our favorite flower-care tricks to test-garden visitors, there's one that never fails to create a real stir: cutting back perennial clumps by a third to a half in early summer. Admittedly, it looks pretty drastic to whack perfectly healthy-looking perennials back so drastically. But when those same visitors come back in late summer to see the results, they never fail to try this technique in their own gardens the following year!

This tough-love trick works best on bushy perennials that normally bloom after midsummer—especially those with tall stems that tend to flop by flowering time, like asters. The harsh trim encourages the stems to branch out instead of shoot up, so the resulting clumps are shorter and seldom need staking. Plus, each single stem turns into two, three, four, or even more new shoots—and that means lots more flowers to enjoy!

Cutting back in early summer works wonders with many perennials. But before you start using it on everything in sight, keep this in mind: It only works on those with branching flower stems. We've tried it on just about every perennial and learned that it definitely doesn't work on those that have single-stemmed blooms, like hostas, peonies, or daylilies—or true lilies (*Lilium*), for that matter. They won't branch, and you'll be stuck with a bunch of stick figures—all stems and no blooms!

## PERENNIAL PRUNING POINTERS

We all know that snipping off spent flowers is a great way to keep many annual bloomers looking super all season long. But would you believe that this same secret can keep many *perennials* in flower for weeks longer—or even months longer—than they'd normally be? It's true! When you're removing spent flowers or cutting back your perennials, look for tiny buds in the joints where the leaves connect to the stem. Cut just above these joints, and you'll have new flowers in a jiffy! We've found this trick works especially well on the following summer favorites:

**Balloon flower** (*Platycodon grandiflorus*)

**Peach-leaved bellflower** (*Campanula persicifolia*)

**Phlox** (*Phlox*)

**Pincushion flowers** (*Scabiosa*)

**Shasta daisy** (*Leucanthemum × superbum*)

**Speedwells** (*Veronica*)

**Stoke's aster** (*Stokesia laevis*)

**Yarrows** (*Achillea*)

## A SPECIAL DELIVERY

Don't you hate it when you head out to work in your flower beds, only to find that you've forgotten your trowel or clippers? That happens to us way more often than we care to admit, so we came up with a spot-on solution: We mounted a few old mailboxes on posts set throughout our flower gardens, then dressed them up with flowering vines like clematis and honeysuckle (*Lonicera*). Besides providing convenient storage for small tools, string, seed packets, and all those other little items that are so easy to lose track of, the mailboxes also make fun garden accents!

## TAKE YOUR TIME

Daylilies are definitely the backbone of our sunny summer beds and borders, because these sturdy plants bloom for weeks or even months with minimal fuss from us. The only thing that really helps improve their looks is removing the wilted flowers, but with each plant producing dozens of blooms that last only one day, keeping these spent blooms picked off can become a real chore. Our solution? Don't worry about daily cleanup; simply go out once a week and remove all the dead flowers you can find, along with any developing seedpods. Then, when no new buds are left, snip off the flower stalks close to the leaves. This minimal maintenance will help keep your daylilies looking great all summer long!

### Undercover Mulch Booster

Wood chips, shredded bark, sawdust, and any other wood-based materials can make great mulches for flower gardens—*if* you know how to use them properly! Applied alone, they'll steal nutrients from the soil (and in turn, from your flowers) as they decompose. But we've found an easy way to avoid this problem; simply overspray with this mulch booster.

**1 can of beer**
**1 can of regular cola (not diet)**
**1 cup of dishwashing liquid**
**1 cup of antiseptic mouthwash**
**$^1/_4$ tsp. of instant tea granules**

Mix these ingredients in a large bucket, then pour into a 20 gallon hose-end sprayer. Apply liberally over all of your flower beds to thoroughly saturate the mulch and wet the soil underneath as well. Your plants will stay happier *and* healthier—from just one application!

**Q** I love having lavender plants in my garden, but they sure don't like me! I set out new plants each year, and they look great in the summer, but they're always dead by the following spring. Any suggestions?

**A** You bet! We used to have the same problem in our test gardens, until we finally discovered the secret to long-lived lavender: well-drained soil! Lavenders hate growing in wet ground, especially in winter. Planting in raised beds is a great way to keep your lavender plants high and dry. Don't want to build up your whole flower bed? Then just make individual mounds of sandy soil right in the garden, and plant your lavenders on top!

# EXTREME MAKEOVERS

Ever notice how some of the most flower-filled perennials can look rather ratty once their flowers fade? Well, you don't have to spend the summer trying to ignore those ugly ducklings! We've found that giving early-flowering perennials an extreme makeover is an easy way to turn them into beauties again. After the main flush of flowers has faded, use your pruners or hedge shears to trim the following perennials down to 2 or 3 inches above the ground. They'll bounce back with handsome, compact mounds of foliage that won't flop over—and many will even send up another round of flowers, to boot!

**Candytuft**
(*Iberis sempervirens*)

**Catmints**
(*Nepeta*)

**Columbines**
(*Aquilegia*)

**Hardy geraniums**
(*Geranium*)

**Lady's mantle**
(*Alchemilla mollis*)

**Mountain bluet**
(*Centaurea montana*)

**Pinks**
(*Dianthus*)

**Spiderworts**
(*Tradescantia*)

**Thread-leaved coreopsis**
(*Coreopsis verticillata*)

**Test Garden**

Would you believe that you can get better blooms by pinching *off* some flower buds? Sounds crazy, we know, but it works—honest! On perennials that bear their flower buds in clusters, pinching out the smaller side buds directs all that stem's energy into the main bud, so you get a bigger bloom. We've tried it with great success on mums, dahlias, peonies, and roses, too. If you'd rather have *more*, but slightly smaller, blooms, do just the opposite: Pinch out the main bud on the stem, and let the smaller side buds get all the growing energy.

And here's a bonus tip: Pinching off different flower buds on the same plant is a super way to extend its bloom season for several days, or even weeks. On some stems, remove the side buds; on others, remove the main buds. The larger buds will open first, followed by the smaller, side buds!

# A MULCH BETTER IDEA

We're mighty proud of our beautiful perennial borders here at the test gardens, but we'll be the first to admit that we can't take all of the credit. So what's our secret? It's *mulch*—and lots of it!

Besides making the beds look neat and tidy, mulch keeps the soil moist and cool; that provides perfect conditions for great root growth and cuts down on our watering chores, too!

Mulch also smothers weed seeds, so our weeding chores are practically nil. For every hour we spend mulching in mid- to late spring (it comes out to just a few minutes for each bed), we're guaranteed to save dozens of hours over the course of the growing season.

Compost is a marvelous mulch, and it's easy to make, or you can buy it bagged. Shredded bark is another great mulch; pine needles are nice, too. And don't overlook one of the all-time best mulches for perennial gardens: chopped leaves. There's always a plentiful supply of leaves in the fall, and you can run 'em through a leaf shredder, or chop and gather them in one easy step with a bagging lawn mower.

## Perennial No-Pest Potion

People love perfumed perennials, but pests sure don't! So the next time you're out in your flower garden, gather the ingredients for this aromatic pest-control spray.

**1/2 cup of fresh tansy or mugwort (*Artemisia vulgaris*) leaves**
**1/2 cup of fresh lavender flowers and/or leaves**
**1/2 cup of fresh sage leaves**
**Boiling water**
**2 cups of room-temperature water**
**1 tsp. of Murphy's Oil Soap®**

Place the herbs in a 1-quart glass canning jar; fill with boiling water, cover, and let it sit until cool. Strain out the leaves and flowers, and add 1/8 cup of the liquid to the 2 cups of room-temperature water and the Murphy's Oil Soap. Pour into a hand-held sprayer, and apply to your plants to keep pests at bay.

## TRY THIS TRAFFIC-STOPPER

Of all the beautiful perennials in our test gardens, there's one that never fails to grab the attention of all our visitors: common rose mallow (*Hibiscus moscheutos*). This shrub-sized perennial is simply impossible to ignore, with huge pink, red, or white flowers that range from 6 to 10 or more inches across. Each bloom opens for only one day, but plants produce many, many buds, so they stay in bloom for about six weeks in mid- to late summer. One word of warning: It's easy to dig into the crowns of this hardy hibiscus by accident in spring, because the plants don't sprout until most other plants are already up and growing. We learned this the hard way, so now we always use labels to mark the clumps, or else surround 'em with a ring of sturdy stakes, as a "Don't dig here!" reminder.

## TAKE A STAND

If staking flowers is your least favorite garden job, here's the best advice we can give you: Choose compact cultivars that don't need your support! Unlike their taller parents, these low-growing cultivars stand up straight all on their own:

**Balloon flower**
(*Platycodon grandiflorus*): 'Apoyama', 'Mariesii', 'Sentimental Blue'

**Blanket flower**
(*Gaillardia × grandiflora*): 'Baby Cole', 'Dazzler', 'Kobold'

**Common sneezeweed**
(*Helenium autumnale*): 'Butterpat', 'Crimson Beauty', 'Moerheim Beauty'

**New England aster**
(*Aster novae-angliae*): 'Purple Dome'

**New York aster**
(*Aster novae-belgii*): 'Niobe', 'Professor Anton Kippenburg'

**Shasta daisy**
(*Leucanthemum × superbum*): 'Little Miss Muffet', 'Snow Lady'

With so many folks traipsing through our test gardens every day, we take safety very seriously. But safety isn't just for big gardens; it is just as important at home, especially where kids play. One potential danger you may never have considered is the pointed tips on the stakes you use to support your perennials. Someone leans over to sniff or pick a bloom, and "Ow!"—they get poked in the arm or eye. Fortunately, there's a simple solution: old tennis balls or racquetballs! Simply cut a slit or small hole in each ball, and stick one over the top of each stake. We usually spray-paint the balls black or dark green before putting them in place; that way, they're hardly visible at all!

# EARS LOOKIN' AT YOU!

Looking for people-friendly plants that are as nice to touch as they are to look at? The "please-feel-me," furry foliage of lamb's ears (*Stachys byzantina*) makes it a favorite with young folks—and the young at heart, too! This dependable perennial also has flowers—spikes of small, purplish pink blooms in summer—but it's really the soft, silvery leaves that steal the show. Lamb's ears is one of our favorite edging plants at our test gardens, and we know you'll love it, too.

One hint: If hot, humid weather causes some of the leaves to turn dark and mushy, don't worry—the damage isn't permanent! Simply cut off all the top growth close to the ground, and fresh new leaves will sprout up in a few weeks. In fact, it's smart to shear your lamb's ears like this each fall if you didn't do it earlier; that'll stop the fungi from getting a foothold during wet winter weather.

## FEED THE LEAVES

Are your perennials lookin' a little frazzled by midsummer? Do what we do: Give 'em a snack they can sink their leaves into right away! Foliar feeding—spraying liquid fertilizer right on their leaves—is a quick and easy way to get nutrients right where they're needed most. Simply fill a hose-end sprayer with compost tea or diluted fish emulsion, and spray the plants thoroughly, until the liquid starts dripping off of the leaves.

## Test Garden SECRET

We love to have birds come to our test gardens, for their beautiful songs as well as for their insatiable appetite for bad bugs. So we encourage 'em every way we can—and one of those ways is planting perennials with lots of seeds that birds like to eat! We've found that one of the best of the bunch is black-eyed Susans (*Rudbeckia hirta*), a spectacular summer bloomer with glorious golden yellow flowers. The seeds of these delightful daisies are a favorite food of goldfinches and purple finches, as well as chickadees, cardinals, sparrows, and nuthatches, to name a few. Just remember to spare the clippers where you're cleaning up around the plants at the end of the season; if you get too tidy and cut off the brown cones, you'll be taking away all those energy-packed seeds, too!

# Awesome Autumn Perennials

### Fall Bedtime Snack

Fall is a super season to get started on a new flower garden. To make sure your planting area will be as loose and fertile as possible, treat it to this snack as soon as you finish digging.

**25 lb. of gypsum**
**10 lb. of organic garden food (either 4-12-4 or 5-10-5)**
**5 lb. of bonemeal**

Mix these ingredients in a wheelbarrow, then apply the mix to every 100 square feet of soil. Work it into the soil and cover with a thick blanket of leaves, straw, or other organic mulch. This rich mixture works miracles for lightening up heavy clay soil, but it's also a good booster for average and sandy soils, too.

## CUTTING REMARKS

Let's face it: No flower says "Welcome, fall!" like chrysanthemums! So when we plan our perennial beds here at the test gardens, we're always sure to include plenty of mums for our autumn display. One thing that visitors never fail to ask about is how we manage to get our mums to stand up straight and tall without staking. After a bit of experimenting, we've found that pinching off the stem tips twice—once in late spring, and again toward the end of June—does the job. Just remember never to pinch after the Fourth of July; if you did do that, the plants probably wouldn't have time to make flower buds and bloom before cold weather sets in. This trick works great on asters, too, by the way!

## MUM'S THE WORD

One of the biggest problems folks seem to have with growing mums is having them die off over the winter. According to the perennial experts at our test gardens, the secret isn't *how* you grow them, but *which ones* you choose! The big-bloomed "florist mums," usually sold as potted gift plants, are normally suited only for Zones 7 to 9. They take longer to bloom than most garden mums, so in cooler areas, the flower buds are often killed by freezing weather before they open. "Hardy" or "garden" mums, on the other hand, are the ones you see for sale in late summer; these should survive the winter just fine in Zones 5 to 9. Some mums are even hardy in Zones 3 or 4; one clue is a name that starts with "Minn" (like 'Minnpink').

## PLAN A FALL FLING

Mums are awesome for autumn color, but they're not the only late bloomers that can brighten up your fall flower beds! For something different, we like to add lots of anemones to our test garden borders. Chinese anemone (*A. hupehensis*), Japanese anemone (*A.* × *hybrida*), and grape-leaved anemone (*A. tomentosa*) all bear dogwood-like blooms in shades of pink and white, and they're a snap to grow in either full sun or partial shade in Zones 4 to 8. Looking for more fall flowers? Asters, goldenrods (*Solidago*), monkshoods (*Aconitum*), and Russian sage (*Perovskia atriplicifolia*) are all fantastic for ending the growing season with a blast of blooms!

## PUT OUT THE LIGHTS

A couple of years ago, we had a real puzzle on our hands here at the test gardens. We had set out a bunch of mums in one bed in spring, and the plants grew like gangbusters, but they never bloomed! We thought maybe it was just a fluke, until the same thing happened again the following year. Finally, one of our clever helpers figured out the problem! It turns out that mums don't set flower buds at just any old time: They need short days and a long period of darkness at night for the process to begin. Normally, nights are long enough, and days short enough, for flower buds to start forming by late July. But these mums were planted under a street light near our parking lot, so they never got enough nighttime darkness to make buds and blooms! We moved 'em to a spot without a night light, and the next year, those mums were as flower-filled as we could wish.

### From Our Readers

*This works wonders on slugs. Take an old spray bottle, and rinse it well. Fill the bottle one-third full of household ammonia, add cool tap water to the top, replace the sprayer, and shake well. Set the spray nozzle on "STREAM." Anytime slugs appear, especially in the evening, walk around your yard giving each slug a squirt. You will be delighted at what this mix does to the nasty critters!*

Doris S.,
Ridgefield, WA

## Divide-and-Conquer Tonic

Fall and spring are both great times to divide your perennials. To get 'em back on track in a flash, give 'em a bath in this time-tested tonic.

**1 can of beer**
**1/4 cup of instant tea granules**
**2 tbsp. of dishwashing liquid**
**2 gal. of warm water**

Mix these ingredients in a bucket, and soak newly divided perennials in this tonic for about 10 minutes just before replanting them. When you're finished, dribble any leftover tonic around your newly settled divisions. It'll get 'em off on the right root and growin' like gangbusters!

## DON'T BE TOO TIDY

When cold weather finally calls a halt to your chrysanthemums, don't be in a hurry to cut 'em down. Trim off the dead flowers if you want, but leave the stems standing until early spring. We've tried treating them both ways—we cut some to the ground and left others with the stems on—and we found that leaving the stems made a big difference in the winter survival rate. So from now on, when we put the test gardens to bed in the fall, we keep our clippers off the chrysanthemums!

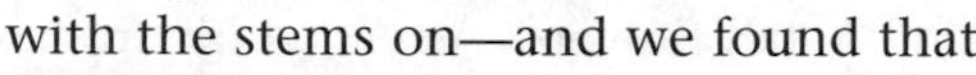

## BRING NEW LIFE TO TIRED PERENNIALS

By fall, things are a lot less busy as far as yard work goes, so it's our favorite time to take a good, long look at our test-garden flower beds. One thing we make a special point to watch for is perennials showing the "doughnut syndrome": a ring of healthy growth surrounding a dead-looking center. If we find a perennial with this problem, we know it's time to divide it, pronto! Here's how:

**Step 1.** A day or two before we plan to divide, we give the ground around the clump a good soaking. We also cut back any top growth, down to about 6 inches above the ground, so the plant will be less likely to wilt before it settles into its new home.

**Step 2.** The next day, we dig up the entire clump and cut or break it into several sections. We keep only the healthy parts from the outside of the clump; the old, dead area from the middle gets sent to the compost pile.

**Step 3.** When we replant the healthy parts, we toss a handful of dry oatmeal and human hair into each planting hole first. Sounds odd, we know, but we've found it really helps the divisions get off to a great start!

## TLC FOR FALL DIVISIONS

Late summer and early fall are ideal times to divide crowded clumps of spring-flowering perennials, since they'll have plenty of time to get settled in before their flowering time comes 'round again. The only disadvantage is that these later divisions may *not* have time to grow deep, well-established roots before the cold weather sets in, so alternating freezing and thawing can pop them right out of the ground!

To keep your fall divisions in good shape, do what we do: Tuck them into their beds with a thick blanket of loose, lightweight mulch, such as straw or evergreen boughs. And if you do spot any clumps that have been heaved out of the soil, press them back in when the ground is thawed out during winter warm spells.

## FALL FOR IRISES

Sure, irises are beautiful in summer borders—but would you believe you can enjoy them in your fall garden as well? It's true! The iris lovers at our test gardens have tracked down a few *reblooming* cultivars: bearded irises that will bloom a second time from late summer into fall if you treat them right!

Two of the easiest-to-find rebloomers are pale yellow 'Baby Blessed' and pure white 'Immortality'. There are many others worth seeking out; some of our favorites include purple-and-white 'Autumn Tryst', bright yellow 'Harvest of Memories', and silvery white 'Lo Ho Silver'. We've found that all of these rebloomers are much more likely to flower again in fall if we give 'em an extra dose of fertilizer after their first early-summer show; keeping 'em watered during summer dry spells seems to help, too.

### Test Garden SECRET

Did you ever plant a white (or pink, or red) cultivar of garden phlox for late summer and early fall color, only to end up with a bunch of purplish pink blooms after a few years? We've had the same thing happen—*and* we've found a way to prevent it! Despite appearances, the original plant doesn't magically change color; rather, its seedlings come up and crowd out the pretty parent plant. To keep this from happening, try this garden-tested trick: Always cut off the spent flower heads after your plants are done blooming. This simple step is guaranteed to keep those pesky seedlings from getting started!

**Q** My aster plant was growing great, but then it started to droop, even though the soil is plenty moist. What can I do to save it?

**A** A nasty fungal disease called aster wilt is probably at work. You need to act fast: Take cuttings of stem tips for rooting, but dig and destroy all the rest of the clump—including the roots, where this fungus resides. It's also smart to avoid planting other asters in the same spot for at least three years.

## FOREVER FLOWERS

Even though our test-garden beds are filled with flowers right through the fall months, we always know that winter is right around the corner. One year, we thought it would be fun to dry some of our favorite fall flowers for cold-weather craft projects; but when we tried air-drying, the results were disappointing—probably because the air was already too cool for quick drying. We tried a store-bought product called silica gel, and it kept the colors looking bright, but it was really expensive, too. So we experimented a bit, and we came up with a great homemade drying powder that costs practically nothing!

Simply mix 3 parts Borax® with 1 part cornmeal, and use some to cover the bottom of a sealable container. Place a single layer of freshly picked flowers in the container, and cover them completely with more of the mixture. Let stand for four to five days, then remove the dried blooms, dust them off with a fine paintbrush, and enjoy them in bouquets or crafts.

## PLUMBAGO CRAZY

Over the years, we've tried just about every blue-flowered perennial we could find, and while we've liked them all, there's one we'd never be without for fall color: plumbago (*Ceratostigma plumbaginoides*). Also known as leadwort, this tough-as-nails perennial is a true beauty, with clusters of small, electric blue blooms starting in late summer. But that's not all! In September and October, the green leaves turn amazing shades of orange, red, and wine-purple that rival the showiest tree or shrub for fall color, all while the plant's still flowering. Plumbago will grow in just about any well-drained site (even dry shade) in Zones 5 to 9. Give it a try—we know you'll love it as much as we do!

# MASTER YOUR ASTERS

Asters are a classic choice for fall flower gardens, and with good reason. Thanks to the efforts of dedicated plant breeders and nurserymen, these colorful perennials have gone from being scrawny roadside weeds to personality-packed garden plants. We should warn you, though, that asters set loads of seeds, and unfortunately, most of the fancy cultivars grown in gardens don't come true. (In other words, the seedlings won't look like the plants they came from.)

The obvious solution is to cut off all the flowers when they fade, to keep seeds from forming—but if you do that, you'll lose a great source of free food for birds that visit your garden in winter! Fortunately, our test-garden crew has found the perfect solution: Wait until early spring to cut back the plants, then mulch around them right away to smother any dropped seeds before they sprout.

# GO FOR THE GOLDENRODS

Late-season visitors to our test gardens are always surprised to see us growing goldenrods (*Solidago*) in our perennial beds. Sure, they're pretty, they say—but don't the flowers bother your allergies? Well, we're here to set the record straight: Goldenrods are *not* to blame for fall hayfever! The real culprit is ragweed (*Ambrosia*). It flowers at the same time as goldenrod, but nobody notices its dull green blooms.

So, now that you know it's safe to enjoy goldenrods in your sunny autumn garden, go wild! Two of our favorites are the low-growing 'Golden Fleece', with masses of branching golden blooms atop 1- to 2-foot-tall stems, and the much larger 'Fireworks', with bright yellow flowers growing on 3- to 5-foot-tall plants.

## Flower Garden Nightcap

When it's time to close up your flower beds for the season, cover the frozen ground with finely mowed grass clippings or chopped leaves, then overspray with our time-tested tonic to settle them in for a long winter's nap.

**1 can of regular cola (not diet)**
**1 cup of baby shampoo**
**1/2 cup of ammonia**
**2 tbsp. of instant tea granules**

Mix these ingredients in your 20 gallon hose-end sprayer, and saturate the mulch blanket. This tonic feeds the mulch, which in turn will feed your garden, while it protects your perennials all through the winter.

## TREES' COMPANY

Besides casting lots of shade, tall trees add another challenge: dense root systems that can suck the water and nutrients right out of any garden you plant directly underneath 'em. If your trees have deep roots, like oaks (*Quercus*) do, you're in luck. But shallow-rooted trees, like maples (*Acer*), can be a real pain to plant under.

To figure out what's underfoot *before* we add a new flower bed at the test gardens, we use a small spade to gently dig around the tree we're considering planting under. If a solid mass of roots makes digging too tough, we don't try to fight Mother Nature; we simply move out farther away from the trunk, until the digging is easy. Besides making the initial site preparation easier, keeping the flower bed away from the tree roots drastically cuts down on water and fertilizer needs later on!

**Test Garden SECRET**

When planting a perennial in a pot or planter, try this terrific trick we swear by at the test gardens: Leave a 2-inch space between the top of the potting soil and the rim of the container, then spread an inch or so of mulch over the soil. Just as it does in the garden, the mulch will help keep the roots cool and cut down on moisture loss, so you'll spend less time watering and more time enjoying your pretty potted perennials!

## GARDENING BY THE CLOCK

Scorching summer heat doesn't just wilt gardeners; it's also tough on our plants. To keep your beds and borders colorful all summer long, it helps to remember that shady spots aren't all the same. A garden that receives morning sun and afternoon shade usually is cooler than one that's shaded in the morning, and then baked by the sun all afternoon. We've found that shade-loving plants that can stand a bit of sun—like hostas—usually grow best in areas that receive morning sun and afternoon shade, or dappled, all-day shade. In sites with shade in the morning and sun in the afternoon, we stick with sun-lovers that can stand a bit of shade—like coreopsis.

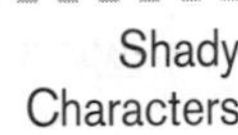

## ASTILBES LOVIN' YOU!

If you're looking to add some sparkle to a shady corner, astilbes are hard to beat! Even if they didn't flower, we'd grow 'em just for their glossy, fern-like leaves. But we're sure happy that they *do* bloom, with their feathery plumes in shades of red, pink, lilac-pink, and white from late spring well into summer. We're even happier to report that they need almost no care in return for all this beauty. All you need to do is keep an eye out for the woody crowns (the part where the roots meet the shoots) peeking out of the ground in summer or fall. If you spot them, do what we do: Cover 'em with a few handfuls of a 50-50 mix of soil and compost to protect 'em through the winter, then lift and divide the clumps the following spring. That's all it takes to grow awesome astilbes!

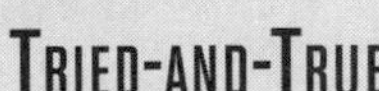

### TRIED-AND-TRUE

Smart deep-South gardeners know they can't believe everything they read about what particular perennials need—specifically, the amount of sun they can take. Plants that prefer full sun in most parts of the country may need partial shade, or even full shade, in hot, humid climates. So unless you're sure that a newly purchased perennial is suited to growing in sun in your area, try it in a bit of shade first! The reverse is true for far-northern gardens: Plants that demand shade elsewhere may languish in cool conditions unless you give 'em lots of light. My Grandma Putt never hesitated to move her perennials around if they didn't thrive where she thought they would at first—and neither should you!

## WONDERFUL WINTER BLOOMERS

As soon as the ground starts thawing after a long, bitter winter, you can be sure that our test-garden crew is ready to get out and start looking for the first roses. Roses in the snow? You bet! In mild-winter climates, Christmas rose (*Helleborus niger*) can start blooming as soon as early winter. In colder areas, the flowers tend to wait until late winter, but they're still out weeks earlier than most flowers. Lenten roses (*H.* × *hybridus*) pick up where Christmas roses leave off, flowering from late winter to early spring. Once the flowers are done, the clumps of leathery, deep green foliage look great all through the rest of the year.

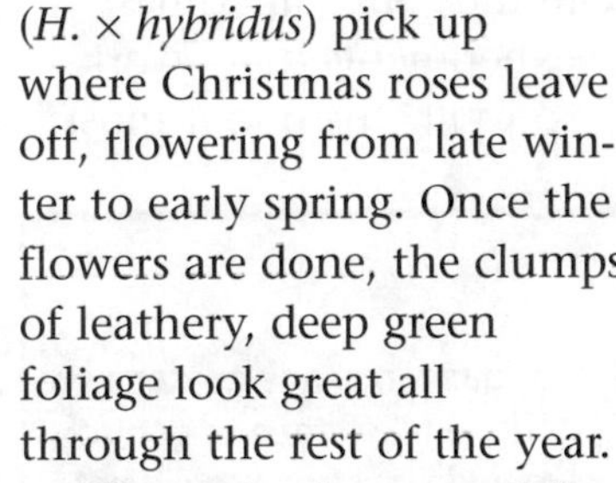

These sturdy perennials are a snap to grow in Zones 4 to 9: Just give 'em partial to full shade and average garden soil. Pests and diseases don't bother 'em, and neither do pesky critters like deer and rabbits! Best of all, the clumps seldom need division, so you can just plant 'em and forget 'em!

## PARTY HARDY

If you enjoy growing annual begonias in your shady gardens, you'll *love* this gem we've found: hardy begonia (*Begonia grandis* ssp. *evansiana*). Unlike most begonias, which shrivel away at the slightest touch of frost, this one can survive the winters outdoors as far north as Zone 6—or even Zone 5, if you give it a sheltered site and a thick blanket of leaves for the winter. Each year, you'll enjoy the 30-inch-tall clumps of wing-shaped leaves topped with arching clusters of pink or white flowers from late summer through fall—all without having to replant each spring!

## PRIDE IS A JOY

We're always experimenting with new plants in our test garden beds, and usually, we're pleased as punch with the results. But sometimes, our experiments don't work out so well! One of our most memorable mistakes was planting yellow archangel (*Lamiastrum galeobdolon*). Believe us: This one is no angel! It looked great in a pot, with trailing stems clad in handsome silver-and-green leaves; but when we planted it in our gardens, it sent out rooting stems in all directions. By the end of that season, it was starting to crowd out less-vigorous companions, so we ripped it all out. Curiously enough, 'Hermann's Pride', a cultivar of the same plant, has proven to be a real winner. It's far more mannerly than its parent, with the same fabulous foliage and bright yellow blooms, but on a dense, clump-forming plant. So take our advice: If you're looking to strike silver in the shade, give 'Hermann's Pride' a try.

### Slugweiser

Slugs love the cool, moist conditions found in shady gardens, so they can be a real problem if you don't take steps to control them. Beer is the classic bait for slug and snail traps; but what attracts the slimy thugs isn't the alcohol in the beer, or even the hops and malt—it's the yeast. So fill up your traps with this simple potion, and don't bother wasting a perfectly good brewski on the enemy!

**1 lb. of brown sugar**
**$^1/_2$ package ($1^1/_2$ tsp.) of dry yeast**
**Warm water**

Mix the sugar and yeast in a 1-gallon jug, fill it with warm water, and let the mixture sit for two days, uncovered. Then pour it into your slug traps, and watch the culprits belly up to the bar!

## MAKE FRONDS WITH FERNS

Think ferns are delicate and hard to grow? No way! We've tested just about every hardy fern we could find, and we've discovered eight great ones that make terrific, fuss-free groundcovers for shady sites. Give these a try and see if you don't love 'em as much as we do!

**Broad beech fern**
(*Thelypteris hexagonoptera*)

**Christmas fern**
(*Polystichum acrostichoides*)

**European lady fern**
(*Athyrium filix-femina*)

**Flowering ferns**
(*Osmunda*)

**Japanese painted fern**
(*Athyrium niponicum*)

**Male fern**
(*Dryopteris filix-mas*)

**New York fern**
(*Thelypteris noveboracensis*)

**Ostrich fern**
(*Matteuccia struthiopteris*)

*For extra color without taking up extra space, plant early-blooming bulbs, such as tulips, daffodils, and hyacinths, under hostas. The bulbs will come up and bloom first, then the emerging hosta leaves will hide the dying bulb leaves. When I divide the hostas, I divide the bulbs as well.*

Lois B., Sioux Falls, SD

## MADE FOR THE SHADE

Most phlox are real sun-worshippers, but guess what—shady-site gardeners can enjoy these beautiful bloomers, too! The secret is to choose your plants wisely. Two that we won't be without are wild blue phlox (*Phlox divaricata*), with clusters of fragrant, lavender-blue flowers, and creeping phlox (*P. stolonifera*), in pink, lilac-blue, or white. Both spread to form broad clumps that'll really knock your socks off when they do their thing in spring!

**Test Garden SECRET**

Granny's bonnets, doves-around-a-dish, or simply columbines—call them what you will, these old-fashioned favorites are a perfect choice for early-summer color in partly shady sites! Columbines (*Aquilegia*) are a snap to grow from seed, and they'll delight you each summer with elegant and intricate flowers in a rainbow of colors. We've found that these pretty perennials have one alarming habit, though: After three or four years, the plants tend to simply disappear, no matter what you do for them! We're not sure why this happens, but we've found a simple way to get around it: Let the flowers go to seed, then crumble the browned seedpods around the parent plants, so you always have new clumps coming along. It never fails!

### All-Purpose Varmint Repellent

Deer, rabbits, and rodents will snack on just about anything in your flower garden. Whatever the culprit, we've got just the cure.

- 1/2 cup of Murphy's Oil Soap®
- 1/2 cup of lemon-scented dishwashing liquid
- 1/2 cup of castor oil
- 1/2 cup of lemon-scented ammonia
- 1/2 cup of hot, hot, hot pepper sauce
- 1/2 cup of urine

Mix these ingredients in a 20 gallon hose-end sprayer, then apply to the point of run-off over any area that needs protecting. Reapply every other week or so (or after a rain) to keep this odiferous mix doing its thing.

## SIZE MATTERS

When you're finding a place for hostas in your beds and borders, keep in mind that you can never really tell how big hostas are going to get while they're still in a pot. We've found that it takes two to four years after planting for them to reach their full size. So, before you stick potted hostas into any old spot, look at the label to see how big they'll get when full-grown, and make sure you give 'em the space they need to spread their wings! If the label doesn't list the spread, then use our handy guide to help you figure out how big your hostas might get, and how far apart to plant them:

- "Dwarf" hostas usually mature at 8 to 10 inches tall. Plant them 8 to 10 inches apart.
- "Small" hostas generally grow 10 to 15 inches tall. Space them 10 to 15 inches apart.
- "Medium" hostas range from 15 to 24 inches tall. Set them 18 to 24 inches apart.
- "Large" hostas are over 2 feet tall when mature. Plant them 2 to 3 feet apart.

## SPOTS AND SPLASHES

When it comes to flower gardening, many folks think of shade as a problem. We like to think of it as an opportunity! Shade provides ideal conditions for all kinds of fantastic perennials that simply can't take the heat of a full-sun site. The secret to successful shade gardening is simple: Use lots of multicolored—or variegated—leaves! You see, perennials need lots of energy to produce abundant blooms, and in shady sites, many perennials can't get all the sunlight they need to support fabulous flowers for very long. Fortunately, leaves need less light, so plants with variegated foliage look great from spring to frost, providing plenty of color all on their own. Green with white edges, gold with green stripes, green and yellow with red splashes—the various combinations of colors and patterns are practically endless!

## HOW SWEET THE SCENT

Did you know that hostas can do more than just look leafy? They can fill your garden with fragrance, too! The sweetly scented varieties tend to do better with a bit more sun than most hostas; heavy shade can discourage flowering, and fewer flowers mean less fragrance. Most fragrant hostas have white flowers, and their perfume is most intense in the evening, so they're great planted around a deck or patio where you relax after a hard day at work.

In our tests, we've found that some of the best hostas for pleasing perfume include 'Aphrodite', 'Fragrant Blue', 'Fragrant Bouquet', 'Fried Bananas', 'Fried Green Tomatoes', 'Guacamole', 'Honeybells', *H. plantaginea,* 'Invincible', 'Royal Standard', 'So Sweet', 'Sugar and Cream', and 'Venus'.

## WATCH OUT FOR WALNUTS

If the shade in your yard comes from a black walnut (*Juglans nigra*) tree, you need to pay extra-special attention to the perennials you plant underneath. According to the experts at our test gardens, walnut trees produce a substance called juglone that discourages many other plants from growing near them. Fortunately, we've discovered that not all perennials are equally sensitive to this stuff. Keeping dropped nuts and leaves picked up helps minimize the amount of juglone that leaches into the soil. But if your plants still aren't thriving there, consider sticking with perennials that have proven to be walnut-tolerant in our tests:

**Astilbes** (*Astilbe*)

**Bee balm** (*Monarda*)

**Bugleweeds** (*Ajuga*)

**Heucheras** (*Heuchera*)

**Hostas** (*Hosta*)

**Jacob's ladders** (*Polemonium*)

**Lungworts** (*Pulmonaria*)

**Solomon's seals** (*Polygonatum*)

**Sweet woodruff** (*Galium odoratum*)

**Wild gingers** (*Asarum*)

### Test Garden

Hostas are classic shade favorites, and they're typically trouble-free, except for one problem: Slugs love 'em! Sure, you can try to foil these slimy slitherers with sprays and traps, but why not stop the problem before it starts? In our test-garden beds, we've discovered that hostas with thick-textured leaves are *far* less likely to get chomped by slugs than those with thin leaves! So if you're tired of slugs making Swiss cheese out of your hosta leaves, give these a try: hybrids 'Blue Umbrellas', 'Invincible', 'Krossa Regal', 'Regal Splendor', and 'Sum and Substance', as well as *H. sieboldiana* 'Elegans' and 'Frances Williams'.

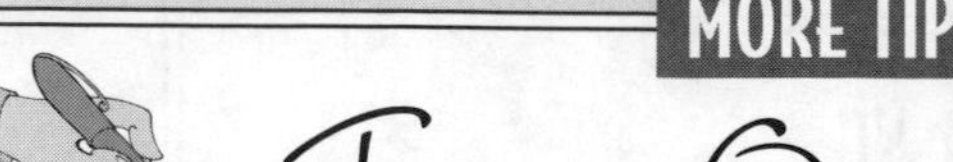

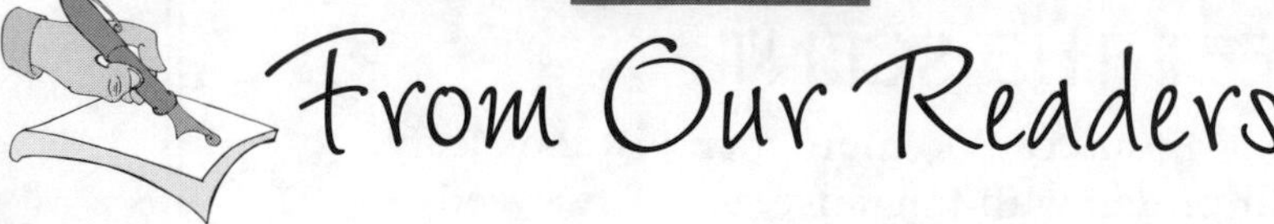

# MORE TIPS From Our Readers

## POINSETTIA CARE

Poinsettias need alternating periods of light and dark to keep them going after their blooming season. I have found that putting them in a closet with a fluorescent light on a timer keeps them going and helps them bloom again. But while they are in a closet and out of sight, don't forget to water them!

***G. P., Niagara Falls, NY***

## WIND BREAKERS

As winter arrives, I like to set up windbreaks in front of my rhododendrons. I've found a quick, easy, and inexpensive way to accomplish this with boards and burlap. I use precut 2 × 2-foot boards for posts (you can even use leftover branches that have fallen from your trees). To attach the burlap, I use a hand-held post stapler. It makes quick work of setting up many windbreaks in just a few minutes! I also make a couple of slits in each windbreak to take the stress off of the end posts when the wind blows.

***Perry N., Michigan City, IN***

## EASY WEEDER

This spring, I discovered so many weeds growing very close to my perennial plants that my trusty three-pronged garden fork was useless, and my dandelion digger wasn't any better. Then I discovered the perfect way to reach into close spots, like around iris rhizomes: I went to my local discount store and bought a 12-inch-long, two-pronged kitchen fork with a wooden handle. I could hardly believe how easy it was to use it to weed in tight places! If I found a taproot, I would place the root between the tines and then rotate the fork, and it would bring up the whole root. Why I never thought of this before, I don't know.

***Richard H., Middlebury, VT***

## LEAF THE WEEDS

Last fall, I put fallen leaves all around my roses and perennials. This spring, I swept up the leaves and had no weeds to dig out. It was a really big help for me.

***Helen B., Wilkes-Barre, PA***

# From Our Readers

## SLEEP TIGHT

After Christmas, I recycle my tree by sawing off the branches and laying them over my already sleeping perennials. Cupping the branches upside down over the plants will protect them from snow, frost, etc., and I can lift the branches from time to time to check on my sleeping beauties.

***Jeannie L., Olathe, KS***

## OH, MY OLEANDERS!

I sprayed diluted baby shampoo on my oleanders to rid them of curly leaf and fungus. It worked so well that I think I may have actually brought an oleander back to life!

***Stanton P., Penn Valley, CA***

## PICKLED GARDENIAS

Each time I finish a jar of pickles, I dump the pickle juice over my gardenia bush. My flowers love it!

***Mike L., Crofton, MD***

## SALTY SECRET

When watering my African violets, I use a pint of warm water mixed with a pinch of Epsom salts. My violets have not stopped growing since, and are growing so fast that I can't believe it!

***Mildred S., S. Sioux City, NE***

## PERK UP YOUR VIOLETS

Always water your African violets from the bottom. Fill a container with warm water, and then place the plant pot inside. Your plants will love you for it.

***Marianne N., Omaha, NE***

## BAG THE BUGS

Are bugs eating your gardenia buds? The culprits are probably grasshoppers—they come in at night to munch on the buds. I cover my gardenias with a garbage bag in late evening, and take it off again in the morning. The grasshoppers aren't able to eat the covered buds, so my flowers are saved.

***Jo Ann A., Lufkin, TX***

MORE TIPS

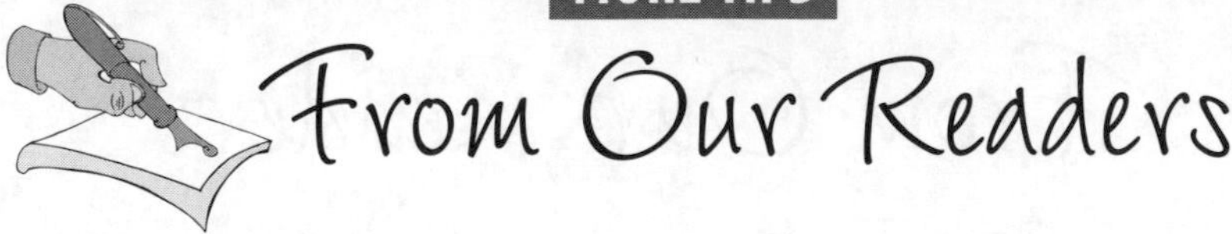

# From Our Readers

## VOILÀ, VIOLETS!

To keep your African violets blooming year-round, simply place an old rusty nail in the soil. Presto! Beautiful blooms without fertilizing!

*Mary-Beth Q., Islip, NY*

## LILY LOVIN'

Leave bamboo stakes in the ground to remind you where your lilies are planted. In the spring, tie three or four strips of material to the bamboo stakes so you'll have the ties right at your fingertips when you need them to support your tall blooms.

*Shirley H., Alpine, CA*

## FLOWER EXTENDER

To make woody-stemmed cut flowers (like lilacs, roses, and honeysuckle) last longer, take a hammer and crush at least an inch of the cut stem. That allows the fibers to soak up more water, and your flowers will look good for many days.

*Julie S., Milwaukee, WI*

## MAGIC MAYO

My hibiscus had been heavily infested with whiteflies, and nothing seemed to help. Then, as a last resort, I placed plastic grocery bags over the infected branches and left them on overnight. The next morning, the dew in the bags had already trapped and killed many of the adult flies. Removing the bags as I went, I wiped the nests off the underside of the leaves with a paper towel dipped in mayonnaise. I then attached sticky traps inside the bush. It was a task, but the bush has been loving life ever since.

*Camille B., N. Hollywood, CA*

## CACTUS BLOOMERS

If you have trouble getting your Christmas cactus to rebloom the next winter, try this: Put 2 tablespoons of castor oil around the roots of the cactus in October, and it will bloom in December. This always works for me.

*Jaclyn B., Monroe, LA*

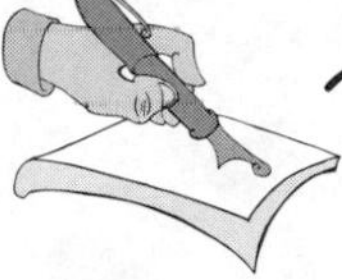

# From Our Readers

## FANTASTIC FLOWERS

Whenever I need a flowering shrub, such as a forsythia or weigela, I don't go out and buy one—I make one! In the fall, I take a long branch at the bottom of an exisiting shrub and bury the bent stem next to the plant. By spring, it will have made new roots of its own. Then, I cut it away from the original plant and dig it up. To make a bushier plant, I bury several branches and plant all the newly rooted ones together.

***Virginia R., Artemus, KY***

## WINTER TENTS

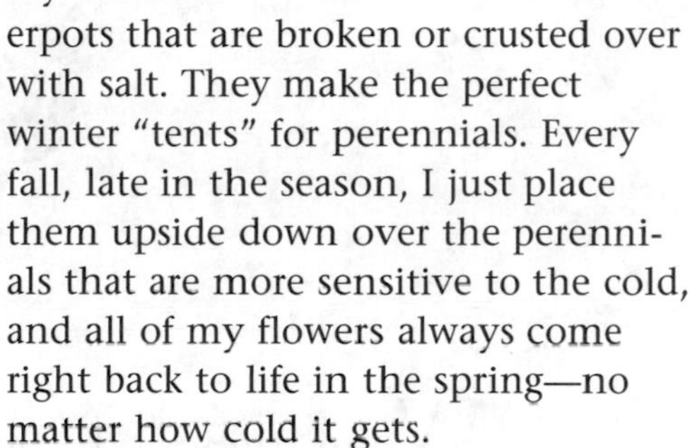

I never throw out my old flowerpots that are broken or crusted over with salt. They make the perfect winter "tents" for perennials. Every fall, late in the season, I just place them upside down over the perennials that are more sensitive to the cold, and all of my flowers always come right back to life in the spring—no matter how cold it gets.

***Madeline K., Poughkeepsie, NY***

## LOVE THAT LITTER!

The azaleas that I planted last year were really pale and sickly come spring—I knew they needed an acidic boost. So I started emptying my cat litter (after I scoop the poop out of it!) around them. Now they are bright and pretty!

***Deb W., Yulee, FL***

## TAME ROWDY ROOTS

I put most of my perennials for the garden into pots first, then plant the pots right in the dirt. That way they're easy to move when it gets cold. But, in order to stop the roots from going wild and spreading out the pot's drainage hole, I've learned to first put a few layers of newspaper in the bottom of the pot, before the plant goes in. The plants don't seem to mind, and the roots stay under control.

***Sandy S., Tampa, FL***

# Chapter 7

# More Bounce from Your Bulbs

When it comes to pure flower power, bulbs are tough to beat. They sure don't look very promising at planting time, but we know we can depend on these little prewrapped packages to produce a bounty of blooms year after year. From dependable daffodils and tantalizing tulips to glorious glads and lovely lilies, bulbs are foolproof enough for even the most novice gardener, and diverse enough to satisfy the most experienced expert. Over the years, we've tried a boatload of these Dutch dandies, so we know what it takes to get the best from bulbs, and now you will, too!

## BREAKING THE RULES

What's the No. 1 rule of planning a beautiful flower bed? Put short plants in front, and tall plants in back! But when it comes to bulbs, we think this rule is made to be broken. Why? Well, the only problem with growing early-flowering bulbs is the fact that you have to look at the yellowing leaves as they die back after bloom. And when those bulbs are right up front, that ugly foliage is all the more visible. But when you plant 'em near the back of the border, they'll bloom well before the big guys start to sprout, then the emerging perennial leaves will cover up the declining bulb foliage. Try it, and see if you don't love this trick as much as we do!

## PILE 'EM ON!

Think you don't have room to add bulbs to your beds and borders? Think again! We've found a great way to fit two, three, or even four times the number of bulbs in the same amount of space—*and* save loads of time digging planting holes, too! Simply dig one hole about 10 inches deep, then set in some large bulbs, like those of lilies, crown imperials (*Fritillaria imperialis*), or giant onions (*Allium giganteum*). Add enough soil to just cover those bulbs, then set in some slightly smaller bulbs, such as daffodils or tulips. Replace more soil, then add a layer of still smaller bulbs, like grape hyacinths (*Muscari*); cover them, too. If you still have room, finish up with a layer of very small bulbs, such as crocuses. Come spring, scatter seeds of sweet alyssum (*Lobularia maritima*) or some other low-growing annual over the area, and you'll enjoy months of color from minutes of work!

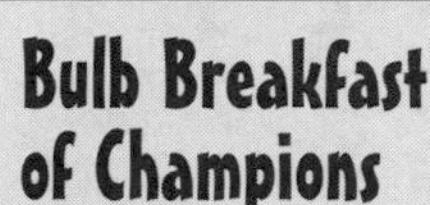


### Bulb Breakfast of Champions

Give your newly planted bulbs a boost with a taste of this terrific tonic. It's packed with enough nutrients and organic matter to provide a small, but steady, supply of food—just what's needed for balanced bulb growth.

**10 lb. of compost**
**5 lb. of bonemeal**
**2 lb. of bloodmeal**
**1 lb. of Epsom salts**

Mix these ingredients in a wheelbarrow. Before setting out your bulbs, work this hearty meal into every 100 square feet of soil in your bulb-planting beds. Or, if you're planting bulbs individually, work a handful of this mix into the soil in each hole before setting in the bulb.

**Q** Hey, Jer—how come I have luck with some bulbs and not others in my deep-South garden?

**A** We've found that some bulbs—notably tulips and hyacinths—need a period of chilling to grow and bloom properly, and they don't get that if your soil stays warm in winter. But you don't have to break the bank buying "precooled" bulbs—it's easy to do the job yourself! Buy new bulbs each year in early fall, then put them in the vegetable drawer of your refrigerator for five to six weeks. Plant them in December, and they'll bloom right on schedule in spring!

## A PERFECT PAIR

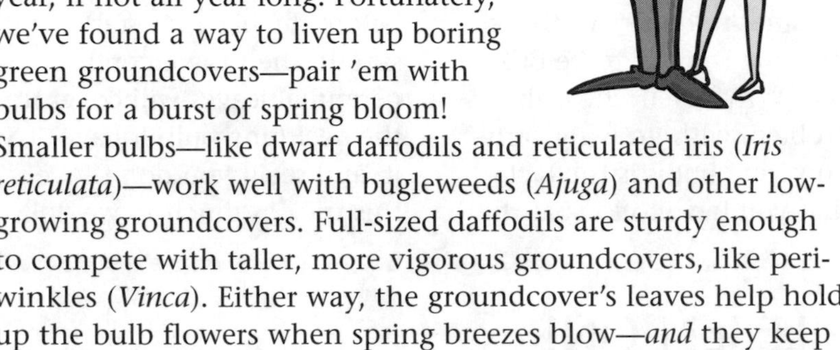

Here at the test gardens, we're always looking for ways to enjoy a beautiful landscape with a minimum of work—and that means we use groundcovers wherever we can. The only drawback to these hardworking plants is that many of them are plain green for most of the year, if not all year long. Fortunately, we've found a way to liven up boring green groundcovers—pair 'em with bulbs for a burst of spring bloom! Smaller bulbs—like dwarf daffodils and reticulated iris (*Iris reticulata*)—work well with bugleweeds (*Ajuga*) and other low-growing groundcovers. Full-sized daffodils are sturdy enough to compete with taller, more vigorous groundcovers, like periwinkles (*Vinca*). Either way, the groundcover's leaves help hold up the bulb flowers when spring breezes blow—*and* they keep soil from splashing up on the flowers when April showers fall!

## WILD ABOUT SAFFRON?

If you've ever purchased saffron at the store for cooking, you know this distinctive spice costs a small fortune. But did you know that you can grow it yourself, right at home? Those little red "threads" (properly called *stigmata*) are harvested from the flower of saffron crocus (*Crocus sativus*), a pretty little bulb that's hardy in Zones 5 to 8. Plant new corms in a sunny site as soon as you get them in late summer for blooms in fall. When they flower, pick the red stigmata, dry them, and store in an airtight glass jar for later use. We've found that saffron crocus does best in very well-drained soil, and may not return in spring if the soil stays wet. But even if we occasionally have to buy new bulbs, we wouldn't be without this little gem in our test gardens!

## THIS END UP!

When we have new helpers in the test gardens at bulb-planting time, we always take a few minutes to review the basics—including which end of the bulb is up! With some bulbs, it's tough to tell, but for most of them, there's a definite difference. The top of the bulb comes to a point, while at the base, there's usually some sign of roots, or the flat plate that the roots grow out of. Setting a bulb upside down won't kill it, but the new shoot has to put more energy into righting itself, and that can weaken the bulb.

### Test Garden SECRET

One of the trickiest parts of growing bulbs is remembering where you planted them! After all, when it comes time to buy and plant more bulbs, or to dig up and divide the perennials they're planted with, the bulbs that are already in your garden have long since disappeared underground. After losing far too many bulbs by digging into them by accident, we knew we had to come up with a better plan. We tried a couple of different methods, but the most reliable was also the simplest: We took lots of pictures of our bulbs in bloom! Besides giving us something nice to look at during the winter, those photos provide a perfect record of what was planted where. It also makes fall bulb shopping a snap, because we can see exactly what colors and kinds of bulbs we need more of, and we know right where we can put them!

## CUT YOUR COSTS

Tulips, gladiolus, lilies, and other bulbs produce some of the most exquisite—and expensive—cut flowers you can imagine! But there's no need to spend a fortune at the florists', when you can grow all that you need right at home. Do yourself a favor, though: Plant the bulbs you plan to cut in a corner of your vegetable garden, or some other out-of-the-way site. That way, you can make beautiful bouquets to your heart's content without ruining the colorful display in your yard.

### TRIED-AND-TRUE

Every time Grandma Putt sent me out to plant lilies, she'd come with me to make sure I picked a good planting spot. She had two special rules: Never plant new lily bulbs where other lilies failed to grow, and never plant 'em in soggy soil. Where the soil was on the heavy (clay) side, here's a little secret that never failed to do the job: She'd have me tilt each bulb a bit in its planting hole, so water couldn't collect between the scales and cause the bulbs to rot. This trick works great for spring-blooming crown imperials (*Fritillaria imperialis*), too!

## TRY A LITTLE TENDERNESS

If you're lucky enough to get some potted bulbs as a gift, don't toss them when they're done flowering! With a little TLC, those bulbs can return to bring you more beautiful blooms in years to come. We suggest treating them like any other houseplant—give 'em lots of light, regular watering, and occasional fertilizing—until after the last frost date, and then plant them in the garden. It may take a year or two for them to flower again, but then they'll come back better than ever to brighten your flower beds with a bounty of bodacious blooms!

## DON'T DELAY

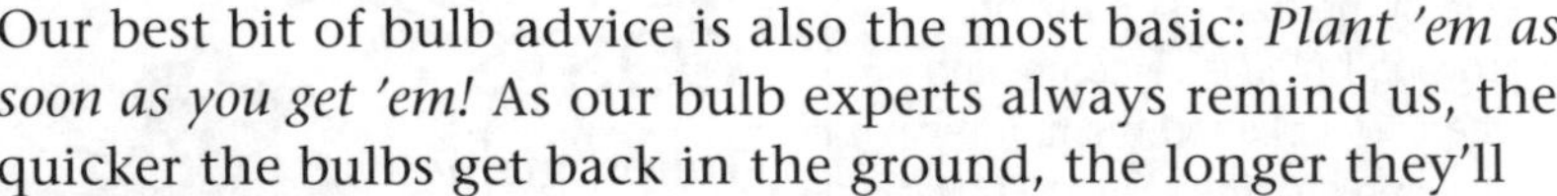

Our best bit of bulb advice is also the most basic: *Plant 'em as soon as you get 'em!* As our bulb experts always remind us, the quicker the bulbs get back in the ground, the longer they'll have to produce a good root system while the soil's still warm, and the better they'll grow later on. But despite our best efforts, we sometimes find ourselves with a few bags of still-unplanted bulbs when cold weather settles in. If this happens to you, don't be tempted to toss them in a corner and plant in spring; yes, there's a small chance they could still bloom after spring planting, but it's more likely not worth the bother. We've found it's far better to plant them even in late fall or early winter—so, as long as the ground isn't frozen, go ahead and get 'em out there!

MIX IT UP!

### Bye, Deer! Tonic

Once deer develop a taste for your garden, they're likely to come back again and again. So *before* they make your beautiful bulbs part of their breakfast, give our garden-tested tonic a try.

**1 cup of fish emulsion**
**3 tbsp. of kelp**
**3 tbsp. of dishwashing liquid**
**Water**

Mix these ingredients in a 3-gallon pump sprayer, and fill the sprayer to the fill line with water. Apply to plants to the point of run-off. Reapply every 7 to 10 days or following any heavy rain that washes the mixture off plant leaves.

## LOVE THOSE GLOVES

Here at the test gardens we like to get our hands dirty, so you'll seldom find us wearing gloves, *except* at bulb-planting time. We've found that some bulbs—hyacinths, most notably, but also crown imperials (*Fritillaria imperialis*), checkered lilies (*F. meleagris*), and other fritillarias—can irritate the hands of folks with sensitive skin. No need to wear clumsy, thick leather gloves, though; disposable gloves seem to work just as well. They're inexpensive, and they're form-fitting enough that you can easily pick up even small bulbs without fumbling. Buy a small box of these gloves in the painting-supplies section of your local hardware store, and you'll have plenty for years to come!

## BULB-BUYING POINTERS

We like to buy most of our bulbs locally so that we can see exactly what we're getting. We've found, though, that it's important to shop early—ideally within the first week or so that the bulbs appear in stores. Otherwise, they can dry out quickly and won't bloom as well the following year. And here's another smart-shopping tip: Check each bulb carefully. Steer clear of any with mushy gray spots on them, as well as those that seem exceptionally lightweight compared to others of the same size; these bulbs are damaged and aren't worth bringing home, even at a discount. It's okay if the bulb's papery skin is loose, though. And don't be concerned about a few nicks—they won't affect the development of otherwise healthy bulbs.

*After I plant my bulbs, I replace most of the soil in the planting area, then add a secret ingredient: chicken wire or rabbit fencing. I lay it out over top of the bulb bed, and cover it with the rest of the topsoil. If cats, dogs, or squirrels try to dig there, they quit when they run into the wire, but the bulbs can come right up through with no problem.*

Patti C.,
Ferndale, WA

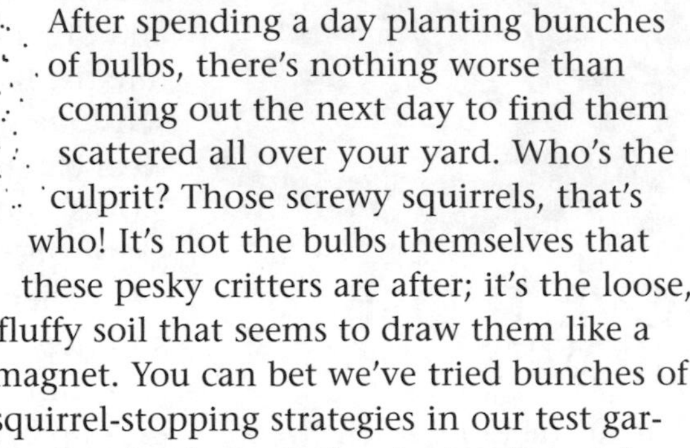

## PEPPER 'EM UP

After spending a day planting bunches of bulbs, there's nothing worse than coming out the next day to find them scattered all over your yard. Who's the culprit? Those screwy squirrels, that's who! It's not the bulbs themselves that these pesky critters are after; it's the loose, fluffy soil that seems to draw them like a magnet. You can bet we've tried bunches of squirrel-stopping strategies in our test gardens, and most times, the simplest solution is simply to take a powder! As soon as you're done planting, sprinkle hot pepper, black pepper, paprika, or even medicated baby powder over the disturbed soil. The stinky stuff is usually enough to keep these furry fiends away from your bulb beds!

### JERRY'S Q&A

**Q** It's not even early winter yet, and some of my bulbs are starting to poke their buds out of the soil! What should I do?

**A** Not to worry! Grape hyacinths (*Muscari*) and several other hardy bulbs often make an extra-early appearance, but they're used to the cold. Their leaf tips might get a little tattered, but the flowers will be just fine come spring.

## THE MORE, THE MERRIER

Just like perennials, many hardy bulbs appreciate being divided every few years. Besides relieving crowded conditions, dividing and replanting provides a great opportunity to work more nutrients into the soil. And since each original bulb will have multiplied into two or more parts by this point, it's also a great way to double or even triple your initial investment in just a few years! Most books suggest waiting until the bulbs have gone completely dormant before dividing them, but then you have to do some guesswork to find the clump. We've found that it's a whole lot easier to dig up the clumps *after* the leaves have yellowed, but *before* they've turned brown and withered away. It's a snap to spot the exact location of the bulbs, so we're far less likely to cut into the clump by accident!

## THE EARLY BULB GETS THE BLOOM

After a long, cold winter, it seems like the first flowers of spring simply can't come too soon! So in our never-ending quest to enjoy bright blooms as soon as possible, we've learned a few tricks over the years! First, we start with the very earliest-blooming crocuses, including snow crocus (*Crocus chrysanthus*), cloth-of-gold crocus (*C. angustifolius*), and *C. tommasinianus*. Then we snuggle 'em up close to a south-facing wall, where the soil will be warmed by even the slightest bit of sun. These two simple steps give us beautiful blooms at least a week before most other bulbs are even thinking of making an appearance!

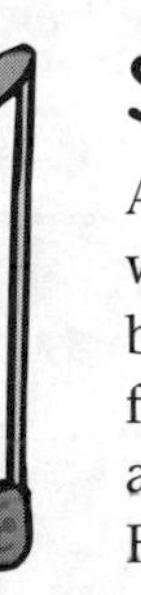

## SIZING THINGS UP

A daffodil is a daffodil is a daffodil, right? Not when it comes to shopping for bulbs! When we buy new daffodil bulbs for our test gardens, we first decide where we're going to plant them, and then select the best size for our needs. Here's what we look for:

■ "Landscape-sized" or "single-nose" bulbs are three years old and produce one flower stem the first year. They're inexpensive and usually a good buy for planting in grassy areas, in large patches of groundcovers, and in cutting gardens (bulbs planted for use as cut flowers).

■ "Bedding-sized" or "double-nose" bulbs are four years old and produce two flower stems per bulb. They're good for most garden uses, including backyard beds and borders.

■ "Exhibition-sized" or "triple-nose" bulbs are five years old. These are the most expensive, but each bulb will produce three or more flower stems—that's three times the flower power of a "single-nose"! This makes them the best choice for planting in high-visibility sites, such as front-yard gardens, as well as in container plantings.

### Bulb Bed Booster

Every spring, serve up this hearty lunch to your hardy bulbs. It'll give them all the nutrition they need to put on a really big show!

**10 lb. of compost**
**5 lb. of bonemeal**
**1 lb. of Epsom salts**

Mix these ingredients in a bucket, stirring them together with a shovel. Scatter the mixture over established bulb beds in early spring, just as the shoots start to emerge from the ground. (This recipe makes enough for 100 square feet.) For an extra treat, add up to 5 pounds of wood ashes to the mix.

## LEAF 'EM BE

It's easy to admire the fabulous flowers of daffodils, tulips, and other spring bulbs; but the yellowing foliage that follows is another matter altogether. Unless you're planning to buy all new bulbs for next year, though, don't even *think* of cutting off the leaves before they're completely yellow! The bulbs need all the time they can get to make food for the following spring's flowers. Instead, do what we do: Pair 'em with perennial buddies that'll come up later and cover up the dying bulb leaves, or else tuck annual transplants around the declining bulb foliage. This clever camouflage trick works every time!

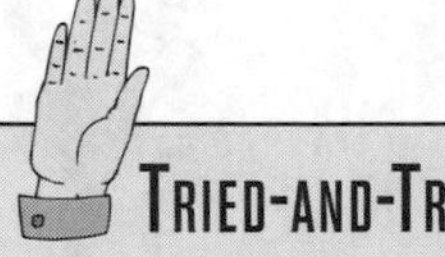

### TRIED-AND-TRUE

Need a cheap, nearly instant groundcover to fill in after tulips, hyacinths, or other spring bulbs die back? Grandma Putt always depended on sweet alyssum (*Lobularia maritima*), and so do we! You can scatter the seeds around the emerging bulb shoots, or buy transplants and pop 'em in around already-blooming bulbs. Either way, they fill the space in a flash and crowd out weeds in the process. As a bonus, this little beauty blooms for months, with tiny but abundant white, pink, or purple blooms that can perfume your whole yard. What more could you ask for?

## GO DOTTY OVER DAFFODILS

If you're a new gardener who's nervous about growing bulbs, take our advice: You can't do better than daffodils! These bulletproof bulbs are just about the easiest plants you can grow: Pests and critters rarely bother 'em, and they'll grow just about anywhere. In fact, just about the only place daffodils *won't* grow well is in soggy soil. If your soil tends to puddle up for more than a few hours after a rain, dig extra-deep holes at planting time, then replace some of the loosened soil before adding your bulbs. Setting the bulbs an inch or two closer to the surface than usual can help, too. An even easier solution is to grow your daffodils on slopes or in raised beds, so they'll sit high and dry!

### Test Garden

What could be better than having a beautiful garden filled with an abundance of delightful daffodils? Having enough to bring indoors, as well! We love to cut these spring beauties for bouquets, and of course we want them to last as long as possible. We've found that the most important factor is *when* you cut them. Don't wait until the flowers are open; that's way too late. Watch the emerging buds, and snip 'em as soon as they're held at an angle to the main stem (they point straight up at first). They'll open quickly once you bring them inside, and easily last well over a week!

## FEEDING FOR FULLER FLOWERS

Ever notice that hyacinth flowers are really full the first year, but then they get looser spikes with fewer blooms in the following years? Many gardeners prefer the more natural-looking effect, but if you want to keep your blooms at their brand-new best, do what we do: Feed 'em with a balanced fertilizer (like 5-10-5) as soon as the leaves emerge in spring. Or, if you want a perfect display of big, full flowers, plant new bulbs every year and move the old ones elsewhere in your yard.

### All-Around Disease Defense Tonic

Most common flower-garden diseases are caused by fungi—microscopic life forms that exist as parasites on our beloved plants. These funky fungi invade plant tissues, destroy cells, and drain the energy out of leaves, then release thousands of spores that germinate and infect the plants, too. The best way to stop these diseases dead in their tracks is to keep a close eye on all your flowering plants and douse them often with this tonic.

**1 cup of chamomile tea**
**1 tsp. of dishwashing liquid**
**1/2 tsp. of vegetable oil**
**1/2 tsp. of peppermint oil**
**1 gal. of warm water**

Mix these ingredients in a bucket, then pour into a hand-held sprayer. Mist-spray your annuals, perennials, and bulbs every week or so before the really hot weather (75°F or higher) sets in. This elixir is strong stuff, so test it on a few leaves first—then wait a day or two to make sure no damage has occurred—before applying it to any plant.

## WHICH WAY DO THEY GO?

If you've ever tried to plant Grecian windflowers (*Anemone blanda*), you know that they can be a bit of a puzzle at planting time. The woody tubers of these spring-blooming anemones look more like chunks of bark than bulbs, and it's practically impossible to tell which side goes up. Fortunately, we've found a simple solution, we plant 'em on their sides and let 'em figure it out for themselves! Here's a bonus tip: Soak 'em in warm water overnight before planting. This seems to really help 'em get off to a great start!

## HANDLING TULIP TRAGEDIES

All leaves and no flowers make tulips mighty dull, indeed! So what happened? It's likely that the bulbs you bought weren't stored or handled properly. Tulips exposed to temperatures above 70°F in storage don't bloom well—*if* they bloom at all. There's not much you can do except be patient; you should have flowers the following year.

If you don't even see leaves where your tulips are supposed to be, suspect voles, mice, or chipmunks, all of which consider tulips a tasty treat. The next time you plant, try one of our favorite tricks: Surround your tulip bulbs with sharp, crushed gravel before you cover them with soil at planting time. Or, for a more permanent solution, line planting beds with ½-inch hardware cloth before you set out your tulips, or plant groups of bulbs in wire-mesh baskets. Yes, it's extra work, but believe us—it's all worthwhile when you see those beauties strut their stuff in spring!

### From Our Readers

*I want to pass along an old trick my mother taught me about how to straighten the stems of tulips after cutting them for arrangements: Simply wrap the stems firmly in old newspaper, starting about a quarter of the way up from the bottom of the stem, and place them in an inch or so of water. Make sure the paper is above the water level, keep them in the water for several hours, and then remove the paper. The result? Perfectly straight stems!*

D. D., Milford, MI

## RING AROUND THE BULBS

Tired of having rascally rabbits snacking on your bulb shoots as fast as they appear? Once these critters get a taste for those tender treats, repellents usually aren't enough: It's time to put up some serious bunny barriers! We've had good luck using black plastic nursery pots (the kind you buy perennials in) with the bottoms cut out. We slip one cylinder over each group of shoots, then push the bottom inch or so of each cylinder into the soil to secure it in place. From a distance, the dark pots blend into the mulch, so they're not visually objectionable—and they do a bang-up job of keeping hungry bunnies at bay!

## ALLIUMS FOR EVERYONE

Guess what, folks? Onions aren't just for the vegetable garden anymore! If you're looking for amazing summer-blooming bulbs, ornamental onions (*Allium*) can really spice up your life. Here's how we make the most of 'em in our test gardens:

■ We particularly enjoy growing chives in our borders—both the pink-flowered common chives (*A. schoenoprasum*) and the white-flowered, later-blooming garlic chives (*A. tuberosum*). Both do double duty, providing beautiful blooms for our gardens *and* tasty foliage for our kitchens. (Just make sure you snip off the spent flowers, so you don't end up with lots of unwanted seedlings!)

■ Garlic is fun to grow, too, with its curiously curved flower stalks. (When we grow garlic in our veggie gardens, we clip off the bloom stems to get bigger bulbs—but in our flower beds, we think they make an amazing accent!)

■ Among the more usual ornamental onions, our favorite is giant allium (*A. giganteum*), with globe-like flower heads that can be 6 inches or more in diameter! After the blooms fade, we let 'em dry right in the garden, then use 'em in arrangements.

## DOUBLE YOUR DAHLIAS

Here's a little trick we use each year to double or even triple the dahlia display at our test gardens! Start the tubers in pots indoors in early spring, and keep 'em warm and moist. When the shoots are about 6 inches tall, cut 'em off about an inch above the soil line, then stick 'em halfway into a mixture of half sand and half compost. After watering lightly, cover the potted cuttings with a clear glass jar, and set 'em in a place with bright, but indirect, light. In four to six weeks, they'll be rooted and ready for the garden. And the original plants? They'll sprout new growth and be even better for the trim!

**Test Garden SECRET**

Most tender bulbs—gladiolus, tuberous begonias, and the like—don't cost much, so you might decide to treat them like annuals and just buy new ones each year. But we've found that it's easy to keep 'em from season to season—a great way to ensure that we always have our favorites, and to save some money, too! As soon as their leaves start to turn color in fall, simply dig 'em up and set 'em in a shady spot to dry off for a few days. Pack 'em in paper bags or in boxes of dry peat moss or vermiculite, and keep 'em in a cool (40° to 45°F), dry place until spring. And here's a bonus tip: Dust your tender bulbs with medicated baby powder *before* you pack them away. It's a surefire way to keep dastardly diseases at bay!

# ABOUT-FACES

After years of growing all shapes and sizes of dahlias, we've noticed a curious trait of theirs: Most dahlia flowers will face the sun—that means south and west. With a little planning, you can use this secret to your advantage! On the north and east sides of your home, plant your dahlias out toward the edge of your property, so the blooms will face toward your house. On the south and west sides, keep the plants next to the house and facing into your yard, so they won't be turning their backs to you as you walk by!

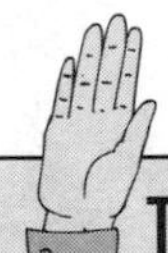

## TRIED-AND-TRUE

Grandma Putt loved all of her flowers, but she always had a special fondness for the exotic beauty of tuberous begonias. Everyone was amazed at how her begonia blooms were twice as big as anyone else's, but I was the only one she shared her secret with—and now I'll share it with you! First, a little botany lesson: Most tuberous begonias produce clusters of three flowers—one male flower flanked by two females. (The female flowers have a swollen seed capsule right behind the petals, while the male doesn't.) When the blooms are still small buds, pinch off the two female flowers. All the growing energy in that stem will go into making one huge, long-lasting male bloom, instead of being shared with the smaller, seed-producing flowers. Yep—it's really that easy!

# GIVE 'EM A JUMP START

In the garden or in a planter, the big, bright blooms of tuberous begonias are hard to beat. You can buy these beauties as started plants, but why spend the dough—it's a snap to start them yourself! The secret to success is making sure you plant 'em properly: The new shoots come from the concave (pressed-in) side, and the roots grow out of the rounded side. So normally, you'll plant these tubers with the rounded side down, with the base of the tuber an inch or so below the surface of the potting soil. But if you buy tubers that don't have any new growth buds visible, try this trick we swear by: Plant them *bottoms up,* right on top of the potting soil. Keep 'em in warm (70°F), humid conditions for about a week, then flip them over and plant them shoot-side up. That'll get them off to a super-fast start!

*For terrific Christmas presents, in early September, grab some 6-inch pots and plant six tulip bulbs in each. Stick them in the back of your refrigerator for 16 weeks (check them once in a while to make sure the soil stays moist). Then, come Christmas, wrap them up and give them to friends and family. The pots will be filled with bright blooms in only a few weeks!*

Sally S., Elk City, OK

## TERRIFIC TIME-SAVERS

No matter how many helpers we have here at the test gardens, it seems like there's always more work than there are hands to do it. So you can bet that when we find a way to save time and still have great-looking gardens, we use it! Recently, one of our staff discovered "self-cleaning" cannas, and now, we wouldn't be without 'em. No, they don't clean up the whole garden for us, but they at least keep themselves tidy, by dropping their spent blooms on their own. (On most cannas, you need to clip off the spent blooms.) They'll look great throughout the season with no deadheading—and that translates into terrific time savings, too!

## DON'T GET BORED

Bearded irises are fantastic for summer color, but they have a big problem, too: iris borers. These pesky moth larvae hatch on the leaves in spring, and then tunnel down through the plants. Once they start snacking on the centers of the rhizomes, bacterial soft rot isn't far behind, causing smelly, slimy, rotted rhizomes. But don't let these buggers get you down—just try our three garden-tested tricks for keeping these plump, pink caterpillars from irritating your irises:

**Choose the right site.** To keep your irises growing strong, give 'em full sun and well-drained soil. And when you plant, make sure the upper half of each rhizome is *above* the soil surface; they don't like to be buried!

**Give 'em a pinch.** If you notice borers tunneling through the leaves, squash 'em between your thumb and forefinger. Also, dust the rhizomes with pyrethrin to kill any emerging larvae.

**Keep 'em clean.** When you divide your irises, discard (don't compost) *all* rhizomes with rot or visible larvae. At the end of the season, cut back and destroy old leaves, and rake up any debris around your irises, to get rid of winter hiding places for these pests.

### Bug-Off Bulb Bath

Used *before* planting, this super spa treatment will help gladiolus, cannas, and other summer-blooming bulbs fend off diseases and pesky pests.

**2 tsp. of baby shampoo**
**1 tsp. of antiseptic mouthwash**
**1/4 tsp. of instant tea granules**
**2 gal. of hot water**

Mix these ingredients in a bucket, then place your bulbs into the mixture. Stir gently, then remove them one at a time and plant them. When you're done, don't throw the bath water out with the babies: Your trees, shrubs, and evergreens would love a little taste, so don't let it go to waste!

## CANNA GET ENOUGH? TRY THIS!

No doubt about it: Cannas are some of the best bulbs for summer flowers and foliage. But buying new plants of high-quality cultivars each year can really break the bank—a single rhizome can cost $10, $15, or even more! Fortunately, there's no need to buy your favorite cannas more than once. Just do what we do: In early spring, chop each rhizome into pieces with at least two growing points on each, then pot up the pieces and grow them indoors until the weather warms up. After a few years of chopping and potting, you'll have as many starts as you could ever use from that one rhizome—plus plenty to trade with your gardening buddies!

Lilies make top-notch cut flowers, but they cost a bundle if you buy 'em from a flower shop. So, save yourself some money, and plant some extra lily bulbs just for cutting. But before you bring the blooms indoors, use this trick that professional florists swear by: Pick or snip off the anthers—those orange, pollen-covered bits that dangle on long stalks from the center of each flower. Otherwise, the pollen will drop off, and trust us: It can be a real hassle to clean off of fabric and furniture!

## CONSIDER THE LILIES

A garden with too many lilies? There's no such thing! Tall or small, traffic-light bright or delicately pastel, these spectacular summer bulbs have long held a place of honor in our summer test-garden beds and borders. But if you love lilies as much as we do, you know that it can get pretty pricey to buy all the lilies you'd like to have.

Well, we've discovered a great way to get around this little problem! You see, most lilies produce small, baby bulbs right above the main bulb, just below the soil surface, and they'll grow into blooming-sized bulbs in no time with just a little help. All you need to do is loosen the soil carefully with a garden fork, pick off the baby bulbs, and plant 'em in a holding bed or a corner of your vegetable garden. Give 'em a year or two to bulk up, then move 'em back to the garden for a stunning show year after year!

## DINNER-PLATE DAHLIAS

If you've ever wondered how to get your dahlias to produce huge, eye-popping blooms, it's no great mystery. Just look for the largest flower bud on each stalk, then pinch out (or snip off) the buds that appear on either side of it. Pinch out any side shoots that come off of the main stalk, too! Then stake the stems before the remaining buds open, because those dinner-plate-sized blooms are mighty heavy!

## FOR SOMETHING COMPLETELY DIFFERENT

Along with lilies, glads, and other classic summer bulbs, we like to experiment with some unusual ones as well—just to keep our test-garden visitors on their toes! One that never fails to amaze gardeners of all ages and experience levels is foxtail lilies (*Eremurus*). These thick, spider-like tubers rocket up from ground level to 4, 5, or even 6 feet tall by early summer, with slender stalks topped with long spikes of white, yellow, pink, or orange blooms.

Most foxtail lilies don't mind winter cold (they can survive the winter as far north as Zone 5), but once they start growing in spring, they *hate* getting nipped by frost. So, do what we do: Cover 'em with 3 to 4 inches of compost, sand, or sawdust in late fall, after the ground has frozen, to discourage early sprouting. (If the spring shoots show above this layer while frosts are still possible, protect them with evergreen branches or large cardboard boxes overnight.) Once all danger of frost has passed, carefully pull away the protective mulch layer, too—and *voilà:* Foxtail lilies to amaze even the most jaded gardener!

### Bulb Bedtime Tonic

Instead of spending your hard-earned money on new tender bulbs each year, why not simply keep the ones you already have? As soon as their leaves start to turn color in fall, dig 'em up and wash them in this tonic before storing them in a frost-free place for the winter.

**2 tbsp. of baby shampoo**
**1 tsp. of hydrogen peroxide**
**1 qt. of warm water**

Mix these ingredients in a bucket and then gently drop in your bulbs. Let them soak for a minute or so, then remove and set on a wire rack to drain. Be sure to let them dry thoroughly before you put them away for the winter; otherwise, they'll rot.

## Pre-Plant Bulb Soak

After sitting around in a garden center for a few weeks, hardy bulbs can get pretty dried out by the time you get them home. To get them plumped up again, give 'em a dip in this super solution just before planting.

**1 can of beer**
**2 tbsp. of dishwashing liquid**
**1/4 tsp. of instant tea granules**
**2 gal. of water**

Mix these ingredients in a large bucket. Let your bulbs soak for a few minutes, then get busy planting!

## PLAN BEFORE YOU PLANT

Planting bulbs in grassy areas (also known as "naturalizing") is a fun way to brighten up boring turf, but trust us: This trick works better in some areas than in others. We thought it would be great to welcome our test-garden visitors with naturalized bulbs in the lawn area by our entrance, and when the flowers were in full bloom the first spring, the effect really was spectacular. We forgot, though, that bulb foliage needs to ripen fully before it's cut—and that meant we wouldn't be able to mow the grass there until early summer! That simply wasn't an option, so we went ahead and mowed as usual; sure enough, very few of the bulbs came back the following spring. Now, we keep our naturalized bulbs in more informal areas, where we can enjoy the colorful bulbs and not worry about the grass getting a little tall before mowing—a much better solution!

## TRY THESE TRICKS!

Crocuses, squills (*Scilla*), and other small bulbs are some of our favorite bulbs for naturalizing here at the test gardens—partly because they are so pretty, but also because they are so simple to plant! To quickly make holes for little bulbs like crocuses, we simply stick a big old screwdriver or asparagus fork a few inches into the ground, swirl it around to make a hole, and drop in the bulbs. Or, if we want to plant a bunch in one spot, we use a spade to cut three sides of a square in the turf, peel back the grass "carpet" (the uncut side acts like a hinge), and set the bulbs in the exposed soil. Then, it's simply a matter of dropping the sod flap back into place and pressing it down with one foot. Presto—perfectly planted bulbs every time!

## A PERFECT SOLUTION

Warm-season lawn grasses look wonderful in summer and fall, but they turn a bland brown color soon after the first frost, and they're slow to green up again in spring. Well, we've found that adding naturalized bulbs is a terrific way to perk up that blanket of beige! Two of our favorite partners for warm-season grasses are lady tulips (*Tulipa clusiana*) and reticulated iris (*Iris reticulata*), but many other small, spring-blooming bulbs work well, too. And unlike cool-season grasses, warm-season grasses grow much more slowly in spring, so they'll be ready for their first mowing right about the time the bulb leaves die back!

## TROWEL WITHOUT ERROR

Have just a few dozen bulbs that you want to naturalize? A sturdy garden trowel makes a super-handy planter for bigger bulbs, like daffodils. To use it like the pros do, grab the handle so the inner curve of the blade faces you, pointing downward. Then stab straight down into the soil as if you're using an ice pick. (The depth of the blade when plunged to the hilt should sink to about 8 inches, the perfect depth for planting larger bulbs.) Just pull back on the trowel to open a pocket in the soil, tuck the bulb in with the pointed end up, remove the trowel, and smooth the soil down. You won't believe how quickly you can get those bulbs in the ground!

**Test Garden SECRET**

Every year, we add hundreds, if not thousands, of bulbs to our test gardens, so you can bet we know a thing or two about how to do the job right—and fast, too! Our all-time favorite bulb-planting tool is a planter bit: an inexpensive item that looks a huge drill bit and fits any 3/8-inch or larger electric drill. This bit makes a perfect 3-inch round hole so quick, you won't believe it! Look for planter bits in garden-supply catalogs, or on our website at www.jerrybaker.com.

**Q** I planted a few dozen daffodils in a grassy area last fall, and I was delighted with the ones that came up—but not all of them did. Any idea why?

**A** Well, daffodils are pretty tough bulbs, and they're seldom bothered by bugs or critters, so I'd rule out those as possible causes. My bet is that you didn't make sure the bottom of each bulb was in firm contact with the bottom of its planting hole. If it isn't, then there will be an air pocket between the two. The roots won't develop properly, and the bulb will rot—a sad return for your effort. So next time, take a few extra seconds to make sure your bulbs are well nestled into the soil before you cover 'em up, and they should be just fine!

MORE TIPS

# From Our Readers

## DISCOURAGE BULB-EATING VARMINTS

Here's how to keep munchers away from your valuable bulbs: Build a bulb box. Take 1/4-inch vinyl-coated hardware screen, and cut out four pieces to make a box to fit over your cluster of bulbs. Tie the screen sides and bottom together with those notched plastic ties that can only be removed by cutting them. Lower the box into the ground with the open side up, and add 1/2 inch of soil to the bottom. Then, place your bulbs on the soil and tie the top on. Inside the box, your investments will be safe from chewing pests, and the emerging foliage will be able to come up through the screen.

***Carl S., Madison, WI***

## CHARCOAL CLEANER

I like to root hyacinths in a glass of water. I've found that adding a lump of horticultural charcoal to the water keeps it clean and clear.

***Erin A., Pine Ridge, SD***

## MONITOR MOISTURE

If stored tender bulbs dry out, they won't be any good next year. I check mine once a month. If they look like they're starting to shrivel, I sprinkle a little water on them to perk them up.

***Anna W., Albany, NY***

## ANOTHER AMARYLLIS

To get more blooms out of your amaryllis, take it out of the soil after the entire plant has died off. Cut off the foliage and let the bulb rest in a cool, dry place until the planting season. When spring planting rolls around, plant your amaryllis, leaving just a bit of the bulb showing (about a third) at the top. Keep watered and, by July, there will be glorious blooms again. Remove the bulb immediately after the first frost, and let it rest until the end of October. Then replant in a pot indoors, and *voilà*!—another Christmas miracle!

***Maureen C., Ontario, Canada***

# From Our Readers

## WONDERFUL WINDOW BOXES

I just love planting tulips in my window boxes so I can see the blooming bulbs from inside my home. I especially like to fill the boxes with bulbs that complement my curtains. Then, when they bloom in the spring, I have beautiful window box blooms that match my interior decorations. Try it—it's as pretty as a picture!

***Vivian L., Toledo, OH***

## GIVE 'EM A PINCH

I've found that pinching off faded daylily blooms helps the bulb store more energy for better blooming the next year. So pinch away!

***Myrtle K., Owensboro, KY***

## GROW MORE GLADS

For a longer season of gladiolus, plant the corms every two weeks, starting after the last frost date and continuing until two months before the first expected frost. You'll have beautiful blooms all season long!

***Gail T., Rockford, IL***

## DAHLIA DEPRESSORS

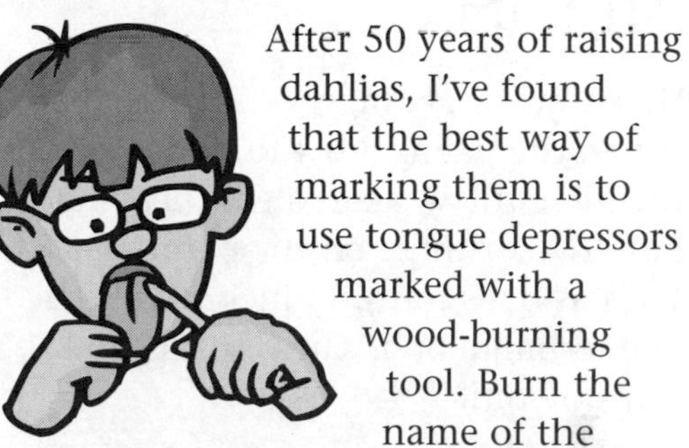

After 50 years of raising dahlias, I've found that the best way of marking them is to use tongue depressors marked with a wood-burning tool. Burn the name of the dahlia on one side, and the color and type on the other (or use a permanent marker). Drill a small hole in the top of the stick, tie a string to it at planting time, then retie the stick to the tuber at storing time.

***Charles W., Port Huron, MI***

## RODENT REPELLER

Rodents used to eat all my tulips, but not anymore. Now I put a piece of mesh with large holes right over my bulb bed, and then I mulch on top. The foliage grows up through the mesh without a problem, but the critters can't dig down to get at the bulbs beneath the soil surface.

***Peter V., Bakerton, PA***

MORE TIPS

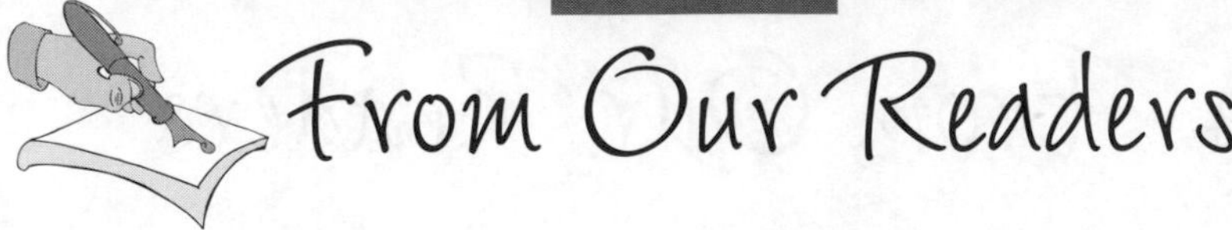

# From Our Readers

## GIANT-SIZED BLOOMS

Here's how I get bigger dahlia flowers: When the plants are 4 to 6 inches tall, I remove the weakest stems, leaving only two or three on the plant. As soon as buds form, I pinch off all but one terminal bud. The result is one giant bloom!

***John H., Fairmount, IN***

## PEAT PROTECTION

If a spring cold snap threatens my daffodils, I cover them with a mound of dry peat moss. I remove it when the frost threat has passed, and my daffodils are just fine.

***Eric N., Mason City, IA***

## WHY WAIT?

I'm always anxious to see my glads bloom. I've found that I can get them to bloom earlier by pinching out the top bud on each spike.

***Marsha N., Buffalo, NY***

## GET A HEAD START

I start my tender, summer-flowering bulbs outdoors before the last spring frost has passed, by planting the bulbs in a bag of peat moss! I cut the bag open, wet down the peat, and set the bulbs inside. Then, if a cold spell threatens, I just cover the opening in the bag with an old sheet or thin board. The results are amazing!

***Gerri V., Green Bay, WI***

## BASIC BULB REPAIR

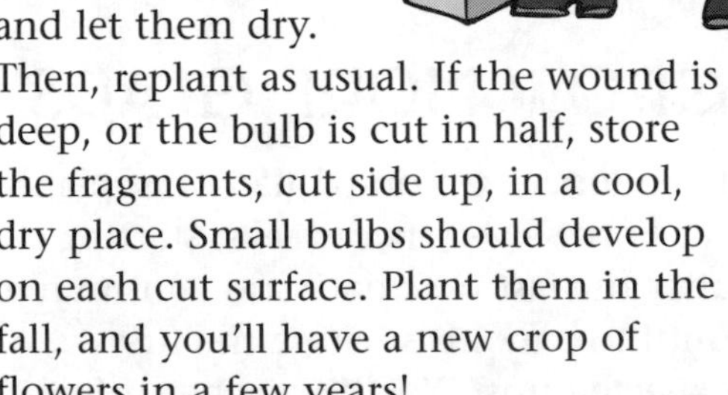

If you accidentally slice into a hyacinth bulb while digging, don't throw the bulb away! Dust minor bulb wounds with wood ashes and let them dry. Then, replant as usual. If the wound is deep, or the bulb is cut in half, store the fragments, cut side up, in a cool, dry place. Small bulbs should develop on each cut surface. Plant them in the fall, and you'll have a new crop of flowers in a few years!

***Leslie J., Baltimore, MD***

# From Our Readers

## FORCING FOIL

When forcing crocus bulbs, I give them the darkness they need by setting them on a cool windowsill and covering them with a cone of aluminum foil. I keep the soil moist, and remove the foil when the crocus shoots are 2 inches tall.

***Jennifer B., Newark, NJ***

## STANDING TALL

I found a way to get my hyacinths to form longer stems! Before the flowers bloom, I put a cardboard toilet paper tube over each stem. The stems then grow taller as they reach toward the light. When they reach the height I want, I take off the tube. Then I get a tall bloom display.

***Tom B., Erie, PA***

## MARKER MAGIC

After lifting my tender bulbs, I use a felt-tip marker to write the plant name and bloom color right on the bulb. That way, I won't make any mistakes at planting time!

***Luke S., Racine, WI***

## EASY LIFTING

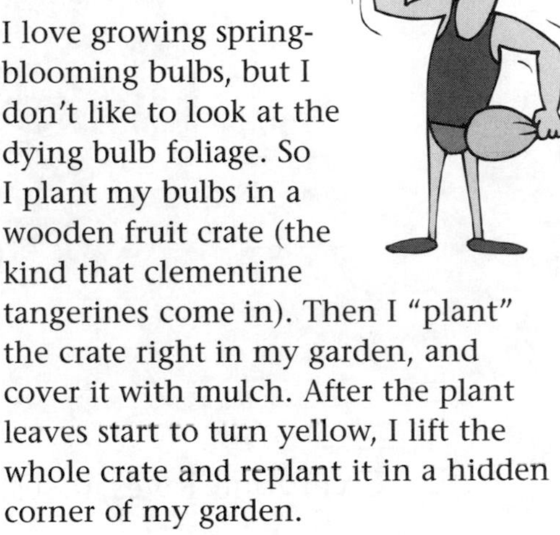

I love growing spring-blooming bulbs, but I don't like to look at the dying bulb foliage. So I plant my bulbs in a wooden fruit crate (the kind that clementine tangerines come in). Then I "plant" the crate right in my garden, and cover it with mulch. After the plant leaves start to turn yellow, I lift the whole crate and replant it in a hidden corner of my garden.

***Diane B., Detroit, MI***

## SUPER STORAGE

I've discovered the perfect storage method for gladioli and dahlias. After lifting my tender bulbs, I arrange them in layers in a box of sawdust (but don't let them touch one another), and store them in an old refrigerator I keep in my garage. It works great!

***Sally S., Toledo, OH***

# Chapter 8

# Ravishing Roses

Everyone loves roses, so why don't more folks grow 'em? We think it's because these beauties have a bad reputation for being prima donnas, demanding frequent feeding, watering, pruning, spraying, and all manner of maintenance to look halfway decent. While this is still true for a few roses, most modern roses are way ahead of those problem-prone selections, with excellent disease resistance, greatly extended bloom seasons, and more. With smart plant selection—plus our surefire garden-tested tips—you, too, can enjoy gorgeous roses without the fuss.

## PERFECT PARTNERS

When visitors to our test gardens ask to see our rose beds, they're often surprised to hear that we don't have any. Oh, we have lots of roses, all right—but we don't believe they should be kept off in a corner by themselves! Roses look simply wonderful paired with perennials, annuals, bulbs, and other flowering plants. Besides providing lots of color when the roses are taking a break, lower-growing plants do a super job covering the "bare ankles" of many roses. (They also practically eliminate the unpleasant chore of having to weed around those thorny stems—a big plus!) In our experience, the roses themselves seem a lot happier to have bed buddies, too. So why not try mixing things up in your own garden? We guarantee you'll love the results!

## BARE'S WHERE IT'S AT

When it comes time to add new roses to our test gardens, and we have a choice between bare-root and container-grown roses, we always go for the bare-root ones. Why? We've tried both, and we've discovered that bare-root bushes seem to settle in quicker than their potted counterparts. We've also found that bare-root roses from mail-order suppliers are a much better bet than those from a local source, because the roots haven't been chopped to fit into a tiny bag or box for display.

### From Our Readers

*To make a beautiful rose arch, tie the ends of the canes to a peg in the ground. You'll have a lovely, blooming "tunnel" in no time!*

Ethel M.,
Corinth, MS

## PLAN AHEAD FOR SPEEDY PLANTING

While we're telling you how great bare-root roses are, we need to be honest and confess the one drawback: their planting time. Bare-roots are available only when the roses aren't actively growing, so they're typically shipped in either late fall or very early spring, when the weather is pretty chilly—not an ideal time to be out in the garden! But we've found an easy way to get around that: We get the beds ready ahead of time. In early fall, we decide where our new roses are going to go, then dig the holes and get the soil all ready for planting. When the roses finally arrive, it takes just a few minutes to get 'em settled in their new homes, and they're ready to grow when the warm weather returns!

### Rose Transplant Tonic

The best time to move established roses is when the bushes are dormant—that is, when the leaves have dropped and scales have formed over the growth buds for next year. Late fall is okay, but many professional rose growers prefer to move roses in early spring, before new growth starts. Whenever you transplant roses, ease the transition with this terrific tonic.

**1 can of beer**
**1 tbsp. of ammonia**
**1 tbsp. of instant tea granules**
**1 tbsp. of baby shampoo**
**1 gal. of water**

Mix these ingredients together in a bucket or watering can, and add 1 cup of the solution to each hole at transplant time. It'll help soothe the shock and get them settled in again in a flash.

## HOW LOW SHOULD YOU GO?

Most times, the roses you buy will be grafted plants—the top growth of a desirable rose growing on the roots of another rose. You can tell this when you look at the base of the bush: Grafted roses have a knobby-looking area just above the roots. It's important to pay attention to the graft union, because it tells you how deep you need to plant. In the North (Zone 6 and colder), we set the graft union 3 inches below the soil surface. In the South, set it 1½ inches *above* the soil line.

## LOCATION, LOCATION, LOCATION

Believe it or not, you can prevent 90 percent of rose-growing problems *before* you even get the bushes in the ground! Here are three points we always consider when selecting the right site for roses:

■ First, give 'em as much sunlight as possible: *at least* 6 hours per day, and ideally 8 or more, throughout the growing season. (Yes, some roses can survive in less, but they seldom bloom well there, and they'll be much more prone to disease problems, so don't chance it.)

■ Good soil is important, too! If your site is soggy or has hard, heavy clay, consider building raised beds, and fill 'em with a mix of good-quality topsoil and compost.

■ An open, airy site goes a long way toward keeping dastardly diseases from getting a foothold. A south- or east-facing site, with some sort of shelter or windbreak to the northwest side, is the perfect spot for growing great roses!

## A SALTY SOLUTION

When new helpers join us at the test gardens, they're often surprised to see that we always keep a good supply of Epsom salts on hand. No, we don't use 'em to soak our tired muscles (well, we *do*—but not until we get home!). In the gardens, we use 'em to give our roses a boost! We rake the mulch away from our roses in early spring, then sprinkle two or three tablespoons of the salts around each bush, out toward the tips of the branches. We scratch the Epsom salts lightly into the soil with a hand fork, then replace the mulch. Try it on your own roses, and prepare to be amazed. You'll notice a big difference in just a few weeks!

### Test Garden SECRET

Hey, cold-climate rose lovers—have I got a tip for you! Whenever you can, buy roses that are grown from cuttings (called *own-root* roses), instead of grafted ones. It may take a bit of searching, but I promise it'll be worth it! You see, if cold winter weather kills the top of a grafted rose, any new shoots you get will be from the roots, not the desirable top growth you chose the rose for. But if an own-root rose dies back, the new shoots will be the same rose you started with! And here's a bonus tip: Set the crown of own-root roses (the point where the roots and stems join) 1 inch below the soil surface to give it extra protection from severe winter weather.

Q Every year, I find lots of little greenish insects clustered on the shoot tips and buds of my roses. What are they, and what should I do about them?

A Sounds like you have an aphid problem! It's often simplest to pinch off the parts that are covered with aphids, because they probably won't recover anyway. To protect the rest of your rosebushes, blend 1 medium-sized onion with a quart of water, strain off the clear juice, and mix 2 tablespoons of it with a gallon of water. Toss in a teaspoon of dishwashing liquid, then spray your roses thoroughly to keep these suckers from dining on your pride and joy!

## WATER IN THE CAN

If your goal is to grow the best-looking roses on the block, it's important to keep the plants supplied with plenty of food and water. But that doesn't mean you need to spend all summer with a garden hose in your hand—just try this time-saving secret! Cut both ends off a large, empty juice can, push it all the way into the ground between every two rosebushes, and fill it halfway with pea-sized pebbles. Pour directly into the can each time you water, and once a month during the growing season, add a small amount of rose food. This trick keeps your plants well fed *and* well watered—in one easy step!

## TRASH OR TREASURE?

After break time here at the test gardens, it's not unusual to see us head back out to the flower beds with our leftovers in hand. Believe it or not, roses just *love* two common kinds of kitchen waste: banana peels and used tea bags! Tucked into the mulch underneath the plants, these waste materials are magic as far as our rosebushes are concerned. Why? Well, the tannic acid in the tea helps make the soil slightly acidic, which roses really appreciate. And the bananas skins are loaded with potassium, which helps the plants fend off pests and diseases.

**Test Garden**

If you've never spent time with real rose aficionados, you'd be amazed at some of the secrets they use to keep their garden stars in prime form. One of the pro-grower tricks we've used with great success is stunningly simple: a drink of alfalfa tea! To try this bloom-boosting solution for yourself, toss a shovelful of compost into a 5-gallon bucket, add two heaping handfuls of salt-free alfalfa pellets (available from animal feed stores), and then fill the bucket with water. Let the mixture sit for at least two days, stirring once or twice a day. If needed, dilute it with water until the tea is light brown before using it to give all your roses a good, long drink. Once the liquid's gone, spread the solids from the bottom of the bucket on the soil around your roses for an extra nutrient boost.

## STEP UP TO FUNGUS-FREE ROSES

Roses are notorious for being disease magnets, but you don't have to be a slave to your sprayer if you know how to keep foul fungi at bay right from the start. Here's our garden-tested, four-step solution to keeping rose woes to a minimum:

**Step 1.** Start with disease-resistant plants, and give 'em the best possible site: well-drained soil, full sun, and good air circulation.

**Step 2.** Keep leaves dry when you water. Soaker hoses wet the soil, not the plants, so they're a much smarter irrigation option than sprinklers.

**Step 3.** If you see only one or two diseased leaves, pick them off and destroy them; that way, you might stop the problem before it starts. But if the fungi have gotten a head start on you, don't wait to spray—get out there as soon as possible to stop the spores from spreading to still-healthy shoots.

**Step 4.** At the end of the growing season, give your rose beds a good, thorough cleanup by raking up all the dropped leaves, so the fungi don't have a place to hang out over the winter.

## PUNCTUAL PRUNING

Based on the questions we get from our test-gardens visitors, pruning has to be the most puzzling part of the rose-growing process. And one of the most confusing things is figuring out the right *time* to prune. We follow this basic rule of thumb for almost all of our roses: We prune 'em in late winter or early spring—just as some of the buds on the largest canes are beginning to swell, but before the plants are sending out shoots and leaves. The one exception is roses that bloom only in late spring to early summer, including many old roses and some shrub roses. We know that pruning once-bloomers in spring cuts off all of this year's blossoms—so you can bet we wait until after flowering to prune those roses!

### TRIED-AND-TRUE

Grandma Putt never skimped when it came to feeding her roses—but she also knew when to call it quits! Come August 15, she'd put the fertilizers away for the rest of the season, because she knew that feeding after that date would produce tender growth that was prone to winter damage. She *did*, however, apply a mixture of 1 cup of bonemeal and 1/2 cup of Epsom salts around the base of each bush before mulching it for the winter. This organic snack wasn't rich enough to promote new shoot growth, but it was prefect for giving the still-growing roots a good boost before their long winter's nap!

## SAY "SO LONG" TO THRIPS!

We love growing white and pastel-flowered roses in our test gardens—and unfortunately, tiny pests called thrips love feeding on them! Brown streaks on the petals are our first clue that these little buggers are at work. To do a double-check, we cut off a damaged blossom, lay it on a piece of white paper for a few minutes, then shake it. If little brown specks fall out, we're sure that thrips are around, and that we need to take action immediately! First, we snip off all the damaged, open blossoms and put them in the garbage; then we give all the rosebushes a good bath with our Double-Punch Garlic Tea (at left). This two-step program does a bang-up job keeping troublesome thrips at bay!

### Double-Punch Garlic Tea

If thrips, aphids, or other bugs are driving your roses buggy, don't pull any punches. Deliver a knock-out blow with this powerful brew.

**5 unpeeled cloves of garlic, coarsely chopped**
**2 cups of boiling water**
**½ cup of tobacco tea***
**1 tsp. of instant tea granules**
**1 tsp. of baby shampoo**

Place the chopped garlic in a heatproof bowl, and pour boiling water over it. Allow it to steep overnight. Strain through a coffee filter, and then mix it with the other ingredients in a hand-held mist sprayer. Thoroughly drench your plants to thwart those pesky pests.

*To make tobacco tea, place half a handful of chewing tobacco in the toe of an old nylon stocking, and soak it in a gallon of hot water until the mixture is dark brown. Store leftover liquid in a tightly capped jug or bottle for later use.

## GIVE BEETLES A BATH

Are Japanese beetles making mincemeat of your rose blossoms? Do what we do: Head out first thing in the morning with a bowl of soapy water, and tap the beetles into it. (Don't wait until later in the day, because once the beetles warm up, they'll fly away as soon as you disturb them; in early morning, they're still dopey and are easy to knock off.) The season for these bad boys lasts only about six weeks, so with a little midsummer attention, your roses will still have plenty of time to produce beautiful blooms in late summer.

## IN GOOD COMPANY

Here at our test gardens, we're big believers in the benefits of companion planting—and not just in the vegetable garden! We've found it works wonders for our roses, too: in particular, pairing them with onions and their relatives to protect the roses from black spot and mildew, as well as aphids. Ordinary onions aren't attractive enough for the flower garden, but there are lots of other options that seem to work just as well. Common chives, for instance, have pretty pink flowers that look super with all kinds of roses. Other low-growing, ornamental onions that make great rose companions include yellow-flowered lily leek (*Allium moly*) and rose-purple to pink-flowered nodding onion (*A. cernuum*).

*While I was living in Colorado, my garden was infested with earwigs. I found that little cans (like tuna or cat food cans) filled with molasses were a great hit with them—they climbed in and died there!*

Pat S., Chino Valley, AZ

## THINK AHEAD FOR BEDTIME

What's our secret for getting roses through the winter with flying colors? Advance planning, that's what! First, we stop fertilizing in midsummer, although we keep watering all through the fall, because we don't want our roses to go to bed in bone-dry soil. Plus, we stop removing spent flowers in late summer or early fall, three to five weeks before the first frost. That tells the roses it's time to stop blooming and start getting ready for winter.

## PERFECT PRUNING, 1-2-3!

When you think about roses, what comes to mind? For most folks, it's the elegant, full-petaled flowers of classic hybrid tea roses. We've found that the secret to getting the very best blooms is keeping the plants properly pruned—and here's how:

**Step 1.** Prune off all but three to six of the youngest, healthiest canes. In the North, cut the remaining canes back to 12 to 14 inches; in the South, leave them 18 to 24 inches tall. (Floribunda and polyantha roses do better if you leave a few more stems, so we usually keep six to eight of the youngest canes.)

**Step 2.** If you see crossing or rubbing canes, prune out one of them. (Repeated rubbing can cause wounds, which are an open invitation for disease problems.)

**Step 3.** Cut off spindly or weak branches. Scrawny stems won't bloom well, so there's no point in keeping them!

### JERRY'S Q&A

Q I know I'm supposed to remove dead stems from my roses each spring. But since the plants aren't growing yet, how in the world can I tell what's dead and what isn't?

A You can tell the health of the stems (called canes) by their color: green and light brown or gray canes are alive, while black or dark brown canes are dead. If possible, prune dead and dying canes back to healthy wood (where the center of the cane is white); otherwise, cut them off right at ground level.

## TRY THESE UNDERCOVER PARTNERS

Roses may be the queens of the flower garden, but let's face it: The plants themselves aren't much to look at! Hybrid teas, floribundas, and grandifloras—three of the most commonly grown types of roses—are particularly prone to losing their lower leaves, leaving ugly thorny stems that detract from the beautiful blooms. But here at our test gardens, you won't see any "bare ankles" on *our* roses, because we cover 'em up with lower-growing flowers! Aromatic-leaved herbs, such as catmints (*Nepeta*) and lavenders, are especially nice. Besides adding beautiful, purple-blue flowers that look great with all colors of roses, their aromatic leaves seem to help keep pests at bay, too!

## GET THOSE SUCKERS

When extra-vigorous canes shoot up from grafted roses, take a close look at 'em—they're probably suckers. Root suckers usually have leaves and thorns that look different from the grafted part of the plant, along with slender, more arching canes. They'll also have different flowers. To keep these suckers from taking over, you need to get rid of them, *pronto!* Dig next to the plant to see where they're attached, then pull or snap them off by hand. If you can't find where the sucker is attached, cut it off as deeply as possible. And never cut off root suckers right at the soil line—this simply encourages 'em to grow right back!

### THANKS, BUD!

Normally, we want our roses to produce as many blooms as possible, and we're not too concerned about how big the individual flowers are. But if we want to produce a few truly showstopping rose blooms to amaze our visitors, we use this simple trick: Pinch off all but the topmost bud on each stem while the buds are still very small. That tells the stem to send all of its energy into the one bud that's left—and we end up with a truly awesome bloom as a result!

## PUT YOUR BUSHES TO BED

Keeping hybrid tea roses healthy and happy isn't just a spring-to-fall job—putting 'em to bed properly for winter is critical, too! Here at the test gardens, we first rake up all fallen leaves and petals from beneath the bushes to minimize lingering bugs or diseases. Then we hang a piece of no-pest stripping from the canes, and cover the plants with straw to insulate them. These simple but effective steps help our hybrid teas sail right through the worst winter cold with no problem at all!

### TRIED-AND-TRUE

Every year, my Grandma Putt had the most glorious roses you could ever imagine, and they just kept coming all summer long. What was her secret? Brewer's yeast! She'd dissolve 3 tablespoons of brewer's yeast in 2 gallons of water, and soak the roots of each bush after their first big flush of flowers. Try it yourself, and see if you're not as amazed by the results as all of Grandma's neighbors were!

# A SWEET TREAT

A beautiful bouquet of perfect rosebuds from your own garden is a real treat—but what can you do if those buds are slow to unfurl into beautiful blooms? Do what we do: Stir a spoonful of sugar into their water, and they'll be open before you know it!

## Basic Baking Soda Spray

No need to spend a bundle buying chemical sprays to treat rose pests and diseases. This simple spray does it all—*and* the ingredients are as close as your kitchen!

**1½ tbsp. of baking soda**
**1 tbsp. of dishwashing liquid**
**1 tbsp. of canola oil**
**1 cup plus 1 gal. of water**
**1 tbsp. of vinegar**

Mix the baking soda, dishwashing liquid, and oil with 1 cup of water. Then add the vinegar last because the mixture may bubble over. Pour the mix into a pump sprayer, and add the remaining water. Thoroughly spray your roses, covering the tops and bottoms of leaves.

# KEEP 'EM SNUG

Take it from those of us who have learned the hard way: Don't be in a hurry to uncover your hybrid tea roses in spring! Taking off the protective covering tells the plants it's time to grow again, so if you jump the gun, their new shoots might get nipped by late frosts. Here in Michigan, we generally wait until nighttime temperatures stop dipping much below 25°F, then pull back part of the covering on a few bushes every few days to see how they're coming along. Once we see the new buds popping, we know the roses are ready to grow, and that it's time to get the coverings off quick!

# DAIRY DOES IT

Nothing can ruin the look of ravishing roses faster than a fungal disease called powdery mildew. It looks just like it sounds: dusty, grayish white spots that start on the leaves and spread to the whole plant. But there's no need to resort to harsh chemicals if you spot this problem on your rosebushes; simply head for your refrigerator! Believe it or not, we've found that spraying a 50-50 mix of milk and water once a week does a bang-up job keeping this nasty disease at bay. You can't get much safer than that—and it really works!

## THEY THRILL IN THE CHILL

For many years, far-north gardeners got left out of the rose-growing game, because many of the classic hybrid teas simply can't take severe winter weather. Well, that's all changed! Even cold-climate gardeners can now enjoy lots of gorgeous blooms, thanks to busy Canadian plant breeders who have developed beautiful, super-hardy shrub roses. Look for Prairie Series roses, produced in Manitoba—'Prairie Dawn' is one of our favorites. Other super-tough shrub roses definitely worth trying include 'Champlain', 'Cuthbert Grant', 'Henry Hudson', 'John Cabot', 'Morden Fireglow', and 'William Baffin'.

## THROW YOUR SPRAYER AWAY!

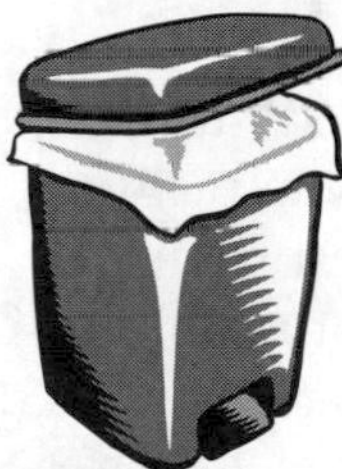

Think you can't grow great-looking roses without fussing with fungicides? Then give rugosa rose (*Rosa rugosa*) a try—this trouble-free shrub actually *hates* being sprayed! Give it full sun and well-drained soil, and it'll return the favor with an abundance of fragrant, white, pink, or purplish flowers from late spring into fall, followed by large, orange-red "hips" that last well into winter. Add in glossy, disease-resistant foliage, and it's easy to see why rugosa rose is one of our favorite shrub roses.

## SHRUB PRUNING MADE SIMPLE

Deciding when to prune once-blooming shrub roses is a no-brainer—simply trim them as soon as their flowers fade! In early to midsummer, cut out one or two of the oldest canes at ground level to make room for vigorous new growth. Then trim off the top third of each remaining cane. Finish up by snipping back the side shoots by up to two-thirds.

### Test Garden

Shrub roses are pretty pest-resistant, and we've found that they're seldom bothered by anything that our homemade pest-control tonics can't handle. But if we do need to apply insecticides, we typically use powdered materials rather than sprays, and we apply the dust early in the morning or late in the evening. At those times of day, the air is still, and the dew on the leaves helps the dust stick better, so we know the pest-control product stays right where it's needed.

## A TERRIFIC TIME-SAVER

With all the myths and misinformation about gardening, the issue of proper rose pruning has to be one of the most confusing. In the course of growing shrub roses for many years in our test gardens, we've found that some of the "rules" actually don't matter much! For example, the classic advice is to always cut just above a bud, and slope the cut at a 45° angle *away* from the bud. But guess what? We've found that simply whacking whole plants back by half with hedge trimmers does just as well! Admittedly, the plants don't look as nice at first, but once they leaf out, you'll hardly notice the difference!

### Baker's Best Rose Chow

Roses are the hardest-working flowering plants in your garden. These beauties bloom only for the sake of showing off as much as they can, for as long as they can. When you follow this simple feeding routine, your roses will have everything they need to keep those blooms comin' along!

**4 cups of bonemeal**
**1 cup of 5-10-5 garden fertilizer**
**1 cup of Epsom salts**

Mix these ingredients in a bucket, then give each bush 1 heaping tablespoon in mid- to late spring, or work in 4 pounds per 100 square feet of rose bed. (Store any leftovers in a tightly sealed container.) Follow up with our Rose Ambrosia (see page 177) to really energize this dry mix.

## DON'T LET 'EM GO THIRSTY

Shrub roses are pretty forgiving plants; but if you really want to get the best from them, be sure to provide 'em with a steady supply of moisture. Here at the test gardens, we try to make sure that our bushes get the equivalent of 1 inch of water every 7 to 10 days throughout the growing season. (If it only rains a ½ inch, for instance, then we'll water long enough to add another ½ inch.) And to make sure the water gets right to the roots (not on the leaves, where it can encourage diseases to develop), we use soaker hoses to slowly and steadily moisten the soil. The flowers we grow around our roses really seem to enjoy the extra water, as well!

## SHARE THE WEALTH

Have a treasured old rose plant you'd love to share with family and friends? Try taking cuttings! It's easier than you might think—especially with this trick one of our test-garden old-timers shared with us: Snip off 6- to 8-inch-long stem tips after the flowers have fallen in summer, and remove all of the leaves except for one or two at the top. Stick the cut end into a potato, then plant the cutting (potato and all) with half of its length below the ground. Water thoroughly, then invert a small jar over it. Remove the jar the following spring, and you'll have a new little rosebush, complete with roots!

## IT'S A WINNER!

If you'd like to try your hand at growing roses, but you don't want to spend your summer spraying, pinching, and pruning, we have the perfect selection for you: a bright-flowered beauty called 'Knock Out'. We're just crazy about this rose, with its beautiful, deep green leaves and dazzling, reddish pink flowers that appear from late spring all the way through frost. Best of all, it's practically immune to black spot and other fungi that can make rose growing a real hassle. Give this rose a try in your own garden, and see if you don't love it as much as we do!

### From Our Readers

*My husband and son-in-law are avid fishermen, so when they bring in a good catch, my daughter and I take all the fish 'innards' and bury them under and around our roses. Our neighbors are amazed at our beautiful blooms, all thanks to the fish!*

Wilma D., Middlesboro, KY

### Test Garden SECRET

One often-quoted piece of rose-pruning advice is to always cut above a bud that faces toward the *outside* of the bush. Well, that makes sense in most cases, because you want to allow for good air circulation through the middle of the plant. But we've found that if there's a big gap in the center of a shrub rose, cutting above a bud that faces *inward* (or in whichever direction we'd like to have a new stem form) works great, too!

## GROW OUT, NOT UP

When we talk about roses with our test-garden visitors, many are surprised to learn that climbing roses don't actually climb on their own—they need to be tied to a support to grow properly. But even more surprising to most folks is that climbers actually bloom better when they're tied to a *horizontal* support, such as a fence, rather than to a narrow, upright trellis. And the canes will produce the best blooms of all when they're trained in the shape of an arch (with the stem tips lower than the middle of the canes). It's really not hard to do, as long as you work with the canes while they're still young and flexible. Have an old climber that you'd like to retrain? Try cutting out a few of the oldest canes at ground level to get a fresh crop of new, easy-to-bend canes.

### TRIED-AND-TRUE

If one of your roses dies, it's mighty tempting to rush right out and buy another one to fill the very same spot. DON'T DO IT! My Grandma Putt always used to say it's a bad idea to plant a new rose in a dead rose's grave, and I've seen for myself that it's true—probably because the diseases, insects, or other problems in that location attack the new plant just like they did the old one. So go out and buy a new plant to replace the one you lost, but find a new place to plant it!

## TWO FOR THE SHOW

Want to have your climbing roses do double-duty? Pair 'em with clematis vines to get twice the bloom in the same amount of space! The rose makes a perfect living trellis that's easy for the clematis to climb, while the clematis flowers will add loads of sparkling summer color. Pair a clematis and rose that bloom at the same time for one spectacular show, or choose kinds that flower at different times to extend the display. In our experience, smaller hybrid clematis (those that mature at 8 to 10 feet tall) are the best partners for climbers. This double-up trick works great with shrub roses, too—and the bigger the rosebush, the bigger the clematis it can support!

## BIG OR SMALL? IT'S YOUR CALL!

Sometimes, it's embarrassing to admit to all the rose-growing mistakes we've made over the years, but we figure that if it helps even one gardener avoid the same mistake, it's worth it! So here's another piece of advice we learned the hard way: Remember to read the fine print on the label *before* you buy any climbing rose, and make sure it won't outgrow the room you have for it. A climbing rose that's too big for its space will need frequent, heavy pruning to keep it in check, and trust us—trying to deal with those long, floppy canes can be like trying to wrestle an octopus (and this octopus has thorns)!

### Rose Ambrosia

Dry fertilizers, like our Baker's Best Rose Chow (see page 174), are great for long-term rose feeding. But if you really want to get all your roses off to a rousing start *and* keep 'em full of flowers through the summer, follow up with this power-packed liquid formula.

**1 cup of beer**
**2 tsp. of instant tea granules**
**1 tsp. of 5-10-5 fertilizer**
**1 tsp. of fish emulsion**
**1 tsp. of hydrogen peroxide**
**1 tsp. of dishwashing liquid**
**2 gal. of warm water**

Mix these ingredients in a bucket or watering can, then water each plant with 1 pint of the solution in the morning once every three weeks; store the liquid in a tightly capped jug or bottle between uses. It'll keep those beautiful blooms comin'—*guaranteed!*

## ROOM TO BREATHE

Flower-filled climbing roses look fantastic growing against a home, but they can do more harm than good if you don't take a few precautions at planting time! Training the canes right against a wall makes it difficult to maintain the siding. On wood siding in particular, the dense leaves hold in moisture and can lead to discoloration or rotting. The poor air circulation is really bad for the rose, too! We've found that it's much better to train climbing roses to a trellis that's held about 6 inches away from the wall. Besides keeping the siding clean and dry, this allows air to flow behind the canes—and that'll go a long way toward stopping rose-ruining diseases in their tracks!

## A SIMPLE SOLUTION

Over the years, we've discovered that climbing roses growing on freestanding trellises, fences, or arbors seem to have many fewer disease problems than their shrubby cousins. Why? We think it's because breezes can circulate freely around the leaves and canes, quickly drying any moisture and discouraging disease development. But if you do find that powdery mildew is turning the leaves of your climbers from rich green to dusty gray, we have the answer: Simply mix 1/4 cup of baking soda and 1 tablespoon of vegetable oil in 2 quarts of water. Spray your roses early in the morning at the first sign of trouble, and every two weeks from then on to keep the disease from spreading.

### Rose Clean-Up Tonic

Fall is the best time to set back the insects and diseases that plague roses. So, after your plants have shed their leaves, but before you mulch them, treat them with this cleansing tonic.

**1 cup of baby shampoo**
**1 cup of antiseptic mouthwash**
**1 cup of tobacco tea***

Mix these ingredients in a 20 gallon hose-end sprayer, and spray your plants well from top to bottom. That'll get your bushes squeaky clean for the winter and let them get off to a healthy start next spring.

*To make tobacco tea, place half a handful of chewing tobacco in the toe of an old nylon stocking, and soak it in a gallon of hot water until the mixture is dark brown. Store leftover liquid in a tightly capped jug or bottle for later use.

## MUST-HAVE MUSKS

For most roses, the rule is: Give 'em sun, and lots of it! But what if you have a site that only gets a half-day of sun? There are several incredible climbers for you, too! Most "hybrid musk" roses make great small-scale climbers (to about 8 feet), and they're often quite fragrant, to boot. Some of our favorites include 'Buff Beauty', 'Cornelia', and 'Kathleen'. In our test gardens, we've found that these sturdy beauties can flower respectably with as few as 4 hours of sun a day!

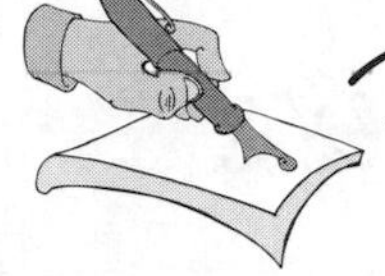

# From Our Readers

## ROSES ALIVE!

I have two secrets for keeping rosebushes alive over the winter. First, mound lots of oak bark shavings around the cut-back branches. Second, during the first week of October, sprinkle ½ cup of a sulphur-potassium-magnesium product around the base of each shrub and gently work it into the soil.

***John K., Sullivan, WI***

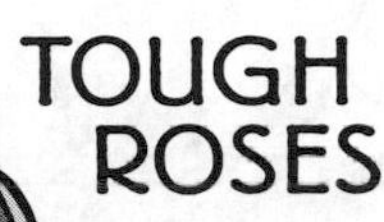

## TOUGH ROSES

Roses must be "toughened" to make it through the winter. Here's my list of do's and don'ts: Don't over-water during the summer. Never fertilize after August. Don't prune in the fall or cut after September—you don't want to encourage weak, late growth. Don't cover your roses: I don't, even here in Michigan; just dump a quart of soil on the center of the plant in late fall and that will be enough protection.

***Kathy W., St. Johns, MI***

## MORE APHID CONTROL

Here's how I protect my roses from aphids—I plant marigolds in between the rosebushes. This simple secret really does the job.

***Barbara T., Carthage, MO***

## A SCENT-SIBLE DECISION

My father gave me this hint: If you have rosebushes that flower but have no scent, go to the hardware store and buy powdered glue. Dig a hole to the root of the bush, and put in one teaspoon of powdered glue. Your roses will have a nice scent. Try it—it really does the trick!

***A. K., Nashua, NH***

## ADIOS, APHIDS

To eliminate aphids from roses, I hang banana peels over the rose canes. It works like a charm.

***W. R., Colorado Springs, CO***

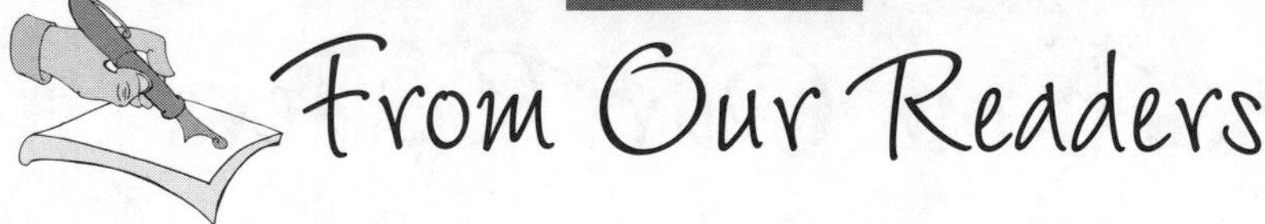


## LONGER LIFE

Cut roses will last longer if you remove the leaves and thorns that will be underwater in the vase. Try it!

***Mary S., Bangor, ME***

## ROSY BEDS

When trimming your rosebushes, save the trimmings and place them around your garden. Cover them with a little soil or bark dust. The prickly terrain is a great way to discourage cats from hanging around and digging in your garden beds. Plus, you get to recycle your trimmings!

***Cathy B., Tualatin, OR***

## SUPER CEDAR

Here's something that works for me: Put cedar mulch around your roses and flowers to help keep bugs away.

***T. W., Florence, NJ***

## SAWDUST SUCKER

When I go to uncover my roses in the spring, it's really hard to get all the sawdust up. So, I use a wet/dry vacuum to suck up the sawdust. When it becomes full, I dump the sawdust into a bag and save it for the next year. You can put a little screen over the end of the hose so you don't suck up a lot of dirt and mulch.

***Debbie Z., Clintonville, WI***

## PEP 'EM UP!

If your cut roses start to droop, use this trick to revive them: Soak the stems in hot water for a few minutes. It works every time!

***Rachel G., Syracuse, NY***

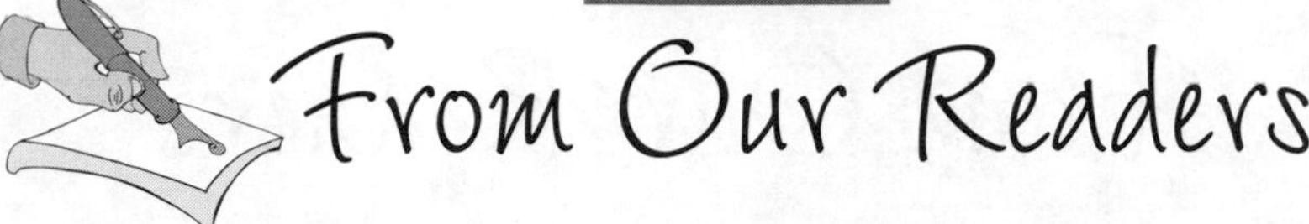


## SPRAY SAVER

I soak used dryer-sheet squares with dishwashing liquid, and tie them to all the tomato cages and posts around my rose garden. Later, when I spray the garden with one of your liquid formulas, these sheets soak it up, which extends their effectiveness.

***Mike M., Greenville, SC***

## GARLIC TO THE RESCUE

Here is a neat trick. If you put one or two garlic cloves in your rosebushes, they will never be bothered by aphids or any other insects. It works for me!

***Carmen G., Silver City, NM***

## CORNMEAL CURE

I have the best tip for getting rid of black spot on roses—use cornmeal "tea." Just soak a cup of cornmeal in a gallon of water for about an hour. Drain the liquid, and then go nuts spraying it all over your roses. I've never found a better way to beat black spot!

***Renee F., Sioux Falls, SD***

## BANANA BONANZA

I've always loved Jerry's tip to bury banana peels in your rose beds. But my family doesn't always love eating bananas—especially, it seems, just when my roses could use the boost. So, when we do eat bananas, I put all the leftover peels in a zip-top plastic freezer bag and toss it in the freezer. I also ask my friends to freeze their banana peels for me. When my roses need a snack, I thaw out the peels and dig them in. Easy!

***Doris F., Eugene, OR***

## FUNGUS AMONGUS

Here's a tip for rose gardeners who are dealing with fungus problems. When you're cleaning up all of the debris and leaves from your sick roses, don't forget about the mulch! It took me a couple of years to open my eyes to the fact that the mulch was part of the problem, spreading the fungus around. So don't forget to rake up all of the surrounding mulch, and start fresh every year.

***Paula A., South Orange, NJ***

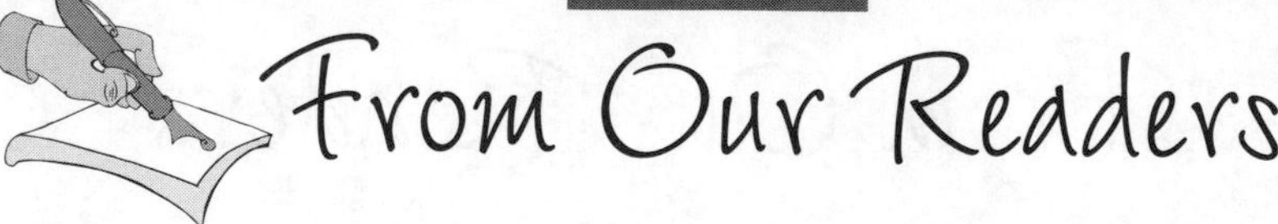

MORE TIPS

# From Our Readers

## ALL POTTED UP

To grow roses that will survive winter for sure, plant them in containers, and bury the entire container—pot and all—right in the garden. When cold weather moves in, pull up each container, and move the whole thing indoors, where it'll be safe and warm.

***Matt D., Akron, OH***

## ROSE REVIVAL

Cut roses are about as pretty as they come, but mine never seem to last too long. So I asked around and got some great advice. First, always cut the stems underwater before putting them in your vase. And recut the stem every single day. I do this when I change the water. And the best trick of all is that if your roses start looking droopy really soon after cutting, just cut them again and dunk them in some warm water—the blooms, stems, everything. Shake them around a little in the water, and some air bubbles will come up. After that, your roses should perk right up.

***Marian L., Gary, IN***

## OVERFED ROSES

Not long ago I tried growing a rosebush for the first time. Like a fool, I put down a lot of fertilizer, thinking the roses would shoot right up. Boy, was I wrong! And it cost me my roses. The local nursery workers told me I had overdone it with fertilizer that was just too strong for my roses. So I'm passing along the lesson I've learned—now I never give new rosebushes any fertilizer, except for bonemeal, and I haven't had any problems since.

***Monica G., Schenectady, NY***

## QUICK SOIL DRAINAGE TEST

Before planting roses, you should always check the soil drainage. To do this, I go out on a dry, mild day, dig a hole to the same depth my roses will be planted at, and pour in enough water to fill the hole. Then I wait to see how long it takes for the water to soak through. A couple of hours is okay. If it takes a day or two, though, then I know that my roses will die right off in that soil, and I pick another planting spot.

***Amanda M., Aurora, IL***

# Part Three

# Just Veggin'

Lawns are lovely to look at, and flowers feed the soul—but when suppertime comes, it's the vegetable garden that takes center stage! Maybe you enjoy the peace of mind you get from feeding your family healthy, home-grown food, or perhaps you simply prefer the fantastic flavor of fresh-from-the-garden produce that no shrink-wrapped, store-bought veggie can ever match. Whatever your reasons, the secret to successful vegetable gardening is the same: knowing what works and what doesn't, so you can depend on a steady supply of tasty leaves, roots, seeds, and fruits all through the growing season. In these chapters, you'll learn more than simply *what* to do and *when* to do it; you'll discover time-tested tips and exciting new techniques for getting the most out of your garden every minute of garden time, every month of the year. So what are you waiting for? 'Tis the season to get your veggie garden growin'!

# Chapter 9

# Vegetable Gardening from the Ground Up

From cool, crisp lettuce straight from the garden to juicy, sun-ripened tomatoes fresh off the vine, home-grown edibles offer colors and flavors that tired, old grocery-store veggies simply can't compete with. Whether you have a tiny deck with a few planters, or a backyard garden big enough to feed the neighborhood, the basics are the same: Build up your soil, plant at the right time, and provide plenty of food and water to keep the harvest comin'. And take advantage of our many years of test-garden experience to get the healthiest plants, highest yields, and best-tasting veggies ever!

## RAISING THE ROOTS

When most folks think of a vegetable garden, they think of a big patch of ground that's all tilled up, with the crops arranged in long rows. Well, that's how we *used* to arrange our test gardens, too, until we found a better way: building raised beds! Creating these permanent planting areas—beds framed with stone or timbers and filled with several inches of good topsoil—has completely changed our veggie growing habits, and we know you'll love 'em too. Here's why:

**Terrific time-savers.** Forget about digging up all the ground every year! Build the beds once, and the soil in them will stay loose and fluffy year after year. We don't even need a trowel to plant in our raised beds; we can just scoop aside the crumbly soil with our fingers!

**Say "so long" to mud.** Since the beds are permanent, the paths around them are, too—and that makes it easy to cover them with straw, wood chips, or some other material to keep your feet out of the mud.

**Veggies just love 'em!** Besides allowing excellent drainage even where the soil is normally heavy clay, raised beds give your crops extra room for good root growth. And of course, the bigger the root system, the healthier the plant—and the more abundant the harvest!

**Planning made perfect.** No more guessing where you grew your tomatoes or your beans last year. With permanent beds, it's easy to remember exactly which crops you grew where the previous year, so you don't grow the same veggies in the same spot season after season (and that's the best way we know to avoid soil-borne diseases!).

MIX IT UP!

### Spring Soil Energizer

After you dig, but before you plant your vegetable garden, fortify the soil with this potent potion. Take my word for it—it'll really get things cookin'!

**1 can of beer**
**1/2 cup of regular cola (not diet)**
**1/2 cup of dishwashing liquid**
**1/2 cup of antiseptic mouthwash**
**1/4 tsp. of instant tea granules**

Mix these ingredients in a 20 gallon hose-end sprayer, and saturate the soil. Wait two weeks before you start planting. (This recipe makes enough to cover 100 square feet of garden area.)

### Tried-and-True

**W**hether you garden in raised beds or in classic in-ground rows, take some advice from Grandma Putt: Pay close attention to how high your crops will eventually get before you decide where to plant them. If she was growing a tall crop like corn or staked tomatoes, for instance, she'd try to keep them on the very northern edge of the vegetable garden so that they wouldn't shade out lower-growing, sun-loving crops, like bush beans. Or, she'd take advantage of the shade for heat-sensitive crops, like lettuce and peas, by keeping them to the north or east side of taller companions.

## THE STRAIGHT AND NARROW

Raised-bed gardening isn't just for large yards; it'll work just as well in smaller areas, too! Here at the test gardens, most of our raised beds are 6 to 8 feet long; but yours can be any length you want. Just be sure to keep them narrow enough that you can reach into the center comfortably without stepping on the planting area (that means 3 to 4 feet for most folks). Why? Because stepping on cultivated soil packs it down—and that defeats the whole purpose of creating raised beds in the first place!

## VEGGIES ON THE MOVE

You rotate the tires on your car, so why not rotate the veggies in your garden? Moving your crops to different spots each growing season ensures that soil-borne pests and diseases don't build up to damaging levels, and it also helps ensure that vital soil nutrients don't get depleted. Here at the test gardens, we use a three-year rotation plan, and it's been giving us fantastic results. Here's our simple system:

**Year One.** Add fresh barnyard manure in fall, or compost in spring, and dig it into the soil. Then plant "heavy feeders" (crops that need lots of nutrients), such as cabbage, peppers, or squash.

**Year Two.** Plant the bed with "moderate feeders," such as tomatoes or beans.

**Year Three.** Follow up with "light feeders," like garlic, onions, or radishes.

We've divided our test-garden beds into three groups (corresponding to the three years), so we have places for each kind of crop each growing season. That means we only need to add manure or compost to one third of all the beds each year—a big time- and money-saver, too!

## STAY AWAY FROM TREES, PLEASE!

When you're selecting a site for a new veggie garden, keep this in mind: Trees and vegetable gardens definitely don't make good partners. Why? Well, for one, lots of sun is a *must* for healthy vegetable growth and top yields. Six hours a day is really the minimum, unless you're going to stick with leafy crops like lettuce and spinach; even then, they still need as much light as they can get. But beyond the shade they cast, some trees can actually be lethal to some vegetables. Both black walnut and English walnut trees produce a chemical called juglone that's toxic to many plants, including potatoes and tomatoes. Believe us, we learned this the hard way—so you can bet that we keep our test-garden veggie beds far away from these big, bad trees!

## CUTWORM CURE

Starting a new vegetable garden in an area that used to be lawn? Then you need to know that planning is key! You see, adult cutworm moths lay their eggs around the bases of weeds and grasses, so you can expect serious cutworm problems when growing edibles in new beds that were previously grassy areas. (Cutworms, in case you don't know, are soil-dwelling caterpillars that like to chomp on the tender stems of veggie seedlings and transplants.) So to minimize the risk, do what we do: Prepare the bed in fall or in early spring. That'll move the cutworms up close to the soil surface, where birds can spot them, zero in, and have the pesky pests for lunch before they can munch on your crops.

**Q** Digging up the soil in my vegetable garden each spring sure is a lot of work, so I'm thinking of buying a rototiller. But I've heard that repeated tilling can cause major soil problems—is this true?

**A** Sure enough, tilling at the same depth year after year can produce a "hardpan": a dense, tightly packed layer of earth right under the fluffy, tilled soil, which interferes with drainage and root growth. To prevent this, go ahead and till one year, but then hand-dig the next. Or better yet, make your life easy and build permanent planting beds!

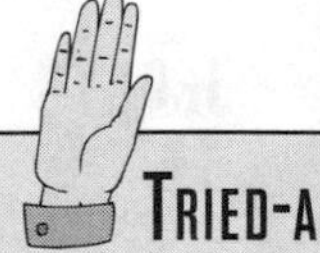

### Tried-and-True

**W**hen it came to planting her vegetable garden, Grandma Putt did more than watch the weather; she'd check the almanac for the moon phases, too! According to old-time gardening wisdom, the best time to plant leafy and fruiting crops (like lettuce, peas, and tomatoes) is when the moon is increasing (waxing); the days of a decreasing (waning) moon are best for bulbs and root crops (such as onions and potatoes). Why not give this trick a try and see if it doesn't work as well for you as it did for Grandma Putt?

## SINK OR SWIM

Before you count on last year's saved seeds for this year's harvest, do what we do: Let 'em go for a swim! We've found that if you pour the seeds into a glass of water, the ones that sink have a good chance of growing up big and strong. Those that float to the top are losers, so toss them on your compost pile. Then sow the good seeds right away, because they'll have soaked up some water and be well on their way to sprouting.

### SOS—SAVE OUR SEEDS!

If you find yourself with leftover veggie seeds after the spring planting season, don't throw them out! We've found that most store just fine for at least a year if you seal them in their original packets, put them in small, airtight jars, and tuck them in the refrigerator. Be sure the temperature stays between 36° and 45°F, and there's a good chance you can get another year's worth of crops out of a single packet of seed!

## TESTING, TESTING

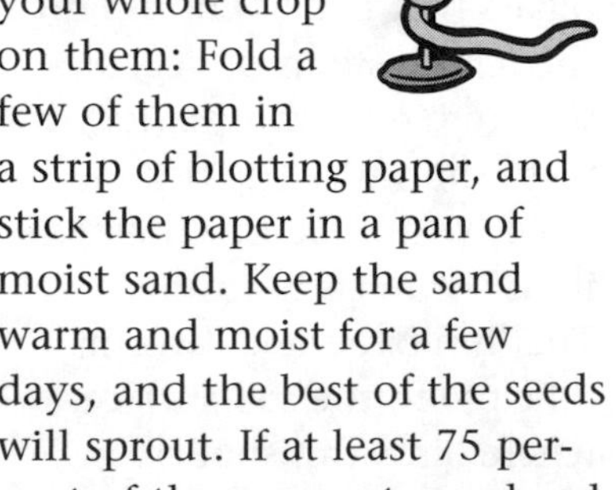

Here's another option for testing saved seeds before you stake your whole crop on them: Fold a few of them in a strip of blotting paper, and stick the paper in a pan of moist sand. Keep the sand warm and moist for a few days, and the best of the seeds will sprout. If at least 75 percent of them sprout, go ahead and plant the rest of the pack as you normally would; otherwise, we suggest buying a new packet.

## SUPER SEEDLING HOLDERS

If there's one thing you can say about our test-garden crew, it's that we're all pretty frugal. We don't see any need to waste money on fancy gardening gadgets when we can use everyday household items instead! So when we're ready to start our veggie transplants indoors, you won't find us buying fancy seed-starting pots; instead, we raid our kitchen scrap pails. Here are two of our favorite recycling tricks:

**Seeds with a-peel.** Instead of tossing citrus peels into the compost pile, clean out each half-rind, and poke a few holes in the bottom to provide drainage. Fill with your favorite seed-starting medium, then plant your seeds in them. Once the plants are up and growing, simply plant them out in your garden, rinds and all!

**An egg-cellent idea.** When you break an egg, carefully remove only the top third or so, then poke a hole in the bottom of the shell. Rinse it out and set it back into an empty egg carton to dry. Come planting time, fill the shells with seed-starting medium, and plant your seeds. At transplanting time, gently crack the shell so the roots can get out easily, then plant the whole shebang in your garden.

## GIVE 'EM THE OLD BRUSH-OFF

Ever wish your indoor-grown veggie transplants could look as full and stocky as those sold at your local garden center? Then use this trick we picked up from some professional greenhouse growers: Simply brush your hand across their tops several times a day, or else set a small fan to blow across them. Besides simulating wind to promote stronger stems, the improved air circulation from the fan will make damping-off and other dastardly seedling diseases a thing of the past!

*Recycled cardboard tubes from toilet paper and paper towels make great seed starters. Just cut them to size and fill them with soil—they hold together well and retain moisture. Best of all, I've found that this method reduces transplant shock because you can plant the tubed seedlings right in your garden without disturbing their roots.*

Robert F.,
Hopkinton, MA

Here at the test gardens, we start hundreds of veggie transplants each spring. So, when it comes time to harden them off, you can imagine that we're kept busy setting them outdoors every morning and bringing them back in at night. Luckily, we've found a way to make the job easier, with a bunch of old kids' wagons! Each wagon can hold several trays of seedlings, and it's a snap to roll them whenever it's movin' time. Give this trick a try—we think you'll love it!

## RUN FOR COVER

When it's time to set your vegetable transplants outdoors, you need to be an eagle-eyed weather watcher. But don't assume that just because the thermometer says the temperature's above freezing, your carefully nurtured veggies will be safe from mean ol' Jack Frost. We made that mistake one year—figuring that since our thermometer read 45°F, our seedlings were plenty safe. Well, when we found all of our baby plants frosted the next morning, we learned our lesson! We did a little research and found out that a thermometer set 5 feet above the ground can read as much as 15° higher than at ground level! So take our advice, and be prepared to cover tender transplants until nighttime temperatures are well settled into the upper 40s. Sure, it's a little extra work—but trust us, it's far better to be safe than to risk losing your entire crop!

*I find 1-gallon plastic vinegar jugs to be perfect for covering transplants. These jugs are a lot sturdier than milk jugs, and they last several years. I cut the base off just above the bottom ridge, then string the empty jug tops on a cord until I need them. After I transplant broccoli, cauliflower, cabbage, and other seedlings, I place the jug tops over the plants, pushing them into the soil a little way so the wind won't blow them off. After the plants have settled in and are growing strong, I take the jug tops off of the plants, replace them on the cord, and hang them on a large nail in my garden house to use again the following year.*

Edith L., Carpenter, WY

## GROUNDS FOR SUCCESS

Small veggie and herb seeds can be a real challenge to sow evenly, especially when you're trying to plant them directly in the garden. To keep them from clumping up, try this garden-tested secret: Mix 'em with dried coffee grounds before you sow them. They'll be as easy to handle as the biggest of the big guys!

## BAG IT!

Don't spend a bundle buying frost protectors for your tomatoes, eggplants, and other tender veggie seedlings! It's easy to create on-the-spot plant protectors with paper grocery bags. Dig a large planting hole, then set the bag inside so that 10 inches or so sticks up above the surface. Fill the bottom of the bag with soil, roll the sides down, and plant your seedling inside. If frost threatens, roll up the sides and fasten them with a clothespin or two to keep your seedling safe and warm. Once the weather has settled, we usually tear off the aboveground part of the bag; the part buried in the soil will simply rot away.

## GIVE 'EM AN EDGE

Tired of spring rains washing away your newly planted veggie seeds? Then try this great trick: Snip some old mini-blind slats into 6-inch pieces, then slip them into the soil between rows of just-sown seeds to make little edgings. That'll keep the rain from washing the seeds from one part of the bed to another, so they grow right where you sowed 'em!

## EASY AS PIE (PANS)

Here at the test gardens, we're always searching for new and better ways to keep track of which crops we've planted and where. The old-fashioned trick of slipping the seed packet over a stick at the end of the row works okay for a few weeks, but with the combination of sun, rain, and wind, they usually fade or blow away after that. We've tried a lot of other labeling options, but the one that works best is also one of the simplest: We cut strips from the base of aluminum pie pans, then use an old ball-point pen to "engrave" the name of the crop into the metal and thumbtack each one to a stick to mark the rows. These tags last practically forever—and best of all, they're free!

### TRIED-AND-TRUE

Just before you set out your vegetable transplants, give Grandma Putt's secret seedling shaper-upper a try: Water them with a solution of half a tablespoon of salt or baking soda per gallon of water. This will temporarily stop growth and increase their strength, so they can stand right up to the changing conditions that they'll face outdoors.

## PROVIDE A BALANCED DIET

Keeping your veggie crops well fed is the key to keeping them healthy, productive, and high-yielding. It's important to remember, though, that not all fertilizers are created equal! Those that contain lots of nitrogen—such as bloodmeal, or commercial fertilizers with a high "N" number, like 10-5-5—are great for leafy crops, like lettuce and spinach. But for other veggies, it's best to go easy on the Big N. If they get too much, they'll lose interest in setting fruit (like squash or melons) or producing big, plump, tasty roots and tubers (like carrots, turnips, and potatoes). For these crops, you'll get a far better harvest by using a balanced organic material. We like composted manure, but a 5-10-5 commercial fertilizer will do the trick, too!

### Compost Booster

Whether you use it as a mulch for your veggies or dig it into the soil, you can never have too much compost! To keep your pile cookin', and the compost comin', try the following formula.

**1 can of beer**
**1 can of regular cola (not diet)**
**1 cup of ammonia**
**½ cup of weak tea water***
**2 tbsp. of baby shampoo**

Mix these ingredients in your 20 gallon hose-end sprayer, and saturate your compost pile every time you add a layer of new ingredients to it. This'll really get things goin'!

*To make weak tea water, soak a used tea bag in a solution of 1 gallon of warm water and 1 teaspoon of dishwashing liquid until the mix is light brown. Store leftover liquid in a tightly capped jug or bottle for later use.

## QUICK KITCHEN COMPOST

No time to tend to a full-scale compost pile? Try this great garden-tested trick: Save your table scraps—peels, shredded vegetables, eggshells, and the like (just no meat or fat). Every few days, place the scraps in a food processor or blender and cover them with water. Add a tablespoon of Epsom salts to the mix, and liquefy. Pour this compost cocktail onto the soil in your garden, lightly hoe it in, and all your plants will jump for joy!

## MANURE MAGIC

As far as we're concerned, there's nothing like good, old barnyard manure to keep veggie garden soil in top-notch shape. But fresh manure can burn tender roots—*and* it's usually loaded with weed seeds, too—so we never use it directly on our crops; instead, we compost it first. Here's how we make our super soil booster weed-free, and—believe it or not—almost odor-free!

**Step 1.** Spread a big tarpaulin on the ground in a location downwind from your house, and dump the manure on top. Fold up the edges of the tarp around the pile of manure.

**Step 2.** Lay another tarp across the top, and add a few rocks so that it stays put. Cut three or four slits in that tarp so the heat can get out.

**Step 3.** Let it sit for six months or so, and—presto!—you've got the best food a garden could ask for. Work it into the soil in spring before planting (we spread a 1- to 2-inch-thick layer on the beds, then dig or till it in), or else use it as a mulch around already-planted veggies. You'll be amazed at the results!

## FORK IT OVER

Keeping vegetable plantings free of weeds is about more than just good looks—it's about protecting them from aggressive plants that steal the nutrients, water, and sunlight that your crops need to thrive. And that goes double for veggie seedlings and newly set-out transplants, because their small size puts them at a big disadvantage against speedier-sprouting weeds. Here at the test gardens, we've found a perfect tool for cultivating around our baby veggies: an old table fork! It's lightweight and easy to hold, and the sharp tines make it a snap to scratch up the soil while leaving our young vegetables standing tall and proud.

### Test Garden SECRET

Don't live near a ready supply of barnyard manure? You can still make a great veggie-garden soil improver right at home—known as leaf mold—with something most folks have an abundance of: fall leaves! We've tried a variety of ways for making this super stuff, and here's what we've found works best: Shred the leaves with a lawn mower (small pieces decompose faster), spray them with a hose to dampen them, and scoop them into garbage bags. Close the bags, poke a few holes in the side with a pitchfork, then set them in an out-of-the-way place and go about your business. Come spring, you'll have a great supply of super-chow to feed your crops!

## A TASTY TREAT

Are your veggies lookin' a little frazzled by midsummer? Foliar feeding—spraying a liquid fertilizer or tonic right on their leaves—gives them a quick snack they can sink their leaves into right away. Simply fill a 20 gallon hose-end sprayer with your favorite liquid formula—we usually use our All-Season Green-Up Tonic (see page 69), but compost tea or diluted fish emulsion can work great, too—and spray away!

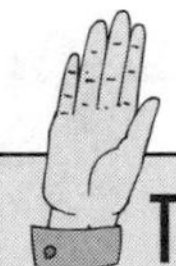

### Tried-and-True

The only problem with using a hoe, garden fork, or other cultivator to scratch up the weeds is that stirring the soil simply brings more weed seeds to the surface. And since many of these seeds need just a short exposure to light to trigger sprouting, weeding this way can be a never-ending job. So if you want to try stopping the sprouts before they start, try this trick that old-time veggie gardeners swear by: Do your work in the dark! You'll obviously need *some* light—you don't want to hoe up your veggies along with the weeds—so bring a large flashlight or a lantern with you, but keep it as far away as you can to avoid waking up those wicked weed seeds!

## HEAT BEATS WEEDS

If you can't weed at night (see "Tried-and-True," at left), we've found that a hot, windy day is the very best time for weeding. Why? Because weeds don't care for that kind of weather any more than most folks do. So when you hoe 'em out, they'll dry out and go belly-up in a big hurry!

## PLEASE DELAY—DON'T PLANT TODAY!

Here's a sneaky way to get a jump start on veggie-garden weeds: Trick 'em into sprouting before you plant your crops! When you've prepared your garden plot in spring, don't be in a hurry to sow seeds right away; instead, water the area thoroughly, or else sit back and wait for some rain. Within a few days, your garden beds will be chock-full of baby weeds, and you can pull 'em right up. Trust us: This advance attack will save you a whole lot of weeding time in the long run!

### Test Garden

Not sure how to tell the weed seedlings from your veggies? Try one of our favorite tricks: Plant radishes around each bed or row. These speedy sprouters will be up and growing in no time, and they'll show you exactly where your other veggie seedlings should come up. Anything else that raises its head outside the border is a candidate for elimination by the Weed Patrol!

## HALT! WHO GOES THERE?

The secret to being an effective weed warrior is to know your enemy! Annual garden weeds, like purslane and chickweed, are pretty easy to control if you keep after them. The important thing here is to get them out *before* they have a chance to flower and produce more seeds. Perennial weeds, like dock and dandelion, are pretty easy to get out when they're little. As they grow, they produce a deep taproot that they use to store food; if you pull off the tops of the plants, the roots will usually resprout. Their stash of stored energy is at its lowest just before the plants flower, though. So, if you've got a crop of strong-rooted villains, lay down the law when they're just about to burst into bloom, and chances are, they won't come back!

### Wonderful Weed Killer

Veggie garden paths are a perfect place for weeds to get started, and from there, they can quickly spread into the loose, rich soil of your growing beds. So keep those paths free of weeds with this elixir, and you'll help keep your weeding chores to a bare minimum!

**1 gal. of white vinegar**
**1 cup of table salt**
**1 tbsp. of dishwashing liquid**

Mix these ingredients in a bucket until the salt has dissolved. Pour it along cracks to kill weeds between bricks or stones in your garden walkways. Caution: Don't spray it on your crops or other plants that you want to keep, and don't pour it on soil that you plan to garden in anytime in the near future!

## EVERYTHING'S COMIN' UP CLOVER

What could be better than a trick that not only solves a common garden problem, but provides a bunch of extra benefits as well? We've found that planting white clover in the pathways between our vegetable garden beds has worked like a charm: Not only do the paths stay mud-free, but the clover grows so thickly that weeds don't stand a chance! Plus, the flowers attract a bunch of beneficial insects, which stick around to help keep veggie pests under control. Best of all, we don't need to mow the clover often, but when we do, we've found that the clippings make a fantastic, nutrient-rich mulch that our crops just love!

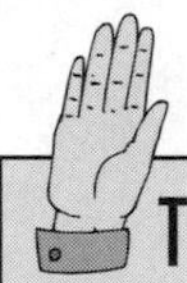

### Tried-and-True

Grandma Putt had to rely on well water to keep her gardens growing when rain was lacking, so she was always careful to make the most of every drop. For the first week or two after planting, she made sure to keep the soil evenly moist so the young plants got off to a good start; after that, she watered only during the most critical growth stages. For leafy crops, like lettuce, that meant the week or two before they were ready to pick. For fruiting crops, such as beans, squash, and tomatoes, it was during the flowering period. And for root crops, such as onions and potatoes, it was the time when the roots started to swell. With these handy rules of thumb, Grandma was able to have a healthy, high-yielding garden every year!

## HEAD 'EM OFF AT THE PASS

Okay, we've just given you some of our favorite, garden-tested weeding tips, but now it's time to reveal our very best tip of all: The easiest way to keep all of your garden weeding chores to a minimum is to stop the weeds from getting started in the first place! And you know how we do that? We mulch! We've found that covering the soil with just an inch or two of organic mulch (chopped leaves, straw, and grass clippings are our favorites) has cut our veggie garden weeding chores by over 90 percent! And that's not even considering all the other great benefits that these mulches provide. They prevent soil moisture from evaporating, which minimizes watering, and they build up the soil's organic-matter levels as they decompose, which improves fertility. Plus, they prevent soil from splashing on crop plants, which minimizes the development of some diseases, and makes for a cleaner harvest, too!

We simply can't say enough good things about mulch, so we'll simply tell you: Try it, you'll like it! And here are two more tips we've learned: Be sure to weed thoroughly *before* you mulch, because it may not smother existing weeds. And remember to check the mulch depth a few times during the growing season, and add more to keep it between 1 and 2 inches deep. You'll be amazed at the results!

## THE TOUCH TEST

To encourage deep rooting—and cut down on your watering time—the trick is to water your veggies thoroughly, and then not water them again for a week or so. To make sure you've really delivered the goods when you water your garden, stick a finger down into the soil after you think you've watered enough. If it's wet several inches down, it's time to quit; if not, water for a few more minutes, then check again until the soil is evenly moist.

## From Our Readers

*When you're dragging a hose through your garden to water your crops, it's hard to keep from knocking over the plants on the ends and corners of the beds or rows. I keep the hose under control with an 18-inch metal pipe (or heavy stake) driven 12 inches into the ground at each corner of the bed. Then I take some old tennis balls, cut a hole in each one, and stick one on top of each pipe. Besides making the pipes more visible, so you don't trip over them, the tennis balls prevent the hose from rolling up over the pipes as you pull it through the garden.*

Gerald M., Mascoutah, IL

## BABY YOUR VEGGIES WITH A BOTTLE

Big, bushy plants, like tomatoes, peppers, cucumbers, squash, and melons, really appreciate a steady supply of water—but who wants to spend all summer doing nothing but watering their veggies? We use a quick recycling trick that saves us loads of time, and keeps our plants happy, too! During the year, we save our plastic soda bottles and caps (the 2-liter sizes work best) and cut off the bottoms, saving the hard plastic bases. We use a nail to poke a hole in the screw-on bottle caps, and then put them back on the bottles. After we plant our crops, we dig a hole next to each transplant, place an upside-down bottle in it (so the lower half to two-thirds is buried), and push the soil back to secure the bottle in place. After filling the bottles with water or a liquid feeding tonic, we use the cut-off bases to act as lids. The water drips slowly through the perforated bottle caps, eliminating the need for us to go out there with the garden hose. Now we have no more thirsty veggies, and lots of free time for us!

## Test Garden SECRET

You've probably heard about gardening in raised beds—but what about sunken beds? Sounds crazy, maybe, but we've found that they're a smart solution where water is scarce. For best results, start in a low-lying area of your yard, then loosen the soil with a rotary tiller or turn it over by hand. (While you're at it, dig in plenty of compost or peat moss; that'll help the soil hold onto whatever moisture it does get.) Use some of the loosened soil to build up a low ridge around the edge, so the surface of the bed is an inch or so below the surrounding soil level, then plant your crops as usual. *Voilà*—you've got yourself a sunken bed that'll catch and keep plenty of rainwater for happier and healthier veggies!

## DON'T FENCE 'EM IN

Thanks to years of testing all kinds of pest-control tips, we've discovered a bounty of great ways to keep flying, crawling, and creeping pests from spoiling our harvest. One pair of nasty nogoodniks that's never failed to challenge our ingenuity is slugs and snails. If you have trouble with these slimy slitherers too, try this permanent solution: Surround your raised beds with mini-fences! Thin copper sheeting works best, because it gives the rascals a jolt of electricity when they try to squirm over the top. Just make sure you get every last slug *out* of the bed before you put up the barrier. Otherwise, they'll have a field day inside the ballpark!

### Flea-Beetle-Beater Brew

Our ancestors thought tomatoes were poisonous, so they avoided them like the plague—and flea beetles still do. So if these little buggers are doing a number on your other veggies this year, just spray 'em with this timely tonic and kiss your flea-beetle battles good-bye!

**2 cups of tomato leaves, chopped**
**1/2 tsp. of dishwashing liquid**
**1 qt. of water**

Put the leaves and water in a pan, and bring the water to a simmer. Then turn off the heat and let the mixture cool. Strain out the leaves, and add the dishwashing liquid to the water. Pour the solution into a hand-held sprayer, and spritz your plants from top to bottom. This potent potion also repels whiteflies, asparagus beetles, and cabbageworms. (As with all repellent sprays, though, you'll need to renew the supply after every rain to keep the scent fresh.)

## ROUND UP SLUGS WITH RINDS

Need a quick way to reduce your slug and snail population? Trapping is a super solution. Here at the test gardens, we like to use the citrus rinds left over from our breakfasts; cabbage leaves work well, too. Simply set the rinds or leaves (domed side up) right on the soil around your plants in the evening. (It works even better if you water the soil before you put the trap down, because slugs *love* lots of moisture.) During the day, the pests will take shelter from the sun by clustering under the trap, so you can simply scrape them into a bucket of hot, soapy water to dispose of 'em for good!

## SPRAY 'EM AWAY

Need a way to zap slugs that aren't making it into your traps? We've found a surefire cure: Pour 1½ cups of ammonia, 1 tablespoon of Murphy's Oil Soap®, and 1½ cups of water into a hand-held sprayer. Shake well, then take aim and fire—and say so long to slugs!

## GOLD FOR YOUR GARDEN

If nematodes are bugging your crops, you won't *see* them, but you're sure to see the damage they cause: stunted, yellow, and/or wilted plants, often with distinctly knotted and possibly rotting roots. There's no safe chemical cure for these microscopic, soil-dwelling worms, but we've found an all-natural option that can really help: marigolds! But not just any marigolds—the French types (*Tagetes patula*) are what you want. Plant 'em in rows or blocks between your crops, and you'll enjoy their flowers all season long. Then, in fall, till the plants into the soil instead of pulling them out. When you're done, fill your 20 gallon hose-end sprayer with a can of beer and drench the soil. By spring, the beds will be in great shape for planting, and pests should be a thing of the past!

## A QUICK COVER-UP

Here's a surefire way to prevent bag bugs from taking a bite out of your harvest: Cover up your crops! No need to buy special protectors from garden-supply companies, though; we've discovered that old pairs of pantyhose make perfect crop covers! We just snip off the legs, and then slip 'em over the plant parts we want to protect—whole heads of cabbage or cauliflower, for instance, or individual fruits on eggplants, peppers, and tomatoes. The nylons are stretchy, so they'll expand easily as your crops mature. And pests can't get through, so you'll get a picture-perfect harvest every time!

Worrying about nasty pests is one of our least favorite things to do in the garden, so we're always on the lookout for ways to prevent problems in the first place. Luckily, one of the most reliable ways we've discovered is not just effective, but it makes our test gardens look lovely, too! What's our secret? We grow lots of flowers and herbs along with our veggies! From a practical standpoint, these plants provide plenty of pollen and nectar, which many beneficial insects feed on during their life cycle. As another plus, we have lots of extra herbs and blooms to harvest for use in crafts and cooking! Many flowers and herbs will work, but we've noticed that some attract more beneficial bugs than others—especially borage, chamomile, dill, fennel, hyssop, lemon balm, tarragon, and thyme.

# REPEL PESTS WITH SMELLS

Take our word for it: It's a *whole* lot easier to keep bad bugs away than to control them once they cause problems. It's not tough to take preventive measures, either: The fixin's are as close as your kitchen! Here are two of our favorite formulas for keeping pests at bay:

- The strong smell of garlic offends as many bugs as it does people! To make a pungent pest repellent, cut up six cloves of garlic, and mix with 1 tablespoon of baby shampoo and 1 quart of warm water. Spray it on your plants, and you can be sure the bugs will stay away.
- To send pests packin', put 1 tablespoon of mustard (the hotter, the better) in 1 quart of warm water, and mix it thoroughly. Pour it into a hand-held sprayer, and lightly spray your vegetable plants at the first sign of trouble. Pests can't take the heat, so they'll skedaddle right out of your garden!

## Paralyzing Pest Salsa

Here's a super-spicy, south-of-the-border surprise that'll sock it to any pest that is plaguing your veggie garden.

**2 lb. of ripe tomatoes**
**1 lb. of chili peppers**
**1 large onion**
**2 cloves of garlic**
**1 cup of vinegar**
**1/2 teaspoon of black pepper**

Chop the tomatoes, chili peppers, onion, and garlic, then liquefy them in a blender. Add the vinegar and pepper to the mixture, then strain out the solids. Pour the liquid into a hand-held sprayer and apply directly onto any pests that you see in your garden.

# A ROCKY SOLUTION

Are tunneling critters like mice and voles your main pest problem? Never fear: We've found the answer! Dig a trench around your garden—we make our trenches 1 foot wide and 8 inches deep—then fill it with gravel. The stones keep the critters from burrowing their way in; plus, the gravel-filled strips make a good-looking, weed-free perimeter for your veggie garden!

*I've found an excellent remedy to control the invasion of my garden by dogs, cats, foxes, possums, raccoons, armadillos, rabbits, groundhogs, and any other like-size critters: Surround the garden with a barrier of 2- or 3-foot-tall chicken wire or similar material that is leaning outward at a 45-degree angle. As the critters get close to the fence, they suddenly feel trapped, so they are more interested in getting away than in going over or under it!*

Robert D., St. Augustine, FL

## DASH DISEASES WITH GARLIC

No matter how much garlic we grow every year at the test gardens, it seems we never have enough. Besides the generous quantities we harvest for cooking, this odiferous onion relative provides a key ingredient for many of our garden tonics! You see, garlic's not only a great insect repellent—it's also an *amazing* antibiotic for sickly plants. So when we see spots, speckles, or other signs of possible disease problems on our veggies, we mince several large garlic cloves and soak them overnight in mineral oil. The next day, we strain the mixture, mix 2 teaspoons of the oil and 2 teaspoons of dishwashing liquid in 1 pint of warm water, then put it in a 20 gallon hose-end sprayer and fill the balance of the jar with warm water. We spray every two weeks in the evening, and find that this does a bang-up job keeping our crops healthy *and* pest-free as well!

### TRIED-AND-TRUE

To keep rabbits and other small critters out of your crops, wrap bunches of dog hair or cat hair in old nylon stockings, and hang them around your garden. The varmints will think that Fido or Fluffy is on duty, and they'll keep their distance.

## DAIRY DOES IT

Luckily, it's pretty easy to prevent most vegetable-garden diseases, because we sure don't want to deal with spraying heavy-duty chemicals on crops that we're going to eat! Choosing disease-resistant varieties, planting them in well-drained soil at the recommended spacing, and using soaker hoses instead of overhead watering (to keep the plants dry aboveground) all play a big part in our battle plan for foiling fungi.

Unfortunately, viruses are tougher to prevent. One of the most common kinds—known as tobacco mosaic virus—is best known for infecting tomatoes and their close relatives, including eggplants, peppers, and potatoes. Symptoms include slow growth, greatly reduced fruit set, and thickened leaves mottled with various shades of green. If we suspect that this virus is lurking in our garden, we keep a bowl filled with a half-and-half mixture of milk and water near us when we're working. Every few minutes, we dip our hands and tools into the liquid. Believe it or not, this one simple step can stop tobacco mosaic virus and others right in their tracks!

# COVER YOUR BASES

Of course, bad bugs aren't the only enemies you have to contend with in the veggie garden. There are also lots of four-legged critters who are only too happy to do your harvesting for you! If you're faced with these rascals taking a chomp out of your crops, our best advice is to simply buckle down and install a fence if you can. Trust us: We've learned the hard way that the time, energy, and expense involved in building a fence around your veggie garden is *far* less than what you'll spend trying to keep animals out with repellents and scare tactics.

But what if a fence simply isn't possible or practical? Then get yourself some "floating row cover," also simply called "garden fabric." This relatively inexpensive, reusable material is easy to drape over your crops (set stones or boards on the sides so it doesn't blow away), and the covering rises up with the plants as they grow. Light, air, and water can easily get through to your plants, but chomping critters can't! Granted, it won't keep super-determined varmints from digging under; but in most conditions, we've gotten great results using it to protect a wide range of veggie crops. As a bonus, it keeps most bad bugs away, too—talk about a two-for-one deal!

## Fungus-Fighter Soil Drench

Garlic does more than just protect the tops of your plants; it can do a good job belowground, too! So, when foul fungi are fussin' around in your soil, causing your veggies to produce poorly, to wilt, or worse, just polish 'em off with this potent potion.

**4 garlic bulbs, crushed**
**1/2 cup of baking soda**
**1 gal. of water**

Mix these ingredients in a big pot and bring to a boil. Then turn off the heat and let it cool to room temperature. Strain the liquid into a watering can, and soak the ground around fungus-prone plants. Go *very slowly,* so that the elixir penetrates deep into the soil. Then dump the strained-out garlic bits onto the soil, and work them in gently, so as not to disturb any plant roots.

## SPRING INTO THE SEASON

If you're like us, you simply can't wait to enjoy the first harvest of the year from your veggie garden. Well, we've found a fantastic way to get a real jump start on the growing season, and it's amazingly easy. Here's how:

**Step 1.** Prepare a bed or two for planting *in the fall,* so you won't have to wait for the soil to dry out enough in spring for digging.

**Step 2.** In late winter, cover the prepared beds with a sheet of clear plastic. It's okay if there's still snow on the ground; it'll melt in a hurry, because heat will build up as the sun shines on the plastic.

**Step 3.** After a few sunny days, use a soil thermometer daily to check the temperature under the plastic. For lettuce and radishes, the soil needs to be at least 35°F, while peas prefer a slightly warmer 40°F.

**Step 4.** When the soil temperature is right, take off the plastic and sow your crops—then enjoy your first harvest two to three weeks earlier than your neighbors!

## SOW SHORT

Speedy-growing crops, like lettuce and radishes, are super for quick harvesting, but their peak harvest period is pretty short, and they don't keep well for long once you pick them. Luckily, there's an easy way to spread out your harvest: Spread out your sowing times! Instead of sowing the entire seed packet at one time, do what we do, and plant short rows or small patches every 10 to 14 days through the spring. As soon as you're done picking the first batch, there'll be another in peak form for harvesting, and you'll have a steady supply of salad fixin's well into the summertime!

### Test Garden SECRET

While beans, corn, tomatoes, and other classic summer crops thrive in warm temperatures, cool-weather crops such as lettuce, spinach, and peas just can't take the heat. Well, our test-garden crew put their ingenuity to work a few years ago, and they discovered that the secret to extending the harvest season for spring crops is simply to give 'em some shade! Since then, we've made sure to plant tall-growing, staked, or trellised crops on the south side of our cool-season crops. The bigger bed buddies do a bang-up job of providing afternoon shade, which helps spring veggies keep their cool and stay productive for a whole lot longer into the summer!

## WE'VE GOTCHA COVERED

*Really* in a hurry to get your garden growing? Then start some of your crops indoors! Setting out transplants can easily speed up your harvest time by several weeks—and possibly even a month or more—but the trade-off is that you have to shield those tender transplants during spring cold snaps. Fortunately, we've found a perfect product to protect our crops at the test gardens: floating row cover! It's light enough to let sun and water through, but it's substantial enough to provide 4° to 6°F of protection—and that's enough to get many crops through those touchy early-season nights when frost threatens. It's easy to set up, and best of all, it's amazingly inexpensive—just pennies per square foot—and you can reuse it for years. So why not give floating row cover a try on your crops this spring? You'll be amazed at the results!

### Hurry-Up-the-Harvest Tonic

When I know that Old Man Winter is waiting in the wings and my plants are still chock-full of unripe veggies, I give my garden a big drink of this tonic.

**1 cup of apple juice**
**1/2 cup of ammonia**
**1/2 cup of baby shampoo**
**Warm water**

Mix these ingredients in a 20 gallon hose-end sprayer, filling the balance of the sprayer jar with warm water. Then apply the tonic on your garden to the point of run-off to speed up the ripening process.

## ALL THROUGH THE FALL

Don't let the return of cold weather call a halt to your harvests! In our trials, we've discovered some super-hardy crops that can take light frost, and even some snow, and still stay tasty. These performance plants include Brussels sprouts, cabbage, chard, chicory, endive, kale, and spinach, too! Believe it or not, you can enjoy these garden-fresh veggies on your Thanksgiving dinner table—and maybe even later if you cover them during cold snaps.

## SET YOUR PRIORITIES

There's nothing more exciting than crunching that first fresh lettuce leaf or savoring that first vine-ripened tomato fresh from your garden. After a while, though, keeping up with your harvesting can get tricky, especially considering all the other fun things there are to do during the summer! When we start to get overwhelmed here at the test gardens, we use the following guidelines to decide what to pick, and when:

**Every day or two:** Perishable crops quickly pass their prime, so it's worth checking them often. This group includes fast-growers like fresh beans, broccoli, cauliflower, cucumbers, peas, summer squash, and sweet corn.

**Once or twice a week:** You can spread out the harvest a bit on slower-growers, such as lettuce, melons, peppers, spinach, and tomatoes.

**As time allows:** Harvest timing on this group isn't quite as critical, so when time is limited, these crops can wait a little while: carrots, shell beans, onions, potatoes, and winter squash.

## ELEVENTH-HOUR SAVE

Has this ever happened to you? The weather takes an unexpected cold turn during the night, leaving your uncovered veggie crops to Mother Nature's mercy. If it happens again, don't panic and rip out what's left of your garden—you may be able to revive hardy crops like chard, collards, and mustard. Simply sprinkle the plants gently with water from your garden hose *before* the sun shines on them. That may be enough to prevent damage, so you can keep on harvesting a while longer.

### From Our Readers

*When frost is near, I pick all of my remaining cherry tomatoes and put them in an egg carton, one tomato per "cup," to keep until I'm ready for them. The tomatoes don't touch one another, and they're out of the sunlight, so they store well. Plus, the cartons stack for convenient storage, and they are easy to access!*

Debbie L., Echo, OH

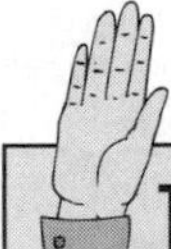

## TRIED-AND-TRUE

**G**randma Putt always depended on lettuce, spinach, and other fast-growing crops because they were so quick to produce a good harvest. While most of her neighbors enjoyed these crops only in spring, Grandma got a double harvest by sowing again in mid- to late summer to get a fall harvest, too! She'd mark her calendar to remind herself to sow heading-type lettuces about 10 weeks before the usual first fall frost; leaf lettuces could be sown as late as 7 weeks before frost, while spinach would still produce with just 5 or 6 weeks of growing time. Grandma knew, though, that the seeds often had a hard time sprouting in summer's hot, dry soil, so she'd soak 'em in cool water overnight before sowing—and they'd be up and growing in no time!

## BEAT THE BIG CHILL

Is Jack Frost threatening to make a return appearance before you're done with your harvest? Never fear! We've found that the same floating row cover we use for protecting transplants from spring frosts works great against fall frosts, too, preventing plant damage even when the air temperature is as low as 28°F. Of course, the crops are a lot taller now, so if the pieces of row cover aren't large enough to completely cover the plants, we simply staple two pieces together. Don't have any floating row cover on hand? Then try this: Drive a stake into the ground at each end of the bed or row, and stretch a rope or wire between the stakes. Then toss an old sheet over the rope to make a tent to protect plants from frostbite at night; remove the sheet during the day.

## STAY GROUNDED

If you've run out of storage space for your carrots, parsnips, or rutabagas during the winter, take heed: We've found that it's possible to leave these crops right in the ground! The trick is to cover them with leaf-filled trash bags, or else straw bales left over from Halloween and Thanksgiving decorating, to insulate them from freezing temperatures. When you're ready to harvest, simply remove the covering, dig up what you need, and replace the cover to protect the rest of your harvest. This super secret lets you enjoy garden-fresh root veggies all winter long!

# From Our Readers

## MANURE TEA

My dad used to fill a 55-gallon water container halfway with fresh cow and horse manure. Then, he'd fill the rest with water, and we'd use that mix to water our vegetable garden. We always had great results!

***Albert S., Rock Hill, NY***

## SLUG REPELLENT

To deter slugs and snails in your vegetable garden, sprinkle wood ashes around any plants where a vegetable would lie on the ground. The slimy pests won't cross the line.

***Clettyce S., Marion, IN***

## CUTWORM CONTROL

Instead of wrapping your vegetable plant stems, just stick some small, 3-inch-long twigs in the ground by your plants to keep cutworms away. I've been doing this for years. You can find them in the garden or nearby fields. I've never lost a plant!

***Thomas S., Tappahannock, VA***

## EASY AS PIE... COLLARS

Here's an easy way to make plant collars: Take a pie pan from a store-bought pie, and make a slit from the edge to the center. In the center, cut a circle about the size of a quarter to handle the plant stems. When a plant is 2 inches high, use the pan as a collar, placing it on the ground around the plant stem by spreading the pan open at the slit.

***Margaret H., Tacoma, WA***

## CONTAINER GROWING

Here is the really lazy way of "container" growing: Take a large bag of professional soil mix, lay it on its side on a board, make a few "X" slits in the bag, and plant a seedling in each X. I've raised small tomatoes this way for many years. When the frost season comes, just carry the board inside in the evening and out during the day. This will extend the growing season.

***Clair B., Decorah, IA***

MORE TIPS

# From Our Readers

## CARPET YOUR GARDEN

Use carpet padding between the rows in your vegetable garden. Water can penetrate the pad, and your feet stay clean when the ground is wet. At the end of the season, hang the carpet pad to dry, hit it with a broom or use a wet/dry vacuum to get out the dirt, and then just roll it up and store it. It will last for several years.

***Jane C., Lincoln, NE***

## CUTWORM COLLARS

I make cutworm collars for plants from the advertisement post-cards that fall from magazines. Fold them in half lengthwise, and put them around the plants, fastening the ends with a piece of tape. It's a good way to recycle, too!

***Ron S., Green Town, PA***

## CROP BASKET

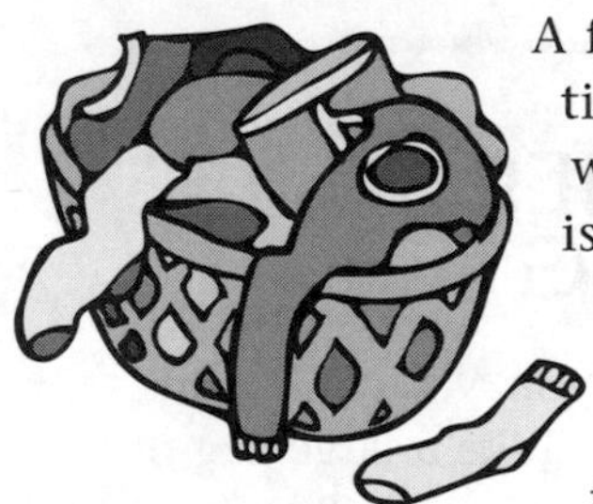

A fast and effective method for washing crops is to put them in a plastic laundry basket. Spray them with a garden hose, and rotate and shake the basket. Because of the openings in the basket, you'll be able to hit all sides with water, and all of the dirt will come off.

***Jessi V., Montgomery, AL***

## HOMEMADE CELLAR

To store fruits and vegetables, bury a barrel or galvanized garbage can upright with approximately 4 inches showing aboveground. Be sure the site is well drained; you may need to make a ditch so that surface water is diverted away from the container. Place the produce you want to store—potatoes, beets, carrots, turnips, or apples—in sacks or perforated polyethylene bags, then put the bags in the can. Put on the lid, cover it thickly with straw, and lay a waterproof canvas or plastic sheet over it. This will keep your produce fresh through the winter.

***John B., Laramie, WY***

## SEÑORITA SALAD

- $1\frac{1}{4}$ lb. of ground beef, browned and drained of fat
- 1 can (16 oz.) of Mexican or chili beans
- 1 can (8 oz.) of tomato sauce
- 1 can ($4\frac{1}{2}$ oz.) of green chilies
- 1 head of lettuce, chopped
- 3–4 tomatoes, chopped
- 1 large onion, chopped
- 12 oz. of grated cheddar cheese
- 1 large bag of Doritos®, crushed slightly

Add the beans, tomato sauce, and green chilies to the browned meat. Keep warm. Then place the lettuce, tomatoes, onion, and grated cheddar in a large serving bowl. Pour the warm meat-and-bean mixture over all. Add the crushed Doritos, toss, and serve.

*Dorothy W., Dubuque, Iowa*

## GARDEN-FRESH SALSA

- 16 firm Roma tomatoes
- 2 red bell peppers
- 3 green bell peppers
- 4 mild onions
- 2–6 jalapeño peppers (2 for mild salsa, 4 for medium, 6 for hot)
- 2 yellow banana peppers
- 4 Anaheim green chilies
- 2 fresh garlic cloves, minced
- 1 cup of white vinegar
- 1 cup of fresh cilantro
- 6 tsp. of garlic salt
- 2 tsp. of black pepper
- 2 cans ($14\frac{1}{2}$ oz. each) of diced tomatoes with Mexican seasonings, drained

Using a food chopper or a sharp chef's knife, coarsely chop and seed all of the cleaned fresh vegetables. Mix with the vinegar, spices, and canned tomatoes. Place in a 1-gallon glass jar, cover, and refrigerate. This is so delicious, it won't last long! Plus, it's a great way to use those healthy and fat-free garden veggies.

*Phyllis W., Great Falls, MT*

## ITALIAN BAKED VEGETABLES

2 crookneck squash, sliced 1/4" thick
2 zucchini, sliced 1/4" thick
1 small onion, sliced 1/4" thick
1 tomato, sliced
5 fresh basil leaves, chopped
2 tbsp. of Parmesan cheese
1/2 tsp. of dried thyme
Salt and black pepper to taste

Preheat oven to 350°F. Toss all ingredients in a 1 1/2-quart ovenproof casserole. Bake 20–25 minutes.

*Leah N., Mesa, AZ*

## PUFF THE MAGIC PIE

2 tbsp. of margarine
2 eggs
1 cup of lowfat milk
1 cup of all-purpose flour
1/4 tsp. of salt
3 cups of fresh chopped vegetables, any combination (such as cauliflower, broccoli, carrots, celery)
1/4–1/2 tsp. of dry Italian herb seasoning
Dash of black pepper
1 cup of shredded Monterey Jack cheese

Melt the margarine in a 9- or 10-inch deep-dish pie plate. Mix the eggs, milk, flour, and salt in a bowl, and pour into the greased pie plate. Put the chopped vegetables in a bowl and mix with Italian herb seasoning and the black pepper. Spoon the vegetables on top of the egg mixture in the pie plate. Top with the shredded cheese. Bake at 400°F about 25 minutes, or until golden brown. Serve warm.

*Mildred W., Poland, OH*

## TEXAS CAVIAR

2 cans (7 oz. each) of black-eyed peas, drained
1 can (7 oz.) of hominy, drained
1 bunch of green onions, chopped
1–2 fresh tomatoes, chopped
1/2 cup of fresh parsley
1/2 cup of fresh cilantro
1–3 jalapeño peppers or green chilies, chopped
1 cup of Italian salad dressing

Mix all ingredients in a large bowl, cover, and refrigerate overnight. Serve with tortilla chips.

*D. M., Des Moines, IA*

# Chapter 10

# Love Those Leaves

Packed with flavor—and lots of nutrients, too—leafy crops are a must-have for any vegetable garden. From ready-in-a-flash salad greens to Brussels sprouts that are worth waiting for, it's easy to find the perfect variety to fill your harvesting needs. We've tried 'em all, and we've gathered up our best hints and tips to help keep you "in the green" all year-round!

## COUNTDOWN TO SPROUTS

Unlike most veggies, Brussels sprouts actually taste *better* when they've been touched by a bit of frost. But you don't want them to freeze hard, so it's important to get 'em growin' at the right time. Here's our no-fail formula for getting perfect, tasty sprouts every year:

**Step 1.** Find out the average date of the first fall frost in your area (ask at your local garden center or check with your gardening neighbors).

**Step 2.** Check the seed packet for "days to maturity."

**Step 3.** Subtract the number of days to maturity from the frost date to find out the ideal transplanting date, then sow your seeds indoors four to five weeks earlier. It's that easy!

### TRIED-AND-TRUE

Back in the good old days, gardeners knew how to keep maggots, club root, and all sorts of good-for-nothing lowlifes away from Brussels sprouts, broccoli, cauliflower, cabbages, and similar crops—simply by sprinkling wood ashes liberally around the base of the plants. Yep, it was (and still is) that easy!

## STRETCH OUT SPROUTS

If you're like us, you want to enjoy your harvest over the longest possible period. Here are three super secrets we've discovered for making the most of our sprouts:

- Select midseason and late-maturing cultivars, such as 'Rubine'.
- Give your plants plenty of space—set 'em about 2 feet apart. (Here's a bonus tip: Sow a crop of leaf lettuce around the transplants to get an extra crop before the sprouts need all their space.)
- Once you've harvested all the sprouts, cut off the leafy top and use it just like you would cabbage!

## HURRY UP THE HARVEST

Do you plan on freezing your crop for tasty winter meals? Then you want all of your sprouts to mature at the same time! Follow these three steps to get a bumper crop of top-quality sprouts that are ready to pick all at once:

**Step 1.** Choose an early-maturing variety (we like 'Oliver').

**Step 2.** Space the plants 18 inches apart (a little closer than usual).

**Step 3.** Pinch out the growing tip of each plant in late summer to speed ripening.

### Super Sprout Weed-Stop

By early spring, any remaining winter-stored sprouts are probably too tough to eat. But don't throw 'em out: Use 'em to mix up this super weed-suppressing tonic!

**1 cup of Brussels sprouts**
**½ tsp. of dishwashing liquid**
**Water**

In a blender, combine the sprouts with just enough water to make a thick mush. Add the dishwashing liquid, then pour the mixture into cracks in your sidewalk and driveway, or any place you want to stop weeds before they pop up. Just don't use it in places where you want flower, herb, or veggie seeds to grow.

## KEEP 'EM COMIN'

Sure, sprouts love the cold, but even they have limits! Fortunately, we've discovered several ways for holding over the harvest when temps are set to fall below 25°F. Where winters aren't too severe, you can transplant your Brussels sprout plants to a cold frame so they can keep growing. Elsewhere, bring the plants into a bright, unheated porch or garage, and pile moist sand around the roots. If that's not a good option for you, then cut off the leaves and roots and store the "logs" in a cool, dark place (35° to 45°F).

# Cabbage

## PILE IT ON!

When it comes to getting a great cabbage crop, the secret is to feed the *soil,* not the plants! Trust us: If you skimp on soil preparation, it doesn't matter how much or how often you fertilize once the plants are in the ground; they just won't grow to their potential. Here are two ways to get your soil in tip-top shape for the biggest and best cabbages on the block:

■ Spread a 3- to 4-inch-thick layer of fresh farm manure over the soil in fall. Work it into the soil then, or let it sit on top for the winter and work it in a few weeks before planting.

■ If fall preparation isn't an option, spread 3 to 4 inches of compost over the soil in late winter or early spring, and dig or till it into the soil about two weeks before planting.

Either way, the super-enriched soil will produce a larger and healthier cabbage crop than you ever thought possible!

### From Our Readers

*Looking for an easy way to label your veggie crops? Use a laundry marker (which won't wash off) to write the date and name of each plant on a plastic knife, fork, or spoon. Stick the plastic silverware down by the plant and you'll never have to guess what variety it is!*

Vera B.,
Robeline, LA

## DON'T WASTE SPACE!

To make your garden space do double-duty, just use cabbage as a follow-up for early crops, like lettuce, peas, beets, spinach, or potatoes. Set out the cabbage transplants as soon as you harvest the earlier crop, and you'll enjoy a second harvest from the same space in fall!

### BY THE WAY...

Cabbages are closely related to broccoli, Brussels sprouts, cauliflower, and kale (as a bunch, they're known as "brassicas"), and they share the same pests and problems. So when you see tips for one crop, they'll usually work just as well for all of its relatives, too!

## Test Garden SECRET

Cabbage sure loves cool weather—but it likes a long growing season, too! So how do you help your plants keep their cool even during the dog days of summer? In our test gardens, we've found that a 6- to 8-inch-thick mulch of straw or dried grass clippings provides perfect growing conditions for cabbage. That means happier plants—*and* a bigger harvest for you!

## THINK A-HEAD

Cabbage needs to be harvested as soon as it's ready—but what do you do with two dozen heads of cabbage all at once? Unless your family *really* likes pickled cabbage for breakfast, coleslaw for lunch, and sauerkraut for dinner, we suggest trying one of these tips in the spring to spread out your harvest later on:

- Start a small batch of seeds every two to three weeks, so the plants mature at different times.
- Set transplants or thin seedlings of early cabbages to stand 6 inches apart. A few weeks later, start harvesting every other plant for use as greens; then pick the rest as the heads firm up.
- Plant late-maturing cabbages 1 foot apart. Harvest every other plant while the heads are small, then let the rest reach full size.

## PLEASE DON'T SQUEEZE

**Cabbage is ready to pick when the** heads are nice and solid—but how can you tell? Whatever you do, *don't* pinch them! We've learned the hard way that pinching the heads bruises the leaves, making them prime targets for rotting during storage. Instead, simply press down on the top of the head with the back of your hand. This firmness test does the trick without damaging your crop in the process!

### Jerry's Lime Rickey

Back in my Uncle Art's day, lime soda rickeys were all the rage. Well, this rickey isn't made with soda, but it *will* make cabbage maggots rage!

**1 cup of garden lime**
**1 qt. of water**

Stir the lime into the water, and let it sit overnight. Then, pour the solution around the root ball of each maggot-plagued plant. Before you can say "Put a nickel in the jukebox," those maggots'll be history!

## "X" MARKS THE SPOT

Want to know how we double our cabbage crop? At harvest time, instead of pulling cabbages up by their roots, we just cut the heads off, leaving as much stalk behind as possible. Then we cut a shallow X in the top of the stump. Usually, a cluster of small heads will grow out of the stalk that's left behind. We clip these off when they're as small as Brussels sprouts, or let 'em grow larger and enjoy their mild, tender leaves in a tossed salad.

Kitchen **CLASSICS**

Looking for something lighter than creamy coleslaw for summer picnics? Try tossing shredded cabbage with apple or pear wedges in a creamy citrus vinaigrette. Or, mix 3 cups of shredded cabbage with 1/4 cup of shredded carrots, 2 tablespoons each of chopped peanuts and sunflower seeds, and 1/2 cup of low-fat sesame-ginger salad dressing; refrigerate for at least 1 hour before serving. Both of these quick-and-easy recipes are sure to be a hit when it's hot!

## KEEP YOUR HEADS TOGETHER

Unless you're planning to preserve your cabbage crop, you'll probably need only a head or two every few days. So what can you do if several heads mature at the same time? If you leave them unpicked, they're likely to crack open! Here are two techniques that we've used to hold ripe heads outdoors for up to a week:

- Grasp a ready-to-pick head between your two hands, then give it a quarter- to half-turn while lifting up slightly.
- Plunge the blade of a trowel, spade, or shovel into the soil on one side of the plant to cut some of the roots.

Remember: You'll still want to harvest the heads as soon as possible. And if they do crack, don't worry—they're no good for storage, but they're still A-OK for fresh eating!

## TICKLE YOUR TASTE BUDS

If you enjoy the crisp taste of just-picked lettuce but are looking for something with a little more zip, why not give Chinese cabbage a try? This multipurpose green is as tasty enjoyed fresh in salads as it is boiled or steamed, stir-fried, or shredded for slaw. It's easy to grow in spring, just like lettuce, but we actually prefer to grow it in the fall. It makes a super follow-up to summer crops that are done producing by August, such as early bush beans, so we get a second harvest from the same amount of garden space!

## BRANCHING OUT

Like other cabbage relatives, Chinese cabbage can be bothered by pesky caterpillars, which chew unsightly holes in the leaves. Luckily, sparrows and other birds love to feed on these pests, so we do all we can to entice feathered helpers to consider our test gardens home. One of our favorite tricks is to push 4-foot-long branches into the soil in our Chinese cabbage patch to give birds a place to perch. We figure if the birds pause there for a second, they'll spy a caterpillar or two for a tasty snack!

## SMUG WITH A RUG

Want to make muddy garden paths a thing of the past? Roll out the red carpet...or any other color carpet, for that matter! Cut your old carpeting and rugs into strips, and lay them down in your vegetable garden between the rows. They'll keep weeds down *and* act as a mulch around your veggies, too!

### From Our Readers

*I harvest my lettuce by cutting the leaves off about 1 inch above the ground. That way, more leaves will grow back in a few weeks, and I get a second harvest from the same plants!*

Tom L., Roanoke, VA

## THE BIG FRAME-UP

Need an easy way to keep cabbage butterflies off of your kale crop? Make a frame out of wood or PVC that stands several inches above the plants, then double up some bird netting and drape it over the frame. Anchor the sides to the ground with rocks or boards—anything that's easy to move when you want to lift the sides to reach the plants. It sure beats picking those darn cabbage loopers off by hand!

## A VARIETY OF VARIETIES

Here at the test gardens, we like kale so much that we've tried just about every variety we could get our hands on. Believe it or not, we've found a few that are worth growing for their good looks alone—never mind that they taste great, too! Here are three of our favorites; try 'em for yourself, and see if you don't agree that they're as pretty as they are productive.

**'Lacinato'.** Also known as 'Nero di Toscana', Tuscan kale, and dinosaur kale, this heirloom Italian favorite has deep blue-green, crinkled leaves that are truly eye-catching in the garden. And the plants themselves look like miniature palm trees!

**'Ragged Jack'.** Another old-time favorite, also known as 'Russian Red', this variety has jagged-edged, blue-green leaves with pinkish red veins and stems; it's very hardy, too.

**'Redbor'.** Our all-time favorite, this big beauty easily reaches 3 feet tall or more, with frilly edged, reddish leaves with deep purple veins and stems. When touched by frost, the whole plant turns a rich violet-purple. This variety looks fantastic paired with fall mums for an unforgettable autumn display!

Kale can last well into winter through much of the U.S.; but north of Zone 7, even this sturdy crop can get frozen out by extended periods of freezing weather. Well, we've found a great way to enjoy these sweet leaves all winter long! We sow a batch of seeds in late summer or early fall, then pot up the seedlings and bring them indoors after a few light frosts. Kept in a sunny window in an unheated porch or room, the plants will keep producing long after other crops are just a memory!

## HOW SWEET IT IS

Poor kale has a really bad reputation as a tough, boring, bland-tasting green. Well, we're here to change all that! Our secret for growing great-tasting kale is simple: Patience! Instead of rushing to pick in midsummer, we harvest our other greens at that time and leave our kale for later. Once cool weather returns—and particularly after a touch of light frost—those tough, stringy leaves will be so sweet and tender, anyone who tastes it will be a kale fan for life! This super-hardy green is so sturdy, you can even harvest when it's frozen; just toss the leaves right into your steamer or a pot of boiling water, and you've got a great-tasting, garden-fresh side dish even in the middle of winter. Yum!

### Pest-Away Garlic Spray

A few aphids aren't a serious problem, but when they start congregating on veggie shoots and damaging tender leaves, it's time to take action. This garlicky spray will halt an aphid invasion faster than you can say "Hold it right there!"

**1 tbsp. of garlic oil***
**3 drops of dishwashing liquid**
**1 qt. of water**

Mix these ingredients in a blender, and pour the solution into a hand-held sprayer. Then take aim and fire on infested plants. Within seconds, those aphids'll be history!

*To make garlic oil, mince one whole bulb of garlic and mix it in 1 cup of vegetable oil. Put the garlic oil in a glass jar with a tight lid and place it in the refrigerator to steep for a day or two. Then, strain out the solids and pour the oil into a fresh jar with a lid. Keep it in the fridge and use it in any tonic that calls for garlic oil.

## COLLAR 'EM

Protect your kale (and other veggie) seedlings from cutworms with collars of 4-inch-wide, corrugated, black plastic drainpipe. Buy it in a 50-foot roll (it costs about $20), then cut it into 6- to 8-inch-long pieces, and place one collar over each plant. Besides shielding transplants from cutworms, nibbling animals, and drying winds, the collars also help keep the plants warm, because the dark color absorbs the sun's heat. They also work great to protect newly planted trees and shrubs from rabbits, voles, and other critters; just cut them a little longer (I usually make mine about 12 inches long), then slit them lengthwise to get them around the tree trunk. Best of all, these collars can be used over and over again, year after year!

## SHAKE IT!

Lettuce is a rewarding crop for beginners and experts alike, because it grows quickly and needs little fussing to produce an abundant, tasty harvest. But actually getting it *started* can be a little challenging; the seeds are so small, it can be tough to sow them evenly. Well, we've found a super solution: We put the seeds in an old salt shaker, then simply sprinkle them over the prepared soil. Voilà—perfectly spaced seeds, so we hardly have any thinning to do later on. (Try this trick with carrot seeds, too!)

## A SOW-SOW SECRET

Sow early, and sow often: That's our test-gardens trick to enjoying a steady supply of lovely lettuce! Instead of scattering a whole packet of seeds at one time, we make it a habit to spread out our lettuce sowings: every 10 to 14 days from early spring until late summer. (In mild climates, you'd have better luck sowing from fall through to early spring.) So, how much should you sow? Well, that really depends on how much of a lettuce harvest you want to reap. Most of the folks here at the test gardens like to enjoy salads every day, so we figure on a generous crop—about 2 feet of row per person at each sowing. But if you make salads only every few days, a foot of row per person per sowing should serve the purpose without leaving you with lots of leftover lettuce!

### JERRY'S Q&A

**Q** Hey, Jer—can you tell me why the tips of my lettuce plants suddenly turned brown? Is it some awful disease?

**A** Relax: Funky fungi *haven't* invaded your garden! It's a condition called tip burn, caused by a combination of heat and an irregular water supply. To prevent it, water regularly to keep the soil evenly moist, and put up some kind of barrier between your tender plants and the brutal sun—a piece of lattice or a heat-loving crop growing on a trellis would be just the ticket!

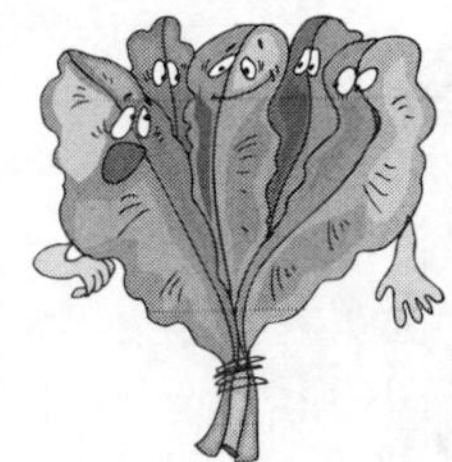

## RX FOR LETTUCE WOES

Having trouble getting your lettuce going? Here at the test gardens, we've found that we can almost always trace the problem to the same two causes: either light (not enough of it) or heat (too much of it)!

**Let there be light.** Lettuce seeds need light to sprout, so planting them too deep (with more than 1/4 inch of soil over them) is sure to keep them from germinating. To prevent that, we usually just scatter the seeds on the soil surface, rake the area lightly, then pat the soil with our hand to firm up the seedbed before watering.

**Keep 'em cool.** No doubt about it: Lettuce is a cool-weather crop! When temperatures are above 75°F, its seeds simply don't want to sprout, or else the seedlings are weak and spindly. The best way to avoid this is to sow early in the season, as soon as the soil is at least 35°F. To get later sowings going, we've found two ways to beat the heat: Watering the seedbed every few hours for the first day or two to keep the soil cool, or, if you don't have the time to spend on such frequent watering, starting the seeds in a cool spot indoors and setting out transplants. Works every time!

MIX IT UP!

### All-Purpose Critter Control

No doubt about it: There are lots of wily veggie-gulpers just waiting to sink their sharp teeth into your harvest. But gophers, skunks, and just about any other critter will turn tail and run when they get a whiff of this powerful tonic!

**2 eggs**
**2 cloves of garlic**
**2 tbsp. of hot chili pepper**
**2 tbsp. of ammonia**
**2 cups of hot water**

Mix these ingredients in a bucket, then let the mixture sit for three or four days. Paint it on fences, trellises, and wherever else unwanted varmints are venturing.

## THE TIP OF THE ICEBERG

One of the best things about growing lettuce at home is the variety of leaf shapes, colors, and flavors there are to choose from. But if you're a fan of the classic 'Iceberg' head lettuce, you might be surprised that this everyday favorite is actually one of the most difficult varieties to grow well at home; it demands careful attention to watering, and it's quick to bolt (go to seed and become bitter) during hot weather. Over the years, we've tried a number of other varieties to replace 'Iceberg' in our test gardens, and we've found a winner: 'Great Lakes'. It gives us large, tight heads of crispy leaves with that classic 'Iceberg' crunch, but *without* the tendency to bolt so quickly. Another favorite from our trials is 'Mini Green': It forms great-tasting heads that are perfectly scaled down to tennis-ball size—just right for a single salad!

### JUST CHILLIN'

Lettuce sure tastes great right out of the garden—but what if you aren't able to use it right away? There's no need to make do with limp lettuce: Simply pull up the whole plant—roots and all—and set it in a glass of water, just as you'd do with a cut flower. Then put a big plastic bag over the whole shebang and set it in the fridge. Treated this way, it'll keep that fresh-from-the-garden crispness for nearly a week!

## CUT AND COME AGAIN

Want to get twice—or even three times—the harvest from a single lettuce sowing? We've found a fantastic trick for getting leaf lettuces to be extra-generous: It's called "cut and come again," and it works just like it sounds. We wait until the leaves are salad-sized, then instead of snipping off individual leaves (which takes forever), or pulling out the clumps by the roots (which kills the plants), we use a knife to cut off the whole top about an inch above the roots. Harvesting this way takes just minutes, and the remaining roots quickly sprout a second crop of tasty leaves. And if the weather stays cool, we sometimes even get a third harvest this way. That's a lot of lettuce from just a few cents' worth of seeds!

## DIVE INTO ENDIVE

Looking for something a little different to pep up your green salads? Endive is one option: It has the same great crunch as lettuce, but it's a lot less fussy about warm weather! Actually, there are two types to choose from: The name "endive" is usually saved for frilly leaved types, while "escarole" refers to those with broad, smoother leaves. We grow both here at the test gardens and plant 'em just like lettuce: sowing directly in the garden every two weeks, starting in early spring. Both endive and escarole tend to taste stronger than lettuce; but if you find them *too* bitter for your liking, try harvesting them earlier (the young leaves are more tender), or do what we do, and enjoy a milder flavor by waiting for cooler weather.

## MIXED GREENS TO GO

If you love the flavors of mixed greens as much as we do, you'll *love* growing "mesclun." This one-size-fits-all term basically means a mixture of different salad greens harvested when they are young and tender. Standard favorites include chicory, collards, endive, kale, lettuce, mustard greens, and spinach, but there is a world of other possibilities; you can combine the seeds of your favorite greens to make a custom mix, or buy a premade mesclun seed mix. Either way, you'll enjoy the amazing combination of colors, textures, and flavors. Best of all, the greens are already mixed up at harvest time, so all you have to do is add your favorite salad dressing and you're good to go! For even more zip, do what we do, and add a pinch of some of your favorite herb seeds before sowing; basil, chives, dill, fennel, and parsley are some of our favorites.

### Kitchen CLASSICS

We love to come up with new ways to enjoy our abundant harvest of greens every year, and our impromptu taste-testing sessions make the test gardens a popular place around lunchtime! Two of our most popular uses for greens? One is placing them between the layers in our favorite lasagna recipe; it's a great way to add more flavor, not to mention lots of calcium, beta carotene, and Vitamins C and K as well. Or, for a cooling summer side dish, we like to substitute greens for cabbage in slaw; use your family's favorite slaw recipe, or try combining 4 cups of shredded mixed greens with 4 tablespoons of mayonnaise, 4 teaspoons of Dijon mustard, and a pinch or two of celery seed—yum!

## CALL ON COLLARDS

Where summer heat is too tough for more tender greens, collards are the crop to call on! This sturdy cabbage relative usually roots more deeply than other greens—one trick it uses to help beat the heat—so preparing a deeply dug seedbed is key. Collard seeds won't sprout until the soil is at least 50°F, so we've found that it's smart to start our spring crop indoors in early spring, then set out the transplants once the soil temperature is right. For a fall crop, sow directly in the garden, about three months before the first expected frost. (In the Deep South, plant in fall for a winter harvest.) Collard greens are remarkably cold-tolerant, too; in fact, a touch of light frost actually makes them sweeter!

### Kitchen CLASSICS

Need a healthy appetizer for a summer party? Finely chop 2 heads of radicchio in a food processor, then mix in 1 1/2 tablespoons of extra virgin olive oil and 1 tablespoon of balsamic vinegar. Stir in 1/2 teaspoon of dried oregano, plus salt and pepper to taste, then spread this colorful mixture on thin, lightly toasted slices of crusty bread. It's deliciously different!

## RADICAL RADICCHIO

If you tried to grow radicchio years ago and thought it was too much bother, it's time to try again! Until recently, the plants needed to be cut back hard in fall—or even dug up and forced to grow again indoors—to produce those beautiful, brilliant red, white-veined heads that add so much flavor and color to green salads. We gave up on growing radicchio until recently, when one of our test-garden crew found seeds of 'Fiero' and 'Indigo', two newer varieties that supposedly don't need to be cut back. Well, we tried 'em, and now we're radicchio fans for life! This crop likes to mature in cool weather, so it makes a super late-season crop; we sow every two weeks from midsummer until two months before our first fall frost date.

*This trick works well on mustard, turnip, and kale: As the plants begin to go to seed, take a lawn mower, and run over the rows or patch of greens. Follow this up with a thorough watering, and, if your soil is not very rich, a good dose of compost. In a matter of days, you will be picking tender, new greens.*

Gerald M., Mascoutah, IL

## JUMP-START FOR SPINACH

If you're one of those gardeners who can't wait to enjoy the first harvest of the spring, then spinach is the crop for you! This speedy leaf crop is typically ready to harvest in about seven weeks from sowing—you can't get much quicker than that, right? Well, we've experimented with a variety of tricks for getting our spinach off to an even faster start, and believe it or not, we've shaved a week or more off of that time! How? We prepare the soil in our spinach beds *in fall,* and sow the seeds right then. A light mulch of straw and/or chopped leaves protects the seeds over the winter, and as soon as the soil thaws in early spring, they're ready to get growing!

MIX IT UP!

### Seed and Soil Energizer

Over the years, we've found that encouraging speedy sprouting gives all of our seed-grown crops a great jump-start for the growing season. So once we've sown our veggie or herb seeds, indoors or out, we give 'em an energy boost with this elixir. Try it in your own garden, and be prepared for your best veggie garden ever!

**1 tsp. of whiskey**
**1 tsp. of ammonia**
**1 tsp. of dishwashing liquid**
**1 qt. of weak tea water***

Mix these ingredients in a bucket, and pour the solution into a hand-held sprayer. Shake it gently, and apply a good misting to the surface of newly planted seedbeds or plant containers.

*To make weak tea water, soak a used tea bag in a solution of 1 gallon of warm water and 1 teaspoon of dishwashing liquid until the mix is light brown. Store leftover liquid in a tightly capped jug or bottle for later use.

## A DIFFERENT SPIN ON SPINACH

If you like spinach as much as we do, you miss its flavor-packed leaves during the dog days of summer. Well, we've discovered a substitute: New Zealand spinach. The flavor's very close to the real thing, from a plant that absolutely *loves* hot weather! We sow it right in the garden around the last frost date in spring, and it's ready in about 60 days. Harvesting is easy: Simply snip off 4- to 6-inch shoot tips and leaves, or cut off the whole top of the plant just above the roots and let it resprout for a second harvest.

# TRICKIN' FOR PROLONGED PICKIN'

Looking to extend your harvest of this tasty cool-season veggie? Here are our two favorite ways to trick spinach into producing abundantly, even when conditions are less than ideal:

**Made for the shade.** If your spinach crop will be ready to pick in mid- or late summer, plant it on the north side of a tall crop, such as corn, trellised cucumbers, or pole beans. The afternoon shade will help keep your spinach cooler, so it'll be less likely to go to seed before you get a good harvest.

**Give it a chill.** Sowing spinach again later in the season is a smart way to go, because it'll be very happy maturing in the cooler temperatures of fall. Unfortunately, the perfect time for sowing in late summer often seems to coincide with the last major warm spell of the season, so spinach seeds are too hot to sprout. If this happens to you, try this trick: Freeze a few spinach seeds in water in each "cell" of an ice-cube tray, then plant 'em directly in your garden, cube and all. Spritzing the seedbed frequently with water helps, too!

Kitchen CLASSICS

Does your family cringe at the thought of having spinach with dinner? To make a super-easy side dish that's sure to change their minds, wash and remove the heavy stems from about 10 ounces of fresh spinach, then steam it for 5 minutes (or just until wilted). Drain thoroughly and return to a dry pot, then add 1/2 cup of halved Thompson seedless grapes, 1 teaspoon of butter, and a dash of ground nutmeg. Toss until well mixed, then garnish with lightly toasted pine nuts (pignoli). This simple recipe makes two super-tasty servings.

# SO LONG, SAND!

Sandy soil is a delight to dig into, but it can be a real drag when you're trying to grow clean spinach greens! Those little bits of sand love to work themselves into the crinkles on the leaves, and there's nothing worse than trying to chew gritty greens. We've experimented with various ways of keeping our spinach grit-free, and we've found three surefire tricks:

- Look for varieties with smooth leaves, such as 'Olympia' and 'Space'; there's no place for sand to hide!
- If you really enjoy the texture of savory (crinkled-leaf) spinach, select a more-upright variety, such as 'Melody'; the plants are much less likely to get splashed with soil.
- Cover the soil with a nice, clean mulch, such as straw or chopped leaves; that way, they'll stay sand-free!

## THE UNKINDEST CUT

Of all the tasty leaf crops we grow, Swiss chard wins the prize for the longest productive period from just one sowing. Plant it in spring, and it'll send up a steady supply of foliage from midsummer all the way to frost; in many areas, it can even live over the winter and yield more leaves the following spring! The secret to keeping chard coming? Don't cut it! Instead of slicing off the stems with a knife, which might slip and damage the innermost growing bud, we grab each leaf at the base and give it a quick twist to snap it off. Works every time!

**Test Garden SECRET**

Like its close relative the beet, Swiss chard needs boron in its soil to grow well. If it doesn't get enough, its stems will crack. To make sure your crops have all the boron they need, sprinkle a pinch of borax in and among the rows at planting time to keep 'em growing strong!

## COLOR YOUR WORLD

Swiss chard is one of those veggies that's pretty enough to grow in any flower garden—especially the variety called 'Bright Lights'. Common chard usually has deep green leaves with white stalks, but when you sow 'Bright Lights' seeds, the stalks come in a veritable rainbow of colors: Besides white, they may be rich red, glowing orange, sunny yellow, or even bright pink! You can sow the seeds directly in your garden, but we like to start them in pots; that way, it's easy to separate the seedlings by stem color and coordinate them with the bloom colors of their companions in our flower beds!

**TRIED-AND-TRUE**

Luckily, Swiss chard is seldom seriously bothered by pests, but it does have one major enemy: leafminers. These tiny flies lay eggs on the leaves, then their larvae tunnel between the upper and lower leaf surfaces, producing winding tunnels and unsightly blotches on the foliage. Nowadays, we cover our test-garden chard with floating row cover fabric to keep the flies away from the leaves; but back in Grandma Putt's day, that wasn't an option. She didn't let these thugs spoil her pickin's, though; instead, she'd harvest as usual, peel off the stricken leafy parts, and steam the stems for a super asparagus substitute!

MORE TIPS

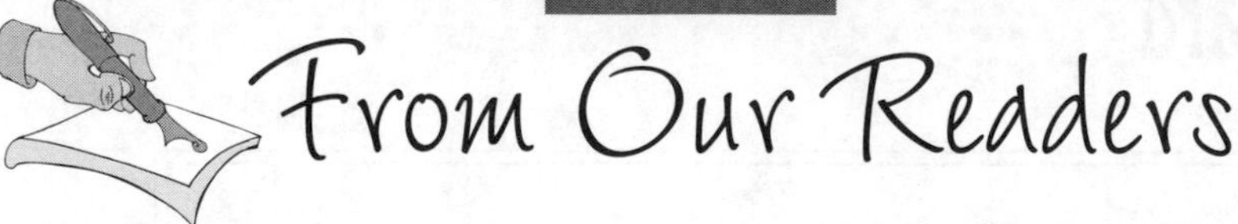

# From Our Readers

## CUTWORM CONTROL

We have found that placing a nail right alongside each cabbage and tomato seedling when they are young will stop cutworms from eating the plants.

***Richard I., Fergus Falls, MN***

## STEADY SPINACH SUPPLY

Want to extend your supply of fresh spinach? Sow short rows of seeds every 10 days. You'll have a steady supply of young, tender leaves for weeks longer than everyone else.

***Jared S., Pittsfield, MA***

## SIMPLE SALADS

For fresh salad fixin's in no time, plant lettuce in a pot out on your deck or patio. If you really want to get creative, set up a salad garden by planting different types of lettuce, and even radishes and small tomatoes, in different pots. It'll make for an attractive, handy, and delicious display!

***Pat S., Roanoke, VA***

## CABBAGE KEEPERS

To keep caterpillars off of your cabbage, make a solution of milk and a little lemon juice or vinegar. Spoon this into the center of each cabbage once a week for an effective deterrent. Still another deterrent for this problem is to place a thin coating of newly mown grass cuttings around the cabbages. This also works to keep broccoli and similar plants caterpillar-free.

***P. R., Jacksonville, FL***

## EGG-STRA SPECIAL CABBAGES

My grandma always grew the best cabbages in town. Her secret? Eggshells! She'd dry and crush all of her eggshells, and work them into the soil around her cabbage plants. The plants thanked her each and every year by producing a bumper crop!

***Phil B., Memphis, TN***

# From Our Readers

## WORM DUST

To get rid of cabbageworms, early in the morning, while the dew is still on the plants, take your flour sifter from the kitchen and lightly sift flour over the cabbage plants. This really works. Why? The worms crawl out on the cabbage and get the flour on themselves, and then when the dew dries, it leaves the worms starched stiff!

***Fae S., Douds, IA***

## SHADY CHARACTERS

Plant your lettuce seeds at the foot of your cornstalks. The tall corn will offer the tender lettuce some much-needed shade.

***Brian G., Northville, MI***

## FAKE SNAKES

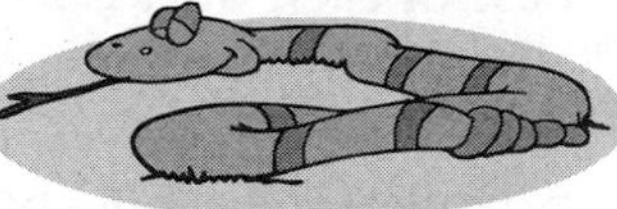

I set lengths of old garden hose between my rows of lettuce and cabbage. Rabbits think they're snakes and steer clear. I move the "snakes" every couple of days to keep the bunnies on their toes.

***Rudy H., Wilmington, DE***

## COOL CABBAGE

I've found that cabbage keeps nicely in the refrigerator if you place it in a large zip-top plastic bag, add a damp paper towel, and seal it shut. That way, it'll stay nice and moist. My cabbages last a full week longer when I store them this way.

***Joan C., Dubuque, IA***

## SWEET LEAVES

I've been growing lettuce for years, so I try lots of different kinds. My new favorite is called "Cos". It's tricky to grow and it took me a few years to get it right. But it's completely worth it when you taste some of this lettuce's leaves. It's *sweeeet* and tasty!

***Katherine H., Canton, OH***

## SHELLS STOP SLUGS

I love to grow lettuce, but I had a lot of trouble with slugs eating most of it. Last year, I started breaking up eggshells and sprinkling them in the garden around my lettuce plants. After that, I had no trouble with slugs at all!

***Laverne P., Cleveland, OH***

## NEW MEXICO HIGH-NOON SPINACH

**1 medium onion, finely chopped**
**1 tsp. of shortening or bacon drippings**
**1 lb. of fresh spinach leaves, with stems removed**
**1 can (16 oz.) of pinto beans**
**1 tbsp. of crushed red pepper flakes**
**Salt and black pepper to taste**
**Bacon bits, optional**

In a skillet, add 1 teaspoon of shortening or bacon drippings and sauté the onions over low heat. Add the spinach, and cook until tender. Rinse and drain the pinto beans; add to the skillet. Add the red pepper flakes (use more or less, depending on your taste); salt and pepper to taste. Stir until heated through. Add bacon bits, if desired, just before serving.

***Jenny R., Satellite Beach, FL***

## ZUCCHINI COLESLAW

**2 cups of shredded zucchini**
**2 cups of shredded cabbage**
**1 medium carrot, shredded**
**2 green onions, sliced**
**1/3 cup of mayonnaise**
**1/3 cup of mild picante sauce**
**1/2 tsp. of ground cumin**

Press the zucchini between layers of paper towels to dry. In a large bowl, combine the zucchini, cabbage, carrot, and green onions. In a small bowl, combine the remaining ingredients. Pour this dressing over the vegetables, and toss well. Cover and chill at least 1 hour.

***Lorraine V., Beaver Dam, WI***

## BRUSSELS SPROUTS SIDE DISH

**1 lb. of small, fresh Brussels sprouts**
**1 tbsp. of red wine vinegar**
**2 tbsp. of fresh dill or 2 tsp. of dillweed, minced**
**Salt and freshly ground black pepper**
**Butter**
**Water**

Preheat oven to 350°F. Trim the sprouts and cut a little cross into the base of each one. Cook the sprouts in a medium-sized saucepan in boiling water for 10 minutes. Drain into a colander, then quickly drench with cold water to prevent further cooking. Put the sprouts into a small, buttered baking dish. Stir in the vinegar, dill, salt, and pepper, and cover. Bake for 10 minutes, then remove the cover and bake for another 5 minutes.

***Kelly B., Springfield, IL***

# TEST GARDEN GOODIES

## EASY SPINACH BAKE

**1 package (10 oz.) of frozen spinach, thawed and squeezed dry**
**1 cup of prepared rice**
**2 eggs, slightly beaten**
**1/3 cup of milk**
**1 tsp. of salt**
**2 tbsp. of chopped onion**
**1 cup of grated cheddar cheese**
**2 tbsp. of butter, melted**
**1/4 tsp. of rosemary**

Combine all of the ingredients in a mixing bowl, blending thoroughly. Pour into a buttered 9 × 9-inch dish and bake at 350°F for 20 to 25 minutes.

***Leah N., Mesa, AZ***

## SUPERB SLAW

**1 medium head of cabbage**
**1 medium onion, thinly sliced into rings**
**1/2 to 3/4 cups of sugar**
**1 cup of cider vinegar**
**3/4 cup of salad oil**
**2 tsp. of salt**
**1 tsp. of dry mustard**
**1 tsp. of celery seed**

In a bowl, alternate layers of shredded cabbage and onion rings. Top with sugar. Do not stir. Place remaining ingredients in a saucepan and bring to a boil. Pour over the cabbage and onion while still hot. Cover and refrigerate 4 to 6 hours. Mix well before serving.

***Alma T., Fort Wayne, IN***

## SPINACH SALAD

**6 slices of fried bacon, minced**
**2 hard-boiled eggs, coarsely chopped**
**1 onion, chopped**
**1 lb. of fresh spinach leaves, with stems removed**

**DRESSING**

**1/4 cup of vinegar**
**1/8 tsp. of garlic powder**
**3/4 cup of sugar**
**1/4 tsp. of salt**
**Dash of black pepper**
**1 tbsp. of Worcestershire sauce**
**1/3 cup of ketchup**
**1/2 cup of salad oil**

Mix the salad ingredients in a large bowl, cover, and refrigerate. Mix the vinegar, garlic, sugar, salt, pepper, and Worcestershire sauce in a pint jar and stir until the sugar is dissolved. Then add the ketchup and oil. Mix thoroughly and refrigerate. Pour the dressing over the salad just before serving.

***Lois M., Chandler, AZ***

# Chapter 11

# THE ROOTS ARE WHAT MATTER

Okay—maybe we're just easily amused, but we have to admit that growing root vegetables is a whole lot of fun. It's easy to see what's happening above the ground, but it's always a delightful surprise to pull or dig up an entirely different-looking root at harvest time. These dependable crops have been staples in the vegetable garden for hundreds of years, so you can guess that they're pretty foolproof. And with our garden-tested growing tips, you can enjoy healthier, more productive plants—and that means a more abundant and flavorful harvest for you!

## A SEEDY SOLUTION

Having trouble getting seeds with woody coats, like those of beets and parsnips, off to a good start? We used to have the same problem, until we found this quick trick: Mix 1 cup of vinegar with 2 tablespoons of dishwashing liquid and 2 cups of warm water. Soak the seeds for 24 hours, then sow them outdoors and cover them with a strip of burlap. This creates a nice warm environment that lets moisture in and encourages sprouting. Lift the burlap daily to check underneath; once the seeds have sprouted, remove the burlap altogether to give the seedlings lots of light and let 'em get growing!

## MEET THE BEETS

Classic garden beets are red and round—but that's just the beginning! We enjoy trying all of the beet varieties we can get our hands on, and we've found some real winners we think you'll enjoy as much as we do. 'Albina Vereduna', for instance, produces sweet, *white* roots, while 'Golden' is bright yellow. Besides their great tastes and good looks, these non-red beets don't "bleed" their color when combined with other ingredients in salads or cooked dishes, as red beets do. 'Chiogga' is another beauty, with roots that are ringed with red and white, just like a peppermint candy. It's a test-garden favorite when shredded raw or sliced thin and tossed into salad, or else roasted. But boiling makes the stripes disappear!

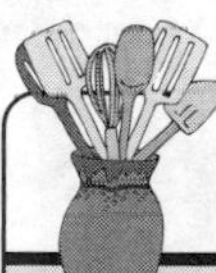

**Kitchen CLASSICS**

Did you know that beets are as easy to roast as potatoes? All of that dry heat locks in the nutrients and brings out the sweetness better than any other cooking method! Our favorite method is to wrap cleaned, whole beets in aluminum foil and put them into a baking pan; then we bake 'em at 350° to 400°F until they're tender (about 1½ to 2 hours). After taking off the foil and letting them stand until just cool enough to handle, we peel 'em and dig in for a tasty treat.

**Test Garden**

Here's the secret to getting the best-quality beets every time: Give 'em plenty of elbow room! Beet "seeds" are actually fruits, made up of clusters of two to six seeds. So when you sow one "seed," you're likely to get several seedlings coming up in one spot, and that means none of them will have the room to develop properly. We make our first thinning when the seedlings are 1 to 2 inches tall, leaving them ½ inch apart. After another week or two, we thin again, based on the type of beet (4-inch spacings are fine for most fresh beets; leave 6 inches for large-rooted storage types). Here's a bonus tip: Don't pull out unwanted seedlings (which can damage those left behind); snip 'em off with scissors and enjoy those tasty trimmings in your fresh salads.

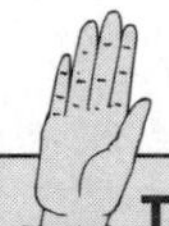

**TRIED-AND-TRUE**

Carrot rust flies may be tiny, but their larvae can cause BIG damage as they tunnel through the roots of your crop. Once they get going, they're tough to control, but fortunately, Grandma Putt knew the secret to getting around them: She simply waited until the apple trees bloomed to sow her carrot seeds. By that time of year, the flies were gone, so they never bothered her crop!

## KEEP 'EM IN LINE

We used to grow all of our test-garden crops in long, narrow rows, but we gradually switched to wide rows or blocks to make better use of our garden space. One exception is our carrot crop—we've found that growing 'em in narrow rows is still the way to go. Why? Trying to thin a bed of carrots takes forever, because you have to allow ample space on all sides of each seedling. But when they're growing in rows, it's a snap to snip out unwanted seedlings in between the ones we want to keep in line!

## THE LONG AND SHORT OF CARROTS

Sure, it's possible to grow gorgeous, long-rooted carrots in your home garden—*if* you're starting with loose, sandy soil, or if you're willing to put lots of effort into creating a deep, rock-free planting area just for them. Well, we don't mind putting work into our garden, but only if it's absolutely necessary—and in this case, it isn't! We simply choose short-rooted varieties, and we get a bumper crop of great-looking carrots every time. So, when you're choosing carrots to grow in your garden, check the seed packet or catalog description for terms like "half long" or "baby"; these are sure to grow just fine in average garden soil. If your soil is really rocky or heavy, consider "ball-type" varieties, such as 'Orbit', 'Parmex', or 'Thumbelina'; they're short enough to grow well even in pots!

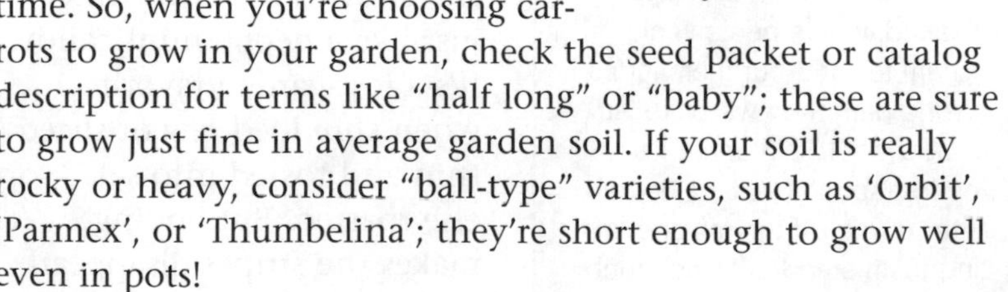

## NO MO' NEMATODES

We get a lot of questions about carrots from our test-garden visitors, and one of the most common concerns is stunted and/or deformed roots. Most often, this is a sign of poor soil preparation; the roots will fork or fail to elongate when they run into an obstruction, like a rock or a clod of heavy clay soil. If you've prepared the soil carefully but are still having bad luck, you probably have a nematode problem. To get rid of these tiny wormlike soil pests, spread 5 pounds of sugar over every 50 square feet of garden area, and work it well into the soil. Then the next spring, overspray the area with a mix of 1 can of beer and 1 cup of molasses in a 20 gallon hose-end sprayer. That should do the trick!

**Q** My carrot patch has been invaded by a bunch of big, black-striped green caterpillars! What can I do to get rid of them before they devour all of the leaves?

**A** Hold on—those caterpillars are actually good guys! Well, it's true that they love to eat carrot greens, but once they mature, they'll turn into beautiful black swallowtail butterflies that will give you hours of pleasurable viewing. Here at the test gardens, we always plant a few extra clumps of parsley or dill just for these caterpillars to feed on. When we spot 'em on our crops, we pick 'em up gently and put them in their special place to feed freely, so we can enjoy the butterflies all summer!

### ASHES ARE THE ANSWER

Fed up with root maggots ruining your early carrot crop? One of our clever test-garden helpers came up with a super solution: Sprinkle wood ashes (or coffee grounds) around your carrots when they are still small. Those vile villains will keep their distance, and your carrot crop will stay blemish-free.

## A SIMPLE TWIST

Has this ever happened to you? You go to pull a carrot out of the ground and end up with nothing but a handful of greens! Well, say goodbye to the frustration of leaving the carrot behind, thanks to this super secret that one of our test-garden old-timers shared with us: After grabbing the leaves, simply push the top of the carrot into the ground a bit, then pull up the root with a twisting motion. Works every time!

## UNDERCOVER CARROTS

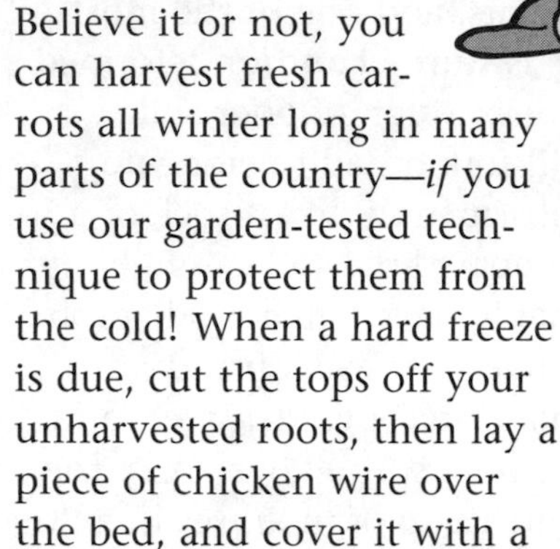

Believe it or not, you can harvest fresh carrots all winter long in many parts of the country—*if* you use our garden-tested technique to protect them from the cold! When a hard freeze is due, cut the tops off your unharvested roots, then lay a piece of chicken wire over the bed, and cover it with a thick layer of straw or dried leaves (about 8 inches deep). When you're ready to harvest, simply lift the covering and dig in! In hard-winter areas, your crop may need extra insulation; we find that setting whole bales of hay or straw on the bed works great.

## THE CARROT-AND-STICK(Y) APPROACH

If carrot rust flies are in a holding pattern around your carrot crop, here's a trick that's sure to catch their attention: Make sticky traps that are yellow-orange, their favorite color. Just glue yellow-orange construction paper to both sides of wooden boards or pieces of heavy cardboard, and attach each board to a wooden stake. Then coat the paper with petroleum jelly, or spray it with Tanglefoot®, and stick your traps into the soil around your carrot plants. The flies will flit over to investigate, and that'll be the end of their egg-laying careers!

## PICK 'EM QUICK

The longer carrots stay in the ground, the more prone they are to attack by root crop nasties like carrot weevils. So pull up those roots as soon as you think they're big enough to eat. You'll be fending off the weevil woes, and getting your carrot crop at its tastiest, too!

### Kitchen CLASSICS

Here's a super-simple recipe for last-minute pasta salad: Cook 1 pound of a medium-sized pasta (such as shells or penne) according to package directions, then drain in a colander and run under cold water for a few minutes. Transfer the pasta to a large bowl, then add 1/2 cup of grated carrot, 1 chopped bell pepper, 2 large chopped tomatoes, and 4 ounces of cubed, part-skim mozzarella cheese. Pour on one 8-ounce bottle of low-fat salad dressing (we like Italian or vinaigrette), toss well, and refrigerate until ready to eat.

## THINK BIG

When you gather your garlic crop, you probably put aside the biggest and best cloves for cooking and save the rest for replanting. But if you really want the best possible harvest each year, you need to change your ways! After years of trials at our test gardens, we've found that we get consistently higher yields when we replant the *largest* cloves and keep the rest for the kitchen. The patches where we replanted smaller cloves also produced smaller cloves, so the harvest was pretty disappointing, and it got worse year after year. So take our word for it: Planting the best cloves to grow is the way to go!

## GO FOR THE GREENS

One year, we forgot to harvest one patch of hardneck garlic in our test garden—so imagine our surprise when we noticed dense clumps of bright green leaves growing there late that fall. We decided to let them grow, and boy, are we glad we did! Ten years later, that patch still supplies us with all of the great-tasting garlic greens we can use. Every four or five years, we divide some of the largest clumps; but otherwise, we just leave 'em alone, except to snip the leaves as we need them. We enjoy the greens in soups, salads, and stir-fry—basically anywhere we'd use regular garlic—but our favorite use for them is as a substitute for basil in pesto recipes. You haven't lived until you've tasted garlic pesto!

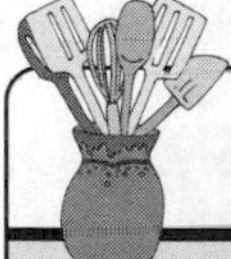

### Kitchen CLASSICS

Looking for a way to pep up a plain pork roast? We *love* this great marinade, and it couldn't be easier to make: Just mix 2 cloves of crushed garlic with 1/2 cup of orange juice, 2 tablespoons of lemon juice, and 1 teaspoon of dried oregano in a large bowl; then add your pork and let it marinate for at least 30 minutes before cooking. (Discard marinade after use.) You won't believe the flavor!

### JERRY'S Q&A

**Q** I need some serious help growing garlic! All I've gotten so far is small bulbs in the ground, with tops like golf balls on the stems.

**A** Dig a hole about a foot across and a foot deep, and fill it with a mixture of 1/3 soil, 1/3 professional potting soil, and 1/3 builder's sand. Plant your garlic in it, and that should do the trick!

Even long-season leeks don't store well out of the ground, so do what we do, and leave 'em until you need 'em! They can stay right in the soil all winter if temperatures stay above 10°F. Need the bed for another crop? Dig 'em up and replant in another spot. Either way, you can enjoy these garden-fresh veggies for months!

## SLOW'S THE WAY TO GO

Having trouble keeping leeks in storage? Maybe you're growing the wrong kind! Short-season leeks, like 'King Richard', grow relatively quickly, so they're great for summer harvesting, but their thinner stems are best used within a few days of harvesting. What you want is a slower-growing, long-season variety, such as 'Alaska' or 'American Flag'; these have thick, cylindrical stems that we find last a whole lot longer!

## KEEP 'EM CLOSE

Compared to most veggie crops, leeks take a long time to mature—but that doesn't mean you have to give up a harvest from that space in the meantime! Instead of setting out our transplants at the recommended 6-inch spacings, we place them just 3 inches apart. Then, when the bases of the plants are about as thick as our pinkie finger, we pull out every other one and enjoy them as scallions. That leaves plenty of space for the remaining leeks to mature—and we get a bonus harvest from the same amount of space!

### GROW IT AGAIN, SAM!

Believe it or not, you can get two harvests from a single leek! As you're preparing your harvested leeks for cooking, slice off the roots with about 3/4 inch of stem, then replant those rooted stem pieces in your garden. Water them well, and they'll produce another whole crop for harvesting!

## SQUEAKY CLEAN LEEKS

Why don't more gardeners grow leeks? We often ask our test-garden visitors that very question, and usually, the answer is that they don't want to bother with the time-consuming trenching or hilling that's recommended for producing the long, white roots. Well, we put our minds to the problem, and we came up with a perfect solution—no digging required! When the leek stems are about 1-inch across, we slip a cardboard cylinder (from the center of a paper towel roll) over each plant by bunching up the leaves with one hand, and sliding the cylinder down over them with the other. Besides producing trouble-free blanching in just one step, it eliminates the chance of soil getting in between the leaf joints, so no more gritty leeks to eat!

### Veggie Power Powder

Think of this powder as comfort food for your garden—kind of like mashed potatoes or macaroni and cheese, only for your soil and all the plants that grow there!

**25 lb. of organic garden food**
**5 lb. of gypsum**
**2 lb. of diatomaceous earth**
**1 lb. of sugar**

Mix these ingredients in a wheelbarrow, and put them into a broadcast spreader. Set the spreader on medium, and apply the mixture over the top of your garden in early spring. Work it into your soil, and then overspray the prepared beds and rows with my Spring Soil Energizer tonic (see page 185). By the time your seeds and seedlings are ready to plant a couple of weeks later, your soil will be rich and mellow, and begging to be filled with great things to eat!

## RINSE AND REAP THE REWARD

Chopped leeks are a great substitute for onions in recipes. If you haven't yet followed our advice and used cardboard cylinders around your plants (see "Squeaky Clean Leeks" above), you're probably going to find soil between the leaves of your harvested leeks when you're getting ready to prepare them. Well, don't spend your time washing off every leaf. Instead, simply chop up the amount of leeks you need, put them in a colander, and rinse well with cool water. That'll clean 'em up quick, and they'll be ready for use in your favorite recipe.

## TREAT 'EM NICE

We're covering onions here in the root crops chapter, because most folks think of them that way. But we've found that onions grow a whole lot better when you treat 'em like leafy crops. Sure, good soil preparation is still very important; but whereas most root crops don't need much water or nutrients, onions really thrive when they get ample supplies of both. So if you've been having disappointing onion harvests, rethink their place in your garden: Try them in well-dug, compost-enriched soil, and keep the water coming during dry spells.

### Test Garden SECRET

If you notice a lot of little flies buzzing around your onions, don't head for your flyswatter; head for your fireplace instead! Gather up some of the wood ashes, then sprinkle them around the base of your onion plants. We've found that this simple garden-tested trick does a good job discouraging the flies from laying their eggs near our onions. This same trick works great against cabbage root maggots, too!

## ALL THE LIVELONG DAY

We know that folks get really confused about the whole "short day/long day" issue when it comes to onions. It's critical to understand the difference, so we're here to shed some light on the subject! Basically, the number of hours of daylight affects how most onion varieties form their bulbs. So if you plant a "long-day" variety down south, your onions may not form bulbs at all, and if you use a "short-day" variety in the north, you may get only tiny bulbs instead of the whoppers you were wishing for. So, whether you're buying seeds, sets, or starts, make sure you are getting a "long-day" variety in the north (where the days are longer in summer) and a "short-day" variety in the south. And if your supplier doesn't know *which* kind of onions they are selling, shop somewhere else!

### NECK AND NECK

If you spot any thick-necked onions as you harvest, set these aside for immediate use (within the next week or two). We've found that these oddballs don't keep well for very long, no matter how carefully we store 'em!

## ISN'T THAT SWEET?

If you've always started your onions from sets, you've never really experienced the great flavor that home-grown onions have to offer. How's that? Sets are available only for the most pungent varieties, so they always produce strong-flavored bulbs. We've found that starting from seed is definitely worth the little extra effort, because that gives us a much wider selection of varieties to choose from—including the classic sweet types that are so great for sandwiches and salads. As a compromise, consider looking for already-started transplants; the selection is not as great as for seeds, but you can set 'em right out in the garden as soon as you get 'em!

## AWESOME ONIONS—1, 2, 3!

Growing onions for storage isn't as simple as just digging up the bulbs and tossing them into a sack for the winter. To get the longest possible storage life—*and* the best overall quality from those bulbs—try this three-step process that we've fine-tuned over the years!

**Step 1.** Once the tops start drooping a bit, stop watering; it's time for the leaves to start turning yellow. To hurry this along, take a spade and insert it at an angle along the row to cut the roots about 2 inches below each bulb.

**Step 2.** When the tops are yellow, pull up the onions and cut off the tops about an inch above the bulbs.

**Step 3.** Lay the bulbs on the soil for a few hours to cure in the sun, then move them to a dry, airy place out of strong sun for a week or so. Store your cured onions in a dark, cool place (just above 32°F), and enjoy 'em all winter long!

### Lethal Weapon Tonic

Garlic and onions are definitely double-duty crops—besides tasting great, they also provide the key ingredients for a perfect pest-fighting spray!

**3 tbsp. of garlic-and-onion juice***
**3 tbsp. of skim milk**
**2 tbsp. of baby shampoo**
**1 tsp. of hot sauce**
**1 gal. of water**

Mix these ingredients together in a bucket, and pour into a 20 gallon hose-end sprayer. Spray on your vegetables every 10 days to prevent aphid problems.

*Make garlic-and-onion juice by chopping 2 cloves of garlic and 2 medium onions. Blend in a blender with 3 cups of water, then strain and use the remaining liquid.

**Q** I've been trying to grow sweet onions for years, and I'm about ready to give up! Every spring, I plant varieties that the catalogs claim are super-sweet, but when I harvest them, the taste is still very strong. Is it something I'm doing, or are they sending me the wrong seeds?

**A** I'll bet my bottom dollar that the problem is in your soil! You see, the strong flavor in onions comes from sulfur, and in acid soil, there's lots of sulfur available. But if you raise the pH, there won't be so much sulfur for the roots to absorb, so the bulbs will have their true sweetness. Have your soil tested (or do it yourself), then add enough lime to raise the pH to 6.5 before you try again. Then you'll be crying with joy instead of from the fumes of your pungent onions!

## WINTER GREENS

Want to enjoy fresh onion greens all year-round? Here's a quirky little trick one of our test-garden crew came up with, and we all enjoy it at home: Set an onion bulb on top of an open jar, and add enough water to barely reach the bottom of the bulb. (You want the mouth of the jar to be wide enough so the onion can nestle into it a bit, but not so big that the onion will fall in.) Set the jar in a sunny window, and keep adding water as needed; pretty soon, new roots will grow from the base and greens will grow from the top. Snip the greens as needed for use in salads or cooking. Once that bulb stops producing, toss it in your compost pile, and start over with a new bulb to enjoy another crop of tasty greens!

## SPREAD 'EM

Did you know that the spacing you choose for your onions at planting time has a big effect on the harvest you end up with? Six-inch spacing is the best if you want the biggest possible bulbs; the downside is that the crop takes up a lot of space this way. In our test gardens, we prefer to plant our seedlings 1 to 2 inches apart. That way, we can pull out some of them to enjoy as scallions through the summer, and still have good-sized onions to dig and store in the fall.

**Test Garden SECRET**

Good air circulation is the best way to avoid storage rots on your onions (garlic, too)—but that's tough to provide when they're piled into a box or sack. Well, we've come up with a great way to provide perfect storage conditions—*and* save space, too! Grab an old pair of pantyhose, drop an onion in the toe, and tie a knot above it; add another onion, tie a knot above it, and so on, until the leg is filled. Hang this leggin' in a cool, dry place. Then, when you need an onion, simply cut below the knot. What a great way to store an abundance of onions!

## YOU SAY POTATO, WE SAY WOW!

While we think the flavor of homegrown produce is superior for just about every vegetable, sometimes it's just not practical to rely on your own garden for all of your needs. Potatoes are a good example of this—at least the traditional white potatoes that are a staple in so many kitchens; it takes about 3 feet of row to produce just 10 pounds of potatoes. Instead of trying to grow all the ordinary potatoes we'd need for the whole winter, we prefer to save our garden space to experiment with special varieties not commonly available in stores. We've tried dozens over the years, but three have emerged as clear favorites with our test-garden crew. Why not try them yourself, and see what all the fuss is about?

**'All Blue'.** For something completely different, 'All Blue' can't be beat! With deep blue skin and lavender-blue flesh, this oddball is a beauty in potato salad and amazing for fries.

**'Rose Finn Apple'.** We can't decide what we like better about this variety: its color (pink on the outside and yellow on the inside) or its long, fingerlike shape, which makes it super-easy to slice! Boiled, baked, grilled, or fried, it's a winner!

**'Yukon Gold'.** With yellow skin and buttery yellow flesh, 'Yukon Gold' is a super all-around variety. It's a special favorite with those who like their fries golden brown, since they start out that color!

### Must-Have Mustard Tonic

No potato beetle worth her stripes will lay eggs in your vegetable garden if you spray your plants with this tea. It works like a charm for repelling cabbage loopers, too!

**4 whole cloves**
**1 handful of wild mustard leaves**
**1 clove of garlic**
**1 cup of boiling water**

Steep these ingredients in a bowl for 10 minutes. Let the elixir cool, then strain out the solids. Pour the liquid into a hand-held sprayer, and spray the plants thoroughly. Repeat after a rain to keep the repellent action fresh.

# TERRIFIC TUBERS THE NO-DIG WAY!

The secret to raising potatoes the easy way is understanding how they grow—and then helping them along with the least possible effort on your part! The plants produce their tasty tubers along the buried parts of their stems, so the trick is to cover a good amount of the stem without burying the whole plant. The traditional way to do this is to plant the potatoes in a trench, then fill it in with soil as the sprouts grow, continuing to "hill" more soil around the stems as they elongate. Well, as far as we're concerned, that's just *way* too much work!

So now, we simply place our potato sets right on top of the ground. Every week or so, as the sprouts grow, we add enough chopped leaves or clean straw to cover the tops about halfway (if they've grown 4 inches over the last layer, for instance, we add 2 more inches of mulch). Surrounding the patch with a ring of low wire fencing helps keep the thick mulch layer in place. Besides completely eliminating digging and hilling, the mulch method makes harvesting new potatoes a snap; we can reach in and harvest clean, young tubers anytime.

## TRIED-AND-TRUE

**T**o help your sweet potato slips shake off the stress of transplanting, try this garden-tested trick that Grandma Putt swore by: Dip the roots of each one into a pan of muddy water just before planting. This protects the roots with a coating that prevents them from drying out while being handled, and it also ensures direct contact with the soil once they're planted.

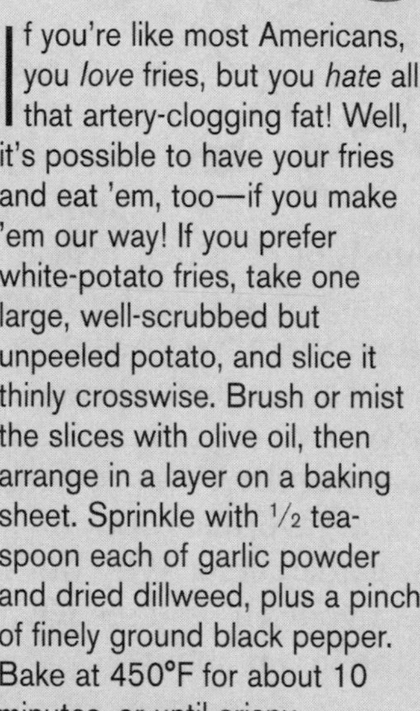

## Kitchen CLASSICS

If you're like most Americans, you *love* fries, but you *hate* all that artery-clogging fat! Well, it's possible to have your fries and eat 'em, too—if you make 'em our way! If you prefer white-potato fries, take one large, well-scrubbed but unpeeled potato, and slice it thinly crosswise. Brush or mist the slices with olive oil, then arrange in a layer on a baking sheet. Sprinkle with 1/2 teaspoon each of garlic powder and dried dillweed, plus a pinch of finely ground black pepper. Bake at 450°F for about 10 minutes, or until crispy.

Rather try something really different? We're crazy about sweet potato fries! Take four clean but unpeeled sweet potatoes, cut 'em in half and then into long wedges, and place on baking sheets treated with cooking spray. Mist the wedges with additional cooking spray, then sprinkle with 1 teaspoon of ground cinnamon, 1/2 teaspoon each of ground nutmeg and ground black pepper, and 1/4 teaspoon of kosher salt. Bake at 425°F for 30 to 40 minutes, or until brown and soft, turning once. Try serving them with applesauce for dipping—delicious!

## DOUBLE THE FUN

We may think of potatoes as only a summer crop, but you folks in mild areas can get *two* crops of spuds! Make your first planting in late winter (make sure the soil is at least 40°F) for a late-spring to early-summer harvest. Then, plant again in late summer (about 12 weeks before average date of your first fall frost) to enjoy a second crop. Be sure to plant the second crop in a different spot than the first, to reduce the chance of soil-borne diseases spoiling your harvest!

## SLIPPING AWAY

Sure, you can buy sweet potato "slips," but why not grow your own? It's a snap to do, and a real hit with the young folks! Simply plant a sweet potato tuber in moist sand four to six weeks before outdoor planting time and keep it in your kitchen or another warm room (around 75°F is ideal). Once the sprouts are about 6 inches tall, with four to six leaf joints and some roots, pull or snip them off about ½ inch above the tuber (but below the roots). Plant 'em outdoors about two weeks after your last frost date to get your plants off to a great jump start!

## VINES ON THE MOVE

If you don't think you have the space for sweet potatoes, you'll love this trick we learned from one of our test-garden helpers: Grow 'em in an old wheelbarrow! Make sure there are a few holes in the bottom for drainage, then fill it with potting soil, plant your slips, and set it out in the sun. The leafy vines of this morning glory relative look pretty trailing over the side all summer, and they are very forgiving if you forget to water every now and then. In fall, harvesting couldn't be easier: Just roll the wheelbarrow to your back porch and reach in to find those tasty tubers!

### From Our Readers

*I've raised sweet potatoes for a good many years, and I've found that when the vines root where they touch the ground, they don't produce much of a harvest. So now, when the plants start spreading, I put two layers of newspaper between the vines and the ground so they can't root themselves there. (You might have to put some rocks on the paper to hold it in place the first time you put the paper down.) This ensures that the plants root only at one spot, and you'll get a much better yield that way!*

Genevieve B.,
Scales Mound, IL

**Kitchen CLASSICS**

When we have one of our popular Friday-lunch picnics at our test gardens, we always make sure someone brings along this terrific pasta salad, packed with just-picked ingredients! It's easy to make: Simply cook 1/2 pound of medium pasta shells according to package directions, then drain well and rinse with cold water. Transfer to a large bowl, then add 2 cups of chopped romaine lettuce, 1 cup of thinly sliced red radishes, and 1/4 cup of chopped fresh basil. Top that with 4 ounces of diced Asiago (or aged cheddar) cheese and 1/2 cup of olive oil vinaigrette dressing, then mix, cover, and chill for 1 hour before serving. This makes enough for six delicious servings.

## THE EARLY BIRD BEATS THE WORMS

Radishes grow so quickly, bad bugs hardly have time to find 'em! The only serious pest problem we've had with this crop in our test gardens is root maggots, which tunnel through and spoil the radishes. Fortunately we've found the solution: timing our planting so the roots are ready to pull by June 1. If we're using a variety that matures in 25 days, for instance, we'll count back four weeks (25 days plus a few extra to allow for the harvesting period), then sow no later than May 1. Try this trick yourself, and you'll never have to deal with maggoty radishes again!

## KEEP YOUR COOL

When you bite into your radishes, do they bite back? If you have trouble with your crop getting too "hot" or too pithy by harvest time, try these three garden-tested tips:

**Keep the water comin'.** Evenly moist soil is a must for sweet, crispy radishes!

**Give 'em a sunscreen.** Help your crop keep its cool by providing midday shade. (We do this by planting our radishes on the north side of our pea trellises.)

**Pile on the mulch.** You don't want to cover the plants themselves, of course—just the bare soil. That'll help keep the moisture *in* and the hot sun *out,* so your radishes will retain tip-top flavor.

## FALL INTO RADISHES

We've always thought of radishes as a quick-and-easy spring crop, but guess what—they're great in fall, too! So, whenever we're left with an empty space after harvesting a summer crop, such as bush beans, we scatter a few pinches of radish seeds to get an additional harvest from that spot. Besides the usual fast-growing varieties, we also enjoy a special one called 'China Rose', with long, oddly shaped, mild-flavored roots. It takes longer to mature (about 55 days), but it also lasts well in storage after a late fall harvest—perfect for perking up winter salads!

## QUICK FIXIN'S

Here's a dandy tip that'll have you munching on fresh salad even as the snow flies: Grow your radishes indoors! Plant radish seeds 1/4 inch deep and 1 inch apart in a 9 × 12-inch cake pan filled with soil. Scatter lettuce seeds on the surface of the soil in another cake pan, and cover with 1/8 inch of soil. Set both pans in a sunny windowsill and keep the soil damp. The plants will be ready for your salad bowl in just 8 to 10 weeks, and you can enjoy fresh-picked salad fixin's even in the dead of winter!

## RAPID RADISHES

Here's a trick some of our longtime test gardeners swear by for getting radishes off to a super-speedy start. Before planting, soak radish seeds in water for 24 hours. Then put them in a brown paper bag and set the bag in the sun. Within a day, the seeds will sprout, and they'll be ready to get in the ground and get growing.

### From Our Readers

*Don't sow your whole packet of radish seeds at once—you'll have a whole bunch of radishes all at one time. Instead, sow 1/4 of the packet every 10 days for a longer harvest.*

Hellen K.,
Rutland, VT

## TERRIFIC TURNIP TIPS

If you've only ever eaten turnips from the grocery store, you simply haven't lived! Those tough, flabby roots are nothing compared to the crisp crunch of turnips fresh from your own garden. We've found that the secret to top-quality turnips is simple: Keep 'em cool! When temperatures are over 75°F, turnip roots are sure to turn bitter and woody. For an early-summer crop, plant as soon as you can work the soil in spring. (Sometimes we even prepare the beds in fall so they're all ready to go for the early spring sowing.) And for a fall crop—which often tastes even better, thanks to the cooler weather—sow about two months before the average date of your first fall frost. Trust us—this'll ensure that you get top-notch turnips!

**JERRY'S Q&A**

**Q** My turnip crop grew big, beautiful roots last year, but they sure didn't taste as good as they looked. How can I stop this from happening again?

**A** When it comes to turnips, bigger *isn't* better! If you're tired of tough turnips, try harvesting earlier—when the roots are larger than a golf ball but smaller than a tennis ball. You'll enjoy these smaller roots a whole lot more!

## QUALITY CONTROL

Having trouble producing turnips that look as good as those shown on the seed packet? Careful soil preparation is the key to growing picture-perfect roots every time. In regular ground-level beds, you'll want to dig the soil 10 to 12 inches deep, and make sure that you've removed all of the rocks, sticks, and hard clods you can find. We prefer to grow our turnip crop in raised beds, because we know the soil there is already deeply dug and rock-free, so we have a lot less work to do at planting time! If your soil is *really* rocky, then try your turnips aboveground—grow 'em in containers! We've discovered that small-rooted turnips, such as 'Market Express' and 'Tokyo Cross', can grow great crops in a container as small as 1 foot wide and 1 foot deep!

## TURNIPS ARE TOPS!

Did you know that turnip tops make tasty greens, too? One way to enjoy them is to use the small plants you remove when you thin your root crop. (Root turnips need room to spread out a bit, so we thin ours to stand 2 to 4 inches apart when they are 4 inches tall). You can also pick a few leaves off the tops of your growing root crop; just don't take too many, or the roots will suffer. If you *really* love these sweet leaves, you're better off with a variety grown just for its leaves (we like 'Shogoin'), then snip the plants down to 1 inch when they get 4 to 6 inches tall. They will resprout, so you can get two or three harvests from just one sowing!

### Test Garden SECRET

If aphids torment your turnips (or any other crop) year after year, do what we do: Plant some hairy vetch next to your veggies! To a ladybug, a big patch of hairy vetch is palatial living quarters, and a ladybug's idea of a four-star restaurant is a plant full of aphids. It's a simple equation: More ladybugs = fewer aphids!

## TUNNEL TROUBLE

If your turnips (and other root crops) are looking a bit out of place, like they're being pulled from below, they probably are—and the culprits are gophers. These toothsome troublemakers love nothing more than to chow down on root crops by munching on them from belowground, where they travel safely out of sight. Short of erecting barriers that reach at least 18 inches underground, your next best bet is to mix up a batch of Gopher-Go Tonic (at right) and dribble it into all of the places where you suspect that gophers are carrying on.

MIX IT UP!

### Gopher-Go Tonic

We've had amazing results with this tonic, so give it a try.

**4 tbsp. of castor oil**
**4 tbsp. of dishwashing liquid**
**4 tbsp. of urine**
**1/2 cup of warm water**

Combine these ingredients, then stir the mix into 2 gallons of warm water. Pour the tonic over any areas where gophers gather, and they'll soon be gone!

MORE TIPS

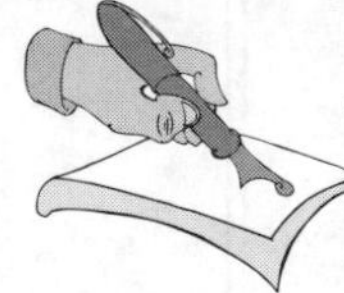

# From Our Readers

## CARROT WEEDING CONTROL

If you have trouble weeding your carrots, next season, just lay two 1 × 4-inch boards side-by-side over the area where you want to plant your carrot row. When you are ready to sow, separate the boards, sow the seeds, and close the boards back over the row. When the seeds sprout, separate the boards just enough for the seedlings to grow in between. The boards will prevent weeds from growing.

***Gerald M., Mascoutah, IL***

## BEET BONANZA

Fresh-from-the-garden beets are my favorite vegetable of all, so I've found a way to extend the season. I harvest all of my beets just before the first frost, and store them in a box of sand in my basement. They stay fresh and crisp all winter long, so I have crisp, sweet beets for months!

***Michael F., Quincy, IL***

## LAZY ONIONS

If you have a hammock, you can store onions in it. Just load it up with your onions and throw a blanket over the hammock at night to keep the dew off. If it's about to rain, put a sheet of plastic over the hammock. When the onions are dry, bring the hammock inside and hang it from the rafters in your basement, garage, or attic. The air will continue to circulate through the onions, and keep them firm for use all winter long.

***Tony L., Mount Pleasant, MI***

## RUB-A-DUB-DUB

Here's a tip I've been using for a long time. When I need to scrub dirty carrots or potatoes, I wash them in the sink using a plain stainless-steel scrubbing pad. Using this method, I can get off all the dirt on the vegetable's skin, and I don't need a separate vegetable brush.

***Valerie N., Buffalo, NY***

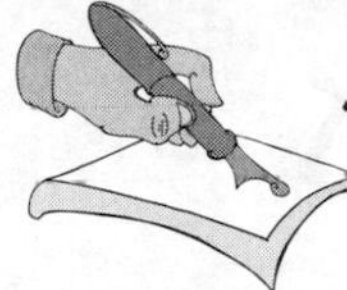

# From Our Readers

## ELIMINATE ONION TEARS

Rub your dry hands on a stainless steel sink before you peel onions, and you won't be crying over those slices.

*Sue E., Commerce, MI*

## RADISH REGIMEN

I never liked planting radishes because I always got them too close together and lost a lot because I had to thin them out. So, now I use five sheets of toilet paper, some flour, and a ¼-inch wire screen for sifting soil (12 inches by 12 inches). I take ½ teaspoon of flour, put it in a saucer, and add enough water to make a paste. I then sprinkle radish seeds in it. Using tweezers, I remove each seed and put it on the toilet paper, with four seeds to a row, 1 inch apart. I stagger the rows and get five rows on one sheet. They will dry and stick to the toilet paper. Set the paper aside until ready to plant. Prepare the rows, lay down the toilet paper on the ground, shovel soil on your screen sieve, and shake until the toilet paper is covered.

*Joseph M., Morris, PA*

## BANISH BEETLES

To get rid of potato beetles, fill a jar with garden lime, poke some holes in the jar lid, and replace the lid. Then use it as a sprinkler to apply lime to potatoes or other nightshade-family plants. Repeat every two weeks, or anytime after a rain.

*Alan E., Harrisonburg, VA*

## ROOT-MAGGOT MAGIC

When planting your radishes, crush some bran cereal and put it in the planting holes. Then sprinkle more around your radish plants. It'll keep root maggots away.

*George D., Phelps, KY*

## MIX 'EM UP

When planting your vegetable garden, mix radish seeds in with your carrot seeds to mark the rows. Radishes sprout faster than carrots, so you will know where you planted your carrots before they come up.

*Mike F., Beverly Hills, MI*

# TEST GARDEN GOODIES

## LOVELY POTATO SOUP

2 cups of sweet Vidalia onions, diced
1/2 cup of de-strung, grated celery
1 tbsp. of butter
1/2 tsp. of powdered ginger
4 cups of Idaho potatoes, peeled, rinsed in salt water, and coarsely diced
3 cups of hot water
2 tsp. of salt
1 cup of hot milk
1/2 tsp. of white pepper
1/2 tsp. of ginger
2 oz. of softened cream cheese
Fresh chives for garnish

In a 6-quart nonmetallic saucepan, combine the onions, celery, butter, and ginger. Cover and cook until soft, stirring as needed. Then add the potatoes and stir to combine. Add the hot water and salt, cover the pan, and cook over medium heat until the potatoes are soft but not mushy. Stir several times during cooking. Take the pan off the heat and stir in the hot milk, pepper, ginger, and cream cheese until blended. Ladle into serving bowls and garnish with the chives.

*Helen S., Hershey, PA*

## PEACHY KEEN SWEET POTATOES

1 qt. of canned peaches
2 lbs. of cooked sweet potatoes or yams
1/4 cup of butter
2 tsp. of orange peel
1/2 cup of brown sugar, packed
2 tsp. of brandy extract
3/4 cup of raisins
1 tsp. of salt
1/4 cup of chopped pecans

Drain the peaches, reserving 1/2 cup of the juice. Slice the peaches and place in the bottom of a flat casserole. In a large bowl, mash the sweet potatoes, then mix the butter, 1/4 cup of the brown sugar, the 1/2 cup of peach juice, brandy extract, raisins, and salt into the sweet potatoes. Spoon the sweet potato mixture over the peaches. Sprinkle the top with the remaining 1/4 cup of brown sugar and the chopped pecans. Bake at 375°F for 15 to 20 minutes, and serve.

*Ruth F., Centre Hall, PA*

## BAKED ONIONS

**1 medium white onion (per person)**
**1 beef bouillon cube**
**Salt and black pepper to taste**
**Butter**

Remove the outer skin from the onion and cut a small core out of the onion's top. Then place the onion on a square of aluminum foil that's large enough to wrap the onion completely. Place the bouillon cube in the hollowed-out onion core and add salt and pepper, if desired. Top with a pat of butter, then seal the onion in the foil. Bake at 350°F for 1 hour.

*Violette W., Lynchburg, VA*

## HARVARD BEETS

**1/2 cup of sugar**
**1 tbsp. of cornstarch**
**1/2 cup of vinegar**
**1/2 cup of water**
**2 cups of diced beets**
**Butter**
**Salt and black pepper to taste**

Mix the sugar, cornstarch, vinegar, and water. Cook until thick; add the beets, and heat through. Remove from the heat and add a small lump of butter, salt, and pepper.

*Agnes W., Marshalltown, IA*

## SWEET POTATO NUT BREAD

**1 cup of butter**
**1 1/2 cups of white sugar**
**1/4 cup of brown sugar**
**4 eggs**
**2 1/2 cups of cooked, mashed sweet potatoes**
**3 cups of flour**
**1 1/2 tsp. of cinnamon**
**1/4 tsp. of nutmeg**
**2 tsp. of baking powder**
**1 tsp. of salt**
**1/2 cup of chopped nuts**
**Raisins (optional)**

Cream together the butter and sugars. Add the eggs and sweet potatoes, then add the flour, cinnamon, nutmeg, baking powder, salt, and nuts. Mix well. Divide the batter between two greased loaf pans, and bake at 350°F for 55 minutes. Test with a toothpick for doneness.

*Lorraine J., New Carlisle, IN*

# Chapter 12

# Classic Veggie Crops

Of all the crops we grow here in our test gardens, this group of fruiting and seed-bearing veggies has to be our favorite—and we're not alone! The rich tang of vine-ripened tomatoes, the succulent sweetness of sun-warmed watermelons, and the cool snap of fresh-picked peas are just a few of the fantastic flavors treasured by folks all over the country. We've rounded up some of our favorite garden-tested tips and tricks to help you grow the best crops you've ever had—with less work than you would've ever thought possible!

## SOW SMART

Garden-fresh green beans are one of the easiest summer crops you can grow—and they're plenty productive, too! Don't expect them to keep you supplied with beans all summer, though: Bush beans produce well for only two to three weeks once the plants mature. To keep 'em coming for months, do what we do—separate your seeds into two or three batches, then sow the batches two to three weeks apart. As one batch finishes, the next will be ripe for picking!

## SHAKE, RATTLE, AND GROW

Most folks think of bacteria as bad guys, but when it comes to beans, bacteria actually do your plants a big favor! There is a certain type of "nitrogen-fixing" bacteria living on the roots of beans (peas, too), which help supply their host plants with growth-boosting nitrogen. If you've been growing beans for a while, these bacteria are already in your soil, so you don't need to do anything special. But if you're planting beans for the first time, or if you're sowing in a bed where you've never had beans before, we think it's smart to add them. It's easy to do—simply buy some "inoculant" powder (available from garden centers and mail-order seed companies). To treat your seeds, pour some of the powder into a small paper bag, add your seeds, and shake away! Plant as usual, and your beans will grow like gangbusters with their beneficial bacterial buddies.

### Test Garden SECRET

If there's one thing beans hate, it's cold feet! We've learned that there's no point trying to rush the bean-planting season, because these summer-lovers simply won't sprout unless the ground is warm enough—at *least* 60°F, and ideally around 80°F. We don't worry about measuring the exact temperature, though, because the answer is right under our feet. If it's warm enough to walk outdoors while barefoot, we know it's warm enough to sow our bean seeds!

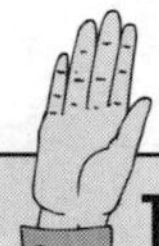

## Tried-and-True

When I was a boy, I spent much of my summer picking beans for Grandma Putt. Maybe that's why, unlike most young folks my age, I actually wished for rainy days! You see, Grandma knew that working around wet bean plants was a surefire way to spread rust and other diseases among the plants, and that could quickly wipe out the rest of the harvest. So until everything was completely dry, Grandma's bean patch was strictly off limits—and I was free to go have fun!

## BEAN THERE, DONE THAT?

Part of our mission here at the test gardens is to share all of the great tips and tricks we've come up with over the years—and another part is to get folks excited about out-of-the-ordinary options we've discovered for traditional garden crops! So if you enjoy growing beans but are looking for something a little different to try, here are three fun *and* flavorful alternatives to plain old pole beans:

**Hyacinth bean.** This climber is as pretty as it is productive, with green or purple leaves and showy clusters of purplish pink flowers. But the real thrill is its amazing pods, which are a glowing, can't-miss magenta color! You can harvest this versatile beauty as a snap bean (pod and all) when young, wait a little while to harvest as shell beans (fresh from the plant, with the pod removed), or simply let 'em dry on the vine.

**Runner beans.** A classic ornamental climber, runner beans can supply a generous harvest as well! Enjoy the eye-catching clusters of scarlet flowers as they bloom, then pick the pods, either fresh or dried, for a tasty treat. We especially like the cultivar 'Sun Bright', which has bright yellow leaves that make a beautiful backdrop for the fabulous flowers.

**Yard-long bean.** Yep, believe it or not, this vigorous vining bean can produce pods as much as 3 feet long! We like to pick 'em younger, though—at about 1 foot—to get the best flavor for fresh use. Try growing yard-long beans on an arbor to create a curtain-like entrance to your veggie patch.

## GROW UP!

What's the secret to enjoying a generous bean harvest for more than twice as long as you get from classic bush beans? It's simple—grow up! Pole beans take a little longer to start producing (60 to 70 days, as opposed to about 50 days for bush beans), but they'll keep going up until the first frost. That means you get at least double the harvest from just one planting. As a bonus, pole beans are a whole lot easier to pick than bush types, too—no stooping required!

## BEAT THE BEETLES

When we come to our bean patch during tours of our test gardens, we can be sure at least one visitor will ask us what to do about Mexican bean beetles. These nasty nogoodniks look a little like ladybugs, but the resemblance stops there. Unlike ladybugs, which help us out by eating bad bugs, Mexican bean beetles can quickly devour the leaves of an entire planting, leaving behind only lacy leaf veins, and weakened plants that usually don't recover.

We've tried various strategies, and have come up with a few good options for foiling these pests. If we're depending on a large harvest for canning or freezing, we make our first bean sowing a big one, so we can get the crop picked before the main batch of beetles arrives. For later sowings, we've had good luck with protecting the young plants with floating row cover until they start to flower, then handpicking the orange-shelled, black-spotted adult beetles and their yellowish orange larvae daily. Sure, it's extra work, but we don't have to worry about chemical sprays—and we know the great-tasting harvest is worth it!

## PICK EARLY, AND PICK OFTEN

Timing is everything when it comes to getting the best-tasting beans from your garden. Once they start ripening, bush beans need to be harvested every day or two—simply pinch the beans off by hand. You can get away with harvesting pole beans just once or twice a week, but more frequent picking will help ensure the best yields. Snip the pole bean pods off with scissors to prevent damage to the vines. With both bush and pole beans, we like to judge whether they are prime for picking by the *width* of the pod, not the length—about the thickness of a pencil is just perfect. If you miss any and they get bigger than that, remove them right away; if you let 'em stay on the plant, production will slow down and reduce your yield!

### From Our Readers

*Here's how to make a bean trellis from an old bicycle tire rim: Grab a tire rim that's at least 24 inches in diameter. Set a 6- to 8-foot piece of scrap lumber or pipe as a post into your garden, and attach the rim to the top, lying flat. Then set a short piece of wire fence in a 3-foot-wide circle around the base of the post. Tie long pieces of string or twine to the spokes, close to the tire rim, then fasten the free ends to the wire fence. Plant your bean seeds around the perimeter of the wire fence, and the vines will scramble straight up the strings.*

Gerald M.,
Mascoutah, IL

## IT'S NOT EASY BEING GREEN!

For a plant that needs frequent harvesting, beans sure don't make it easy: Trying to find green pods against the green leaves and stems can be like hunting for a needle in a haystack! We find it's a lot more fun to grow beans with colorful pods, because they make harvesting a breeze instead of a bore. For golden pods, we like 'Gold Mine' (a bush type) and 'Goldfield' (a pole type). 'Royal Burgundy' is a beauty of a purple-podded bush bean; 'Purple Pod' is a classic pole variety. Keep in mind that purple-podded beans will turn green after a few minutes of cooking, but they'll still taste great!

### Kitchen CLASSICS

We love snacking on green beans fresh from the plants—so much so that it's a wonder any of them actually make it to our kitchen! But when we do have a bounty of beans, we enjoy making them into a simple—and simply stunning—side dish. Clean and remove the stems from 3/4 pound of fresh green beans, then boil them in a large pot for 4 to 7 minutes, or until tender, but not mushy. While the beans are cooking, heat 2 tablespoons of extra virgin olive oil in a large skillet over medium heat. Then add 2 cloves of garlic (minced) and sauté for 1 to 2 minutes. Add the beans and 1/2 cup of roasted red peppers, and heat for 2 minutes, tossing frequently. Transfer to a bowl, stir in 2 tablespoons of lemon juice, and serve immediately. This colorful concoction yields four servings.

## MORE BEETLE BUSTERS

If bean beetles bedevil your bean crops year after year, confound the rascals by trying these time-tested tricks:

■ No matter what kinds of beans you grow, plow them under at the end of the season. You'll eliminate the beetles' winter homes and add nitrogen to the soil.

■ Next season, plant beans and potatoes together. The spuds will chase away the bean beetles, while the beans will banish the spuds' arch-enemy, Colorado potato beetles. Now that's what we'd call a dynamic duo!

### Knock-'Em-Dead Insect Tonic

This potent mixture will deal a death blow to squash bugs, bean beetles, and any other foul felons that are after your veggies.

**6 cloves of garlic, finely chopped**
**1 small onion, finely chopped**
**1 tbsp. of cayenne pepper**
**1 tbsp. of dish-washing liquid**
**1 qt. of warm water**

Mix these ingredients in a bucket, and let the mixture sit overnight. Strain out the solids, pour the liquid into a hand-held sprayer, and knock those buggy pests for a loop!

## HAVE A BLOCK PARTY

What's the most common mistake folks make when growing corn? Planting it in rows! Sure, that's the traditional way to do it, and it's fine if you're growing a whole field of corn. But when you're growing just a few dozen plants in a garden, planting in rows can lead to small, poorly developed ears. That's because corn drops its pollen from its tassels down to its ears. When the plants are in a long, narrow row, the wind can blow the pollen away before it reaches the silks.

Planting in blocks—we suggest at least 16 plants (4 rows of 4 plants) per block—greatly improves pollination rates, so you'll enjoy perfect, fully formed ears every time!

## BOWLING FOR BETTER GROWTH

Corn is a thirsty crop, especially at that critical stage from flowering to harvest. So, if you live in a dry climate, or if your weather forecast predicts drought this summer, try this trick we swear by—plant your corn in a bowl! Dig a flat-bottomed circle about 12 inches in diameter and 4 inches below the level of the bed, then

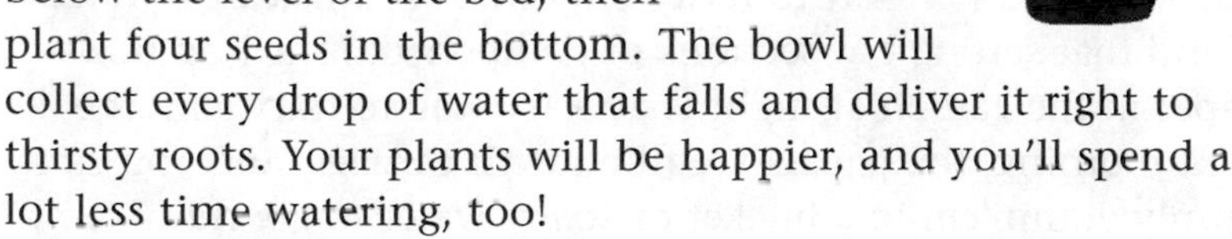

plant four seeds in the bottom. The bowl will collect every drop of water that falls and deliver it right to thirsty roots. Your plants will be happier, and you'll spend a lot less time watering, too!

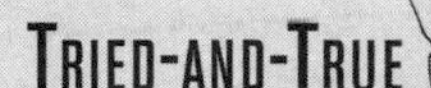

### TRIED-AND-TRUE

**W**hen it comes to getting sweet corn in the ground, haste definitely makes waste! If you sow before the soil is warm enough (it needs to be at least 60°F), the seeds are just as likely to rot as to sprout. Instead, do what Grandma Putt always did—wait until the dogwood trees are in full bloom before you plant your corn. The seeds will sprout up quickly, and as a bonus, you'll stand a good chance of foiling your crop's archenemy, the nasty European corn borer!

Deciding which kind of sweet corn to grow can be as challenging as deciding which car to buy! Varieties with an SU designation have the classic sweet corn flavor, while SE (sugar-enhanced) are—as you might guess—even sweeter, and SH2 varieties are the sweetest of all. Since you obviously want your sweet corn to be...well, *sweet,* you might wonder why anyone would grow anything but SH2 types. We've tried all three types here at the test gardens, and we actually prefer the SU varieties! Besides having a great classic corn flavor, they are a whole lot more forgiving of dry spells and occasional days of cool weather. SH2 varieties also have to be isolated from the other two sweet corn types, as well as from other kinds of corn—and that can make it mighty tough to find a site that'll please them!

## SEPARATE'S THE SECRET

Location isn't just important in real estate—it's critical if you want to get the best out of your sweet corn crop! Be sure to site your sweet corn patch *at least* 25 feet (and ideally 100 feet) from field corn, popcorn, and ornamental corn. Otherwise, they'll cross-pollinate, and your sweet corn will likely be starchy and tough instead of tender and juicy!

## A GRAPE IDEA!

Are pesky birds plucking up your corn seeds as soon as you plant them? Sprinkle grape Kool-Aid® powder, straight from the packet, over the soil where you've seeded. Believe it or not, birds dislike it so much that they'll go elsewhere for lunch!

## PROTECT EARS FROM EARWIGS

Earwigs—long, brownish insects with prominent pincers at their back end—may look nasty, but most times, they're good to have around. They feed on a wide variety of garden pests (including aphids and mites), as well as dead and decaying plant material. Sometimes, though, they can get a little *too* abundant, and then they start making pests of themselves! On corn, they feed on the silks, which then interferes with pollination and leads to misshapen, poorly filled ears. No need to resort to nasty chemicals in this case—we've found that setting out sections of dampened, rolled-up newspaper in the garden at night is an easy way to trap 'em. The next morning, the papers are filled with earwigs, and you can simply dump 'em in a bucket of soapy water to get rid of 'em.

## A LITTLE DAB'LL DO YA

There is nothing more frustrating than heading out to your corn patch expecting to pick some perfect ears, only to find damaged or stripped cobs fit for the compost pile, not the kitchen. Over the years, we've tried all kinds of tricks to keep birds, squirrels, and raccoons from spoiling our corn crop, and we've finally discovered a way that works. As soon as the silks start to wilt and turn brown, slip the toe end of a nylon stocking over each ear of corn, then touch the toe of the stocking with a dab of perfume. One whiff and the thieves will steer clear of your crop—*guaranteed*!

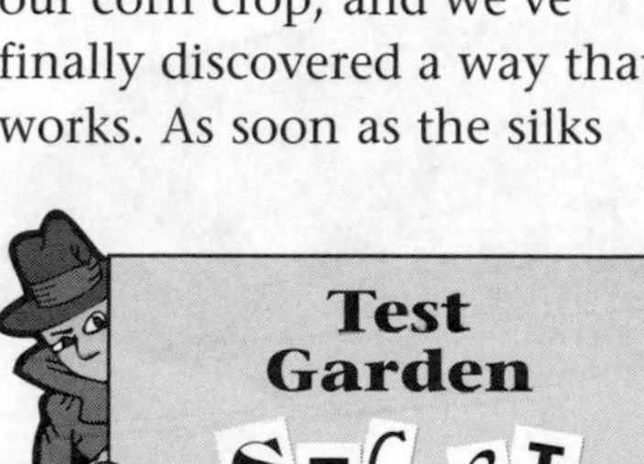


Believe it or not, plain old mineral oil can help protect our corn crop from earworm damage! We apply a drop to the tip of each ear when the silks begin to brown, then repeat the application every five or six days, for a total of three applications per season. This simple solution does a bang-up job of keeping those wicked worms away!

## THE NO-FAIL NAIL TEST

Ask 10 gardeners for the best way to judge the ripeness of sweet corn, and you're likely to get 10 different answers. Here at the test gardens, though, we've found a method we all agree on: Start testing your corn about 15 days after the silk appears. Peel back the husk a couple of inches, and press on a kernel with your fingernail until it pops open. If the juice is milky, the corn is perfect for picking. If it's watery, then give it a few more days. If it's pasty, then you're late, so you'd better get picking right away!

### Vim and Vigor Tonic

Vegetable plants really work up an appetite churning out all that good food for us, and even the most well-balanced diet needs a little kick now and then. So every three weeks during the growing season, feed your garden with our All-Season Green-Up Tonic (see page 69). But for a change of pace, use this tonic once in a while to keep things cookin'.

**1 can of beer**
**1 cup of ammonia**
**4 tbsp. of instant tea granules**
**2 tbsp. of baby shampoo**

Mix these ingredients in a 20 gallon hose-end sprayer, and spray all of your veggies to the point of run-off. It'll turn them into lean, mean, growing machines!

## SILKY SMOOTH

Want to remove silk from your corn quickly and with less mess? Try this trick that one of our test-garden helpers shared with us—rub a damp paper towel along the ear. The silk will cling to the towel, not the corn!

## CHASE THE RAINBOW

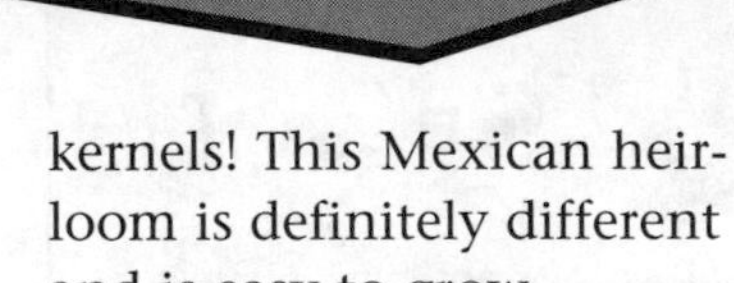

We love looking at our colorful test gardens all through the growing season—so much so that we hate to see the beauty fade after the first frost. That's why we get extra pleasure out of growing crops that can help keep the color coming all through the winter, too! Ornamental corn varieties are some of the best choices for long-lasting beauty—not just in harvest colors for Halloween and Thanksgiving decorating, but also Christmas, Valentine's Day, and even St. Patrick's day! Here are just a few out-of-the-ordinary favorites:

**'Mini Blue'.** Deep blue kernels on 4- to 6-inch-long ears aren't just pretty; they're excellent as popcorn, too.

**'Oaxacan Green'.** Full-sized ears covered in emerald-green kernels! This Mexican heirloom is definitely different and is easy to grow.

**'Red Stalker' (also called 'Seneca Red Stalker').** Large, multicolored ears with bright red husks and stalks. We use the whole plant for holiday decorating.

**'Strawberry'.** Tiny, 2-inch-long ears with deep maroon kernels look like giant strawberries! They make great accents for wreaths, swags, and other decorations. After the holidays, shell the ears and enjoy the kernels as great-tasting popcorn.

### Kitchen CLASSICS

Nothing beats good old corn-on-the-cob—but instead of blasting it with butter, try seasoning it with herb vinaigrette instead. It's a lot more heart-friendly that way! Have an abundance of fresh corn? Cut it off the cob and mix it into a bottle of inexpensive, store-bought salsa for a gourmet taste sensation.

## LET YOUR CUKES GO TO POT

When you consider that cucumbers are nearly 95 percent water, it's hardly surprising that they're one of the thirstiest crops in the veggie garden! To make sure your cukes keep their cool and get the water they need, try this trick that we swear by: Plug the hole of a 6-inch clay flowerpot with a cork or small stick, then sink it into the ground, up to the rim. Plant your cucumber seeds about 2 inches away from the pot, and fill the pot with water daily (twice a day is good in hot, dry weather). The water will gradually seep out of the pot, providing a steady supply of moisture to keep those vigorous vines producing top-quality cukes all summer long.

## SOCIAL CLIMBERS

What's the biggest mistake folks make when growing cucumbers? Trying to get away without a trellis! Trust us—we've tried growing this crop both ways, and the supported plants out-yielded the sprawlers every time. There are lots of other benefits, too:

**Saves space.** A trellised crop takes up just one-fifth of the space of unsupported vines—a big plus in small gardens!

**Discourages disease.** Getting the vines off the ground allows good air circulation around the leaves, stems, and developing fruits, minimizing mildew, rots, and other nasty garden diseases.

**Makes harvesting a breeze.** No more stooping over, stepping on vines, or getting scratched up hunting for ripe cukes, because they're right within easy reach.

**Keeps fruits on the straight and narrow.** Tired of misshapen or curled cukes? When they grow on a trellis, they hang straight, so the fruits are well formed and super easy to slice!

### Test Garden

If you struggle with cucumber beetles every year, you'll *love* this garden-tested secret! Cucumber beetles are drawn to cukes by a bitter compound that most varieties have in their skin. But guess what? Some cucumbers lack this chemical attraction, so the bad beetles tend to steer clear of them! Three varieties we've had great luck with are 'Aria', 'Holland', and 'Jazzer'. But while they aren't attractive to cucumber beetles, they *are* attractive to people; they've given us some of our tastiest harvests ever!

## OH, BOYS!

One of the most common questions we get about cucumbers is why so many of the flowers fall off without producing fruits. No, it's not some horrible disease! Like many other squash-family plants, cucumbers have separate male and female flowers. (You can tell the difference if you look closely. The females have tiny cucumbers just below the bloom, while males don't.) The male flowers start blooming a week or more before the first females open, and they outnumber the females all through the growing season. So don't be alarmed when you see those excess flowers falling—it's only natural!

## SNIP THE TIPS

If you've grown cucumbers before, you've probably noticed that the vines tend to produce more fruits near their tips than at their bases. So, it just makes sense that encouraging the vines to branch gives you more shoot tips—*and* a bigger harvest! We like to pinch off the main tip when a vine has four or five leaves. Instead of one long vine, we end up with four shorter, but more productive, ones. And as a bonus, our trellis doesn't need to be as tall this way!

## REFRIGERATOR PICKLES

Need a tasty snack in a flash? Cut off the ends of two pickling cucumbers, slice them lengthwise into quarters, and put them in a plastic bag with 1 tablespoon of salt and 2 peeled garlic cloves. Seal tightly and refrigerate for a few hours. Here at the test gardens, we like to prepare our "cool cukes" first thing in the morning, then enjoy them as a tasty treat with lunch!

### Kitchen CLASSICS

It seems to take forever for our cucumbers to begin producing, but once the fruits start comin', we always have an abundance to use in the kitchen. One of our favorite ways to enjoy the bounty is in a simple, but flavorful, cucumber salad. Simply peel and chop two medium cucumbers and two large tomatoes, and put them in a mixing bowl. Add 2 tablespoons of chopped fresh basil and 1/4 cup of crumbled feta cheese, then toss with 1/4 cup of reduced-fat Italian dressing. Chill for an hour or two before serving to let the flavors blend, and you've got yourself a super summer side dish!

## FOILED AGAIN!

Believe it or not, plain old aluminum foil can be a gardener's best friend when it comes to protecting cukes and other crops from bad bugs. You see, the shiny foil reflects light, which confuses aphids and lots of other pests, making it difficult for them to find your plants. To put this trick to work in your own garden, simply lay sheets of foil over the soil around your cucumbers (corn and squash are good candidates, too). Use soil or rocks to weigh down the edges of the sheets so they don't blow away. (And don't forget to poke holes a few inches apart in the foil, so water can get down to the roots.) This simple secret works wonders to keep the local pest population away from your veggies!

## CUKES YOU CAN COUNT ON

Once cucumber vines start producing, it can be tough to keep up with the harvest. After just a few weeks, though, that abundance will be just a memory. It's nothing you did wrong, it's just the nature of the beast! Over the years, we've worked out a great strategy to keep us in a steady, but manageable, supply of garden-fresh cukes through a good part of the growing season. We make three sowings about three weeks apart, so the next cucumber crop is coming in just as the previous one is finishing. If you want to try this in your garden, just keep in mind that there's no need to go overboard at planting time—just three plants per sowing can provide plenty of fruit for a family of four! That's assuming you're eating them fresh, of course. If pickles are what you're after, go ahead and make one big sowing to get your harvest all at once.

### Mildew Remover Tonic

Powdery mildew and its kissin' cousin, downy mildew, can spell the end for cucumbers. But you can fight these funky fungi and keep your garden growing great guns by spraying your plants every week with my special spray.

**1/2 cup of baking soda**
**2 drops of dishwashing liquid**
**1 qt. of water**

Mix these ingredients in a bucket, then pour into a hand-held sprayer. Spray plants thoroughly at the first sign of mildew, and any diseases will soon be history.

**TRIED-AND-TRUE**

**W**hether you buy your eggplant transplants or grow 'em yourself, there's no sense in hurrying to get 'em in the ground. The experts say that the average daily temperature should be at least 65°F before eggplants can stay outside safely. But we don't bother keeping track of temperatures—we use Grandma Putt's secret of waiting until the new oak leaves are fully expanded on our trees. By that time, the weather's settled and warm—and we know our eggplants won't get nipped by a big chill!

## GET A JUMP START

When Mother Nature turns up the heat, many veggies slow down or even stop producing—but not eggplants! These summer-lovers thrive during the dog days, which makes them a snap to grow in Southern gardens but a challenge in the cooler North. There, they need a serious head start on the growing season—and that means sowing them indoors as early as 10 weeks before transplanting (about 8 weeks before the last spring frost date). And heating mats are a must for keeping the soil at least 70°F, and ideally 85°F, for the week or so that the seeds take to sprout. But you know what? You don't need to go to all this bother to enjoy eggplants in your own garden! Just two or three plants per person will provide plenty of good eating, so we suggest that folks simply buy transplants. It's not cheating—it just makes sense!

## THANKS FOR THE SUPPORT!

When fully loaded with fruit, eggplants sometimes have trouble holding themselves up, so it's smart to support 'em before they keel over. We've tried a lot of different techniques, and our favorite stake is a small extension-type curtain rod. We stick it in at planting time, and as the plants grow, we can easily adjust the rod upwards so that it is always at the right height. This works great for supporting pepper plants, too!

## EGGING 'EM ON

Hey, cool-climate gardeners—if you're craving the taste of garden-fresh eggplant but are having trouble getting the fruits to ripen before frost, don't despair! Growing eggplants in containers is a great solution. Raised above ground level, the soil heats up quickly, providing ideal conditions for root and shoot growth. To turn the heat up another notch, set the pots on a paved surface, or tuck them against a south-facing wall. You'll be savoring the great taste of home-grown eggplant in no time—and enjoying the pretty purple flowers and colorful fruits in your pots, too!

## EGG-STRA SPECIAL

When you think of eggplants, you probably think of fairly large, plump fruits with purple-black skin, right? Well, that's the picture of classic supermarket eggplants, but when you grow your own, there's a whole world of shapes, sizes, and colors to choose from! Here are just a few that never fail to get *oohs* and *aahs* from our test-garden visitors:

**'Asian Bride'.** Long, slender, pale lavender fruits striped with white; they have a mild flavor and creamy texture.

**'Kermit'.** Egg-sized, green-and-white fruits that are definitely not your average eggplants; great when cooked on skewers.

**'Little Fingers'.** Thumb-sized, light purple fruits that are fantastic for grilling!

**'Rosa Bianca'.** Mild, sweet fruits with skin in shades of pink, lavender, and white. Picked when 5 to 6 inches in diameter, they are superb for stuffing.

### Test Garden SECRET

If the leaves of your eggplants are so full of holes that they look like lace, flea beetles are the likely culprits. But we've found the solution! In the cool of the morning, hit 'em with our Knock-'Em-Dead Insect Tonic (see page 258). Then, for long-term protection, make yellow sticky traps. Paint 1 × 6-inch pieces of cardboard yellow, tack them to sticks, and coat the surfaces with a sticky substance such as honey or Tangle-Trap®. Poke the sticks into the soil among troubled plants to trap flea beetles.

# SHINE ON, EGGPLANT

Based on the questions we get here at the test gardens, one of the biggest puzzlements folks seem to have about growing eggplants is knowing when to harvest them. It's really pretty easy, though, as long as you know what to look for. Pick as soon as the fruit has a nice, glossy sheen on the skin. If you wait until that shine turns dull, the fruit is too mature, and it's going to be tough and seedy inside. Always *cut* the fruits off the stems, by the way. Twisting them off is an easy way to damage the plants and spoil the rest of your harvest!

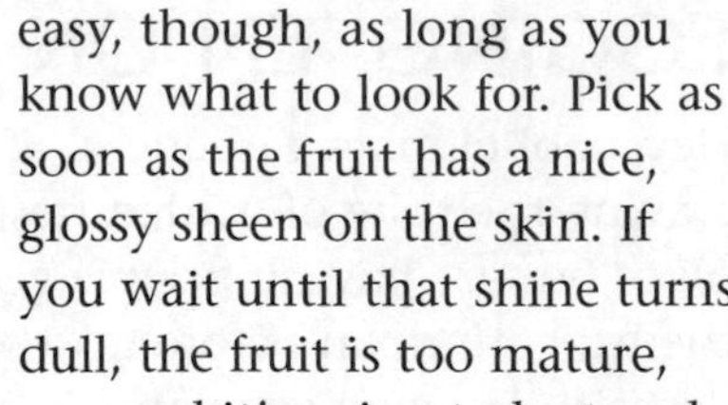

## Kitchen CLASSICS

Cut into sticks, slabs, or wedges, eggplant fries are one of our favorite summer side dishes. The challenge is getting them nice and crispy without having the finished fries dripping in oil. Some of our kitchen whizzes have experimented with different tricks, and they've found that coating the slices with flour, beaten egg, and bread crumbs, then letting them "dry" for a half hour or so in the refrigerator, really helps prevent the fries from soaking up so much oil. Another option is to parboil the slices for a minute or two, then drain and pat dry before frying.

# HANDY HARVEST HELPER

It's a joy to see a happy, healthy eggplant crop chock-full of ripening fruit. But, sooner or later, Jack Frost is going to make a return appearance and spoil your harvest if you don't plan ahead! Snipping off all the remaining blossoms about a month before our usual first fall frost date does the trick. Instead of wasting energy on baby fruits that'll never be big enough to pick, the plants put all of their energy into ripening the fruits that are already formed—and we're assured of a bountiful harvest of top-quality fruit!

# TIME FOR LIME

If flea beetles haven't yet done major damage to your eggplant leaves, there's a simple way to combat the tiny terrors: Use garden lime. Simply dust your eggplants lightly with garden lime early in the morning, when the plants are still wet with dew, so the powder clings better. That'll go a long way toward keeping flea beetles at bay. (If the beetles have already been busy, see the Test Garden Secret on page 267.)

## SMART MELON MANAGEMENT

Why don't more folks grow melons in their home gardens? Probably because these vigorous vines take up so much valuable garden real estate! Watermelons, for instance, can take up as much as 100 square feet—and that's enough room to grow a bountiful harvest of less space-hungry crops. Still, the flavor of home-grown melons is such a treat that we like to encourage folks to give 'em a try—and to that end, we've experimented with a couple of options for fitting them into an average backyard garden.

The obvious solution seemed to be growing bush-type varieties, but that was a bust. Their vines still spread 3 to 4 feet in all directions, so they took up a fair bit of room. Plus, we felt that the flavor was disappointing. Full-sized vines are definitely more satisfying. They have more leaves to support the developing melons, so their fruits are reliably rich and sweet. To give them room to ramble without wasting space, pair them with tall, upright crops, such as staked tomatoes, corn, or sunflowers. That way, the vines can creep along the ground around their bed buddies, and you can get an abundant harvest even where space is at a premium!

### JUGGING ALONG

One of our favorite tricks for recycling plastic milk jugs is using them in the melon patch to prevent the fruit from rotting. Simply cut a jug in half lengthwise, lay one half on the ground, and set the ripening melon inside. Not only will this plastic perch prevent rot, but it will also discourage critters from nibbling on your melons!

### Test Garden SECRET

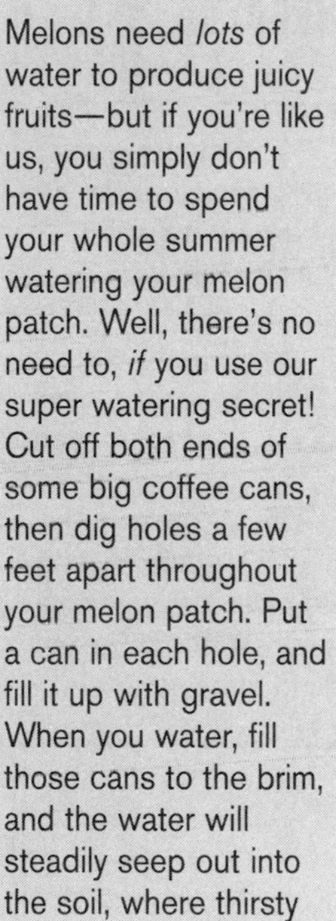

Melons need *lots* of water to produce juicy fruits—but if you're like us, you simply don't have time to spend your whole summer watering your melon patch. Well, there's no need to, *if* you use our super watering secret! Cut off both ends of some big coffee cans, then dig holes a few feet apart throughout your melon patch. Put a can in each hole, and fill it up with gravel. When you water, fill those cans to the brim, and the water will steadily seep out into the soil, where thirsty roots can drink their fill!

## TUCK 'EM IN

What's the secret to keeping melons growing strong? Keeping 'em toasty warm! So on nights when the temperature drops below 65°F after planting, simply toss a blanket over their bed, in the form of floating row cover. In fact, since these covers allow air, light, and water to get through, we leave 'em over our test-garden melon beds full-time during the early growth stages. Besides keeping the vines warm, they help keep bad-guy bugs at bay, too. We have to make sure we whisk the covers off the minute flowers appear on the plants, though. Otherwise, the good-guy bugs wouldn't be able to pollinate them, and we wouldn't have any melons to harvest!

**Q** Hey, Jer—any pointers for telling when muskmelons are ripe for the pickin'?

**A** You bet! Check the blossom end (opposite the stem) by pressing on it. If it's ripe and ready to pick, it should give way slightly and smell kind of sweet.

## TWO'S A CHARM

Where watermelons are concerned, sometimes less *is* more! We've discovered that the best way to ensure the biggest fruits is to leave no more than two fruits to ripen per vine. It's the secret to getting all of the vine's energy to the fruits that are left. Of course, if you're not after blue-ribbon winners, or if you're growing "icebox" varieties (which have smaller fruits), it's fine to leave a few more to develop on each vine. But pinch off all of the remaining blossoms in early fall so the existing fruits will get enough energy to ripen before frost appears.

## A BRICK TRICK

If you just can't wait to slice into a ripe, juicy melon, try fast-forwarding the ripening time. Place your young melons on bricks while they're still attached to the vine, and the heat that the bricks absorb will speed up the ripening process. We've found that this can speed ripening by several days—and that's important when your family is clamoring for fresh melon!

## A SWEET IDEA

While melon plants like lots of water, that doesn't mean they should always get everything that they want—especially if you want the sweetest fruits possible (and who doesn't?). We get the best-tasting melons when we water generously through most of the growing season, until we're about three weeks away from harvest time. Slowing down the water supply for this final ripening period seems to help the plants concentrate sugars in the fruits, so our melons are as sweet as we could ever hope for!

## MULCH BETTER

We suppose it's possible to grow top-quality melons without mulch, but *we* sure wouldn't want to try it! Besides maintaining an even soil temperature and moisture level—which encourages great root growth and healthy, productive vines—mulch also helps keep the developing fruits off of the soil, reducing the chance of rotting and pest damage, and keeping the fruits free of dirt, too. Don't be in a rush to mulch, though, because you do want to make sure that the soil is plenty warm first. We've found that waiting until the vines just begin to spread, then mulching with 6 to 8 inches of straw, turns our melon plants into clean, mean growing machines!

### Marvelous Melon Soil Mix

Melons are mighty particular about the ground they call home, so it's worth putting some extra effort into making their bed. This mixture suits 'em to a T.

**2 cups of coarse builder's sand (not beach or "sandbox" sand)**
**1 cup of compost**
**1 cup of professional planting mix**
**1 cup of Mouthwatering Melon Mix***

Mix these ingredients in a bucket or wheelbarrow. Use the mixture to fill each of your melon planting holes, then get ready to modestly accept your town's Most Mouthwatering Melon award!

*To make Mouthwatering Melon Mix, combine 5 pounds of earthworm castings (available in catalogs), 1/2 pound of Epsom salts, and 1/4 cup of instant tea granules.

Nothing beats a slice of ice-cold, home-grown melon on a sultry summer day. But when your melon vines are at peak production, you'll have plenty of fruits to enjoy, so why not try doing something a little different with them? Here are our favorite ideas:

- Cut watermelon into chunks, remove any seeds, and then puree the chunks in your blender. Freeze the juice in ice-cube trays, and enjoy as a sweet treat to beat the heat.
- Slice seedless watermelon thinly, then use cookie cutters to cut the slices into festive shapes for a fun and flavorful dessert.
- Use a melon baller to scoop out the flesh of your favorite melon, and add to fruit salad. Shape the empty rind into a disposable serving basket for the salad.

## LESS IS MORE

Folks who visit us at our test gardens often ask our opinion on growing seedless watermelons at home. Well, we've tried it, and we think it's worthwhile—*but* it takes a bit more effort to get 'em off to a good start. Here's what you need to know:

**Give 'em a jump start.** *Always* start seedless watermelon seeds indoors. They are very touchy about cool temperatures and soggy soil, so it's critical to provide the best possible conditions for sprouting (an evenly moist, but well-drained seed-starting mix, kept at about 85°F).

**Take their coats off.** The seed coats tend to be thicker on seedless types, so they sometimes cling to the seedlings and interfere with growth. We've found that misting the newly sprouted seedlings lightly a few times a day can help soften the seed coat. If it doesn't drop off on its own after two or three days, pry it off carefully.

**Give them room.** Plan on growing several plants, and allow garden space accordingly. Seedless watermelon plants can't pollinate themselves, so each seed packet contains seeds of a compatible seeded variety to ensure the needed pollen supply for fruiting.

**Time transplanting carefully.** The optimum time for moving seedless watermelon starts to the garden is when the soil is at least 65°F. The seedlings should be three to four weeks old, with two or three true leaves.

Once the young plants get growing, they're actually quite vigorous, so they won't need as much pampering. Just make sure they get plenty of water, because if they get stressed, you may actually end up seeing some black seeds in your "seedless" varieties!

## OKRA ALL THE TIME

Those of you who live in warm to hot climates know that okra is a super summer crop for your neck of the woods. But did you know that with a simple little trick, you can extend your harvest to last for months? To spread out the ripening times, start one batch of seeds in early spring, then sow again in June so you get a steady supply of pods well into the fall months. Or, sow one crop in spring, then cut about half of the plants back to 18 to 24 inches in midsummer and give them a good watering and feeding. The cut-back plants will produce lots of later-bearing side branches, with an abundance of pods that'll be ready to harvest just as the uncut plants start to slow down.

## OKRA UP NORTH

Who says you have to live in the South to enjoy this classic Southern favorite? With a little know-how, it's possible to produce a good okra crop in just about any part of the country! The secret is to give these heat-loving plants a jump start on the growing season by sowing them indoors, three to four weeks before your last frost date. For even speedier sprouting, do what we do—soak the seeds overnight in warm water or nick the seed coat with a file before sowing. Put the seed pots on a heating mat to keep the soil at 85°F until the seedlings appear, then grow them at 75° to 80°F until the weather is warm and settled enough for them to go out into the garden.

**Test Garden SECRET**

If there's a downside to growing okra, it's the spines that cover the plants. They're really tiny, but they can cause a big problem when you brush up against them, causing swollen, irritated skin. Traditional advice is to grow "spineless" varieties, like 'Clemson Spineless'—but what most folks *don't* know is that only the pods of these varieties are spineless. There are still plenty of spines on the leaves and stems. We learned this from painful personal experience, so now we *always* wear gloves and long sleeves when working around our okra plants—"spineless" or not!

**Kitchen CLASSICS**

Have an abundance of tomatoes and okra? Combine these classic summer crops into this tasty side dish! Sauté two cloves of garlic (minced) and half of a red onion (sliced) in 2 tablespoons of olive oil in a large wok. Add five large tomatoes (chopped) and 3/4 pound of okra, cut into 1/2-inch-thick pieces. Cook for 4 to 5 minutes, or until the okra is soft, but not limp. Add 1/4 cup each of chopped fresh basil and sliced olives; cook for another minute. Season with salt and pepper, and you've got yourself a great garden-fresh vegetable dish that serves four.

## JOIN THE POD SQUAD

Harvesting okra at the right time is the key to getting a tender, tasty harvest. The pods of some varieties can get 5 to 7 inches long and still be good, but we prefer to pick them at about 3 inches long; getting them young seems to encourage the plants to produce more pods. They grow fast, so harvesting every other day is about right. But what if you're away for a few days and some pods get too big? No need to waste those pods—simply open 'em up and shell out the seeds. If they're not fully mature, cook them like peas (we like them boiled, or in soups). If the seeds are dark and fully mature, try roasting and grinding them for a great coffee substitute. Talk about "waste not, want not"!

## PRETTY AND PRODUCTIVE

Okra isn't just good to grow in a vegetable garden—it's pretty enough to earn a place in flower beds, too!

With its creamy yellow, maroon-centered blooms, this handsome hibiscus relative makes an elegant companion for many other summer-blooming annuals and perennials in our test gardens. Our particular favorite is the variety known as 'Burgundy', with rich red stems and leaf veins on 4-foot-tall plants. Even the pods are red! If you want to try these beauties, just remember to keep 'em picked to keep the flowers coming, and enjoy 'em raw or cooked. Just be aware that they'll turn green if you cook them!

## PEAS WITH APPEAL

If you're puzzled about all the different types of peas there are to choose from, you're not alone! Here's a rundown of the three main types we grow here at the test gardens:

**Garden peas.** Also known as English or shelling peas, these classic varieties are the kinds you take out of the pods, then eat just the seeds. (Don't toss those pods in the trash, though—they are perfect food for your compost pile!)

**Snap peas.** Also known as sugar peas, these varieties offer the best of both worlds: plump seeds and sweet edible pods that snap just like beans. We love 'em either raw or cooked. Looking for something really different? Try to track down the yellow-podded and purple-podded varieties. They're beautiful, and they're a lot easier to pick because they're easy to see!

**Snow peas.** Grow these peas for their edible pods, picked when they are flat and tender. We like to snack on them right from the plants, but they're super when steamed or in stir-fries, too!

## 'TIS THE SEASON FOR PEAS

If you live in one of the hotter parts of the country, don't fret: Your homegrown peas can be just as tasty as anyone's up north! The secret is to plant your crop in December, instead of March. And for an extra-speedy start, soak the seeds in water overnight before planting. They'll sprout super-quick and get growing in a flash. You'll be harvesting tender, sweet peas before you know it!

### Test Garden

With most spring crops, making successive sowings several weeks apart is the best way to spread out your harvest period for as long as possible. But with peas, we've found that this trick *isn't* the answer. You see, pea plants really prefer cool weather, so late sowings are likely to grow slowly and may not produce any pods at all before the dog days arrive in August. But not to worry, because we've found the answer—sow once, but use seeds of several different varieties with different maturity dates. You might, for instance, plant 'Mr. Big' (which is ready in 58 days), 'Little Marvel' (62 days), and 'Wando' (68 days) all at the same time. By spreading out the maturity dates, you're guaranteed a generous harvest over the longest possible period.

## FIFTY IS NIFTY!

Tradition tells us to get pea seeds in the ground "as soon as the soil can be worked in the spring"—but this is one case where old-time advice may not be the best. Yes, it's true that peas prefer to grow in cool conditions, but they actually sprout quickest when the soil is around 60°F. In early-spring soil (which is around 40°F), they can take three weeks or more to sprout—*if* they don't rot in the meantime. The problem with waiting that long is that the plants will start producing just as summer's heat arrives, and that can cut down on your harvest period. Here at the test gardens, we've had great luck by compromising—we sow our peas when the soil is around 50°F. Since we've been doing this, we've seldom had problems with the seeds rotting, and we've still gotten great yields from our pea patch: a perfect solution!

## STICK IT TO 'EM

Love growing peas, but hate messing with strings, netting, and other trellising materials? Then you'll love this terrific recycling trick—use the branches you prune off your trees and shrubs in spring to make perfect pea stakes! A good trellis branch is about 5 feet long and splits into several sturdy stems. Stuck into the pea row so their branches just overlap, these super stakes are just the kind of support peas need—and best of all, they're *free!*

### DON'T LET THEM DRY

One of our favorite things about this cool-weather crop is the fact that we seldom need to worry about watering our peas. Rainfall is usually abundant in the spring, so Mother Nature takes care of that chore for us. But if there *is* a dry spell, we water regularly as soon as the blossoms fall. Providing peas with plenty of water while their pods are filling can make the difference between a disappointing harvest and generous abundance!

### From Our Readers

*When I noticed that rabbits were eating my peas, I took white pepper and sprinkled it lightly over the tops of the plants. I didn't have any more trouble with the rabbits, and the plants didn't seem to mind a bit!*

Corrine S.,
Villard, MN

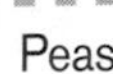

## AUTUMN ABUNDANCE

Over the years, we've had great luck with planting many classic spring crops—such as lettuce and spinach—in mid- to late summer for a fall harvest. These cool-season favorites make super follow-ups for earlier-harvested summer crops, allowing us to get two or even three harvests from the same amount of space. The one challenge we've had is trying to get good results with growing peas this way. It seems they really hate the heat when they're young—even more than when they are starting to produce pods!

Fortunately, we've discovered a few tricks for successful fall peas. First, plant them where they'll get some shade from taller crops, such as corn, sunflowers, or staked tomatoes. And second, mulch them generously. That'll keep the roots from getting baked, and help your pea plants beat the heat!

## BEYOND PODS

Peas produce more than just tasty pods and seeds—their flowers are edible, too! Snack on 'em straight from the plants, or toss the pretty white or purple blossoms into your salads. For something extra-special, snip off the new shoots, too. The tendrils and newest leaves are super-tender and have a fantastic, garden-fresh flavor that's wonderful in salads and stir-fries. Harvesting the blooms and shoots will prevent more pod production, so don't try this until you've enjoyed your fill of peas!

### Veggie Vitalizer

Here's a really out-of-the-ordinary tonic that packs a double punch. It'll get your crops up and growin' to new heights *and* help repel nasty pests, too!

**1/2 can of beer**
**1/4 cup of pepper/onion/mint juice***
**3 tbsp. of fish emulsion**
**2 tbsp. of dishwashing liquid**

Mix these ingredients in a 20 gallon hose-end sprayer, and apply liberally to your vegetable garden every three weeks.

*To make this juice, finely mince 1 green pepper, 1 onion, and 2 tablespoons of mint leaves. Add to 1 quart of hot water, and blend in a blender. Strain, and use the remaining liquid in this tonic.

## Test Garden SECRET

In a hurry for your harvest? The secret to getting peppers to develop faster is providing them with magnesium in a form they can use quickly. To try this in your own garden, mix 2 tablespoons of Epsom salts in 1 gallon of water. Apply 1 pint of this mixture to each plant just as the blooms appear, and you'll get a fantastic set of fruits that'll ripen before you know it!

## DECISIONS, DECISIONS...

With literally dozens of varieties of peppers to choose from, in all shapes, sizes, and colors, how can you even begin to decide which ones to grow? Here are some criteria we use when choosing peppers to try in our test gardens:

**Heat or sweet?** First, we narrow our choices by flavor. Sweet peppers are great for frying, stuffing, or simply enjoying raw in salads, while hot peppers are a must for adding zip to cooked dishes.

**Over the rainbow.** Both hot and sweet peppers come in a variety of colors. Hots are typically green, red, or yellow, while sweets can be green, red, yellow, orange—and even lavender, creamy white, or chocolate brown!

**Sizing 'em up.** Large-fruited peppers tend to be slow to mature—ours usually don't start ripening until late summer—and in most areas, the growing season isn't long enough for them to produce another set of flowers and fruit. Small-fruited types, like cherry peppers, mature quickly and bear generously through the summer. Our suggestion? Plant several varieties of different sizes to have a steady supply of peppers for months!

### FIRE, FIRE!

Here's our little secret to help you get the hottest hot peppers in town. Just before you're ready to harvest, flood their bed with water. This stresses the roots and sends out a signal to "turn up the heat!"

## COLOR CONSIDERATIONS

Sweet peppers are a treat to eat, but growing them provides a bit of a dilemma. Do you pick them when they are green, or wait until they turn color? Fully colored fruits have a mild, evenly sweet flavor, and their bright skins are perfect for adding cheerful colors to salads, stir-fries, and other dishes. All these benefits come at a price, though. While the fruits are ripening, the plants aren't producing more flowers, so you get fewer fruits in the long run. That's why most folks pick their peppers at the green stage, even though the flavor can be a little bitter at that time.

But guess what—we've found a great compromise! We wait until our peppers are just starting to turn color, then harvest them and leave them at room temperature, where they'll continue to ripen. Once they are fully colored, we put them in plastic bags and refrigerate them to stop the ripening process. (They'll keep for about two weeks this way.) With this simple trick, we can harvest an abundance of peppers—*and* enjoy eating them, too!

## PLANNING POINTERS

Even though we've been growing peppers for years, we tend to forget how big the plants get—and how much of our valuable test-garden space they take up! Generally, allowing just three plants per person provides enough sweet peppers for fresh use. (If you're planning to freeze or pickle them, you'll probably want to double or triple that.) For hot peppers, one or two plants per person will provide plenty of fruits. So, unless you are growing enough for a large family, our advice is to skip growing these crops from seed and simply buy a few transplants of different varieties. That way, you can use your valuable seed-starting space for other crops—and you can enjoy a range of pepper shapes and sizes without buying way more seeds than you need!

**Q** My pepper plants look fantastic—big, bushy, and perfectly healthy—but the flowers keep dropping off, so I'm not getting any fruit! Any advice?

**A** Yep—I've got you covered! Or rather, you should keep your *plants* covered, at least when nighttime temperatures drop below 60°F. Simply toss a piece of floating row cover over your pepper patch when a cool night is predicted, and you'll have new flowers and fruits in a week or two!

# MIX AND MATCH

If you're the type who enjoys mixing veggies in with your flowers, then peppers are the ideal crop for you! The plants themselves are nice and bushy, and the fruits—well, their bright colors complement all kinds of beautiful blooms!

Here at the test gardens, we especially like using hot peppers as ornamentals, because their fruits tend to be more abundant, and thus, more visible. One of our particular favorites is 'Bulgarian Carrot', which is filled with pointed, bright orange fruits, which do look just like mini carrots! 'Bolivian Rainbow' is another variety that really lives up to its name, with purplish leaves and violet-purple flowers that turn into small fruits in shades of purple, yellow, orange, *and* red! And for something to really wow the neighbors, how about trying 'Trifetti' ('Variegata')? It sports green leaves liberally splashed with both purple and white, along with deep purple fruits that turn bright red—wow!

## Sweet Success Spray

This sugar-packed spray is sure to lure bees to your veggie plants and ensure pollination. What's more, it'll kill nasty nematodes in the soil. So with this mixture, you get two benefits for the price of one!

**$1/2$ cup of sugar**
**Water**

Pour the sugar into 2 cups of water and bring to a boil, stirring, until the sugar is completely dissolved. Let the mixture cool, dilute it with 1 gallon of water, and pour the solution into a hand-held sprayer. Then spritz your bloomin' plants to the point of run-off. Before you know it, willing, winged workers will fly to your rescue!

# THE BIG BELL SECRET

Trying to get the biggest possible bell peppers for stuffing? Let some of the flowers set fruit, then pinch off the rest of the blooms. That way, your plants will put all of their energy into developing a few huge peppers, rather than a bunch of little ones!

## HOT, HOT, HOT!

Hot peppers don't just *taste* hot—they *feel* hot, too! The juices in the fruits and plants can burn your skin, and take it from us—it hurts. Wearing gloves when handling them in the kitchen is a must, because the capsaicin (the substance that causes the burning) is most concentrated in the inner parts of the peppers. To be extra careful, we wear gloves when harvesting, as well, just in case the peppers get nicked or broken during handling. And no matter *where* you're working with them, always keep your hands away from your face, because you sure don't want to get the juice in your eyes! If you do manage to get some on your skin, despite taking precautions, don't worry—a bit of milk will take the pain away.

## WINTER WONDERFUL

The return of frosty weather doesn't have to signal the end of your pepper harvest! The plants are actually tender perennials, which means that they will keep growing if you bring them indoors for the winter. This isn't too practical with most sweet peppers (although we've had good luck with small-fruited types like 'Jingle Bells'), but it's a super way to overwinter your favorite hot pepper plants. Pot them up in late summer, and trim them back by about a third. Then bring them indoors before the first frost and keep them in a warm room with lots of bright light. Set 'em outside again after danger of frost the following spring, and they'll grow like gangbusters. You'll have enough hot peppers for the whole neighborhood—guaranteed!

### Kitchen CLASSICS

Looking to spice up your life? Try some of our favorite ways to make the most of our pepper harvest!

**Go Italian.** Sprinkle diced red pepper and a small amount of anise seeds on your pizza to mimic the taste of Italian sausage–without the fat. Add pepperoncini to your salad.

**Go Thai.** Mix chilled, thinly sliced filet mignon with garlic, ginger, soy sauce, and fish sauce. Toss with sliced red onions, jalapenos, and some lime juice. Serve on butterhead lettuce.

**Go Hungarian.** Add Hungarian cherry peppers (they're sweet and mild—usually!) to your next pickle and olive tray.

Squash plants (and melons) appreciate the extra warmth they get when you sow them indoors, but they don't take kindly to having their roots disturbed at transplanting time. Here's a terrific trick our test-garden helpers swear by. Dig up a piece of turf that's about 3 inches deep, and cut it into 2-inch-square chunks. Turn the sod pieces upside down, and poke two or three seeds into each piece. When your seedlings are ready to head outdoors, simply transplant them as is—sod and all. They'll never know they've been moved!

## LET'S GET SQUASHED

What's the hardest thing about growing squash? We think it's trying to decide which ones to grow! There are so many kinds to choose from, and so many uses for them, that the whole matter can get mighty puzzling. But it doesn't have to be—here's a quick overview to help you make sense of this confusing crop!

**Summer squash.** These tend to be bushy plants with fast-growing fruits that are harvested when young and tender for use soon after picking. Examples include crooknecks, pattypans (scallops), and zucchini.

**Winter squash.** Typically produced on long, trailing vines (but sometimes on bushy plants), these hard-skinned fruits are harvested when fully mature. They can be used immediately or kept in storage for up to several months. Many types of squash fall into this category, including acorn, buttercup, butternut, cushaw, delicata, and hubbard varieties, as well as pumpkins.

## BE THE BEE

Since only the female squash flowers set fruit, there's no need to worry about the male flowers dropping off of your plants. But if the *females* fall and don't leave a ripening fruit behind, you have a problem! Usually, it means that there aren't enough bees around to pollinate the blooms. But don't worry—you can do the job yourself. Simply pick off a male bloom, peel off the petals, and rub the part that's left against the sticky center column of a female flower. (One male bloom has enough pollen to treat several females.) Pretty soon, you'll probably have more squash than you know what to do with!

## HARVEST BOOSTERS

If you love all kinds of squash as much as we do, it simply makes sense to try for the longest possible harvest! For summer squash, sowing again one month after the first sowing, and again one month after that, guarantees an abundant harvest well into the fall. We probably don't need to remind you that summer squash plants can be very prolific, so don't go overboard at planting time; for each person, figure on one or two plants each, of two or three different varieties, at each sowing to enjoy a steady supply without getting overwhelmed.

Winter squash grow a lot more slowly, so instead of making multiple sowings, plant both early-maturing and late-maturing varieties at the same time to spread out your harvest. Figure on two or three of these productive plants per person.

## TRY A PUMPKIN PILE

We have to admit that our best pumpkin crop of all time didn't actually grow in our test gardens—it grew in our compost pile! We often find various veggie seedlings around the pile, and we usually just pull them out and toss them into the compost. But one year, a couple seedlings came up in an old pile, and we didn't notice them for a few weeks. By then, they were already growing strong, so we decided to leave them and see what they produced. Well, imagine how pleased we were when a few months later, those extra-vigorous, super-healthy vines presented us with a bumper crop of perfect pumpkins—all without any work on our part!

The moral of this story? Next year, consider planting your pumpkins (or squash or melons) right in your compost bin and see if you don't get the same amazing results!

### Kitchen CLASSICS

Looking for a really different side dish to liven up your next summer supper? Give fried squash blossoms a try! First, wash and pat dry 18 to 24 male flowers (they're the ones that don't have small fruit right below the bloom). Next, make the batter. Beat 1 egg with 1 cup of ice water, then add that mixture to 1 cup of flour in a bowl and stir. (The batter should be thin.) Dip the blossoms in the batter and fry in hot oil for about 30 seconds on each side. Drain on paper towels, then add salt and pepper to taste, and enjoy!

## CONTAIN YOURSELF

Think you can't grow squash and pumpkins in pots? Think again! The trick is to select varieties that produce compact, bushy plants with small fruits. That way, the plants themselves will be easy to manage, and you'll get an abundant harvest, too! For summer squash, we've gotten great yields from 'Sunny Delight' pattypans (scallops), 'Multipik' straightnecks, and 'Jackpot' and 'Roly Poly' zucchini. For winter squash, 'Burpee's Bush Table Queen' has been a real winner for us. And for pumpkins in a small space, give 'Bush Spirit' a try. No matter what kind you choose, we suggest hand-pollinating the blooms (see "Be the Bee" on page 282)—especially if the containers are in areas where bees might not be as active.

### From Our Readers

*To save space, I train my squash vines on trellises. I use pantyhose "slings" to tie the fruits to the trellis so they don't break off the vines. It keeps my vines off the ground, and makes harvesting a cinch!*

Chris F.,
Grants Pass, OR

## BYE-BYE, BEETLES!

Cucumber beetles—those tiny yellow bugs striped or spotted with black—don't attack only cucumbers—they'll damage all kinds of squash, too! The larvae eat the roots, while the adults chew into stems and fruits, spreading diseases. If you spot just a few beetles, handpick the ones you can, and drown them in a bucket of soapy water. But if you think your yard has become cucumber beetle heaven, try this trick—plant a small plot of cucumbers to lure the beetles away from your squash. Then just as the cucumber plants reach full flower, go out early and blast those bad beetles with our Knock-'Em-Dead Insect Tonic (see page 258).

### TURN THE TIPS

Running out of room for your squash vines? No need to dig up more garden space! Simply pinch off the vine tips, or turn them gently to encourage them to grow back toward the center of the plant. Either way, you'll enjoy a bumper crop without giving up your whole yard!

## Test Garden SECRET

It's not unusual for squash leaves to droop a bit during the heat of the day, but if your plants start wilting and don't perk up by evening, you've got a *big* problem on your hands! Adult squash vine borers aren't very noticeable, but these brownish moths lay their eggs on stems near the base of the plants. The eggs then hatch into plump, whitish larvae that tunnel into the stems, causing the vines to wilt and die suddenly.

The surest cure is to stop borers *before* they start, by covering young squash plants with floating row cover until they flower. By that time, the plants are ready to start yielding, and they're usually large enough to tolerate some borer damage. But if your established squash vines do get "bored," don't despair. Slit the affected stem with a knife and remove the larvae, then heap soil or compost over that area to encourage new roots and healthy new vine growth.

# DEFINITELY DIFFERENT

The thought of pumpkins usually brings to mind images of Jack-o'-lanterns and holiday pies—but that's just the beginning. Visitors to our test gardens never fail to be amazed by some of the out-of-the-ordinary varieties we grow, and we think you'll have a lot of fun with them, too!

**'Jack-Be-Little'.** Picture a perfect orange pumpkin scaled down until it's small enough to fit in your palm—that's 'Jack-Be-Little'! These pint-sized fruits are delightful for crafts and decorating—and perfect for personal-sized servings of baked pumpkin for Thanksgiving dinners.

**'Lumina'.** Think all pumpkins are orange? Think again! This variety produces 10- to 12-pound fruits that are pure white outside (with orange flesh inside). Want a white pumpkin in a mini size? Then 'Baby Boo' is the pumpkin for you!

**'Triple Treat'.** Talk about an all-purpose pumpkin! It's ideal for Jack-o'-lanterns, great for pies, and super for snacking, because the seeds don't have any hulls. 'Eat-All' and 'Snack Jack' are also hull-less.

## Pest Pulverizer Potion

There's nothing more frustrating than putting a lot of time and energy into your veggie garden, only to have it feasted upon by any and all bugs that walk, crawl, or fly by. Well, here's a way to keep those pesky pests at the proper distance—treat 'em to a little heat!

**3 hot peppers**
**2 tbsp. of baby shampoo**
**1 qt. of water**

Puree these ingredients in a blender, then strain out the solids. Pour the liquid into a hand-held sprayer, then apply to pest-plagued plants to get rid of unwanted bugs and keep 'em from comin' back.

## TINY IS TASTIER

Let's face it—zucchini plants are so prolific, it seems like *everyone* is trying to give them away come harvest time! But it's possible to enjoy a steady supply of tender fruits without being overwhelmed—*if* you pick early, and pick often! If we harvest our zucchini when they are no more than 3 inches long, our plants keep producing these gourmet treats generously, without leaving us with a glut of baseball-bat-sized fruits that are too tough to eat.

## WONDERING ABOUT WINTER?

Judging by the questions we get here at the test gardens, a lot of folks are downright confused about the best way to keep winter squash in storage. Well, just about any winter squash will keep for a few weeks with no special treatment; but if you want to be enjoying superb squash through most of the winter, follow these three simple steps to surefire storage success:

**1.** Wait to harvest the squash until the fruit's skin is hard enough to resist when you try to puncture it with your fingernail. Or, simply wait until the vines begin to die.

**2.** Wipe the outside of the squash with a damp cloth to remove any clinging soil, then dip the squash in a solution of 1 part bleach and 6 parts water. (Make extra-sure that the stem end gets dipped, too!) Let it dry.

**3.** Keep the cleaned squash in a well-ventilated area at room temperature for 10 days to cure. Then move the squash to a cooler spot—between 50° and 55°F—until you're ready to eat 'em!

OK, you've picked the perfect pumpkin. Now, how do you get it ready to eat? Follow these simple steps, and you'll have plenty of pumpkin for quick meals at a moment's notice:

**Step 1.** Wash the pumpkin, then use a large, sharp knife to cut it in half. Scoop out the seeds, then cut the pumpkin into chunks.

**Step 2.** Put the chunks on a well-greased baking sheet, and bake at 325°F for about an hour, or until the pulp is soft.

**Step 3.** Scrape the pulp from the shell, and toss it into your food processor to puree.

To enjoy that great pumpkin flavor, warm the puree with a little butter or margarine, ground cinnamon, and skim milk, then serve like mashed sweet potatoes. Or, add a little salt and pepper to the puree, then use it like gravy over lean pot roast.

## TOMATO TERMS

Every time we show folks around our test gardens, they always want to know what kind of tomatoes we recommend—and we're never sure what answer to give. Choosing the perfect tomato variety is really a matter of personal taste, as well as the kind of climate you live in. So the varieties we swear by here are likely to be disappointing in Texas, or Alaska, or any other area with a significantly different climate from what we have here in Michigan. The one secret we *do* like to share with our visitors—no matter where they live—is the importance of understanding the terms "determinate" and "indeterminate" when selecting varieties to try. Here's the scoop:

**Determinate varieties.** These produce bushy plants that tend to ripen their fruits all at one time. Because they don't get too tall, you can either let them sprawl, or else support them with tomato cages (supporting them keeps the fruits cleaner and less prone to rot). Determinates are a great choice if you plan to do a lot of preserving, because the harvest is concentrated into a short period (about a month).

**Indeterminate varieties.** Once these start growing, they keep growing, up and up and up! Unless you're prepared to deal with a tangled mess, staking or trellising the vinelike stems is definitely the way to go. Indeterminates keep producing new clusters of flowers and fruit until frost, so once the first fruits ripen, you'll get a steady harvest through the rest of the season—ideal for fresh use!

### Test Garden SECRET

Are your tomato plants looking a little purple around the edges? No, it's not a disease or pest problem. Your plants are trying to tell you that they need more phosphorus! This is a common problem early in the season, when the soil is still a bit cool and roots aren't established enough to seek out all the phosphorus they need.

We've discovered a simple solution—spraying our tomato transplants weekly with fish emulsion for the first month or two, and holding off on mulching for the same time period. The spray gives the plants a quick nutrient boost, and the bare soil allows quicker warming to encourage speedy root growth. By midsummer, our plants are growing like gangbusters and their roots are getting all the phosphorus they need.

## CHOOSE QUALITY OVER QUANTITY

What's the most common mistake folks make when planting tomatoes? Planting too many of them! We admit to being guilty of that just about every year; after all, there are just so many fascinating varieties to choose from. But unless you plan on eating tomatoes at every meal (or leaving them on all of your neighbors' doorsteps), two to three plants per person will provide a manageable amount of fruits for fresh eating. For the most versatile harvest, choose varieties with different fruit sizes, colors, and maturity dates. Want enough to preserve for the winter? Add another six or more plants per person of a firm-fleshed, paste-type variety to use for sauces, freezing, or canning.

### Kitchen CLASSICS

Stumped for a healthy appetizer? Our favorite Tuscan tomato-basil spread needs nothing more than a loaf of crusty bread—thinly sliced and lightly toasted—to soak up the delicious drippings. And it's as easy as could be to make. Seed and dice 4 very ripe plum tomatoes, and place them in a medium bowl. Add 2 large leaves (slivered) of fresh basil and 1 tablespoon of extra virgin olive oil, then stir until well mixed. Season with salt and pepper to taste, then enjoy!

## A COOL IDEA

Full sun is generally a must for growing healthy, high-yielding tomato plants. But in some cases, they can get too much of a good thing! Those of you in the South will have much happier plants if you give them a bit of shade during the hottest part of the day. No, you don't need to go out and hold a beach umbrella over them! Simply plant them on the north side of a taller crop, such as corn or okra. That way, they'll still get plenty of light, but they'll be spared the worst of the heat—and they'll produce a whole lot more top-quality fruit to thank you!

### THE ACID TEST

When it comes to that "true" tomato flavor, not all tomatoes are created equal! You see, it's a combination of sweet (sugars) and sour (acids) that gives the fruits their distinctive taste. Some folks like their tomatoes a bit more on the acid side, while others prefer them sweet and mild. How can you guess which varieties are which? It's easy! In general, red tomatoes tend to be more acidic, with gold, yellow, and white-fruited varieties are more on the sweet side.

## TURN UP THE HEAT

Don't worry, northern gardeners—we've got great tips for you, too! Here are some of our favorite garden-tested tomato-boosting tips. Try one, or try 'em all—and be prepared for *amazing* results!

**Gimme shelter.** Plant your tomatoes against a south-facing wall, which will reflect light and radiate heat to help 'em beat the chill.

**Rock and roll.** Place one or two large, flat stones (or a bunch of smaller rocks) around the base of each transplant to keep the tender roots toasty warm, even on cool nights.

**Shine on.** Use aluminum foil as mulch around tomatoes to reflect more light onto the plants. It'll speed ripening and increase yields in cloudy regions, and help repel aphids and some other pests, as well!

## TOMATOES IN THE PILE

If you're like us, you're always looking for new ways to make the most of every precious inch of garden space. Well, then—you'll *love* this terrific space-saving trick! Instead of using solid-sided enclosures, keep your compost in wire-sided bins, then plant your tomato plants around the outside of the wire. As the plants grow, simply tie them to the sides of the bin—no need to fuss with stakes or trellises for support! Tomatoes grown this way seldom need feeding, watering, or mulching, either. The tomato roots will spread happily in the loose, moist, organic-rich soil under the pile, and find all the goodies they need to produce amazingly healthy, fruit-laden plants. So, you'll get a great harvest of tomatoes, *and* still have lots of space to grow other tasty crops, too!

### From Our Readers

*I've come up with a quick recycling trick to help my tomatoes get off to a great start. I set the transplants out in the garden in early spring, then place a ring of water-filled, 2-liter soda bottles around each one. This mini-wall keeps the wind from whipping the plants, and it keeps them warm, too! For extra protection on cold nights, place a cover on top, then remove it the next morning.*

Linda O.,
Le Suear, MN

## KEEPING GOOD COMPANY

Paying attention to your tomatoes' bedmates can make the difference between a so-so yield and a jaw-dropping harvest that'll turn your neighbors green with envy. The secret is to always plant basil, bee balm, and borage near your tomatoes. These aromatic herbs are the best garden partners your tomatoes will ever have, because the scents from these plants repel bugs and boost your plants to new heights!

## TRENCH YOUR TOMATOES

Here's a top-notch planting trick that the old-timers at our test gardens swear by. First, strip off all the tomato plants' leaves except the top two sets, then lay each plant in a trench a few inches deep, covering all but the leafy tip with soil. The shoot will quickly straighten itself out, while the buried stem develops lots of life-giving roots to help boost the harvest! This trick works especially well in cold regions, or when you're trying to get a jump on the season, because the roots grow up close to the soil surface, where the soil is warmer.

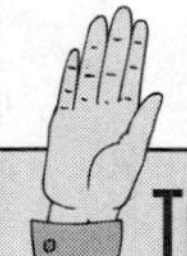

### TRIED-AND-TRUE

If a summer storm knocks a lot of blossoms off your tomato plants, don't panic—you can still get a good crop. Just pollinate the remaining flowers yourself with an old trick Grandma Putt swore by. Rub an old nylon slip to build up static electricity, and lay it on the blossoms of one plant. Then take it off and shake the pollen onto another plant. You'll get 100 percent pollination every time!

## AN A-PEEL-ING IDEA

It may sound crazy, but we swear it's true—tomatoes go bananas over bananas! Have a bunch of overripe ones and no time to make banana bread? Then use 'em whole, or just use the peels. We like to place one in the bottom of each planting hole to provide a growth-boosting dose of potassium at the start of the season. Then, every time one of us polishes off a banana during the growing season, we dig a little hole in the mulch near the base of a tomato plant, lay the peel in it, and cover it up. (We're always careful not to dig much into the soil, because we don't want to damage the shallow roots.) As thick as it is, that peel breaks down in no time, and all of its marvelous minerals go right to feeding our tomato crop!

## TRELLISING'S AS EASY AS 1-2-3!

If you're new to growing tomatoes, you may wonder why folks spend so much time trying to find the best way to support their plants. Well, after you've grown 'em once without any kind of support, you'll understand! Besides taking up a huge amount of space (which could be better used growing other crops), tomato plants allowed to sprawl on the ground are hard to harvest from, and their fruits are far more prone to rot and pests when they're sitting on bare soil.

You can bet we've tried all kinds of support systems over the years, and finally, we've come up with what we think is the perfect tomato trellising system:

**Step 1.** Install 4 × 4 wood posts 8 to 10 feet apart, then run one strand of heavy wire (clothesline wire works great) along the tops of the posts.

**Step 2.** At transplanting time, set your young tomato plants about 2 feet apart between the posts. Then, when they're about 1 foot tall, tie a piece of biodegradable twine to the wire above each plant, and fasten the loose ends to the base of the plants.

**Step 3.** As the plants grow, twine the main stem around the string for support. Keep the suckers pruned off.

Once you're done harvesting in fall, cleanup is a snap. Simply cut the strings off the wire, and toss the whole shebang onto your compost pile. Best of all, there are no space-hogging cages or stakes to take up garage or shed room during the winter!

### SUGAR, MY SWEET!

For the sweetest, juiciest tomatoes in town, take a tip from Mary Poppins—add a spoonful of sugar to each hole at planting time. Your tomatoes will be so lip-smacking good, the kids (and you, too) will be eating them right off the vine!

### Kitchen CLASSICS

Sure, you put tomatoes in your green salad—but then, they're just the supporting cast! To give your garden-fresh tomatoes top billing, try these suggestions:

**Tomato-cucumber salad.** Toss ⅔ cup of chopped tomatoes and ⅓ cup of chopped cucumbers with Italian dressing.

**Tomato-basil salad.** Mix 1 cup of chopped tomatoes with ¼ cup of chopped basil leaves and drizzle with balsamic vinaigrette.

## SKIMMING THE SURFACE

Have your tomatoes been bothered in the past by deadly diseases? Don't give up! We've gotten great results with a super-simple preventive step—treat 'em to a mix of 1 part skim milk and 9 parts water. Apply with a hand-held sprayer to the point of run-off in the early part of the summer, and it'll do a bang-up job discouraging diseases from getting started!

### Tomato Blight Buster

To ward off many common tomato diseases, we use this mix on all of our newly transplanted tomato seedlings—and you should, too!

**3 cups of compost**
**1/2 cup of powdered nonfat milk**
**1/2 cup of Epsom salts**
**1 tbsp. of baking soda**

Mix these ingredients in a bucket, then sprinkle a handful of the mixture into each planting hole. For additional disease defense, sprinkle a little more powdered milk on top of the soil after planting, and repeat every few weeks throughout the growing season.

## GOTCHA, SUCKER!

If you're wondering about the secret to growing whopper tomatoes, the answer's right at your fingertips! Keep your plants pruned by pinching off all of the "suckers" that develop in the crook between the branches and the main stem. These side shoots will simply steal energy away from the rest of the plant, so taking them off will help the whole plant stay stronger and productive. But don't let those unwanted bits go to waste! Here are two ways we've found to put those prunings to work:

**New plants for free.** Root the suckers in pots of growing mix—they'll be growing again before you know it—and then transplant them to your garden to fill space left by earlier-harvested crops, like bush beans.

**Moths-be-gone.** If you already have all of the tomato plants you need, spread the pruned-off suckers on the ground among your cabbages. Freshly plucked tomato foliage gives off an odor that helps repel egg-laying cabbage moths—for a while, anyway!

## WATCH OUT FOR HORNWORMS

Ugh! What's that gigantic green caterpillar on my tomato plant? It's a hornworm, that's what—and that hungry son-of-a-gun can wipe out the whole plant if you're not careful! Watch out for these pests in mid- to late summer. Their green coloration makes them hard to see, but the diagonal white markings on their sides sometimes help give them away. Fortunately, there usually aren't many of them, so control is a simple matter—just pick them off and drop them into soapy water.

One warning, though: If you see a hornworm with little white cocoons on its back, *leave it alone!* Those cocoons are a sign that the caterpillar has been parasitized by a beneficial insect called a braconid wasp. Braconids are harmless to people, but they attack a wide range of garden pests, including hornworms. So leave those infested caterpillars alone (they stop feeding quickly, once affected, so they won't do any more damage), and you'll encourage the braconids that hatch to call your garden their home!

## STOP THE CRACK ATTACK

You've been waiting for that perfect tomato to reach the peak of ripeness, so you hold off on harvesting one more day—only to find a big crack in the fruit in the next day! Fortunately, cracking doesn't ruin the flavor, but you'll want to pick and use that fruit in the kitchen immediately. Otherwise, it's likely to rot before you know it. Next time, pay close attention to soil moisture levels. If there's a dry spell, and then you water thoroughly or get a heavy rain, the sudden flow of moisture into the fruits is what causes the cracking. Keeping your plants well mulched, and making sure the soil stays evenly moist underneath, will practically eliminate those ugly, cracked fruits in the future!

### From Our Readers

*I've heard that using calcium is a sure cure for blossom-end rot—that nasty problem that causes tomatoes to turn black on one end. But I couldn't find plant calcium, so I asked my nephew, a doctor, what I might use in its place. He suggested Tums®, because they have calcium in them. Well, I crushed up two tablets per plant, put them in my watering can, and then watered my tomatoes with the mixture. I no longer have blossom-end rot—just beautiful tomatoes!*

Jewel R.,
Poplar Bluff, MO

## Tomato Booster Tonic

Want to get the best tomato crop on the block? Treat your plants with this tonic, then get prepared for a bumper harvest this year!

**2 tbsp. of Epsom salts**
**1 tsp. of baby shampoo**
**1 gal. of water**

Mix these ingredients in a watering can. Generously soak the soil around your tomato plants in early summer, just as they show a bunch of yellow flowers, to stimulate fruit set.

## DON'T WASTE THE TASTE

Have an abundance of ripe tomatoes, but not the time to can them? Try this super-simple recipe for making great-tasting tomato juice! Wash and core the tomatoes (work in batches of six or so, depending on their size), and cut away any bad spots. Put the tomatoes (peels and all) in a blender, and blend on high speed or puree until smooth. Then can or freeze the vitamin-packed juice to enjoy that home-grown tomato flavor during the winter. It's that easy!

## NOW THAT'S RIPE!

After you've waited weeks for your tomatoes to start bearing fruit, you'll want to keep the harvest coming for as long as possible. So, if Jack Frost is due to appear, gather up all the green tomatoes that are left, wipe off any dirt, and wrap each one in newspaper. Then pack them in a cardboard box, and store in a cool, dry place. Those that had any color at all when you picked them will continue to ripen over the next month or two, so check them often, and use them as soon as they color up. Enjoy those that were still solid green as fried green tomatoes—one of the great late-fall taste treats!

## BEAT THE BITE

Believe it or not, squirrels and other varmints that take big chunks out of your tomatoes are often doing so to quench their thirst. So before you arm yourself with all kinds of pest controls, install a birdbath or other water source in your yard. If you give the thirsty critters an easy drink, they just might leave your tomatoes alone!

## BUTTER 'EM UP

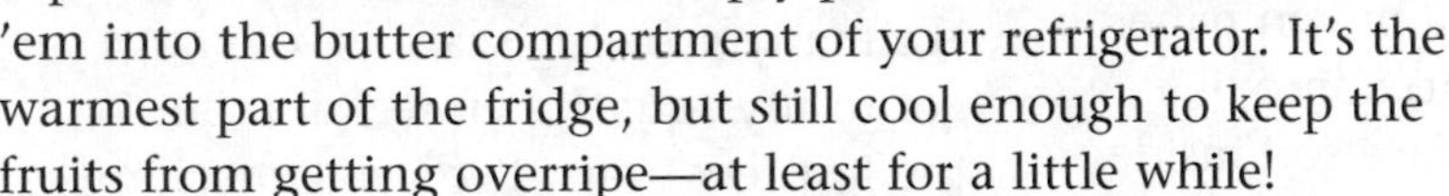

Fully ripened tomatoes keep their best flavor when they're stored at room temperature, but they'll last only a day or two that way. Well, we've found a way to keep 'em in top form for a week or so: Simply put 'em into the butter compartment of your refrigerator. It's the warmest part of the fridge, but still cool enough to keep the fruits from getting overripe—at least for a little while!

What if you have the opposite problem: already-picked fruits that are taking their good old time to finish ripening? Put 'em in a paper bag with an apple or a banana! Those fruits give off ethylene gas, which will speed the ripening process—and you'll have picture-perfect tomatoes in no time!

### Test Garden SECRET

If you don't want to bother with trellising or other heavy-duty support systems, determinate tomato varieties are definitely a good choice for you. The only drawback is that they usually bear fruit for just four to six weeks each summer—a much shorter period than indeterminate varieties offer. But guess what? Determinates can be a lot more than one-hit wonders! We've discovered that by pruning our plants back by a quarter to a third after their main crop, we can encourage new growth and often get another great crop at the end of the growing season. Now how's that for doing double duty?

## PICKY, PICKY

If your tomato plants always have lots of unripe fruits when cold weather returns, don't think you have to make drastic changes. Just try this trick next year—a month before you expect the first frost, start plucking all new flower clusters off of the plants. That way, you'll direct the plants' energy into ripening the tomatoes that are already on the vine, rather than producing new ones that won't have time to mature. To make the remaining fruits ripen even faster, spray 'em with our Hurry-Up-the-Harvest Tonic (see page 204).

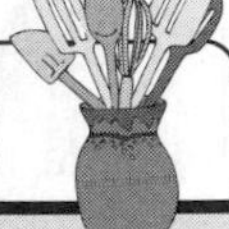

### Kitchen CLASSICS

Serve them as an appetizer, or as a side dish—either way, we guarantee that these oven-roasted tomatoes will become a family favorite! To prepare them, preheat your oven to 300°F, then line two baking sheets with foil, and generously spray the foil with cooking spray. Cut 4 round tomatoes crosswise into 3/4-inch-thick slices, and lay them on the baking sheets. Sprinkle with 2 teaspoons of sugar, 1 teaspoon of dried basil, and 1/2 teaspoon of ground black pepper. Bake for 45 to 55 minutes, or until the tomatoes start to shrivel; then remove from the oven. Sprinkle with 2 teaspoons of grated Parmesan cheese, and return to the oven for 1 to 2 minutes, or until the cheese melts. Serve warm.

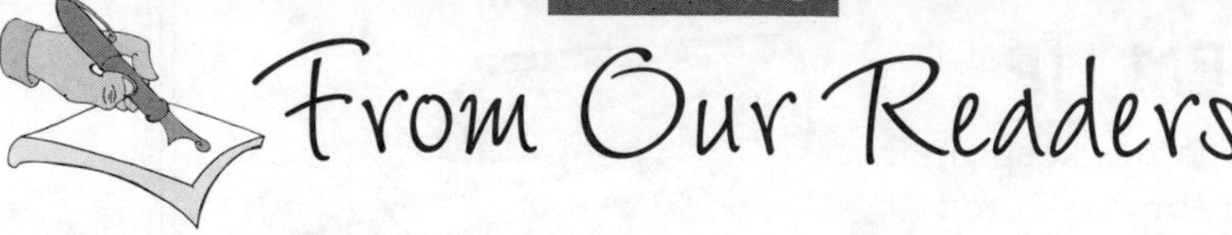

# From Our Readers

## BAGGED TOMATOES

Plant your tomatoes in thin brown paper lunch bags. Bury a brown paper bag (opened and upright) approximately 6 inches deep. Place soil inside the bottom of the bag, and set your tomato plants in the bag. Water well. I've found that the bag helps protect the plants against the elements and insects. And it can be clothes-pinned shut when you're expecting frost. If the bag begins to fold over, roll it down to stiffen the collar. After about four weeks, check to see if the bag is starting to decompose. If not, carefully tear it away from the growing plant.

***Sandy M., Westland, MI***

## BUG-FREE CUKES

Growing cucumbers used to be a problem for me beause of the destructive beetles in our area. After many years, I finally found a way to grow cucumbers without bugs chowing down on them. I start by planting sweet potatoes, and when they get a good start, I plant my cucumbers among the potatoes, where the potato leaves will give them protection. It's amazing, but I get lots of cukes now with no beetles!

***Charles G., Norfolk, VA***

## SQUASH-BUG CONTROL

For many growing seasons, the bugs got to my squash before I did. But in the last few years, I've been checking the squash each day when I can, and when the bugs start drilling holes in the lower stems, I go into organic action. I get out my shovel and bury the squash stems under good soil almost to the leaves, or lower if the bugs didn't get that high. It works, but it takes a little time for the plant to get reorganized. The bugs don't reappear, and there is much squash to be had by all!

***Charles G., Norfolk, VA***

## CORN PROTECTION

A gardening friend told me how to keep raccoons from eating sweet corn from my garden—sprinkle mothballs between the rows. This has kept the varmints from bothering my crops!

***Mike G., Troy, NY***

# From Our Readers

## A SHELL GAME

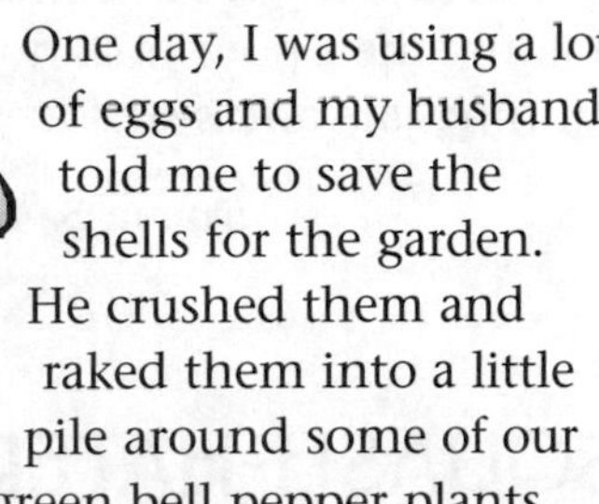

One day, I was using a lot of eggs and my husband told me to save the shells for the garden. He crushed them and raked them into a little pile around some of our green bell pepper plants (he didn't have enough for all of the plants). I had no clue which plants got the shells, but when it came time to pick the peppers, we could really see the difference. The peppers that got the shell treatment were bigger and healthier, their edible parts were thicker, and their taste was just divine.

***Darlene L., West Allis, WI***

## CROP CIRCLES

I've discovered a great way to keep my tomato plants fertilized through the season without a lot of extra work on my part. I dig a hole and fill it with aged manure. Then I plant five or six tomato plants in a circle around the manure. When it's time to water the tomatoes, I water only the manure hole. My tomatoes seem to love it, because I get a bumper crop!

***Denise C., Shiloh, OH***

## SUPER SQUASH!

Here in Albuquerque, we have a terrible problem with squash bugs. I heard about marigolds repelling squash bugs, so I planted a bunch of the flowers and then planted my squash in their midst. (I've found that I have to plant the marigolds first because the squash here grows too quickly.) Imagine my surprise when the plants surrounded with marigolds were untouched by squash bugs!

***Yvonne S., Albuquerque, NM***

## WINTER TOMATOES

For vine-ripened tomatoes in winter, prune pencil-thick branches from your best plants just before first frost in autumn and bring them inside. Strip the leaves from the bottom third of the branch, and remove fruits and any buds. Then place each stalk in potting soil in a large pot. Keep the soil moist, insert tomato cages, and cover with plastic. Place the pots in front of a sunny window. When new growth appears, remove the plastic and add fertilizer. You'll have tomatoes all winter long.

***Gerald M., Mascoutah, IL***

## CORN BREAD PUDDING BARS

1 can (16 oz.) of kernel corn, drained
1 can (16 oz.) of cream-style corn, drained
1 package (8½ oz.) of corn muffin mix
1 cup of sour cream
3 eggs
½ cup (1 stick) of butter, melted

Mix all the ingredients together and pour into to a greased 9 × 13-inch pan. Bake at 375°F for 30 to 40 minutes. Cool slightly, then cut into bars.

*Leah N., Mesa, AZ*

## TOMATO JUICE COCKTAIL

8 lb. of tomatoes
1 cup of chopped celery
½ cup of chopped onion
½ cup of chopped green pepper
1 tbsp. of sugar
2 tsp. of salt
2 tsp. of grated horseradish
2 tsp. of Worcestershire sauce
¼ tsp. of Tabasco® sauce

Peel and quarter the tomatoes. Then cook all the ingredients together until tender. Remove from the heat, and run the mixture through a blender and then a sieve. Heat the juice until boiling, then pour into hot, sterilized canning jars and seal.

*Donna S., El Reno, OK*

## SQUASH-HATER'S DELIGHT

2 lb. of summer squash, cut into chunks
2 green peppers, chopped
2 onions, chopped
½ cup (1 stick) of margarine
2 eggs, beaten
⅓ cup of sugar
1 tsp. of salt
½ tsp. of black pepper
2 cups of soft bread crumbs

In a large saucepan over medium-high heat, boil the squash until tender; drain and mash. Sauté the peppers and onions in the margarine. In a large bowl, mix the peppers and onions into the squash. Stir in the beaten eggs, sugar, salt, and black pepper. Layer the squash mixture with the bread crumbs in a greased 8 × 12-inch baking dish, alternating squash, then bread crumbs, then squash, and so on, ending with a layer of bread crumbs. Bake at 325°F for 1 hour.

*Bill H., Vancouver, WA*

## GREEN-TOMATO PIE

**$1^1/_8$ cups of sugar**
**$^1/_4$ cup of flour**
**$^1/_4$ tsp. of salt**
**$^1/_2$ tsp. of cinnamon**
**$^1/_4$ tsp. of ground cloves**
**$^1/_2$ tsp. of nutmeg**
**$3^1/_2$ cups of cored and sliced green tomatoes (about 8 medium-sized tomatoes)**
**2 tbsp. of lemon juice**
**1 tsp. of grated lemon rind**
**9" unbaked pie shell and top**
**1 tbsp. of margarine**

Combine the sugar, flour, salt, cinnamon, cloves, and nutmeg, and toss with the tomatoes. Add the lemon juice and rind. Pour it into the pie shell, and dot the filling with the margarine. Lay the top crust over the filling. Seal the crusts together, and gently slit the top. Bake at 425°F for 15 to 20 minutes, or at 350°F for 30 minutes.

***William M., Wayland, MI***

## ZUCCHINI CHEESE PUFFS

**6 medium-sized zucchini**
**1 cup of small-curd cottage cheese**
**1 cup of shredded Monterey Jack or cheddar cheese**
**2 eggs**
**$^3/_4$ tsp. of dried dillweed**
**$^3/_4$ tsp. of salt**
**$^1/_4$ tsp. of black pepper**
**$^1/_2$ cup of bread crumbs**
**1 tbsp. of butter, melted**

Cut the zucchini into chunks, or shred. Put in a large saucepan and cover with water. Bring to a boil, and boil for 5 minutes, then drain. Spoon the cooked squash into a shallow $1^1/_2$-quart baking dish. In a large bowl, mix together the cottage cheese, Jack/cheddar cheese, eggs, dillweed, salt, and pepper. Spoon the cheese mix over the zucchini. Bake uncovered at 350°F for 15 minutes. Mix the bread crumbs with the butter and sprinkle over the top. Then bake for another 15 minutes. Serve warm.

***Margaret H., Tacoma, WA***

# Chapter 13

# Heavenly Herbs

Of all the crops we grow here at the test gardens, herbs are closest to our hearts. Besides being beautiful in their own right, these sturdy, productive plants provide a bounty of flavor and fragrance. That means we get twice the benefits from a single planting: pretty leaves and flowers to look at outdoors, *and* terrific tastes to enhance our cooking indoors! And if all that wasn't enough, herbs happen to be some of the most trouble-free plants around. In this chapter, we've gathered up our top tips for getting the very best out of these versatile crops, from planting to harvesting, and beyond!

## A MATCH MADE IN HEAVEN

Most folks know that basil and tomatoes taste great together—but did you know that they make perfect partners in the garden, too? It's true! We'd heard this bit of gardening lore for years and finally decided to try it out; so we planted them together in one of our test garden beds, and planted the tomatoes alone in another bed. Sure enough, that old-time advice was right on the money: The tomato plants with basil buddies looked healthier overall, and we got a bumper crop of both! Besides enhancing each other's growth, growing tomatoes and basil in the same bed makes harvesting a breeze. You can get all the ingredients you need for a classic summer side dish in just one quick trip to the garden!

## JOIN THE BUSH LEAGUE

Here's a super double-duty herb: bush basil! This compact cutie produces dense, bushy mounds of tiny, bright green leaves, looking for all the world like a miniature, closely clipped shrub. Although the leaves are little in size, they're as big in flavor as their larger relatives—and there are a *lot* of them on every plant! A row of bush basil makes a neat edging for a flower garden or vegetable plot, but our favorite way to grow it is in a pot right outside the kitchen door. That way, we can easily reach out and snip a few shoots to spice up a salad or sandwich, even if it's pouring rain!

### JERRY'S Q&A

**Q** I like to start my basil plants indoors to get an early crop, but the transplants I set out never seem to grow well. Any advice?

**A** Yep: Don't jump the gun! Basil is one of those crops that really needs heat, and it hates it when temperatures drop below 45°F. If you really want to start the plants indoors, wait until just two or three weeks before your last frost date, so they're still fairly small when you set 'em out after the weather has settled and nighttime temperatures are at least 50°F. Or, simply wait a week or two *after* the frost date, then sow the seeds directly in your garden. We've found that later-sown plants tend to grow quicker, so they're usually ready to harvest at the same time as indoor-sown plants—with a lot less bother on your part!

# AN ARRAY OF BASILS

In our opinion, the hardest part about growing basil is deciding which ones to try! With dozens of different kinds to choose from, in such a variety of flavors, leaf shapes, and colors, it can be challenging to pick the perfect plants for your needs. To help simplify matters, we like to divide basils into three different groups, and grow a few from each in the test gardens every year:

**Best basils for the kitchen.** For true basil flavor, our favorite is the variety 'Genoa Profumatissima'. Plants labeled "sweet basil" are usually fine for cooking, but their flavors can vary. "Lettuce leaf" basils have extra-large leaves that are ideal for wrapping around fillings to make tasty appetizers; 'Mammoth' and 'Napoletano' are two good varieties. Lemon basil adds a delightful citrus touch to cooked dishes.

**Beautiful basils.** We love growing the purple-leaved basils in our flower garden, because they make a great contrast to both bright and pastel blooms—*and* we can eat them, too! 'Red Rubin' produces the most consistent deep-purple color. 'Purple Ruffles' and 'Dark Opal' can both have some green in the leaves, but they are attractive, too! 'African Blue' produces big, bushy plants (up to 3 feet tall or even higher), with purple-tinged green leaves, and purplish spikes of pink blossoms. The flavor of this one isn't pleasant, so we just let it bloom to enjoy the pretty flowers.

**For something different.** Quite a few other basils aren't our favorites for cooking or for looking at, but they sure make great scents! 'Anise', as you might expect, has a distinct licorice aroma—and yes, 'Cinnamon' smells just like it sounds. Other basils that we enjoy for their fragrance alone include 'Clove' and 'Spice', more commonly known as sacred or holy basil.

What's our No. 1 secret for getting the best out of our basil? Harvest early, and harvest often! We start picking as soon as our plants have at least six pairs of leaves, snipping off the shoot tip just above the first or second pair of leaves. Each leaf joint that's left will produce a new shoot, which is ready to harvest again in just a few weeks. We use so much basil that we usually pick the shoots as fast as they're ready, but sometimes, they get a little ahead of us and start producing buds and blooms. When that happens, that's our cue to get out there and pinch off those shoots *right away*. Otherwise, the plants will stop producing new leaves, and our harvest is over for the year!

## SAVOR THE FLAVOR

Basil plants are real summer-lovers, turning black at the slightest touch of fall frosts. So when the weather forecast calls for temperatures to dip below 40°F, that's your cue to snip off all of the top growth and bring it into the kitchen. If you end up with too much for fresh use, pulverize the leaves in a food processor with just enough olive oil to make a smooth paste. Use the paste instead of butter or mayonnaise on sandwiches for a dash of heart-healthy unsaturated fat. Or freeze it in ice-cube trays, then add it to soups, stews, and pasta dishes all year long.

Don't have time to deal with preserving your harvest right now? Toss a sheet or floating row cover over your basil on the first few chilly nights, and you may extend your harvest for another few weeks into the fall.

### LEAN AND GREEN

If your basil plants look great but taste bland, you're probably being too nice to them! They like fertile soil, but if you're too generous with the nitrogen, their leaves will be low in the oils that give the plant its distinctive flavor. So keep high-nitrogen fertilizers for hungry crops like corn, and use compost to bring out the best in your basil!

## A WINTER WONDER

Dried basil is okay in a pinch, but it doesn't compare to the rich flavor of the fresh leaves. Luckily, it's easy to have that great taste on hand all winter long, by growing the plants indoors! Either take cuttings from your favorite garden basils in late summer, and root them in pots of lightly moist growing medium, or sow a few seeds in pots in mid- to late summer. Make sure you bring your potted basils indoors before frost; then set 'em on a sunny windowsill or under plant lights in a warm room. Keep 'em well pinched to promote bushy growth, and you'll enjoy that summery flavor even in the depths of winter.

### Kitchen CLASSICS

There's no way we could talk about basil without giving you our favorite pesto recipe! We admit that it's incredibly rich, but just a small serving satisfies. To make it, place 1 cup of extra virgin olive oil and 2 large cloves of garlic in a food processor. Using the large blade, blend on high speed until smooth. With the blade spinning, open the chute and gradually add 3 tablespoons of raw pine nuts (pignoli); process until smooth. Gather 2 cups of firmly packed basil leaves (with the stems removed), and add to the food processor, a few at a time, until well pulverized. Add 1½ teaspoons of salt and ¼ teaspoon of ground black pepper, then gradually add 1 cup of freshly grated Parmesan cheese. (If necessary, stop the food processor and stir down the mixture with a stiff rubber spatula.) Continue processing until smooth.

### TRIED-AND-TRUE

**G**randma Putt loved the mild onion flavor of chives so much, she figured out a way to enjoy 'em all year long! She'd dig up a clump or two in late fall, cut all of the top growth back to an inch or two above the soil, and then leave the plants in her cold frame for at least a month to get a good chilling. Then she'd bring 'em inside, pot them up, and set 'em on a sunny windowsill. The leafless clumps would get the signal that spring had already arrived, and in no time they'd be sending up new growth that Grandma could snip for cooking all through the winter months.

## NO FUSS, NO MUSS

If you like plant-it-and-forget-it crops, you'll *love* growing chives! Give 'em a site with full sun and well-drained soil, and they'll produce lots of those tasty leaves without giving you a moment's trouble. After all, no self-respecting pest would chew on chives, and deer don't like 'em much either! In fact, the only thing you need to think about is keeping 'em from being *too* happy and spreading themselves around your whole garden.

Take our word for it: This is one herb that you can harvest to your heart's content all summer long, and it'll keep coming back for more. Be sure to keep the pretty flowers picked, too—they're wonderful crumbled into salads or used to add flavor and color to white vinegar. If the plants produce more blooms than you can use, be sure to snip them off as soon as the flowers fade, or else they'll drop *lots* of seeds everywhere, and you'll have more chives than you could ever use!

## DON'T NIP THE TIPS

What's the most common mistake folks make when harvesting chives? Snipping off the leaves at the tips, rather than the base. We understand why—it's because the young leaves, and especially their tips, are the most tender and flavorful part of the plant. But if you always cut only the tips, pretty soon your whole clump will look like it's had a bad haircut, and you'll only be left with the older leaves for the rest of the year. The secret to smart harvesting is to grab several blades in your fingers and cut them off down low—about 2 inches above the soil. That encourages the plant to send up new leaves, ensuring a steady supply of top-notch chives all through the growing season.

## START-UP SOLUTIONS

Once you've got 'em growing in your garden, keeping chives alive is practically a no-brainer. Getting 'em *started* is another matter entirely! You can try to raise them from seeds, but they take ages to sprout, and then they grow very slowly. Plus, the tiny, grasslike seedlings are a real challenge to handle at transplanting. We get around that by using small (2- or 3-inch) pots, and carefully sowing the seeds evenly over the surface of moistened seed-starting mix, then covering them with another ½ inch of mix. Once the plants are finally up and growing, we can transfer the whole pot of seedlings to the garden as one clump—no thinning required!

Still, it'll take a year or two for a seed-grown patch to be vigorous enough for harvesting—and that's why we highly recommend starting with part of an established clump instead! Seek out a friend or neighbor who already has chives in their garden and ask them to remember you when they divide their plants. These need to be divided every three years anyway, and most folks are glad to find a good home for their extras!

## EXTRA-LIVELY CHIVES

Want to really jazz up your meals? Then you need to give garlic chives (*Allium tuberosum*) a try! The plants look a lot like common chives—except that the leaves are flat instead of rounded, and they have white flowers instead of pink—and they are just as easy to grow. But unlike the oniony flavor of regular chives, the leaves and blooms of this relative have a mild garlic flavor that goes with just about everything except dessert!

### No-Jive Chive Tea

Sure, chives are great in the kitchen—but they're also worth growing to protect your other plants. One of our favorite uses for this abundant herb is this simple solution for spraying on apple and peach trees. It's great for foiling fungi before they can get a foothold on your fruit!

**1 part chive leaves (horseradish leaves work, too)**
**4 parts water**

Put the chives and water in a pan, and bring the water to a boil. Then remove the pan from the heat, let the tea cool, and strain out the leaves. Pour the remaining liquid into a hand-held sprayer. Spray your fruit trees every seven days, and say "Farewell, fungus!"

## LET'S GET FRESH

Once you've tasted the delicate flavor of garden-fresh dill and fennel, you'll never go back to that tasteless dried stuff! But these handy herbs are good for more than just their leaves and seeds—they are fabulous in the flower garden as well. Their fernlike foliage makes a beautiful backdrop for the bright blooms of annuals and perennials, and their lacy yellow bloom clusters add color in their own right. Best of all, the tiny individual blossoms are rich in pollen and nectar, which makes them wonderful for attracting a wide variety of beneficial insects to your yard.

Just be sure to give these tall-growing herbs a sheltered site so the wind can't knock 'em down—then let these triple-duty herbs add flavor to your cooking, beauty to your flower beds, and a pest-fighting punch to your veggie garden!

Normally, we know that when we grow annual herbs, we'll need to replant them every spring. But we don't have to do that with dill anymore, thanks to this great trick! We've discovered that if we set aside a permanent space for our dill, then let some of the plants drop their seeds in the garden, they'll come up year after year in the same spot without us ever having to replant. Talk about a trouble-free crop!

## A DILLY OF A TIP

If you're growing dill to collect the seeds, just about any old kind of seed will do to get the plants growing. But if you're looking for a good harvest of those light, feathery leaves (commonly called "dillweed"), it's worth seeking out some of the newer varieties that are on the market. 'Dukat' has become one of our test-garden standards, due to its exceptionally good flavor (even when dried). And it grows only 2 to 3 feet tall, so it's much less likely to fall over—a big plus! 'Hercules' is our latest favorite, with exceptionally flavorful foliage on extra-vigorous, 3- to 4-foot-tall plants. 'Fernleaf' is a great choice for small spaces, because it grows only 18 inches tall, with lots of lush leaves. Grow it in a pot right outside your kitchen door, and you can have fresh dill on hand all summer long!

## DOUBLE-DUTY FENNEL

If you're like us, you're always on the lookout for ways to boost your harvests without having to dig up more garden space. Well, here's a super double-duty crop—Florence fennel, also known as sweet fennel or finocchio. The lacy leaves have that distinctive fennel flavor, so you can use them just like the regular herb. Then, as the plants mature, you'll notice that they produce a large, swollen base with thickened leaf stalks. This white, bulblike structure tastes something like celery with a licorice-like tang—great for mincing into soups and salads!

## NEED THE SEEDS?

It used to be that when we'd grow dill and fennel for seeds, we'd have a hard time knowing just when to harvest them. If we waited until all of the seeds were brown, they'd fall off as soon as we touched them, and we ended up dropping more in the garden than we collected for cooking! Fortunately, one of our helpers figured out a better way. Here's what we've learned:

**Step 1.** As soon as the dill or fennel flowers start blooming, watch them carefully. Within two to three weeks, the flowers in the outer edge of the cluster (the first ones to start blooming) will have produced seeds. When those seeds start turning brown, you'll know it's time to harvest.

**Step 2.** Use scissors or garden shears to snip off the seedheads, working carefully, so you don't jostle them and knock off the seeds. Be sure to leave a good bit of stem on them—12 to 18 inches is good.

**Step 3.** Carefully gather the seedheads into bunches, and hang them upside down in a dark, airy place. Spread a sheet of newspaper on the floor underneath them to catch the seeds as they drop. Within two to three weeks, pull off any seeds remaining on the plants, then gather up your nice, clean seed harvest!

### Kitchen CLASSICS

Pork tenderloin is about as lean a meat as you can get. But it's too large a cut for most families to eat in one meal, so there are always delicious leftovers. Here's a quickie supper for two that uses up those leftovers—with a little help from your herb garden! Place 2 cups of sauerkraut (rinsed and drained) in a large nonstick skillet with $1/2$ cup of water. Sprinkle 1 tablespoon of fennel seeds evenly over the sauerkraut. Top with 2 cups of split baby carrots, 4 whole, small canned potatoes, and 6 ounces of thinly sliced, cooked pork tenderloin. Cover, bring to a boil, and then simmer for about 5 minutes, or until the carrots are tender and all of the ingredients are hot.

One of our favorite ways to use mint is in ice cubes, as a cool garnish for summer beverages. But if you make ice cubes using tap water, they're often so cloudy that you can't even see the pretty leaf inside. Fortunately, our clever test-garden helpers figured out the secret to getting perfectly clear cubes—by using water that's been boiled, then cooled! Freeze an ice cube tray half full of the water, then top each half-cube with a clean mint leaf. Add a spoonful of water to each one and refreeze, then fill completely and freeze again. This trick works well with many other herbs, too, including bright blue borage blooms and the citrusy leaves of lemon balm or lemon verbena.

## CORRAL THESE CREEPERS

Mints look good, smell great, and taste even better! Give them half a chance, though, and they'll overrun your garden with lightning speed. To make mints behave themselves, try this trick—plant them in large containers sunk into the soil, so that the rim extends about an inch above the soil surface. (The jumbo pots used to grow trees and shrubs are ideal.) Check on them periodically to make sure that the meandering mint roots don't jump the rim and wander where they're not wanted!

## WHAT'S THE DIFFERENCE?

Mints are classic "pass-along" plants: Because they grow so quickly, folks always have plenty to share. Keep in mind, though, that not all mints are created equal; they all have different flavors and uses. If someone offers you a clump of mint but they don't know what kind it is, chances are it's probably either peppermint or spearmint—and it's not hard to tell 'em apart. Peppermint has deep green leaves and purple-tinged stems, while spearmint is usually bright green. If you still aren't sure which you have, rub the leaves and take a good whiff: Peppermint is much more pungent than spearmint. (If you have a choice, by the way, we suggest spearmint over peppermint, because spearmint's milder flavor is much more useful for cooking.)

### SOWING'S A NO-GO

Thinking about starting your peppermint patch from seed? Think again! True peppermint (*Mentha × piperita*) is a hybrid that doesn't produce seed, so the only way to get it started is by dividing or taking cuttings from an existing clump.

## MINT BY THE YARD

If you have a damp, shady spot where other plants just won't thrive, don't despair—you can bet that mints will grow there! Planted where they're allowed to spread freely, these vigorous herbs make beautiful, fragrant, *and* flavorful groundcovers. Put some stepping stones through the patch, and you can enjoy the wonderful scents as you brush by the plants along the path. Once or twice during the summer, put your mower blade on its highest setting and run your mower over the whole area. That will help keep the patch tidy and promote lower, bushier growth. (Here at the test gardens, we take turns mowing the mint patch—the wonderful fragrance of the cut leaves makes it one of our favorite tasks!)

## THE MORE MINT, THE MERRIER

Mints are a perfect herb for impatient gardeners, because you can start harvesting as soon as the new shoots start peeking up through the soil. Little wonder that they are a favorite accompaniment for other early delicacies, such as spring lamb and just-picked peas! Don't hesitate to harvest as much mint as you need. Frequent snipping keeps the plants lush and productive, encouraging the shoots to branch and providing more of those tender, flavorful stem tips. If your plants produce more growth than you can use, try one our favorite tricks: Tie the fresh stems into bundles, and hang them in front of a screen door or open window to scent the summer air the natural way!

### Healthy Container-Herb Tonic

Potted herbs don't have much soil to support them, so they depend on you for a steady supply of food. This mild, but nutritious, tonic fits the bill perfectly!

**1/4 cup of brewed tea**
**1 tbsp. of dishwashing liquid**
**1 tbsp. of antiseptic mouthwash**
**1 tbsp. of ammonia**
**1 qt. of warm water**

Mix these ingredients in a watering can, and water your potted herbs with it once a week. Besides giving your herbs a gentle nutrient boost, it'll help fight insects and diseases, too!

It's fast. It's fun. And it's fall! There's no better dessert for your end-of-the-season cookout or picnic in the park. Simply dice 1 red or green apple and 1 pear (both unpeeled), then peel and slice 1 banana. Add all of the fruit to a medium bowl, then combine with 3 tablespoons of lemon juice and 1/4 cup of chopped fresh spearmint. Cover and chill for several hours before serving. This easy recipe makes four servings, but it's a snap to double it if you have plenty of fruit on hand. (Having enough mint is *never* a problem!)

## CONTAIN YOURSELF!

Where garden space is at a premium—or if you just don't want to let mints loose in your yard—planting 'em in pots is a great way to go. Pots, planters, window boxes, and even hanging baskets can all provide perfect growing conditions for these fragrant favorites. Just remember to put a saucer underneath, or else set them on an impervious surface (like pavement). Otherwise, the roots can creep out of the drainage holes and start spreading before you know it!

Mints grow quickly and will fill even a large planter in no time, so plan on dividing the entire clump every spring. Keep just a quarter of the clump, and replant it into fresh potting soil. Find a good home for the other pieces, or pot them up, too. (One word of warning: Don't throw 'em in your compost pile, or you'll soon have a *mint* pile!)

## AN HERB FOR ALL SEASONS

The return of Jack Frost doesn't have to signal the end of your mint harvest! To extend the season and keep the mint coming, pot up a clump or two of your favorite mint in late summer, then leave the pots outdoors for four to six weeks after the first frost. Once the plants have gotten a good chilling, bring the pots indoors to a bright windowsill, or set them under plant lights. Before you know it, new shoots will appear, and you can enjoy fresh-picked mint all winter long!

## THE NAME GAME

Talk about an identity crisis! These tasty herbs tend to get mixed up with some not-so-flavorful relatives, so it's smart to do your homework *before* you buy:

**Common oregano (*Origanum vulgare*).** Also known as wild marjoram, common oregano is usually what you get if you buy plants simply labeled "oregano," or if you try to grow oregano from seed. Perennial in Zones 5 to 9, the plant typically has purplish pink flowers. Common oregano doesn't have a whole lot of flavor—it varies from plant to plant.

**Greek oregano (*O. heracleoticum* or *O. vulgare* subsp. *hirtum*).** Sometimes called "true oregano," this aromatic, strong-flavored herb is the choice of many cooks for soups, stews, and tomato sauces. It's usually hardy in Zones 5 to 9, but it tends to be less vigorous than common oregano. You can tell them apart by Greek oregano's white flowers and more pungent fragrance when the foliage is rubbed.

**Sweet marjoram (*O. majorana*).** Long favored for use in cooking, due to its milder oregano flavor, sweet marjoram is a tender perennial usually grown as an annual. It, too, has white flowers.

## HARVEST HELPER

Planning on preserving some great flavor to spice up winter meals? Prime time for picking both oregano and sweet marjoram is just before the blooms open. For no-fuss harvesting, simply gather all of the top growth from one clump in one hand, and cut off all the stems about 1 inch above the ground with your other hand. The plants will resprout in no time, and you may even get a second harvest later in the season!

## Test Garden

Many herbs will grow well in the same good soil that you give your veggies and flowers—but not oregano and marjoram! When we tried to grow them among our other plants, with regular watering and lots of fertilizer, these Mediterranean natives tended to get loose and floppy, drop their leaves, and have a poor flavor. So now we're careful to give them a site closer to their native habitat—plenty of sun, and loose, not-too-fertile soil, with a pH around neutral. And when we mulch our other herbs with compost, we pass right by these two. Now, our oregano and marjoram plants are dense and bushy—and positively bursting with flavor!

## From Our Readers

*Looking for a clever way to keep track of your herbs? When setting out plants or sowing seeds, use a permanent laundry marker to write the name and date on the handle of a plastic knife, fork, or spoon. Stick the plastic silverware down into the soil by the plant and you'll never have to guess what it is!*

Vera B.,
Robeline, LA

## LET'S GET GROWING!

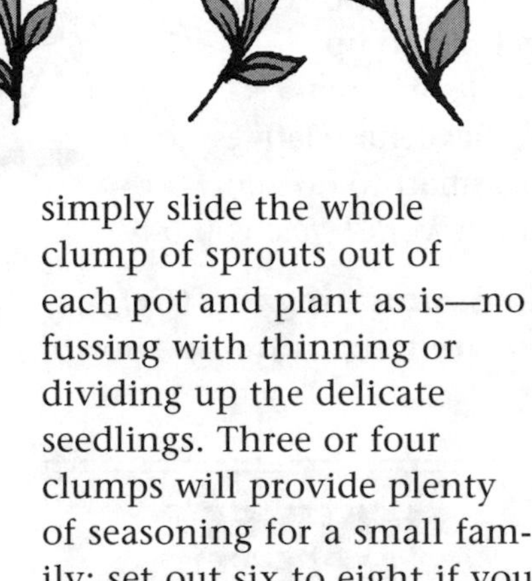

If you want to grow Greek oregano, start with purchased plants, or get a division from a friend who has a clump with a good flavor. Remember that this "real" oregano is strong stuff, so you need only one or two plants for fresh use—or three or four if you want to dry a lot for winter use.

Sweet marjoram, on the other hand, is a snap to grow from seed. We start ours indoors in midspring, scattering the seeds thinly but evenly over the surface of several 2- or 3-inch pots. That way, when all danger of frost has passed, we can simply slide the whole clump of sprouts out of each pot and plant as is—no fussing with thinning or dividing up the delicate seedlings. Three or four clumps will provide plenty of seasoning for a small family; set out six to eight if you have a large family or plan to harvest for drying.

## THE INSIDE SECRET

For a taste of summer even when there's snow on the ground, grow some sweet marjoram indoors through the winter. Sow the seeds in pots in early fall, and keep them in a warm, bright spot on a sunny windowsill, or under lights. Don't want to bother with seeds? It's also a simple matter to dig up your garden-grown clumps in late summer, divide them into several parts, and pot them up to bring inside when the weather gets chilly. Enjoy their flavorful foliage all winter long, and then plant those clumps back outside next spring for an extra-early harvest next summer!

## SPEED 'EM UP

What's the trickiest part of growing parsley? Getting it started! Parsley plants produce a deep taproot, so they generally don't take kindly to transplanting. But when you try to grow them from seeds sown in the garden, you'll find that they tend to take a long time to sprout (sometimes as long as six weeks). We've discovered two amazingly easy ways to fool the seeds into sprouting a whole lot sooner—usually in a matter of days, instead of weeks! If we're sowing from early spring to early summer, we soak the seeds in warm water overnight. (Putting them in a Thermos® helps make sure that the water stays warm for as long as possible.) If we sow from early to late summer for a fall harvest, we freeze the seeds in ice cubes instead (two or three per cube), then plant the whole cubes in the garden. This makes it a snap to space the seeds perfectly, too!

## FLAT'S WHERE IT'S AT

When most folks think of parsley, they picture the frilly bit of green on the side of their dinner plate. That's the kind known as curly parsley (*Petroselinum crispum* var. *crispum*), and while it makes a pretty garnish, it's fine for eating, too. (It also makes a beautiful edging for a flower bed, by the way!) But if you really want the best flavor, we suggest growing Italian parsley (*P. crispum* var. *neapolitanum*) instead. Its flat, deep green leaves aren't as decorative, but they hold up much better during cooking.

### Kitchen CLASSICS

In the heat of summer, when you don't feel like eating anything warm, give this recipe a try. It satisfies like a meal, yet it's refreshingly light. To start, boil 1/2 pound of bow-tie pasta in a large pot until it's al dente. Drain and toss with 3 tablespoons of olive oil, then cool completely. Toss with 1 cup of chopped honeydew melon, 1/2 cup of seedless purple grapes (halved), 1/2 cup of finely chopped fresh Italian (flat-leaved) parsley, and 2 tablespoons of lemon juice. Makes four servings.

# A COOL IDEA

Some herbs, like parsley and basil, are slow to air-dry, and they often lose their pretty green color in the process. Use this trick to dry them quickly—harvest a handful of stalks, and put 'em in brown paper lunch bags. Shut the tops of the bags with clothespins or paper clips, write the herb name on the outside of each, and set the bags in the fridge. Check on the herbs in a few days; they're ready when they're crispy to the touch. You can thank your fridge's dehumidifying action for this quick and easy process. Best of all, you can store the dried herbs—bags and all—right in the same place until you need 'em!

## THE OUTER LIMITS

Knowing the proper way to harvest parsley can make a big difference in the productivity of your plants. Instead of snipping from the center of the clump, harvest the *outer* leaves regularly, even if you don't need them immediately for cooking. (Simply stand the cut stems in a glass of water in your refrigerator to hold them for up to a week.) That way, the plant will keep producing a steady supply of top-quality leaves, and you'll always have plenty of parsley to pick!

# BABY THOSE BUTTERFLIES

Parsley is seldom bothered by pests, but sometimes you'll spot a black-striped, green caterpillar or two chomping on the leaves. Don't be too quick to destroy these colorful caterpillars (commonly called parsleyworms), because they are the larvae of beautiful, black swallowtail butterflies! Here at the test gardens, we plant an extra patch of parsley in an out-of-the-way spot. That way, when we find the caterpillars on our main crop, we can relocate them to our "butterfly nursery." There, they can chew to their heart's content without ruining our harvest!

## From Our Readers

*I have a natural remedy to rid your roses of aphids: garlic-and-parsley tea. Put 2 tablespoons of minced garlic and 1/2 cup of chopped dried parsley leaves in 3 cups of water, boil down to 2 cups, then strain and cool the liquid. Put 1 cup of the liquid in a hose-end sprayer, and spray rose bushes and any other plants that aphids like. Or save yourself a step and just plant garlic and parsley between all your roses; that works, too!*

C. E., Folsom, CA

## ROSEMARY IN A RUSH

If you're ready to get growing with rosemary, take our advice, and don't even *think* about bothering with seeds. It's hard to get them to sprout (we usually get only half of them to germinate, at best), and it can take two or three years for the seedlings to get big enough to harvest from. Since a single rosemary plant can provide enough leaves for most families, it makes a lot more sense to simply buy one. That way, you can choose exactly the plant form you want, too—this herb can have either an upright or a trailing growth habit.

## SNIP IT

Harvesting rosemary is no hassle—it's as simple as a quick snip with your scissors. Just cut off 3 to 4 inches of one shoot tip—that's enough for most recipes. If you need more, go ahead and gather it, as long as you don't take off more than a quarter of the top growth at any one time. Need to store your harvest for a day or two? Wash it, pat it dry, wrap it in a paper towel, and store it in a plastic bag.

If your plants are producing more than you can use for cooking, snip off a few shoot tips that are about 6 inches long, then tie them together. Use the bundle as a brush for applying sauces when grilling meats or vegetables, then toss it onto the coals for the last 10 minutes of cooking to add flavor and aroma.

### BRANCHING OUT

When it comes to keeping rosemary plants looking bushy and producing generously, periodic pinching is the key. Begin pinching or snipping off the growing tips when the plants are 6 inches tall, and repeat after every 4 to 6 inches of new growth. Don't discard these bits, by the way—enjoy the tender trimmings as tasty salad toppers!

### Kitchen CLASSICS

Getting a little tired of eating plain old chicken again? Try perking up that poultry with the heavenly aroma and flavor of rosemary! The secret to this recipe is cooking the chicken with the skin on to keep it moist and juicy. Just toss the skin before you eat, to keep the fat and calories under control. In a heavy nonstick skillet, place 2 chicken breasts (bone in and skin on) with the skin side down. Lay a small branch of rosemary on each. Cover, and cook on medium-high for 10 to 15 minutes, or until the chicken is no longer pink inside and the juices run clear. Remove and discard the skin and rosemary, and lightly season with salt and freshly ground black pepper to taste.

## GET POTTED

For those of you who live in Zones 8 to 10, rosemary is a hardy perennial—you can just plant it once and enjoy it for years. In colder climates, growing this aromatic herb is a bit more trouble; but in our opinion, the flavor of fresh rosemary makes it worth every bit of effort!

The easiest route is to purchase a new plant each spring, plant it in your garden, and then let it die when winter temperatures drop below 25°F. But you know what? This versatile herb can adapt well to life in containers, too! That means you can set a potted rosemary plant outside in spring after all danger of frost has passed—it'll thrive on a hot, sunny site like a patio or other paved surface. Then, in the fall, bring it back inside, so you can harvest all winter long, too! While indoors, rosemary prefers to stay cool (about 45°F), so a sunny but unheated porch is ideal.

### Happy Herb Tonic

Herbs generally don't like a whole lot of food, but they do appreciate a mild feeding every now and again. This tonic is one we swear by for keeping all kinds of herbs happy and high-yielding.

**1/4 cup of brewed tea**
**1/2 tbsp. of bourbon**
**1/2 tbsp. of ammonia**
**1/2 tbsp. of hydrogen peroxide**
**1/2 tsp. of dishwashing liquid**
**1 gal. of warm water**

Mix these ingredients in a watering can, and sprinkle it over your herbs every six weeks during the growing season.

## BURNING FOR YOU

Want to enjoy fantastic fragrance from your herb garden even in wintertime? Save the dried stalks of rosemary and tie them into bundles with cotton string. Toss a bundle or two into your fireplace for a heavenly reminder of summer. Other perfect plants to dry, bundle, and burn include basil, bee balm (*Monarda*), lavender, lemon verbena (*Aloysia triphylla*), mint, and thyme.

## A TASTEFUL TIP

It stands to reason that herbs with edible leaves have edible flowers, too! Toss fresh sage flowers (both the common and pineapple kinds) into salads, float 'em in soups, or mix 'em in with herb leaves in pesto for a citrus-mint tang. Other herbs with especially flavorful flowers include basil, borage, chives, cilantro (coriander), dill, garlic, lemon balm, mint, oregano, parsley, rosemary, and thyme.

## DON'T SKIMP ON SAGE

For most families, a single clump of sage will provide plenty of pungent leaves all summer long. But the gray-green leaves and blue blooms are so pretty (and so popular with hummingbirds) that we suggest finding space for sage in your flower gardens, too!

It's a snap to grow all of the sage you need from seed. Sow indoors in early to mid-spring at 60° to 70°F, and you'll see seedlings within a few weeks. The young plants typically take two years to really bush out, but if you have several plants, you can harvest lightly from each during the first year without harming them. In the second spring, trim the woody stems back by one-half to two-thirds to promote plenty of tender new shoots for cooking—and dense, bushy growth to admire in the garden!

### Sage Soap Spray

Aromatic herbs appeal to people, but bugs sure can't stand the smell of 'em! When you combine these fragrant plants with soap to make this tonic, you'll end up with a spray that kills the bad bugs that are already around *and* keeps the others from stopping by, too.

**1 cup of wormwood or tansy leaves**
**1 cup of lavender leaves**
**1 cup of sage leaves**
**1 tsp. of Murphy's Oil Soap®**
**Water**

Put the herbs in a canning jar, and fill the jar with boiling water. Let it cool, then strain out the herbs. Mix 1/8 cup of the liquid with 2 cups of water and 1 teaspoon of Murphy's Oil Soap, pour into a hand-held sprayer, and apply to bug-bothered plants to send pests packin'.

We like to tuck sage plants everywhere in our test gardens—with other herbs, veggies, flowers, and even shrub plantings! So you can imagine that come midsummer, we have a whole lot of sage on hand for harvesting. One of our favorite ways to make the most of this abundance is by making herbal wreaths. We snip off a basketful of 4- to 6-inch shoots, then gather them into small bundles and attach them to a wire wreath form with dark yarn or lightweight floral wire. Once the wreath is completely covered, we hang it from a hook in the ceiling in a dark, airy spot to dry. Once the wreath is completely dry, we have a decorative way to display our dried sage—*and* have it right on hand for seasoning winter meals in style!

## WHAT'S IN A NAME?

If you decide to shop for sage plants instead of growing them yourself, you'll find lots of varieties to choose from! Besides the common culinary sage (*Salvia officinalis*), there is 'Purpurea', with purplish gray foliage; 'Icterina', with yellow-splashed green leaves; and 'Tricolor', with a mix of cream, purple, and green in each leaf. All of these are beautiful and add lots of color to the herb garden, but they tend to be less vigorous and less hardy than the common kind. One selection that we've had really good luck with is 'Berggarten', with broad, silvery gray leaves. It's gorgeous in the garden and grows like a champ, too!

### MOVE IT!

Have an extra sage plant on hand? Put it in a pot! Set it outside during the summertime, then bring it indoors for the winter to enjoy a steady supply of fresh foliage all through the cold months.

## GET FRUITY

Looking for something a little different to liven up your herb garden? Here at the test gardens, we're plum crazy about the out-of-the-ordinary species known as pineapple sage (*S. elegans*). This fruity beauty grows 3 to 4 feet tall, with bright red blooms and an abundance of bright green leaves that smell and taste exactly like…you guessed it, pineapple! This versatile herb complements a variety of dishes, from savory to sweet, but we particularly like the leaves in fruit salads and pound cakes. They make great garnishes as well, particularly for teas and party punch bowls.

## THE REAL THING

Watch out—not all tarragons are created equal! Seed-grown plants of tarragon may or may not smell or taste the way they're supposed to. In fact, some don't have any scent—or flavor—at all! True French tarragon (the type prized for cooking), on the other hand, doesn't set seed, so you have to start with a division from a friend's clump, or with a purchased plant. To make sure you're getting the tarragon that you want, buy your herbs from a reputable nursery—and *always* rub and sniff the leaves before you buy.

## TLC FOR TARRAGON

Here's a handy hint for top-notch tarragon—unlike some common culinary herbs, this one *loves* the rich, moist soil that veggies and flowers thrive in. So give your French tarragon a good spot and a bit of compost to keep it growing vigorously and producing those licorice-like leaves—then save those dry, infertile sites for oregano, thyme, and other tough subjects!

## SCISSORS, PLEASE

You don't need any special tools to harvest tarragon—just a pair of sharp scissors for snipping. You see, yanking on stems damages the plants—especially the roots—slowing down growth and reducing your harvest. But with one clean cut, you'll get damage-free leaves for your kitchen, and the plants that are left can keep producing more for you to pick!

*Here's how I fertilize small areas of my garden. I pour the dry fertilizer into an empty Parmesan cheese canister (the kind with the shaker top). Just twist the top so the opening is covered with the shaker holes, then shake away to sprinkle out the perfect amount!*

Nina C.,
Lexington, SC

Q I've heard that French tarragon is the kind to grow for cooking, and that Russian tarragon is the bitter, less-flavorful substitute you get if you try to grow tarragon from seed. But what in the world is Mexican tarragon?

A Good question! Mexican tarragon (*Tagetes lucida*) is actually a kind of marigold—but it's not like the big-flowered hybrids that fill flower beds everywhere. It does have bright yellow blooms, but they're on the small side, and that's okay—you want the plant mostly for its leaves, anyway. They have a wonderful tarragon-like taste with a touch of cinnamon, too. This pretty herb is super easy to grow from seed, and grows fast enough to be treated like an annual. Best of all, it's a lot more heat-tolerant than French tarragon—so it's a super choice for hot-climate gardeners!

## FOR THE SERIOUS CHEF

When it comes to cooking, dried tarragon can't hold a candle to the delicate flavor of the garden-fresh growth. To have a supply of green, growing tarragon all year-round, pot up a clump in late summer, and leave it outdoors for several weeks after the first frost. Then bring it indoors, trim off the browned top growth, set it in a warm, bright spot, and enjoy the tender new shoots as needed.

## VIM AND VINEGAR

Have plenty of herbs on hand? Preserving that fantastic flavor is as easy as 1-2-3! All you need is some vinegar and fresh herbs, and you've got yourself the fixin's for gourmet-quality marinades and salad dressings. (Tarragon is our favorite for vinegars, but other good herbs to try include chive blossoms, dill, fennel, and parsley.) Just follow these three simple steps:

**Step 1.** Fill clean jars with white wine (or rice wine) vinegar, and add several sprigs of herbs—all of one kind, or a mix of two or three per jar. Close the jars, and set 'em on your kitchen counter or in an out-of-the-way place.

**Step 2.** After several weeks, open the jars and smell the vinegars. If you can detect a rich, herbal aroma, they're ready to use; otherwise, reclose the jars, and check again every week until they are ready.

**Step 3.** For an extra-special look (great if you plan to give the vinegar as a gift), strain out the old herbs, move the vinegar to a fancier bottle, then add a new sprig or two to the new vinegar bottle.

## CONSIDER YOUR OPTIONS

If you need thyme for your garden (and who doesn't?), it pays to do your homework before you choose your plants. Most nurseries sell two types: mat-forming kinds and bushy kinds. The ground-hugging types—including creeping thyme (*Thymus serpyllum*) and woolly thyme (*T. pseudolanuginosus*)—typically have a dense covering of very tiny leaves on thin, trailing stems, making them ideal for growing as ornamental groundcovers. The bushier kinds, such as common thyme (*T. vulgaris*), have a more upright habit and come in a variety of great flavors. They are the types to try when you want tasty thymes for your table!

## PRIME THYME

Overwhelmed by your choice of thymes? You can't do better than starting with common thyme, either from seed or from purchased plants. This versatile herb complements just about any dish, from meats and veggies to breads, soups, and salads. Once you've had some experience growing the common type, consider branching out into some of the more unusual kinds. Here at the test gardens, some of our favorites include caraway thyme (*T. herba-barona*) and lemon thyme—they smell and taste just like their names suggest!

No matter which thymes you try, the secret to success is simple—get the site right. Well-drained, neutral to alkaline soil is a must, and full sun is best, although most thymes can tolerate a half-day of sun and a half-day of partial shade. And don't be too kind to your thymes—abundant water and too-fertile soil will cause them to grow quickly at first, then flop open and rot out before you know it!

### Kitchen CLASSICS

Need something to make tonight's dinner really special? Use this quick-to-fix white sauce over chicken, vegetables, potatoes, noodles, rice, or in casseroles such as chicken potpie. Bring 1 cup of water to a boil, then set aside. In a small saucepan over medium heat, stir together 1 tablespoon of olive oil and 1 tablespoon of flour until well blended. Gradually stir the water into the oil-flour mixture, stirring constantly with a wire whisk. Whisk in 1/2 teaspoon of chicken bouillon granules, 1/3 cup of nonfat dry milk, and 1/2 teaspoon of dried thyme. Stir until the sauce is thick and hot, but not boiling. Yields 2 servings.

## HERBS EVERYWHERE!

Thymes are more than just practical and productive—they're mighty pretty as well! We particularly love growing them along the edges of our test-garden paths, so we can enjoy their scents when we brush by them as we walk. They are also wonderful for planting near veggies or around the base of fruit trees. (Thymes are a favorite with bees, and when these beneficial buzzers come to take in some thyme, they'll stick around to pollinate the crops.) Looking for more ways to work thyme into your life? Try it in containers! The plants look great in patio pots, window boxes, and even hanging baskets. No matter where you plant them, you can't ask for an easier herb to grow—they don't need frequent feeding or watering, and bugs rarely bother 'em!

### Herb-Booster Tonic

Just like people, herbs enjoy a nice, cool drink when the going gets hot. Quench their thirst with this simple summertime pick-me-up.

**1 can of beer**
**1 cup of ammonia**
**1/2 cup of Murphy's Oil Soap®**
**1/2 cup of corn syrup**

Mix these ingredients in a 20 gallon hose-end sprayer, then give your herbs a good dousing every six weeks during the growing season to keep them cool as cucumbers!

## A SNIP IN THYME

Gathering thyme couldn't be easier—simply snip off a few shoots as needed for cooking. (For the best flavor, take the tender, green-stemmed tips, not the woody-stemmed parts.) Planning on drying a bunch for winter use? Gather up all of the top growth, and cut it off about 2 inches above the ground. You can do this when the flowers are open, but we prefer to harvest just *before* the blooms burst, so we won't have to worry about grabbing bees along with the thyme stems! Don't do this full-plant harvesting more than once a year, though, or the clumps may not recover in time to survive the winter.

## SET IN STONE

Our one complaint about thyme? Because the plants grow so close to the ground, they tend to get gritty when heavy rain splashes soil onto the leaves, and that means we have to wash them carefully before using them for cooking. Normally, we'd get around this by covering the soil around the plants with an organic mulch, such as compost or chopped leaves. But thymes tend to take offense at this extra TLC, because these materials hold too much moisture around the base of the plant and promote rot. Well, we found the perfect solution—we spread an inch or so of large gravel or small rocks around the base of each of our thyme plants. They absolutely *love* the good drainage and extra warmth they get from the stone mulch, and the leaves stay as clean as a whistle!

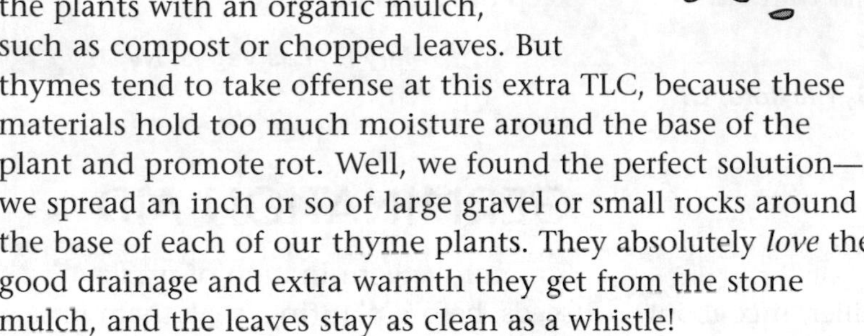

## BETTER BUTTER

We're always on the lookout for new ways to enjoy our herbs, and we haven't found a better treat than homemade herbal butter! It's amazingly easy to make—just combine ½ cup of softened sweet (unsalted) butter with about 1 tablespoon of minced fresh herbs. Wrap the mixture in plastic wrap (tiny crocks and decorative butter molds work great, too), and put in the freezer overnight to harden. Enjoy the flavored butter on warm muffins or toast, or on steamed veggies for a real taste sensation. Thyme, basil, marjoram, oregano, and rosemary all make a super savory butter. For a sweeter treat, try dill, fennel, lemon verbena, or mint.

### TRIED-AND-TRUE

If you've never tried drying herbs at home, you won't believe how easy it really is! Just bundle a few stems of fresh herbs together with a rubber band, and hang 'em upside down until the leaves are crispy. (Thymes are especially quick and easy to dry, because they contain very little moisture to begin with.)

If you're worried about your drying herbs getting dusty, this trick Grandma Putt came up with is just the ticket. Cut a hole in the bottom of a brown paper bag, and cut a few flaps in the sides, too, for ventilation. Turn the bag over, slip it over the stems of an herb bundle so they poke through the hole in the bottom, and hang up the covered bundle. A warm, dark, airy place is perfect for drying herbs. They'll be crispy-dry in about two weeks.

MORE TIPS

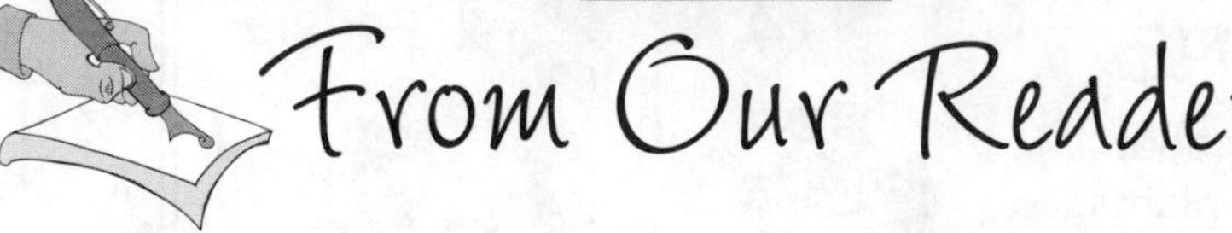

# From Our Readers

## HARVEST EARLY

My grandma always told me to harvest herbs in the morning after the dew had dried, because by later in the day the sun's heat will have depleted their essential oils (their source of flavor). And you know what they say—Grandma knows best!

***Jaclyn B., Hartford, CT***

## BUG BUSTER

For a great mealy bug killer, mix about 1/4 teaspoon of ground cloves with 1/4 cup of rubbing alcohol. Let it steep overnight, then dab the mix right on mealy bugs with a cotton swab to knock 'em dead.

***Tom B., Cochranton, PA***

## TASTIER TOMATOES

Interplant parsley, calendula, borage, and bee balm among your tomato plants to improve their growth and flavor.

***Opal S., Brookhaven, MS***

## SPICY SLUG STOPPER

To keep slugs out of your garden, sprinkle powdered ginger around your plants or wherever the slugs have access. Replace it regularly to keep the slugs out.

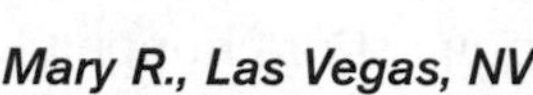

***Mary R., Las Vegas, NV***

## GERMINATION AID

To improve germination of parsley seeds, before planting, soak them for a few hours in a mixture of 1 cup of vinegar, a squirt of dishwashing liquid, and 2 cups of warm water.

***Sue C., Sussex, WI***

## SUPPORT YOUR PLANTS

I came up with a wonderful idea for my bleeding heart plant. After the plant has died back for the winter and before it starts to perk up in the spring, I put a tomato cage over it so the plant will have something to support it once it's up and growing again.

***Karen W., Vancouver, WA***

# From Our Readers

## GREAT GARNISH

When I'm ready to harvest my parsley, I cut the stems as long as possible. I wash the parsley in clear water, gently shake off the excess water, and lay the parsley on a clean dish cloth to dry completely. Then I tie the stems with cotton twine, and place the bunch in a paper bag with the stems sticking out of the bag. I tie the bag tightly, hang it on a hook, and forget about it for a couple of weeks. The parsley stays green and looks almost fresh; it's still attractive as a garnish.

***J. K., Moab, UT***

## CHIVES ON ICE

To store your chives, rinse and dry the tufts, but don't cut them! Hold them in a bundle so they're all facing the same direction. Then just fold the bundle in half, place it in a freezer bag, and pop it in the freezer. When you need chives, just snip some off your frozen stalks, and return the bundle to the freezer again.

***Sylvia P., Jonesboro, AR***

## TIME TO DRY

Need to dry herbs for winter use? Grab an old, clean window screen and set it in a well-ventilated, protected area, like a screened porch. For large-leaved herbs (like basil and mint), strip the leaves from the plant, and place the leaves in a single layer on the screen. For small-leaved herbs (like thyme), dry the whole stem on the window screen and strip the leaves off after they're completely dry.

***Alex Y., Portland, OR***

## HERBAL MOTH REPELLENT

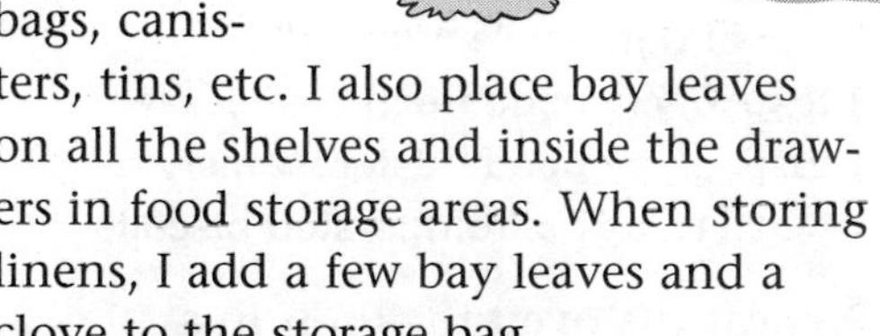

Pantry grain moths and weevils can be kept away by adding a bay leaf or two to all open grain boxes, bags, canisters, tins, etc. I also place bay leaves on all the shelves and inside the drawers in food storage areas. When storing linens, I add a few bay leaves and a clove to the storage bag.

***Suzanne W., Carp Lake, MI***

# Test Garden Goodies

## PERFECT PESTO

**2 cups of fresh basil leaves**
**3 sun-dried tomato slices, rehydrated and drained**
**1 tsp. of minced garlic**
**1/3 cup of fat-free, plain yogurt**
**3 tbsp. of good-quality olive oil**
**Salt and black pepper to taste**
**1/2 lb. of your favorite pasta, cooked**
**1/2 cup of grated Parmesan cheese**

Using the chopping blade of your food processor, process the basil, tomato slices, and garlic until finely chopped. Add the yogurt and mix well. Using a slow, steady stream, add the olive oil while continuing to process. Add salt and pepper to taste. Mix into your favorite hot, cooked pasta, and top with the Parmesan cheese.

*E. M., Overland Park, KS*

## HERB BISCUITS

**1/4 cup (1/2 stick) of butter**
**1 tsp. of Dijon-style mustard**
**2 tbsp. of chopped fresh basil leaves**
**1 tbsp. of chopped fresh rosemary**
**1 pkg. (12 oz.) of refrigerated biscuits**

Preheat the oven to 400°F. In a medium saucepan, melt the butter over medium heat. Remove from the heat and mix in the mustard and herbs. Dip each uncooked biscuit into the herbed butter to cover, and place on a lightly greased baking sheet. Bake 15 to 20 minutes or until golden brown. Serve warm.

*Conne N., Santa Fe, NM*

## GRUNE SOPE (GREEN SAUCE)

**5–10 eggs**
**16 oz. of sour cream or yogurt**
**1–2 tbsp. of lemon juice**
**Salt to taste**
**Pinch of sugar (optional)**
**Handful each of chopped fresh borage, burnet, chives, dill, lemon balm, and parsley**

Hard-boil the eggs for 10 minutes. Cool them enough to handle, then peel and chop. Mix the remaining ingredients with the chopped eggs and serve over hot boiled or baked potatoes.

*Hannelore V., Filmore, NY*

# TEST GARDEN GOODIES

## HERBAL RICE

**6 tbsp. of canola oil**
**1 cup of chopped fennel**
**1 bell pepper, chopped**
**1 onion, chopped**
**2 cloves of garlic, minced**
**2 tbsp. of chopped fresh mint**
**2 tbsp. of chopped fresh rosemary**
**2 tsp. of grated lemon zest**
**1/2 tsp. of ground coriander**
**1 1/2 cups of uncooked rice**
**1 1/2 cups of dry white wine**
**3 1/2 cups of chicken broth**
**1 1/2 tbsp. of lemon juice**
**1/3 cup of Parmesan cheese**
**Salt and black pepper to taste**

In a medium saucepan, heat the oil over medium heat. Add the fennel, bell pepper, onion, garlic, and 1 tbsp. each of the mint, rosemary, and lemon zest. Sauté, stirring, until the vegetables are beginning to soften (about 2 minutes). Add the coriander and rice, and sauté a few minutes more. Pour in the wine and chicken broth, and reduce the heat to medium-low. Simmer uncovered, for 20 to 25 minutes, or until the rice is tender. Remove from the heat and stir in the remaining mint, rosemary, and lemon zest. Add the lemon juice, cheese, and salt and pepper to taste. Wait 10 minutes before serving.

***Jake U., Peoria, IL***

## GARDEN-FRESH PASTA

**2 large, ripe tomatoes**
**4 tbsp. of olive oil**
**1/4 cup of chopped fresh basil leaves**
**1/4 cup of chopped green onions**
**1 tbsp. of chopped fresh oregano leaves**
**2 cloves of garlic, minced**
**1/4 tsp. of salt**
**Fresh-ground black pepper**
**1 lb. of capellini pasta**
**1/2 cup of grated Parmesan cheese**

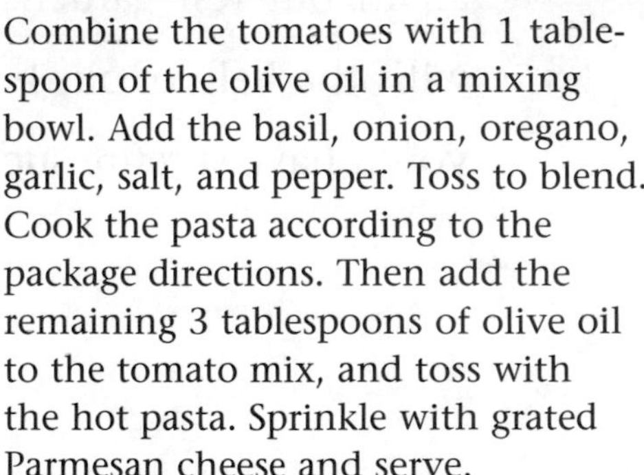

Blanch the tomatoes in boiling water for 30 seconds. Plunge into cold water for 30 seconds to stop the cooking, then peel and core. Remove as many seeds as possible and dice the tomatoes. Combine the tomatoes with 1 tablespoon of the olive oil in a mixing bowl. Add the basil, onion, oregano, garlic, salt, and pepper. Toss to blend. Cook the pasta according to the package directions. Then add the remaining 3 tablespoons of olive oil to the tomato mix, and toss with the hot pasta. Sprinkle with grated Parmesan cheese and serve.

***Joyce F., Cathedral City, CA***

# Chapter 14

# The Best of the Rest

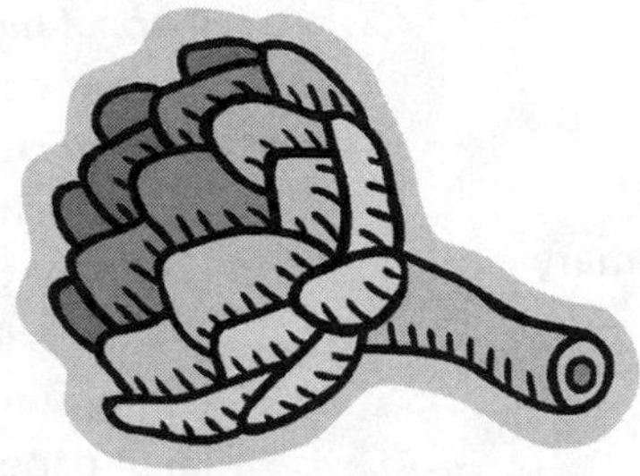

To round out our vegetable-growing tips, here are some of our very favorite veggie crops that tend to defy classification. They're not fruits, they're not seeds, and they're not leaves, but one thing's for sure—they *are* great! We've grown and enjoyed 'em all in our test gardens year after year, and now, with the help of our handy hints and terrific tips, you'll have surefire success with them, too!

## A NEED FOR SPEED

Now here's a crop you don't see in every garden! That's not because artichokes are so fussy, but because they usually can't tolerate cold winters. You see, with this oddball veggie, it's the flower buds that you harvest, and the plants usually don't bloom until they are in their second year. So, if you live north of Zone 8, your artichoke plants may not live long enough to start flowering. Sure, the plants *look* good the first year, but if they aren't going to produce anything useful, then they're just taking up space that could be better used for high-yielding crops.

Well, we've come up with a way to trick our artichokes into *thinking* that they are old enough to flower, even though they're not even a year old! Here's the lowdown:

**Step 1.** In January, soak the seeds in water for 48 hours. Then mix the seeds with a handful or two of moistened sphagnum moss or seed-starting medium in a plastic bag, and place in the refrigerator for one month.

**Step 2.** Remove the chilled seeds from the refrigerator, then plant them in individual pots. Grow them indoors in a cool, bright place, moving them into bigger pots as needed.

**Step 3.** Four to six weeks before your average last frost date, move the pots to a cold frame or sheltered spot outdoors. (Set them out for gradually longer periods each day over the course of several days, so they aren't shocked by the cooler outdoor temperatures.) This cool period simulates winter chilling.

**Step 4.** When all danger of frost has passed and the soil is warm (around 60°F is ideal), transplant the potted plants into a sunny, well-drained spot, spacing them about 3 feet apart. By late summer, your artichokes should be producing lots of tasty buds for you to enjoy well into the fall months!

After we've waited so long for our artichoke harvest, we don't want *any* of those tasty buds to go to waste. So even if we're not ready for them right away, we go ahead and pick the buds when they're at the perfect stage—firm to the touch, but not yet starting to open. Then we place 'em in a vase—just as we would flowers—with their heads sticking out and their stems submerged in the water. This simple secret keeps 'em ready-to-eat fresh for about a week.

## THE BIG COVER-UP

Where winter temperatures fall below 20°F, overwintering artichokes can be a tricky business. Sure, you can dig 'em up and bring them into an unheated porch or garage for the winter, but these big plants need *big* pots, and it's a lot of work to dig 'em up. We've gotten much better results by leaving the plants in place, cutting the tops back to about 1 foot above the ground, and then covering them with an upside-down bucket or bushel basket. Then we pile 8 to 12 inches of loose mulch (like chopped leaves) around the covering. With this kind of protection, artichoke plants may survive as far north as Zone 5, depending on how severe the winter is. We still like to start new plants indoors, just in case—but quite often, we're amazed at how well our established plants survive the big chill under their snug covers!

### Kitchen CLASSICS

Not sure what to do with these funny-looking 'chokes? First, you need to cook them! We like to pop 'em in the microwave—it's by far the quickest way to prepare them. Slice off the stem so the big bud can sit firmly on its bottom, then cut off and discard one-quarter to one-third of the top. Place the prepared artichokes in a deep microwavable bowl, then add water, cover, and microwave on high until done. (For one artichoke, use 1/2 cup of water and cook 5 to 8 minutes; for two artichokes, use 1 cup of water and cook 7 to 11 minutes.) Now, try one of these treats:

**Dip it.** Pull off the "petals" one at a time, and dip them into lemon juice or other dip. Put a petal to your mouth, holding onto the tip. Bite down gently, and use your teeth to scrape off the dip and the tender flesh.

**Stuff it.** With a spoon, scrape the fuzzy center out of your cooked artichoke. Fill the 'choke with something cold, such as chicken or tuna salad, or something hot, such as warm crabmeat, for a super-elegant side dish!

### PRETTY IN PURPLE

Want to try something extra-special in your artichoke patch? The heirloom cultivar 'Violetto' never fails to attract *oohs* and *aahs* from our test-garden visitors. It's a true beauty, with small but perfectly shaped heads of petal-like bracts that are beautifully blushed with violet-purple. They're almost too pretty to pick, but don't let that stop you—the flavor is exceptional!

## BED BUDDIES

Think you don't have room to grow asparagus? Think again! Sure, most folks plant asparagus in their veggie garden, but there's no law that says it *has* to grow there. Here at the test gardens, we decided to try something different—we used ours as a backdrop for one of our flower borders. In the spring, it's easy to reach the spears for harvesting; in summer and fall, the ferny foliage makes a gorgeous backdrop for bright blooms. Asparagus plants thrive with the same regular feeding and watering that flowers love, so these ornamental edibles make positively perfect garden partners!

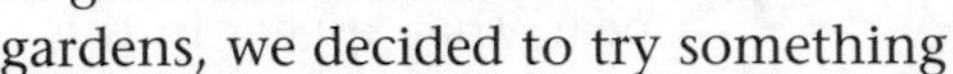

## LET'S HEAR IT FOR THE BOYS!

What's the secret to selecting the most productive asparagus variety for your garden? It's simple—boys are best! You see, some asparagus plants produce only female flowers, while others make only male blooms. The pollinated female flowers then put energy into making seeds, which saps some strength from the plants. Plus, you're stuck pulling out lots of unwanted seedlings every year. With all-male hybrids, the plants put all their energy into their growth instead of seeds. That means you're guaranteed a much heavier harvest with a lot less work, year after year!

### Soak-It-to-'Em Tonic

Don't take a chance that diseases will claim your asparagus crop before you can! Do what we do, and always disinfect newly purchased asparagus roots before planting them by soaking them briefly in this simple solution.

**1 cup of bleach**
**1/4 cup of dishwashing liquid**
**1 gal. of warm water**

Mix these ingredients in a bucket, then drop in your asparagus roots. Let them soak for an hour or so, and then plant them right away.

**JERRY'S Q&A**

**Q** If buying asparagus as one-year-old crowns is a good idea, wouldn't I be better off buying two-year-old crowns instead?

**A** NO! We've tried 'em side by side, and discovered that the older crowns actually take longer to settle in and get growing. By the end of the first growing season, both patches basically looked the same and produced similar yields each year. So save yourself some dough, and stick with the less-expensive one-year-olds.

## DOUBLE DELIGHT

We're absolutely fanatical about asparagus here at the test gardens, so you can bet we've tried just about every trick in the book to get the best possible harvest over the longest possible period. Well, we've found one fantastic trick that beats all the others by a mile—a way to enjoy garden-fresh spears all the way into the fall! The secret is to plant twice as many crowns as usual. Then, once the bed is established, pick spears from just half of it until early summer. Once the plants in the unharvested part have fully leafed out in midsummer, cut all of their tops down. Then harvest the new spears that appear in this half of the bed into October. What a great way to turn the seasons upside down, and enjoy this tasty treat twice as long as usual!

## ASPARAGUS UNDER COVER

Should you leave the tops on your asparagus plants through the winter or not? Many folks like to leave 'em on, because they act like a mulch, protecting the crowns from drying winds and sudden temperature changes. The problem, though, is that nasty asparagus beetles like to hide in the tops in cold weather, so they're ready to chomp on the tender new spears as soon as they appear in spring. We've come up with the perfect solution to this puzzle: We cut down the tops in late fall, then cover the beds with a 1-foot-thick layer of straw or another loose, lightweight mulch. That keeps the crowns safe from Old Man Winter *and* practically eliminates the beetle battle, too!

From Our Readers

*Don't dump the water down the drain after boiling or steaming your vegetables! Instead, let it cool, then use it to water your houseplants. The cooking water is chock-full of vitamins and minerals that houseplants just love!*

Kristen F., Franklin, IN

## FAST ASPARAGUS

With the prospect of those tender, tasty spears in mind, it can sure be tough to wait several years to enjoy your first harvest! Well, it's possible to enjoy garden-fresh asparagus the very same year you plant, *if* you know our two-part time-saving trick:

**Get a jump start.** Instead of growing asparagus from seed, buy one-year-old crowns from a local nursery or mail-order supplier. Now, you're already a full year ahead of the game! (Figure on planting about 25 crowns per person, by the way.)

**Harvest wisely.** Go ahead and harvest the first spring, but only for two weeks, and don't cut any spears that are thinner than a pencil. Extend the harvest period to three to four weeks the second year, and four to six weeks the third year. After that, go ahead and harvest for the full eight weeks—and enjoy every minute of them!

## A PASSION FOR PURPLE

We happen to think that "ordinary" asparagus is actually pretty extraordinary; but for a crop that's really over the top, why not try growing purple or white asparagus as well? The variety 'Purple Passion' is one of our all-time favorites. The flavor is a little sweeter than that of typical asparagus, and the deep purple uncooked spears look absolutely beautiful in salads. (They turn plain green when cooked, unfortunately, but they still taste great!) White asparagus isn't a separate variety—instead, you simply pile soil over the emerging shoots of regular asparagus to keep out the sunlight until harvest. Its incredibly mild flavor is the ultimate gourmet treat!

### Kitchen CLASSICS

No vegetable is more elegant than asparagus! Its distinctive flavor shines when it's prepared simply, as in this easy asparagus-hazelnut salad. Cut 2 pounds of fresh asparagus into $1^1/_2$-inch pieces, and place in a heavy saucepan with just enough water to cover. Bring the water to a boil, then lower the heat and cook the asparagus gently just until tender (4 to 5 minutes). Pour off the hot water, then rinse the pieces in cold water to stop the cooking. Pat dry, and place in a glass or plastic bowl. In another small bowl, combine 3 teaspoons of light soy sauce, 2 teaspoons of walnut oil, 1 teaspoon of honey, and 2 tablespoons of chopped toasted hazelnuts (filberts), then pour over the asparagus. Cover and chill for 30 minutes. Serve on a bed of red leaf lettuce, garnished with grape tomatoes, for a tasty and colorful feast!

# Broccoli and Cauliflower

Sure, you can cook broccoli in gourmet recipes—but who has time for that every night? After a busy day, it's a snap to whip up this simple stir-fried broccoli. It's ready in a flash, and good for you, too—just one serving delivers almost all the vitamin C you need for the entire day! Simply heat 1½ tablespoons of canola oil in a large nonstick wok or skillet over medium heat. Add 2 cloves of minced garlic, and saute for 1 to 2 minutes. Add 1½ pounds of fresh broccoli, cleaned and chopped, and cook for 2 to 3 minutes, or until it turns bright green. Add 3 tablespoons of low-sodium stir-fry sauce and stir-fry for 1 minute. Remove from the pan, season with ¼ teaspoon of freshly ground black pepper, and enjoy!

## WARM THOUGHTS

Visitors to our test gardens always ask questions about these two closely related crops. And that's no surprise, either—we've been growing 'em for years and are *still* learning their secrets! One of our biggest puzzles used to be getting 'em started in spring: If we waited to sow outdoors until the soil was warm enough for good germination, then the weather was *too* warm for good head formation later on. So it turns out, indoor sowing is the way to go! We've gotten great results by starting broccoli and cauliflower seeds indoors 10 weeks before our last frost date, then setting them out in the garden when they are 4 to 5 weeks old (as soon as the soil temperature is at least 50°F).

## EXPLORE YOUR BROCCOLI OPTIONS

Love the flavor of just-picked broccoli, but have trouble getting it to grow well? Give a broccoli taste-alike a try! One, known as "broccoli raab," isn't a type of broccoli at all. It's actually a variety of turnip grown for its leaves, stems, and buds. Sow the seeds in the garden a week or two after you plant your peas. When the broccoli raab plants are about a foot tall, snip off the bud clusters along with a few leaves underneath. The flavor is a bit stronger than true broccoli, so we like to mix the shoots with other veggies in stir-fries or salads.

"Oriental broccoli" or "Chinese broccoli," also known as kai lan or gai lan, is another crop with flower buds and shoot tips that makes a fine broccoli substitute. It grows super-quick, so it makes a great filler crop before or after main-season crops, such as tomatoes and beans.

## AW, SHOOTS!

When buying broccoli at the grocery store, most folks choose the largest heads they can get. But those in the know also enjoy the smaller, more tender sideshoots they can get from their home-grown broccoli. Here are some of our favorite tricks for boosting these super-tasty shoots:

■ After harvesting the large central head, *don't* pull out your plants! Over the next few weeks, you'll get a second harvest of small new shoots that pop up from the remaining stem.

■ Some folks like to spread their broccoli plants out 18 to 24 inches apart, and that's fine if your objective is big main heads. But we've discovered that setting out our plants just 8 inches apart is a much better bet—the central heads are smaller, but the sideshoot population absolutely explodes, giving us a *much* bigger harvest overall!

■ Don't care about the central head at all? Choose varieties described as "sprouting" types. They produce many small clusters of buds that you can harvest all summer long.

## FALL INTO CAULIFLOWER

Having bad luck with your spring cauliflower crop? You're not alone! This touchy crop has very specific ideas about its preferred growing temperatures—ideally between 60° and 65°F, but definitely not below 45°F or above 75°F. We have *much* better luck growing cauliflower for fall harvest. Besides practically eliminating the chance of unexpected cold snaps, sowing in July means that the soil is warm, so we can sow the seeds directly in the garden—and that means no fussing with indoor-grown transplants. Try it for yourself, and see if you don't get the same great results in your own garden!

### Veggie Harvest Bath

Lots of bugs love to hide in broccoli florets and other nooks and crannies in vegetables. Here's an easy way to make sure that your harvest is completely bug-free—give it a bath!

**Fresh-picked broccoli (or other veggies)**
**1/4 cup of salt**
**1 tbsp. of vinegar**
**Cold water**

Pour the salt and vinegar into a sinkful of cold water, and submerge the veggies for 15 minutes or so. The bugs will float up to the surface, where they can be easily picked off. Rinse the veggies with fresh water, and they're ready to eat.

# KEEP IT COMFY!

If top-notch cauliflower is what you're after, don't skimp on watering during dry spells! These plants need steady, even moisture at the rate of about an inch a week all through their growing period. If they don't get enough water, or if the supply is erratic, they'll grow up with a strong—or even foul—flavor.

This high-maintenance crop also demands a good, well-balanced diet. We give ours a good dose of fish emulsion when we first move the transplants to the garden (or when the direct-sown seedlings are a few inches tall). After that, we follow up with our All-Season Green-Up Tonic (see page 69) every three weeks throughout the growing season to ensure strong, healthy growth and high yields.

We're always on the lookout for ways to make our veggie beds more productive—and this one's a real winner! Right after setting out our broccoli and cauliflower transplants, we sow lettuce seeds around them. By the time the other crops start needing the elbow room, all of the lettuce is long gone to the salad bowl!

# GETTING THE WHITE RIGHT

Part of the allure of cauliflower is its creamy white color—definitely different than other common garden crops. Most times, though, that doesn't happen on its own—the heads need to be shielded from the sun (a process called blanching). It's an important step, but not a difficult one. Just wait until the developing head is egg- to fist-sized, then either break off an outer leaf and drape it over the head, or bring several of the outer leaves up and clip 'em with a clothespin.

Once you've blanched your cauliflower, keep a close eye on it. In warm weather, it'll be ready to pick about 4 days after you cover the head. In cool weather, it can take 10 days or so. Cut the head the minute it's ready, or it'll rot!

### THE SHELL GAME

Just like people, broccoli and cauliflower plants need lots of calcium to grow up big and strong. So if your plants look weak and aren't producing well, try mixing some crushed eggshells into the soil around the base of each plant. This'll give 'em a good nutrient boost and help get 'em back on the right track!

### LEAF IT ALONE

Don't feel like bothering with blanching? Stick with a self-blanching variety, such as 'Self-Blanching Snowball', with outer leaves that naturally curl inward to cover the head. Or just grow regular cauliflower and leave it alone. The heads will develop a greenish or purplish tinge—not as attractive as the white, but still okay to eat!

## COLORFUL CAULIFLOWER

Is your family less than impressed with your skill at growing broccoli and cauliflower? (Sometimes our kids wish we had a lot *less* success than we do!) Well, then, why not take a break from plain green broccoli and white cauliflower, and add some color to your dinner table? Here are a few out-of-the-ordinary varieties that we guarantee will become family favorites! If you try any of these, remember—they don't *need* blanching, and furthermore, they don't *like* it.

**Broccoflower.** A hybrid between broccoli and cauliflower, this combo crop has the color of broccoli, but looks more like cauliflower, with a flavor that's sweeter than either.

**'Orange Bouquet'.** Well, it's not exactly carrot-orange, but the pretty golden color is certainly showy, and it sticks around even through the cooking process. Best of all, this variety is loaded with vitamin A!

**'Romanesco'.** These bright yellow-green heads have perfect spiral-shaped florets with a mild cauliflower flavor. Great either raw or cooked.

**'Violet Queen'.** Yep—it's a beautiful purple color! Purple cauliflower is best used fresh in salads or just lightly steamed, because the florets tend to turn greenish when cooked for longer periods.

### TRIED-AND-TRUE

**W**henever you need to sprinkle any non-poisonous powder over cauliflower or other veggie plants, don't spend money on a fancy-schmancy duster. Do what Grandma Putt did: Place the mixture in a small paper bag with about five small holes punched in the bottom. Blow up the bag with air, twist the neck tightly, and shake away!

Kitchen **CLASSICS**

The Waldorf salad was created about a century ago at the Waldorf-Astoria Hotel in New York City, using just apples, celery, and mayonnaise. Since then, chefs have added nuts, and now they sometimes substitute pears for the apples. Here's a recipe we love for late-summer test-garden lunches—a wrap sandwich that gives this old favorite an even more modern twist. Simply slice and core 1 pear, chop 1 medium stalk of celery, and place them in a medium bowl. Add 1 tablespoon of chopped walnuts and 3 tablespoons of light mayonnaise, then combine until well blended. Spread out 2 flour tortillas (8-inch-diameter), and top each one with 2 slices of lean ham or turkey and half of the pear mixture. Wrap each tortilla and serve immediately.

## HEAD-START CELERY

We're all for growing veggie transplants, but sometimes, it's just simpler to buy them—and that's *definitely* the case with celery! This slow-growing crop takes five to six months from seed to harvest, so in most climates, the seeds need a two- to three-month head start indoors to have enough time to mature before frost. If your family's *really* crazy about celery, go ahead and grow your own transplants if you have the space and time. But we usually figure on six plants per person, and for that amount, we find it's cheaper and easier to pick up a few packs of already-started transplants!

## KEEP 'EM DEEP

Want to harvest fresh celery all winter long? Do what we do—dig up your plants with a fair amount of roots attached to them before the freezing weather sets in, and then replant them in a deep cold frame. They'll be easy to reach even when the ground is covered in deep snow!

## BEYOND THE PALE

Back in the old days, most folks blanched their celery to get the stems nice and white. What they didn't know was that left to its own devices, celery has a little more flavor and a *lot* more nutrients! Still, if you don't think celery is celery unless it's nice and white, blanching is easy. Just slip bottomless half-gallon, waxed paper milk cartons over the plants as they're growing. Or plant a variety like 'Golden Self-Blanching'—it'll do the job all by itself!

## DIG IN!

Most veggies enjoy a steady supply of moisture, but celery is one of the few crops that actually *likes* soggy soil! So if you have a low spot where other veggies won't thrive, this can be the perfect choice for planting there. But what if you want to grow celery in a drier area? We've found the secret—dig a shallow trench (about 4 inches deep and 1 foot across) and set your transplants in the bottom, then lay a soaker hose alongside them in the trench. That makes watering during dry spells a snap, and your celery plants will be thrilled with their extra-moist rooting area.

MIX IT UP!

### Blight-Buster Veggie Tonic

A number of different diseases that cause dark spots on leaves, which then wither and die, are called blights. They spread fast, so at the first sign of blight on celery, potatoes, or tomatoes, haul out this powerful weapon and fight back!

**1 tbsp. of light horticultural oil**
**1 tbsp. of baking soda**
**1 gal. of water**

Mix these ingredients in a bucket, pour into a hand-held sprayer, and spray your plants to the point of run-off to keep them in tip-top shape.

## CELERY-WHAT??

Celeriac isn't as good-looking as its close relative celery, but it's just as tasty—and a lot less persnickety, too! It's grown for its large, swollen roots, rather than its stalks. Many folks use it as a cooked vegetable, but we also enjoy it fresh in salads, shredded or sliced up thin.

You can grow celeriac the same way you do celery, and start eating the roots when they get about 2 inches in diameter. But leave most of the crop in the ground until Jack Frost has paid a few calls in fall—it tastes much better then! Lift the roots with a garden fork, cut off the tops an inch or two above their base, and store the roots in your garage or in a container of damp sawdust to enjoy all winter long.

## THIS CROP KEEPS ON COMIN'

If you like growing veggies that don't demand a lot of special care, then you'll *love* having rhubarb around! Once established, this fuss-free crop will give you a generous harvest, season after season. In fact, one of our test-garden clumps has been here 10 years and is still going strong!

All this dependable perennial needs is evenly moist soil, along with a generous mulch of grass clippings or straw. (We spread a layer about 3 inches deep around each clump in spring and fall, making sure it doesn't pile up right next to the stems.) We have several rhubarb plants, so we harvest lightly from each and seldom bother with extra fertilizer. In a home garden, though, we recommend growing just one or two plants (remember, they get *big*), then giving each clump a generous mulch of compost *under* the regular mulch you apply in spring.

**Test Garden SECRET**

We're always on the lookout for ways to extend the harvest season of our veggies, so you can bet we were thrilled to learn this old-time trick for enjoying fresh rhubarb all winter long. Simply dig up a few crowns after the first frost, lay them on the ground, and cover them with a few inches of sand. After seven weeks, dig up the frozen clumps, plant them indoors in large buckets, baskets, or even plastic bags, and keep them lightly moist. The leaves will be yellowish, but the stems (the part you want) will be red and ready to pick in no time!

## PICKIN' AND GRINNIN'

Since rhubarb plants stay in place so long, it makes sense to let 'em get off to a great start—and that includes holding off on harvesting until the second season. And when the time does come, don't even *think* about cutting the stalks off with a knife. No matter how careful you are, it's way too easy to have the blade slip and cut into the crown! Just grab the stalk you want as close to the base as possible, and give it a twist as you pull upward. Stick with the largest, longest stalks your plant has to offer (we like 'em to be at least 10 inches long and an inch thick), and don't touch the leaves that have short and/or thin stalks—save them to feed the plant for next year.

## BYE-BYE, BLOOMS!

When we ask new helpers at the test gardens to trim the flowers off the rhubarb clumps, they usually look at us like we're crazy—after all, whoever would want to remove those beautiful blooms? Well, they change their minds once we explain the reason. You see, it takes a lot of energy to make all those showy flowers—and that's energy the rhubarb plants could be putting into making more of those tasty leaf stems!

## THE THREE-WAY SPLIT

If your rhubarb's leaf stalks are short, stringy, and crowded-looking, that's your cue that it's time to divide the clump. We like to take care of this in early spring, so the divisions have plenty of time to make new roots before winter returns. Dig up the clump—and be prepared, because it's going to take some work to lift that big clump!—then wash some of the excess soil off so you can see what you're working with. If the crowns are loose, you may be able to pull them apart with your hands; otherwise, cut 'em apart with a sharp spade. Generally, we like to divide old clumps into three parts, so we get divisions that are big enough to produce well that same year. Be sure to work a generous amount of compost into the hole when you replant, and your rhubarb will be good to go for several more years!

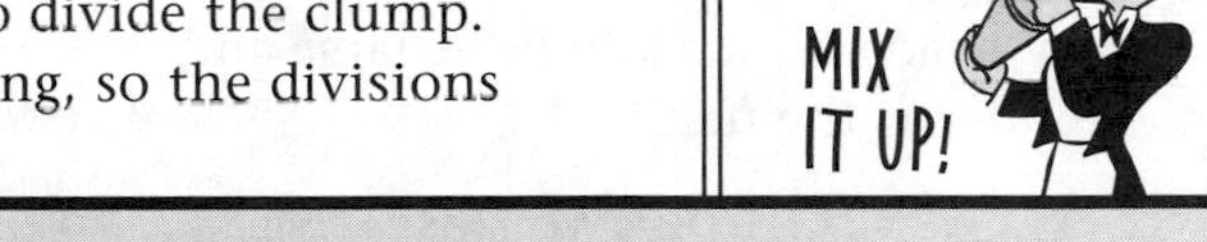


### Robust Rhubarb Tonic

Want to have the most robust rhubarb in town? Treat your clumps to a taste of this terrific tonic twice a year, and be prepared for the biggest and best-looking harvest you've ever had!

**1 cup of brewed tea**
**1 tbsp. of Epsom salts**
**Vegetable table scraps (all that you have on hand—but no meat or fats)**
**1 qt. of water**

Whip these ingredients together in a blender or food processor, then pour the mushy mix over the soil in your rhubarb bed. Serve up one meal in the spring, and another in the fall.

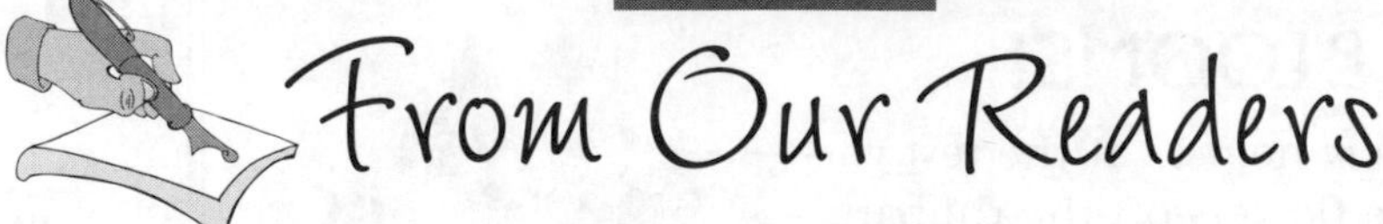


## BETTER BROCCOLI

Pruning broccoli the right way will give you a double crop. When you cut the first head, cut it high on the stalk, leaving as much of the stem and as many leaves on the plant as possible. Then, destroy the buds at the base of all but the bottom leaves by inserting the point of a knife and twisting where each leaf joins the main stem. The undeveloped buds that are lower on each stem will send up large, strong shoots. These will form secondary heads, which will be as large and tender as the first.

***Gerald M., Mascoutah, IL***

## MORNING COFFEE

After I read that artichokes like acidic soil, I started taking the leftover coffee in mugs or in the pot and pouring it right around my artichoke plants in the morning. My reward: a bumper crop!

***Betty D., Hooper, NE***

## RHUBARB INSECTICIDE

Here's a garden/tree insecticide we use to control pests and reduce blight on tomatoes: Take three medium-sized rhubarb leaves, and boil them in 1 gallon of water. Cool the mix, then pour it through cheesecloth to filter out the leaves. Mix in 10 drops of dishwashing liquid. Apply to your plants with a small hand-held sprayer.

***Marlen H., Bellingham, WA***

## FORCING THE ISSUE

Rhubarb is my favorite garden plant—I use it in everything. So I like to force it indoors during the winter so I can have more of it during the year. I just wait until the leaves have died back, dig up one or two plants, and plant them in pots that I keep outside. Once the air's freezing, I move them into the garage. The cool temperature and darkness in there are perfect for getting good stalks. About a month later, my rhubarb's ready.

***Liz T., Atoka, OK***

# From Our Readers

## GIVE CAULIFLOWER A DRINK

I found out the hard way that lack of water can stunt the growth of cauliflower. So if your cauliflower heads are on the small side, next year remember to water them more when the plants are young. You should see bigger heads.

***Bethany M., Duluth, MN***

## A REAL SOUR PUSS

I was having a big problem getting my rhubarb to grow until I got a soil test and found out that my soil was too sweet (alkaline). I just added a little "sour" to the soil in the form of sulfur to make it more acidic, and my rhubarb's been doing great ever since.

***Joan Z., Dover, DE***

## ASHES, ASHES

Sprinkle ashes from your charcoal grill around your cabbage and broccoli plants to keep cabbageworms away. It works for me!

***Shelly M., Rockton, IL***

## BROCCOLI BASICS

As a rule, I always start broccoli indoors. The best way I have found to do this is by filling my container with loose peat. Then I plant the seeds at least 1 inch apart from each other, and at least ½ inch deep. I make sure the container gets plenty of water and bright light, and I'm never disappointed with the results!

***Kathleen M., Colstrip, MT***

## COLORFUL CAULIFLOWER

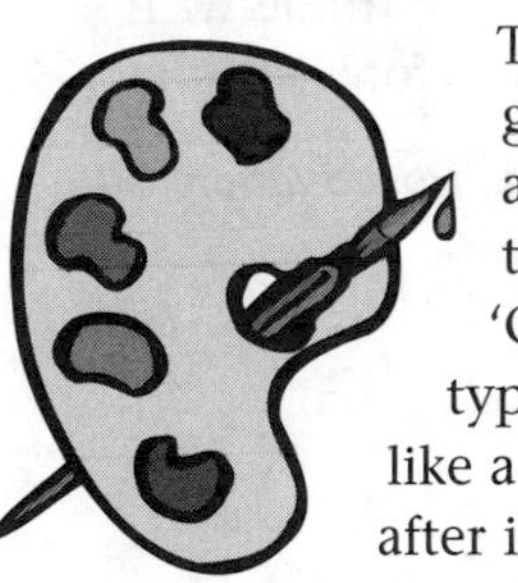

The only way I can get my kids to eat any cauliflower is to grow the 'Orange bouquet' type. Its color is just like a Creamsicle®, even after it's cooked. When I serve this up instead of the plain stuff, it gets eaten fast. And I think its flavor is even a little better than the standard types.

***Jessica T., Richmond, VA***

# Test Garden Goodies

## BROCCOLI-RAISIN SALAD

6 slices of bacon
1/4 cup of sugar
1 cup of mayonnaise
2 tbsp. of cider vinegar
1 large head of broccoli, finely chopped
1 cup of finely chopped onions
1 cup of raisins
1/2 cup of sunflower seeds

Cook the bacon, then chop it up into small pieces and set aside. In a large bowl, mix together the sugar, mayonnaise, and vinegar. Add the broccoli, onions, raisins, and bacon, and mix well. Chill overnight. Sprinkle with sunflower seeds just before serving.

*Pat M., Roscommon, MI*

## ROASTED ASPARAGUS

Small young asparagus spears
Orange juice
Olive oil
Seasoning to taste (I use lemon pepper and garlic salt)
Sesame seeds

Clean the asparagus and cut off the tough ends. In a flat pan or cookie sheet, mix half orange juice and half olive oil—just enough so that when you lay down the asparagus in the pan, it will just be touching the liquid. Gently stir the mixture. Lay the asparagus in the pan side-by-side. Roll it so the spears get coated with the liquid. Season to taste, and sprinkle with sesame seeds. Bake at 350°F until tender.

*C. C., Bloomington, IN*

## EASY RHUBARB CAKE

2 cups of chunked fresh rhubarb, cut into 3/4-inch pieces
2 cups of flour
1 1/2 cups of brown sugar
1 cup of milk
1/2 cup of solid shortening
1 egg
2 tsp. of salt
1 tsp. of vanilla
1 tsp. of baking powder
1 tsp. of baking soda
1/4 cup of granulated sugar

In a large bowl, mix together all ingredients except the granulated sugar. Pour the batter into a greased 9 × 13-inch pan. Sprinkle granulated sugar over the top and bake at 350°F for 45 minutes. Cool before serving.

*Luna W., Spokane, WA*

# TEST GARDEN GOODIES

## RHUBARB PIE

**4 cups of chunked fresh rhubarb, cut into ¾-inch pieces**
**1½ cups of sugar**
**¼ tsp. of salt**
**½ tsp. of nutmeg**
**¼ cup of flour**
**2 tsp. of finely grated orange peel**
**9" unbaked pie shell and top**

Heat the oven to 425°F. Mix together the rhubarb, sugar, salt, nutmeg, flour, and orange peel. Pour into the pie shell. Place the top crust, and crimp the edges to seal. Make a slit in the center. Bake for 20 minutes, then reduce the heat to 350°F and bake for 25 minutes, or until the crust is golden brown.

*Kathleen C., Harpursville, NY*

## CAULIFLOWER DELIGHT

**1 tsp. of salt**
**1 head of cauliflower**
**Mayonnaise**
**Mustard**
**Shredded soft cheese**

Using the teaspoon of salt in water, boil the cauliflower until tender, but don't let it fall apart. In a small bowl, mix some mayonnaise and mustard to taste, until it's as tangy as you want. Drain the cauliflower well and put it on a microwave-safe plate. Using a spoon, spread the mayonnaise-mustard mix over the cauliflower, completely covering it. Next, sprinkle on the cheese. Microwave on high for 10 seconds, or until the cheese is melted. Serve at once.

*Daniel B., West Richland, WA*

## ONE-DISH BROCCOLI CASSEROLE

**2 cups of Minute® rice**
**2 cans (10¾ oz. each) of condensed cream of mushroom soup**
**1 cup of water**
**1 jar (16 oz.) of Cheez Whiz®**
**¾ cup of chopped onions**
**¾ cup of chopped celery**
**½ cup (1 stick) of margarine**
**2 boxes (10 oz. each) of frozen broccoli spears, thawed and chopped**

Mix all the ingredients together in a casserole dish, and bake uncovered at 350°F for 30 minutes.

*Margaret L., Pottstown, PA*

# Part Four

# Mix It Up Tonics

## All-Around Disease Defense Tonic

Most common flower-garden diseases are caused by fungi—microscopic life forms that exist as parasites on our beloved plants. These funky fungi invade plant tissues, destroy cells, and drain the energy out of leaves, then release thousands of spores that germinate and infect the plants, too. The best way to stop these diseases dead in their tracks is to keep a close eye on all your flowering plants and douse them often with this tonic.

**1 cup of chamomile tea**
**1 tsp. of dishwashing liquid**
**½ tsp. of vegetable oil**
**½ tsp. of peppermint oil**
**1 gal. of warm water**

Mix these ingredients in a bucket, then pour into a hand-held sprayer. Mist-spray your annuals, perennials, and bulbs every week or so before the really hot weather (75°F or higher) sets in. This elixir is strong stuff, so test it on a few leaves first—then wait a day or two to make sure no damage has occurred—before applying it to any plant. (For related text, see page 149.)

## All-Purpose Bug & Thug Spray

Very cold winter weather can strike a big blow against the bad bugs that plague your flower beds, but you can't depend on it to kill all of them. You can rely on our all-purpose spray to do the job!

**3 tbsp. of baking soda**
**2 tbsp. of Murphy's Oil Soap®**
**2 tbsp. of canola oil or other vegetable oil**
**2 tbsp. of vinegar**
**2 gal. of warm water**

Mix these ingredients in a bucket, pour into a hand-held sprayer, and mist-spray your plants until they are dripping wet. Apply in early spring, just when the bugs and thugs are waking up from their long winter's nap, and you'll say "So long!" to those bad boys. (For related text, see page 84.)

## All-Purpose Critter Control

No doubt about it: There are lots of wily veggie-gulpers just waiting to sink their sharp teeth into your harvest. But gophers, skunks, and just about any other critter will turn tail and run when they get a whiff of this powerful tonic!

**2 eggs**
**2 cloves of garlic**
**2 tbsp. of hot chili pepper**
**2 tbsp. of ammonia**
**2 cups of hot water**

Mix these ingredients in a bucket, then let the mixture sit for three or four days. Paint it on fences, trellises, and wherever else unwanted varmints are venturing. (For related text, see page 221.)

## All-Purpose Varmint Repellent

Like deer, rabbits and rodents will snack on just about anything in your flower garden. The only difference is that these little critters eat a whole lot less than deer! Whatever the culprit, we've got just the cure.

**1/2 cup of Murphy's Oil Soap®**
**1/2 cup of lemon-scented dishwashing liquid**
**1/2 cup of castor oil**
**1/2 cup of lemon-scented ammonia**
**1/2 cup of hot, hot, hot pepper sauce**
**1/2 cup of urine**

Mix these ingredients in a 20 gallon hose-end sprayer, then apply to the point of run-off over any area that needs protecting. Reapply every other week or so (or after a rain) to keep this odiferous mix doing its thing. (For related text, see page 134.)

## All-Season Clean-Up Tonic

This is the one tonic that you absolutely need to use religiously throughout the growing season. The mouthwash kills bad bacteria and discourages insects; the shampoo cleans your plants and helps the other ingredients stick better; and the tobacco tea contains nicotine, which does a double whammy on those pesky pests.

**1 cup of antiseptic mouthwash**
**1 cup of baby shampoo**
**1 cup of tobacco tea***

Mix these ingredients in a 20 gallon hose-end sprayer, and give everything in your yard a good shower every two weeks in the early evening throughout the growing season. You'll have the healthiest flowers in town—guaranteed!

*To make tobacco tea, place half a handful of chewing tobacco in an old nylon stocking and soak it in a gallon of hot water until the mixture is dark brown. Store leftover liquid in a tightly capped jug or bottle for later use. (For related text, see page 111.)

## All-Season Green-Up Tonic

If your plants are looking a bit peaked, give them a taste of this sweet snack. It's rich in nutrients and packed with energizers, too: just what plants need to stay happy and healthy all summer long. They'll green up in a jiffy!

**1 can of beer**
**1 cup of ammonia**
**1/2 cup of dishwashing liquid**
**1/2 cup of liquid lawn food**
**1/2 cup of molasses or clear corn syrup**

Mix these ingredients in a large bucket, pour into a 20 gallon hose-end sprayer, and spray everything in sight—not just your flowers, but also your trees, shrubs, lawn, and even vegetables. Apply this tonic every three weeks right up through the first hard frost, and your whole yard will come through the hot summer months with flying colors! (For related text, see page 69.)

## Annual Perk-Me-Up Tonic

If summer's heat and humidity have gotten the best of your annual flowers, don't give them up for lost. You can enjoy several more weeks of blooms if you treat 'em right, right now! Cut them back by about half, water them thoroughly, and then dose them with a shot of this tonic. They'll be back in bloom before you know it!

**1/4 cup of beer**
**1 tbsp. of clear corn syrup**
**1 tbsp. of baby shampoo**
**1 tbsp. of 15-30-15 fertilizer**
**1 gal. of water**

Mix these ingredients in a watering can, then slowly dribble the solution onto the soil around all of your annuals. Within two weeks, they'll be real comeback kids—and you'll get to enjoy their lush leaves and beautiful blooms until mean old Jack Frost makes a return appearance in mid-fall. (For related text, see page 100.)

## Aphid-Away Spray

Aphids can strike anywhere at any time, but they're particularly active in northern lawns, especially in shady places during the heat of summer. If they start bugging your yard, give this spray a try.

**2 cups of water**
**2 medium cloves of garlic, finely chopped**
**1 small onion, finely chopped**
**1 tbsp. of baby shampoo**

Put all of these ingredients into an old blender, and blend on high. Let it sit overnight, and then strain through a coffee filter. Pour the liquid into a hand-held sprayer bottle, and apply liberally at the first sign of aphid trouble to send these little suckers scurryin'! (For related text, see page 37.)

## Awesome Annual Feeder Formula

Lively annuals burn up a great deal of energy with their constant flowering, so they need to eat heartily to keep it up. For consistent color all through the growing season, stick with a liquid food that your plants can use right away, such as this terrific tonic.

**1 can of beer**
**2 tbsp. of fish emulsion**
**2 tbsp. of dishwashing liquid**
**2 tbsp. of ammonia**
**2 tbsp. of hydrogen peroxide**
**2 tbsp. of whiskey**
**1 tbsp. of clear corn syrup**
**1 tbsp. of unflavored gelatin**
**4 tsp. of instant tea granules**
**2 gal. of warm water**

Mix these ingredients together in a large bucket, and pour into a watering can. Feed all of the annuals in your yard with this mix every two weeks in the morning for glorious blooms all season long. (For related text, see page 91.)

## Baker's Best Rose Chow

Roses are the hardest-working flowering plants in your garden. These beauties bloom only for the sake of showing off as much as they can, for as long as they can. When you follow this simple feeding routine, your roses will have everything they need to keep those blooms comin' along!

**4 cups of bonemeal**
**1 cup of 5-10-5 garden fertilizer**
**1 cup of Epsom salts**

Mix these ingredients in a bucket, then give each bush 1 heaping tablespoon in mid- to late spring, or work in 4 pounds per 100 square feet of rose bed. (Store any leftovers in a tightly sealed container.) Follow up with our Rose Ambrosia (see page 177) to really energize this dry mix. (For related text, see page 174.)

## Basic Baking Soda Spray

No need to spend a bundle buying chemical sprays to treat rose pests and diseases. This simple spray does it all—and the ingredients are as close as your kitchen!

**1½ tbsp. of baking soda**
**1 tbsp. of dishwashing liquid**
**1 tbsp. of canola oil**
**1 cup plus 1 gal. of water**
**1 tbsp. of vinegar**

Mix the baking soda, dishwashing liquid, and oil with 1 cup of water. Then add the vinegar last because the mixture may bubble over. Pour the mix into a pump sprayer, and add the remaining water. Thoroughly spray your roses, covering the tops and bottoms of leaves. (For related text, see page 172.)

## Beetle Juice

Are beetles chomping at your beautiful bloomers? A dose of this elixir can save the day. This recipe sure isn't for the squeamish, but we've found that nothing beats it for fighting bad beetles!

**1/2 cup of beetles (both larval and adult beetles, dead or alive)**
**2 cups of water**
**1 tsp. of dishwashing liquid**

Collect the beetles and whirl 'em up in an old blender (one that you'll never again use for food) with 2 cups of water. Strain the liquid through cheesecloth and mix in the dishwashing liquid. Pour about 1/4 cup of the juice into a 1-gallon hand-held sprayer, and fill the rest of the sprayer jar with water. Spray your plants from top to bottom, and make sure you coat both sides of the leaves. Wear gloves when handling this mixture, and be sure to clean the blender with hot, soapy water when you're done. (For related text, see page 83.)

## Blossom-Booster Tonics

When flowers fail to perform, it's typically because they're either dirty or tired (or both). Here's a great way to clean 'em up and green 'em up in a hurry. First, perk up your soil with this simple dry mixture.

**1/3 lb. of sugar**
**1/3 lb. of Epsom salts**
**1/3 lb. of gypsum**

Mix these ingredients in a bucket, and apply the mixture to your flower beds with a hand-held spreader. Now, it's time to get those leaves clean and shiny, so they can get back to their job of feeding your flowers.

**1 cup of apple juice**
**1 cup of Gatorade®**
**1/2 cup of ammonia**
**1/2 cup of Pedialyte®**

Mix these ingredients in your 20 gallon hose-end sprayer, and overspray your flower beds to the point of run-off. This'll wash the dirt right off those leaves—and help energize the dry mix at the same time. Before you know it, your flowers will be back to blooming like crazy! (For related text, see page 115.)

## Bug-Off Bulb Bath

Used before planting, this super spa treatment will help gladiolus, cannas, and other summer-blooming bulbs fend off diseases and pesky pests.

**2 tsp. of baby shampoo**
**1 tsp. of antiseptic mouthwash**
**1/4 tsp. of instant tea granules**
**2 gal. of hot water**

Mix these ingredients in a bucket, then place your bulbs into the mixture. Stir gently, then remove them one at a time and plant them. When you're done, don't throw the bath water out with the babies: Your trees, shrubs, and evergreens would love a little taste, so don't let it go to waste! (For related text, see page 153.)

## Bulb Bedtime Tonic

Instead of spending your hard-earned money on new tender bulbs each year, why not simply keep the ones you already have? As soon as their leaves start to turn color in fall, dig 'em up and wash them in this tonic before storing them in a frost-free place for the winter.

**2 tbsp. of baby shampoo**
**1 tsp. of hydrogen peroxide**
**1 qt. of warm water**

Mix these ingredients in a bucket and then gently drop in your bulbs. Let them soak for a minute or so, then remove and set on a wire rack to drain. Be sure to let them dry thoroughly before you put them away for the winter; otherwise, they'll rot. (For related text, see page 155.)

## Bulb Breakfast of Champions

Give your newly planted bulbs a boost with a taste of this terrific tonic. It's packed with nutrients and organic matter to provide a small, but steady, supply of food—just what's needed for balanced bulb growth.

**10 lb. of compost**
**5 lb. of bonemeal**
**2 lb. of bloodmeal**
**1 lb. of Epsom salts**

Mix these ingredients in a wheelbarrow. Before setting out your bulbs, work this hearty meal into every 100 square feet of soil in your bulb-planting beds. Or, if you're planting bulbs individually, work a handful of this mix into the soil in each hole before setting in the bulb. (For related text, see page 141.)

## Clipping Clean-Up Tonic

Do you like to leave the clippings on your lawn after you mow? Then spray it with this clean-up tonic at least twice a year. It'll help the clippings break down more quickly and let your lawn breathe better, too!

**1 can of beer**
**1 can of regular cola (not diet)**
**1 cup of ammonia**
**1 cup of dishwashing liquid**

Mix these ingredients in a bucket and pour them into a 20 gallon hose-end sprayer. Apply to the point of run-off. This'll really help speed up the decomposition process for any clippings left littering your lawn, and help minimize thatch buildup as well. (For related text, see page 9.)

## Compost Booster

Whether you use it as a mulch for your veggies or dig it into the soil, you can never have too much compost! To keep your pile cookin', and the compost comin', try the following formula.

**1 can of beer**
**1 can of regular cola (not diet)**
**1 cup of ammonia**
**1/2 cup of weak tea water***
**2 tbsp. of baby shampoo**

Mix these ingredients in your 20 gallon hose-end sprayer, and saturate your compost pile every time you add a layer of new ingredients to it. This'll really get things goin'!

*To make weak tea water, soak a used tea bag in a solution of 1 gallon of warm water and 1 teaspoon of dishwashing liquid until the mix is light brown. Store leftover liquid in a tightly capped jug or bottle for later use. (For related text, see page 192.)

## Divide-and-Conquer Tonic

Fall and spring are both great times to divide your perennials. To get 'em back on track in a flash, give 'em a bath in this time-tested tonic.

**1 can of beer**
**1/4 cup of instant tea granules**
**2 tbsp. of dishwashing liquid**
**2 gal. of warm water**

Mix these ingredients in a bucket, and soak newly divided perennials in this tonic for about 10 minutes just before replanting them. When you're finished, dribble any leftover tonic around your newly settled divisions. It'll get 'em off on the right root and growin' like gangbusters! (For related text, see page 126.)

## Double-Punch Garlic Tea

If thrips, aphids, or other bugs are driving your roses buggy, don't pull any punches. Deliver a knock-out blow with this powerful brew.

**5 unpeeled cloves of garlic, coarsely chopped**
**2 cups of boiling water**
**1/2 cup of tobacco tea***
**1 tsp. of instant tea granules**
**1 tsp. of baby shampoo**

Place the chopped garlic in a heatproof bowl, and pour boiling water over it. Allow it to steep overnight. Strain through a coffee filter, and then mix it with the other ingredients in a hand-held mist sprayer. Thoroughly drench your plants to thwart those pesky pests.

*To make tobacco tea, place half a handful of chewing tobacco in the toe of an old nylon stocking, and soak it in a gallon of hot water until the mixture is dark brown. Store leftover liquid in a tightly capped jug or bottle for later use. (For related text, see page 168.)

## Drought Recovery Tonic

If the dog days of summer are doing a real number on your lawn, don't despair—this refreshing tonic will soon set things right!

**1 can of regular cola (not diet)**
**1 cup of baby shampoo**
**1 cup of ammonia**

Mix these ingredients in a 20 gallon hose-end sprayer, and saturate the turf to the point of run-off every two weeks until the grass returns to normal. And remember that every time you water, moisture needs to reach 6 to 8 inches below the surface. This deep watering will encourage strong, deep roots that can stand up to periodic droughts. (For related text, see page 51.)

## Flower Garden Nightcap

When it's time to close up your flower beds for the season, cover the frozen ground with finely mowed grass clippings or chopped leaves, then overspray with our time-tested tonic to settle them in for a long winter's nap.

**1 can of regular cola (not diet)**
**1 cup of baby shampoo**
**1/2 cup of ammonia**
**2 tbsp. of instant tea granules**

Mix these ingredients in your 20 gallon hose-end sprayer, and saturate the mulch blanket. This tonic feeds the mulch, which in turn will feed your garden, while it protects your perennials all through the winter. (For related text, see page 129.)

## Fungus-Fighter Soil Drench

Garlic does more than just protect the tops of your plants; it can do a good job belowground, too! So, when foul fungi are fussin' around in your soil, causing your veggies to produce poorly, to wilt, or worse, just polish 'em off with this potent potion.

**4 garlic bulbs, crushed**
**1/2 cup of baking soda**
**1 gal. of water**

Mix these ingredients in a big pot and bring to a boil. Then turn off the heat and let it cool to room temperature. Strain the liquid into a watering can, and soak the ground around fungus-prone plants. Go very slowly, so that the elixir penetrates deep into the soil. Then dump the strained-out garlic bits onto the soil, and work them in gently, so as not to disturb any plant roots. (For related text, see page 202.)

## Gopher-Go Tonic

We've had amazing results with this tonic, so give it a try.

**4 tbsp. of castor oil**
**4 tbsp. of dishwashing liquid**
**4 tbsp. of urine**
**1/2 cup of warm water**

Combine these ingredients, then stir the mix into 2 gallons of warm water. Pour the tonic over any areas where gophers gather, and they'll soon be gone! (For related text, see page 249.)

## Grass Greener-Upper Elixir

When I see a lawn that needs immediate help, I always suggest a good dose of this elixir as a super-quick fix. Trust me, this liquid lunch never fails to get a hungry lawn back on track!

**1 can of beer**
**1 can of regular cola (not diet)**
**1 cup of apple juice**
**1 cup of lemon-scented dishwashing liquid**
**1 cup of ammonia**
**1 cup of all-purpose plant food**

Mix these ingredients in a large bucket, then pour 1 quart into a 20 gallon hose-end sprayer. Apply to your yard to the point of run-off every three weeks during the growing season for fantastic growing results! (For related text, see page 3.)

## Grass Seed Starter Tonic

The secret to getting your grass seed off to a great start is first giving it a good soaking with this tonic. It'll guarantee almost 100 percent germination every time!

**1 gal. of weak tea water***
**1/4 cup of baby shampoo**
**1 tbsp. of Epsom salts**

Mix these ingredients in a large container, drop in your grass seed, and put the whole shebang into your refrigerator. After 48 hours, take the seed outside and spread it out on a smooth, flat surface, such as a clean-swept area of your driveway. Once the seed is dry, it's ready to sow.

*To make weak tea water, soak a used tea bag in a solution of 1 gallon of warm water and 1 teaspoon of dishwashing liquid until the mix is light brown. (For related text, see page 26.)

## Hurry-Up-the-Harvest Tonic

When I know that Old Man Winter is waiting in the wings and my plants are still chock-full of unripe veggies, I give my garden a big drink of this tonic.

**1 cup of apple juice**
**1/2 cup of ammonia**
**1/2 cup of baby shampoo**
**Warm water**

Mix these ingredients in a 20 gallon hose-end sprayer, filling the balance of the sprayer jar with warm water. Then apply the tonic on your garden to the point of run-off to speed up the ripening process. (For related text, see page 204.)

## Knock-'Em-Dead Insect Tonic

This potent mixture will deal a death blow to squash bugs, bean beetles, and any other foul felons that are after your veggies.

**6 cloves of garlic, finely chopped**
**1 small onion, finely chopped**
**1 tbsp. of cayenne pepper**
**1 tbsp. of dishwashing liquid**
**1 qt. of warm water**

Mix these ingredients in a bucket, and let the mixture sit overnight. Strain out the solids, pour the liquid into a hand-held sprayer, and knock those buggy pests for a loop! (For related text, see page 258.)

## Lawn Jump-Start Tonic

Once you've got the soil in great shape for your new lawn, treat it to a taste of this power-packed potion. By the time you're ready to plant, your soil will be rarin' to get that grass growin'!

**1 cup of fish emulsion**
**$^1/_2$ cup of ammonia**
**$^1/_4$ cup of baby shampoo**
**$^1/_4$ cup of clear corn syrup**

Mix these ingredients in a 20 gallon hose-end sprayer, and saturate the soil. Wait several days before you sow seed or lay sod. After planting, spray the area lightly with water three or four times a day. Pretty soon, you'll be rollin' in the green—grass, that is! (For related text, see page 23.)

## Lawn Wake-Up Mix

Want to give your lawn a root-rousing wake-up call? We make it a habit to apply this tonic as soon as possible in spring, and trust us—the results are amazing!

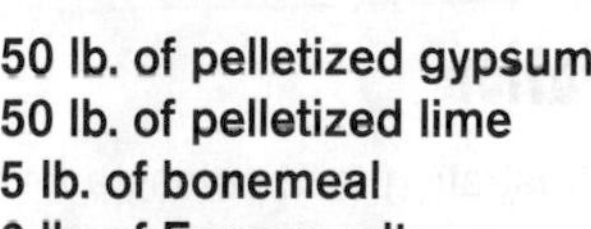

**50 lb. of pelletized gypsum**
**50 lb. of pelletized lime**
**5 lb. of bonemeal**
**2 lb. of Epsom salts**

Mix these ingredients in a wheelbarrow, and apply with your hand-held broadcast spreader. Next, follow up with this energizing mix:
**1 cup of baby shampoo**
**1 cup of ammonia**
**1 cup of regular cola (not diet)**
**4 tbsp. of instant tea granules**

Mix these ingredients in a 20 gallon hose-end sprayer, and apply to the point of run-off. Within two weeks of this treatment, follow up with a good feeding of your favorite dry lawn fertilizer to get your grass off to a great start. (For related text, see page 5.)

## Lethal Weapon Tonic

Garlic and onions are definitely double-duty crops—besides tasting great, they also provide the key ingredients for a perfect pest-fighting spray!

**3 tbsp. of garlic-and-onion juice***
**3 tbsp. of skim milk**
**2 tbsp. of baby shampoo**
**1 tsp. of hot sauce**
**1 gal. of water**

Mix these ingredients together in a bucket, and pour into a 20 gallon hose-end sprayer. Spray on your vegetables every 10 days to prevent aphid problems.

*Make garlic-and-onion juice by chopping 2 cloves of garlic and 2 medium onions. Blend in a blender with 3 cups of water, then strain and use the remaining liquid. (For related text, see page 241.)

## Mildew Remover Tonic

Powdery mildew and its kissin' cousin, downy mildew, can spell the end for plenty of veggies. But you can fight these funky fungi and keep your garden growing great guns by spraying your plants every week with my special spray.

**$^1/_2$ cup of baking soda**
**2 drops of dishwashing liquid**
**1 qt. of water**

Mix these ingredients in a bucket, then pour into a hand-held sprayer. Spray plants thoroughly at the first sign of mildew, and any diseases will soon be history. (For related text, see page 265.)

## Moles-No-Mo' Tonic

Not sure whether you have moles or gophers? Take a good look at the culprit. Moles are much smaller than gophers, with a pointed snout and large, clawed front paws that are well suited for intense digging. You rarely see them, but you'll know they are there when you see the mounds of dirt they push out as they dig their tunnels. To send 'em on their way, try this tonic.

**2 tbsp. of hot sauce**
**1 tbsp. of dishwashing liquid**
**1 tsp. of chili powder**
**1 qt. of water**

Mix these ingredients in a bucket, then pour a little of the tonic every 5 feet or so in the mole runways to make the critters run away! (For related text, see page 49.)

## Perennial No-Pest Potion

People love perfumed perennials, but pests sure don't! So the next time you're out in your flower garden, gather the ingredients for this aromatic pest-control spray.

**1/2 cup of fresh tansy or mugwort (*Artemisia vulgaris*) leaves**
**1/2 cup of fresh lavender flowers and/or leaves**
**1/2 cup of fresh sage leaves**
**Boiling water**
**2 cups of room-temperature water**
**1 tsp. of Murphy's Oil Soap®**

Place the herbs in a 1-quart glass canning jar; fill with boiling water, cover, and let it sit until cool. Add 1/8 cup of the liquid to the 2 cups of room-temperature water and the Murphy's Oil Soap. Pour into a hand-held sprayer, and apply to your plants to keep pests at bay. (For related text, see page 121.)

## Pest-Away Garlic Spray

A few aphids aren't a serious problem, but when they start congregating on veggie shoots and damaging tender leaves, it's time to take action. This garlicky spray will halt an aphid invasion faster than you can say "Hold it right there!"

**1 tbsp. of garlic oil***
**3 drops of dishwashing liquid**
**1 qt. of water**

Mix these ingredients in a blender, and pour the solution into a hand-held sprayer. Then take aim and fire on infested plants. Within seconds, those aphids'll be history!

*To make garlic oil, mince one whole bulb of garlic and mix it in 1 cup of vegetable oil. Put the garlic oil in a glass jar with a tight lid and place it in the refrigerator to steep for a day or two. Then, strain out the solids and pour the oil into a fresh jar with a lid. Keep it in the fridge and use it in any tonic that calls for garlic oil. (For related text, see page 219.)

## Pest Pulverizer Potion

There's nothing more frustrating than putting a lot of time and energy into your veggie garden, only to have it feasted upon by any and all bugs that walk, crawl, or fly by. Well, here's a way to keep those pesky pests at the proper distance—treat 'em to a little heat!

**3 hot peppers**
**2 tbsp. of baby shampoo**
**1 qt. of water**

Puree these ingredients in a blender, then strain out the solids. Pour the liquid into a hand-held sprayer, then apply to pest-plagued plants to get rid of unwanted bugs and keep 'em from comin' back. (For related text, see page 285.)

## Pre-Plant Bulb Soak

After sitting around in a garden center for a few weeks, hardy bulbs can get pretty dried out by the time you get them home. To get them plumped up again, give 'em a dip in this super solution just before planting.

**1 can of beer**
**2 tbsp. of dishwashing liquid**
**1/4 tsp. of instant tea granules**
**2 gal. of water**

Mix these ingredients in a large bucket. Let your bulbs soak for a few minutes, then get busy planting! (For related text, see page 156.)

## Rise 'n' Shine Clean-Up Tonic

Want to bag bad bugs before they get going? First thing in spring, spray down everything in your yard with this tonic.

**1 cup of Murphy's Oil Soap®**
**1 cup of tobacco tea***
**1 cup of antiseptic mouthwash**
**1/4 cup of hot sauce**

Mix these ingredients in your 20 gallon hose-end sprayer, filling the balance of the jar with warm water. Apply to the point of run-off to nail any wayward bugs and thugs that were overwintering in your lawn.

*To make tobacco tea, place half a handful of chewing tobacco in an old nylon stocking and soak it in a gallon of hot water until the mixture is dark brown. (For related text, see page 40.)

## Rose Ambrosia

Dry fertilizers, like our Baker's Best Rose Chow (see page 174), are great for long-term rose feeding. But if you really want to get all your roses off to a rousing start *and* keep 'em full of flowers through the summer, follow up with this power-packed liquid formula.

**1 cup of beer**
**2 tsp. of instant tea granules**
**1 tsp. of 5-10-5 fertilizer**
**1 tsp. of fish emulsion**
**1 tsp. of hydrogen peroxide**
**1 tsp. of dishwashing liquid**
**2 gal. of warm water**

Mix these ingredients in a bucket or watering can, then water each plant with 1 pint of the solution in the morning once every three weeks; store the liquid in a tightly capped jug or bottle between uses. It'll keep those beautiful blooms comin'—*guaranteed!* (For related text, see page 177.)

## Rose Clean-Up Tonic

Fall is the best time to set back the insects and diseases that plague roses. So, after your plants have shed their leaves, but before you mulch them, treat them with this cleansing tonic.

**1 cup of baby shampoo**
**1 cup of antiseptic mouthwash**
**1 cup of tobacco tea***

Mix these ingredients in a 20 gallon hose-end sprayer, and spray your plants well from top to bottom. That'll get your bushes squeaky clean for the winter and let them get off to a healthy start next spring.

*To make tobacco tea, place half a handful of chewing tobacco in the toe of an old nylon stocking, and soak it in a gallon of hot water until the mixture is dark brown. Store leftover liquid in a tightly capped jug or bottle for later use. (For related text, see page 178.)

## Rose Transplant Tonic

The best time to move established roses is when the bushes are dormant—that is, when the leaves have dropped and scales have formed over the growth buds for next year. Late fall is okay, but many professional rose growers prefer to move roses in early spring, before new growth starts. Whenever you transplant roses, ease the transition with this terrific tonic.

**1 can of beer**
**1 tbsp. of ammonia**
**1 tbsp. of instant tea granules**
**1 tbsp. of baby shampoo**
**1 gal. of water**

Mix these ingredients together in a bucket or watering can, and add 1 cup of the solution to each hole at transplant time. It'll help soothe the shock and get them settled in again in a flash. (For related text, see page 164.)

## Seed and Soil Energizer

Over the years, we've found that encouraging speedy sprouting gives all of our seed-grown crops a great jump-start for the growing season. So once we've sown our veggie or herb seeds, indoors or out, we give 'em an energy boost with this elixir. Try it in your own garden, and be prepared for your best veggie garden ever!

**1 tsp. of whiskey**
**1 tsp. of ammonia**
**1 tsp. of dishwashing liquid**
**1 qt. of weak tea water***

Mix these ingredients in a bucket, and pour the solution into a hand-held sprayer. Shake it gently, and apply a good misting to the surface of newly planted seedbeds or plant containers.

*To make weak tea water, soak a used tea bag in a solution of 1 gallon of warm water and 1 teaspoon of dishwashing liquid until the mix is light brown. (For related text, see page 225.)

## Seedling Saver

The tender stems and soft leaves of flower seedlings are easy targets for dastardly diseases, so it's smart to be prepared ahead of time. Put out the "Not Welcome" mat with a batch of our special solution.

**4 tsp. of chamomile tea**
**1 tsp. of dishwashing liquid**
**1 qt. of boiling water**

Mix these ingredients in a bowl, and let steep for at least an hour. Strain out the solids and pour the liquid into a hand-held sprayer. Mist your seedlings as soon as their little green heads poke out of the soil to foil attacks by foul fungi. (For related text, see page 66.)

## Slugweiser

Slugs love the cool, moist conditions found in shady gardens, so they can be a real problem if you don't take steps to control them. Beer is the classic bait for slug and snail traps; but what attracts the slimy thugs isn't the alcohol in the beer, or even the hops and malt—it's the yeast. So fill up your traps with this simple potion, and don't bother wasting a good brewski on the enemy!

**1 lb. of brown sugar**
**½ package (1½ tsp.) of dry yeast**
**Warm water**

Mix the sugar and yeast in a 1-gallon jug, fill it with warm water, and let the mixture sit for two days, uncovered. Then pour it into your slug traps, and watch the culprits belly up to the bar! (For related text, see page 132.)

## Spring Soil Energizer

After you dig, but before you plant your vegetable garden, fortify the soil with this potent potion. Take my word for it—it'll really get things cookin'!

**1 can of beer**
**1/2 cup of regular cola (not diet)**
**1/2 cup of dishwashing liquid**
**1/2 cup of antiseptic mouthwash**
**1/4 tsp. of instant tea granules**

Mix these ingredients in a 20 gallon hose-end sprayer, and saturate the soil. Wait two weeks before you start planting. (This recipe makes enough to cover 100 square feet of garden area.) (For related text, see page 185.)

## Squeaky Clean Tonic

When you catch pest problems early, a mild tonic will usually clean things up lickety-split. If not, then it's time to pull out the big guns with this more potent version of our All-Season Clean-Up Tonic (see page 111).

**1 cup of antiseptic mouthwash**
**1 cup of tobacco tea***
**1 cup of chamomile tea**
**1 cup of urine**
**1/2 cup of Murphy's Oil Soap®**
**1/2 cup of lemon-scented dishwashing liquid**

Mix these ingredients in a bucket, then pour into a 20 gallon hose-end sprayer, and apply to the point of run-off. No matter what bad guys are buggin' your yard, this potent brew will stop 'em dead in their tracks!

*To make tobacco tea, place half a handful of chewing tobacco in an old nylon stocking and soak it in a gallon of hot water until the mixture is dark brown. Pour the liquid into a glass container with a tight lid for storage. (For related text, see page 39.)

## Summer Soother Tonic

If you're like us and enjoy watering your yard by hand from time to time, then why not kill two birds with one stone? By that we mean to water and soothe your grass at the same time with a nice relaxing shower.

**2 cups of weak tea water***
**1 cup of baby shampoo**
**1 cup of hydrogen peroxide**

Mix these ingredients in a 20 gallon hose-end sprayer, and give everything in sight a good soaking. It makes for a really delightful summer shower, and your grass will thank you for it!

*To make weak tea water, soak a used tea bag in a solution of 1 gallon of warm water and 1 teaspoon of dishwashing liquid until the mix is light brown. Store leftover liquid in a tightly capped jug or bottle for later use. (For related text, see page 16.)

## Thatch-Blaster Tonic

Instead of waiting for thatch to build up in our lawns, we stop it from starting in the first place by spraying regularly with this power-packed tonic. Give it a try, and we know you'll be as pleased with the results as we are!

**1 cup of beer**
**1 cup of regular cola (not diet)**
**1/2 cup of dishwashing liquid**
**1/4 cup of ammonia**

Mix these ingredients in a 20 gallon hose-end sprayer, filling the balance of the sprayer jar with warm water. Saturate the entire turf area. Repeat once a month during summer, when grass is actively growing, and that nasty thatch will soon be a thing of the past! (For related text, see page 53.)

## Transplant Recovery Tonic

A sip of this soothing drink will set all your seedlings up right at transplanting time!

**1 tbsp. of fish emulsion**
**1 tbsp. of ammonia**
**1 tbsp. of Murphy's Oil Soap®**
**1 tsp. of instant tea granules**
**1 qt. of warm water**

Mix these ingredients in a bucket and pour into a hand-held sprayer. Mist your little plants several times a day until they're off and growing again. (For related text, see page 67.)

## Weed-Killer Prep Tonic

Sometimes you need to call in the heavy artillery to tackle a major weed invasion—and that's where chemical herbicides come in. To really zing a lot of weeds in a large area, over-spray your turf with this tonic first.

**1 cup of dishwashing liquid**
**1 cup of ammonia**
**4 tbsp. of instant tea granules**

Mix these ingredients in a 20 gallon hose-end sprayer, filling the balance of the sprayer jar with warm water. Apply to the point of run-off, then spread or spray on the herbicide. This one-two punch will make those wily weeds wither away before you know it! And one more tip: Don't water the grass for at least six hours following the herbicide application. (For related text, see page 47.)

## Wild Weed Wipeout Tonic

When you've got lawn weeds that won't take no for an answer, fill a hand-held sprayer with this tonic and take it with you every time you go out to mow your lawn. Zap those pesky weeds right on the spot, and before you know it, your weeds will be history!

**1 tbsp. of white vinegar**
**1 tbsp. of baby shampoo**
**1 tbsp. of gin**
**1 qt. of warm water**

Mix these ingredients in a bucket, and then pour into a hand-held sprayer. Drench each weed to the point of run-off, taking care not to get any spray on the surrounding plants. For particularly stubborn weeds, use apple cider vinegar instead of white vinegar. (For related text, see page 46.)

## Year-Round Refresher Tonic

Do your flowers tend to go hog-wild for a while, then fade out by midsummer? We've found that feeding lightly, but often, with this refresher tonic gives much better results than one big supper of chemical fertilizer at planting time. Our plants grow more steadily, bloom better, and stay healthier than we ever dreamed possible—and now yours can, too!

**1 cup of beer**
**1 cup of baby shampoo**
**1 cup of liquid lawn food**
**½ cup of molasses**
**2 tbsp. of fish emulsion**
**Ammonia**

Mix the beer, shampoo, lawn food, molasses, and fish emulsion in a 20 gallon hose-end sprayer. Fill the balance of the sprayer jar with ammonia, then apply liberally to your flower beds to the point of run-off every three weeks from spring through fall. (In warm climates, you can use it year-round.) (For related text, see page 74.)

# USDA Plant Hardiness Zone Map

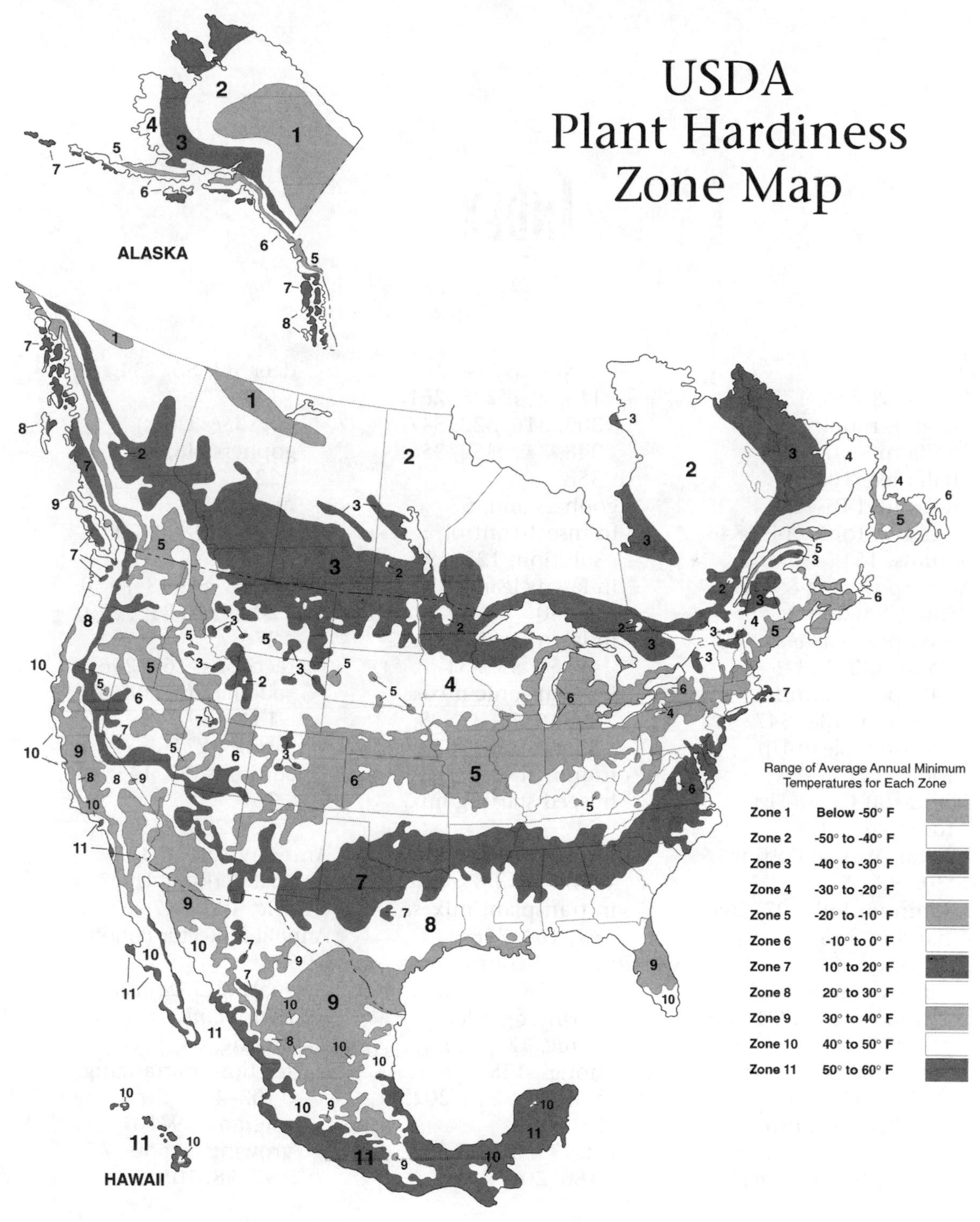

# Index

## B

## C

## D



## E



## F

## G

## H



## I

## J



## K



## L

## M

## N



## O

## P

## R

## T

## U



## V

## W



## Y



## Z